THE EXTERNALS
OF
THE CATHOLIC CHURCH

𝔑𝔦𝔥𝔦𝔩 𝔒𝔟𝔰𝔱𝔞𝔱:

ARTHUR J. SCANLAN, S.T.D.
Censor Librorum

ℑ𝔪𝔭𝔯𝔦𝔪𝔞𝔱𝔲𝔯:

✠ JOHN CARDINAL FARLEY, D.D.
Archbishop of New York

NEW YORK, *August 24*, 1917

ISBN-10: 0-6153709-5-0
EAN-13: 9-7-80615-37095-8

The type and image scans in this book are the property of Nine Choirs Press and except for brief excerpts, may not be reproduced in whole or in part without permission in writing from the publisher.

Printed and bound in the United States of America.
Published by Nine Choirs Press

Distributed by:
IHS Enterprises
PO Box 151
Palenville, NY 12463

www.NineChoirsPress.com

✠ J.M.J. ✠

THE EXTERNALS
OF
THE CATHOLIC CHURCH

HER GOVERNMENT, CEREMONIES
FESTIVALS
SACRAMENTALS, AND DEVOTIONS

BY

Rev. JOHN F. SULLIVAN
OF THE DIOCESE OF PROVIDENCE

NEW YORK

P. J. KENEDY & SONS

1917

COPYRIGHT, 1917
BY P. J. KENEDY & SONS

PREFACE

OUR CATHOLIC LITURGY is a grand and harmonious manifestation of man's homage to God. Its words and ceremonies and devotions are the growth of centuries. The essentials of our Church's worship have been embellished with a wealth of ritual observance, of which each detail is symbolic of the purpose for which that worship is offered. The explanation of these manifold practices is the object of this work.

How little is known, even by fairly well-informed Catholics, concerning the history and meaning of the practices which have been embodied in our Church's majestic ritual! They kneel before the altar of God; they listen to the cadence of psalm and hymn and Preface and prayer; they see the ministers of the Church perform various sacred actions — and in many cases they know little of the origin of what they hear and see, or of the reasons for the ceremonial which adds so much to the beauty of Catholic worship. They receive the Sacraments of the Church, devoutly, indeed, but without ever trying to learn why these are administered with certain ceremonies. They use the sacramentals, and profit by so doing; but how few have had an opportunity of learning the history of these things which our Church sanctifies for us! And when a non-Catholic, interested in these ancient practices of the "Mother Church," asks why and wherefore — how seldom we, the children of that Church, are able to give an accurate and satisfactory answer!

This book is an attempt to put into clear, convenient and readable form an explanation of many practices of our Church. While it covers a wider scope than any one-volume work hitherto issued on the subject in English (or, possibly, in any other language), it has no pretensions to be considered an authoritative or even a complete summary of the matter treated in its pages. The wealth of subjects which might be included in "The Externals of the Catholic Church" is so great that no book of this size could contain even a fragmentary account of each; and so a selection had to be made — the results of which the reader will find in the Table of Contents.

It has not been deemed advisable to cumber its pages with references to authorities, or with footnotes. The facts stated, however, have been carefully gleaned from the most approved sources. First of all, the author wishes to pay a tribute of gratitude to that monumental, marvelous and long-desired work which is the literary glory of the Church in America — The "Catholic Encyclopedia." Extensive use has been made of its many volumes; in fact, without its aid a book like this would have been well-nigh impossible.

He is deeply indebted, too, to that valuable little book, "The Sacramentals," by Father Lambing, and parts of this work will be found to be reminiscent of much that was lucidly treated by that learned and painstaking author. The "Catholic Dictionary" has furnished much from its concise and accurate pages; and the following works have been of more than occasional usefulness in gathering the matter which this book contains: "The Roman Court," by Rev. P.A. Baart; "Roman Documents and Decrees"; "The Law of the Church," by Rev. Ethelred Taunton; the "Acta Apostolicae Sedis"; the "Bibliotheca" of Ferraris; "The New Matrimonial Legislation," by Rev. C. J. Cronin, S.J.; "The Mass: a Study of the Roman Rite," by Father Fortescue; the "Ecclesiastical Dictionary" of Father Thein; "The Holy Sacrifice of the Mass," by Rev. Dr. Gihr; the "Handbook of the Divine Liturgy," by Rev. C. C. Clarke; "Ritual in Catholic Worship," by Father Procter, O.P.; "Christian Symbols," by C. E. Clement; "Lent and Holy Week," by Rev. Herbert Thurston; "The Costumes of Prelates," by Father Nainfa, S.S. — and various other standard works and reference-books on the Church's law and liturgy.

. . . .

If this book shall be occasionally a help to some of his fellow-priests for purposes of instruction, or if through it some knowledge of the beautiful ceremonial of our Church is imparted to our Catholic laity, it will fulfill the intention and the hopes of

THE AUTHOR

CONTENTS

PART I. THE GOVERNMENT OF THE CHURCH

CHAPTER		PAGE
I.	The Pope	3
II.	The Cardinals and the Roman Court	10
III.	The Bishops and the Diocesan Clergy	14

PART II. THE RELIGIOUS STATE

IV.	The Monastic Life	20
V.	The Great Religious Orders	27
VI.	Religious Life for Women	40

PART III. THE ADMINISTRATION OF THE SACRAMENTS

VII.	The Ceremonies of Baptism	44
VIII.	The Sponsors in Baptism	49
IX.	The Ceremonies of Confirmation	54
X.	The Confession of Sins	61
XI.	The Ceremonies of Extreme Unction	69
XII.	The Ceremonies of Holy Orders	74
XIII.	The Ceremonies of Matrimony	87

PART IV. THE HOLY SACRIFICE OF THE MASS

XIV.	The Mass	92
XV.	The Growth of the Mass — I	97
XVI.	The Growth of the Mass — II	102
XVII.	The Growth of the Mass — III	108
XVIII.	The Requisites for the Mass	113
XIX.	Why the Mass is Said in Latin	121

CONTENTS

PART V. THE ECCLESIASTICAL YEAR

CHAPTER		PAGE
XX.	The Church's Calendar	126
XXI.	Festivals	131
XXII.	Advent	137
XXIII.	Christmas Day	141
XXIV.	Lent and Holy Week	147

PART VI. THE SACRAMENTALS

XXV.	The Sign of the Cross	154
XXVI.	The Cross and the Crucifix	157
XXVII.	Holy Water	163
XXVIII.	Vestments	169
XXIX.	The Stations of the Cross	179
XXX.	The Holy Oils	183
XXXI.	Candles	189
XXXII.	The Rosary	193
XXXIII.	Scapulars — I	198
XXXIV.	Scapulars — II	206
XXXV.	The Agnus Dei	212
XXXVI.	Palms	216
XXXVII.	Incense	219
XXXVIII.	Church Bells	223
XXXIX.	Religious Medals	231
XL.	Ashes	235

PART VII. THE LITURGICAL BOOKS

XLI.	The Missal	238
XLII.	The Breviary	243
XLIII.	The Ritual	247

CONTENTS

PART VIII. DEVOTIONS

CHAPTER		PAGE
XLIV.	THE DEVOTION TO THE SACRED HEART	252
XLV.	THE INVOCATION OF SAINTS	257
XLVI.	THE VENERATION OF IMAGES	262
XLVII.	THE VENERATION OF RELICS	267
XLVIII.	THE FORTY HOURS' ADORATION	272
XLVIX.	OUR DAILY PRAYERS	276
L.	THE LITANIES	284

PART IX. MISCELLANEOUS

LI.	SERVICES FOR THE DEAD	291
LII.	THE CHURCHING OF WOMEN	298
LIII.	FASTING AND ABSTINENCE	302
LIV.	INDULGENCES	307
LV.	PILGRIMAGES	313
LVI.	AN UNMARRIED CLERGY	317
LVII.	CHRISTIAN SYMBOLS	322
LVIII.	THE CATHOLIC BIBLE	328
LIX.	CHURCH MUSIC	333
LX.	PSALMS AND HYMNS	346
LXI.	THE MARRIAGE LAWS	351
LXII.	RELIGIOUS SOCIETIES	361
LXIII.	THE CANONIZATION OF A SAINT	370
LXIV.	CHURCH BUILDINGS AND THEIR PARTS	375
LXV.	THE CONSECRATION OF A CHURCH	381
LXVI.	OTHER RITES THAN OURS	388

INDEX 395

THE EXTERNALS OF THE CATHOLIC CHURCH

THE EXTERNALS OF THE CATHOLIC CHURCH

PART I
THE GOVERNMENT OF THE CHURCH

Chapter I

THE POPE

The Catholic Church is a divinely instituted society, of which all the members profess the doctrine of Christ and are united under the teaching and rule of the Roman Pontiff and the Bishops subject to him, that thereby they may cultivate holiness and obtain salvation.

Like all other societies it has, therefore, a system of authority by which it is ruled, and by which its members are directed toward the end for which it was established; and the description of this system will form the matter of these first chapters.

When we read of the Church's government or of its legislative acts we often meet the words "Cardinal," or "Metropolitan," or "Delegate," or "Primate," and we know in a vague way that these are officials of the Church; but the great majority of us Catholics have no very clear idea of the duties or the relative rank of these and other dignitaries. Many of us, doubtless, are far less familiar with the details of the government of our Church than we are with the administrative machinery of our country or city.

The Two Hierarchies. The governing body of the Church's clergy is usually known as the *Hierarchy*, a word derived from the Greek, signifying "priestly rule."

The Divine Founder of our Church did not intend that the "rank and file" of its membership should have authority in it, or a power to perform sacred public functions. To selected members, called the *clergy*, was given the office of offering public worship, or administering most of the sacraments, and of ruling and instructing the faithful; and the clergy (the "chosen ones") are therefore known, first of all, as the Hierarchy of Order, because they receive these powers through the Sacrament of Holy Orders. And in order that there may be system and uniformity, that the work of the whole body may be done in an orderly and effective manner, these leaders of the Church possess also certain legislative powers, on account of which they are known as the Hierarchy of Jurisdiction.

The essential features of the Church's government are the *Papacy* and the *Episcopacy* — the office of Pope and the office of Bishop. These were established by our Blessed Lord. The other grades of the hierarchy and the various details of governmental legislation have been determined by the Church herself in the course of centuries.

The Pope. Every nation has its ruler, be he emperor or king or president. Every society has its legislative head, its centre of authority, its lawmaker and lawgiver. And, as the Church is a society of men, although instituted by God, His wisdom has ordained that at the head of His earthly kingdom there shall be one man, a monarch, endowed with supreme power. This man is the Pope, the successor of St. Peter in the bishopric of Rome. "Upon this Rock I will build My Church." "I will give to thee the keys of the kingdom of heaven. Whatsoever thou shalt bind on earth shall be bound in heaven, and whatsoever thou shalt loose upon earth shall be loosed in heaven." Our Lord Jesus Christ, wishing His Church to be one, instituted the Primacy of Peter to rule it and to cement it into unity.

The Pope's Power. The sovereignty of the Pope over the Church differs from that of the rulers of other societies. He has direct authority over all Catholics, from the most exalted prelate to the humblest layman; and he is obliged to render an account of his administration to no human being. None of his power is derived from or delegated by any one else. According to the Vatican Council, he has "the whole fullness of supreme power, ordinary and immediate, over all and each of the pastors and the faithful." He is the supreme judge in matters of faith. To him belongs the right to regulate all the Church's discipline. He may enact laws for the whole Church and for any part of it, and dispense from them. He can inflict censures, such as excommunication. He can reserve to himself the power of absolving from certain sins. He and he alone can form, suppress and divide dioceses and approve new religious orders. He can dispense from any vow, no matter how solemn or sacred.

The Pope's Infallibility. That the successor of St. Peter may preserve the faith of Jesus Christ free from any taint of error, that the shepherd may guide the flock aright, he has been endowed with a wonderful power and privilege. He is infallible in matters of faith and morals. That is, when by virtue of his Apostolic office he defines a doctrine of faith or morals to be held by the whole Church, he speaks without error or danger of error, being preserved from it by the Spirit of God, Which "teaches all truth" and abides with the Church forever.

Non-Catholics often ask: "Does this mean that the Pope cannot make a mistake?" Others go further, and inquire: "Do you Catholics believe that the Pope cannot sin?" The answer to both questions is, No. The Pope is subject to error, like other men. He can sin, even as we, for he is human. He is infallible only when he is speaking as the supreme teacher and head of the Church, and only when he is defining a doctrine concerning faith or morals and imposing it upon the whole Church to be accepted and held by all the Church's members. He has no immunity from error in other things. He may advocate historical or scientific views that are absolutely false. He may write books which may be full of inaccuracies and misstatements. God protects him from error only when he is exercising his office of sovereign teacher and lawgiver regarding matters which are the doctrine of the Church, whether these be of faith or morals. Such doctrines thus proposed are the teaching of the Church of Christ as soon as the Pope defines them; and any one who refuses to accept them thereby ceases to be a member of the Church.

Here, then, we have the supreme authority, the highest tribunal of appeal, the very foundation of our Church. The man who sits to-day in the chair of Peter is, like him, the rock upon which God's Church is built. He is guided by the Holy Spirit when he is teaching the truths of God to the world. As the Church is our infallible guide in the path of salvation and our infallible teacher concerning God's revealed truth, it is logical and necessary to hold that he who rules the Church must be likewise infallible, free from even the possibility of error, when he is solemnly proclaiming its principles of morals or of faith.

The Pope's Election. The Papacy is a monarchy, differing from other governments of that kind in one important detail; it is not hereditary. It may be termed an elective monarchy. In the first centuries it was the custom to allow the clergy and people of each diocese to choose their own bishop, and this was done at Rome as well as elsewhere; the election, however, required the assent of the neighboring bishops, and the crowning of the new Pontiff was performed by the Bishop of Ostia. The present system of election may be traced back to Pope Nicholas II, for his decree, issued in 1059, restricted the electoral power to the Cardinals. At first the Cardinal-Bishops were the only ones authorized to select the new Pope, but after a time all the Cardinals were allowed to have a share in that important work.

Who may be chosen to fill the office of Pope? Strictly speaking, any male Catholic who has come to the age of reason — even a layman. Strange to say, it would be legally possible to elect even a married man; for the law of the "celibacy of the clergy" is not of divine institution, but is a rule of the Church which developed gradually and was finally made a part of her legal code for the greater part of the world. But there is no danger, in the present state of the Church's discipline, that we will have a Pope with a wife, nor even that any layman will be selected in preference to a cleric. For more than five hundred years the choice has fallen in every instance upon a Cardinal.

Would it be possible for the Pope to nominate his successor?

No; this is expressly forbidden by the Church's law, because it would mean an act of jurisdiction by one who no longer has authority — for a dead Pope is no longer Pope, and any selection made by him has no binding force on the Church after his death.

The Conclave. The election of a Pope takes place at what is called a *Conclave*, which word signifies that the voting prelates (the College of Cardinals) are under lock and key. This is an ancient practice, dating back to the twelfth century.

"Death lays his icy hand on kings," sang the old poet; and he who is more exalted than any king must bow to the same inexorable law. When the Sovereign Pontiff dies, his actual death is verified by a quaint ceremony. One of the Cardinals approaches the bedside and strikes the forehead of the dead Pope three times with a silver mallet, calling him by his baptismal name. The death of the Pope being thus legally attested, the Cardinals are summed to the Conclave to elect his successor.

A part of the Vatican Palace is walled off, and ten days after the death of the Pope the Cardinals begin their work. The balloting is usually secret, and as a two-thirds vote is required for an election, it frequently happens that several ballotings are required.

The governments of Austria and Spain, and others as well, have been allowed at some elections to register their opposition to some proposed candidate, enforcing the withdrawal of his name. This was known as the Power of Veto. It has been definitively forbidden in all elections hereafter.

When a candidate is found to have the necessary number of votes and has manifested his willingness to accept the office, he is thereby Pope. He needs no ceremony of consecration to elevate him to the Papacy.

It would be possible, though far from probable, that a person might be elected Pope who is not already a Bishop. He would become Pope as soon as he was lawfully chosen, and could then perform all the duties of the Papacy which pertain to jurisdiction;

but he could not ordain or consecrate until he himself had been raised to the episcopate by other Bishops.

Within a few days after his election the new Pope is crowned with solemn ceremonies after a Mass of Coronation, in which petitions are offered for the spiritual and temporal welfare of the new Pontiff, and for the prosperity of the Church under his rule.

The Pope's New Name. For about one thousand years it has been customary for each new Pope to change his name. This is said by some to be in imitation of the taking of the name of Peter by the first Pontiff. Usually the name is taken of some preceding Pope whose works and sanctity commend themselves to the new Pontiff, and whose policies, perhaps, he intends to imitate.

Tiara and Keys

Such is the method which our holy Church uses for the perpetuation of her government, continuing through century after century that glorious line of successors to him who received from our Saviour the commission to feed His lambs and His sheep. The powers of evil have conspired against that Church, but they have not prevailed. Storms have raged around the barque of Peter, but it has not been overwhelmed. The enemies of God's Church have tried and are trying to destroy that which is indestructible.

The Pope's Titles. The "Pope" gets that name from the Latin "Papa," a childish word for "Father." By virtue of this office he is also the "Patriarch of the West," the "Primate of Italy," and the "Metropolitan of the Province of Rome," as well as the Bishop of Rome. He is often spoken of as the "Sovereign Pontiff." The word *Pontiff* comes from the priesthood of pagan Rome, and signifies literally "bridge-builder," because the high-priests of Rome, among other civic duties, had charge of the bridges over the Tiber.

The Pope is usually mentioned as "Our Holy Father," and is addressed as "Your Holiness," or, in Latin, "Beatissime Pater" —

"Most Blessed Father." He speaks of himself in official documents as "Servus Servorum Dei" — "Servant of the Servants of God."

The Pope's Insignia. The ordinary garb of the Sovereign Pontiff is white. He does not use the crosier or pastoral staff of Bishops. Among his insignia are the *pallium*, which signifies his rank as a Primate, and the *tiara*, or triple crown In early centuries the Pope wore a simple mitre, like other Bishops; but about the ninth century a crown was added to it, to denote the Pontiff's temporal power as ruler of the States of the Church. Later a second crown was added, and about the year 1365 a third — signifying, according to some, the supreme authority of the Pope in spiritual things, his jurisdiction over the Church considered as a human society, and his dominion as a temporal monarch. According to others, the triple crown typifies his threefold office as teacher, lawgiver and judge.

Peterspence. A part of the revenue of the Holy See at the present day is provided by a yearly contribution from the faithful of various countries. This bears the name of "Peterspence," because in England, in Saxon times, each householder gave a penny. It began in the reign of King Offa, in 787, and spread from England to other nations of northern Europe. At the time of the Reformation it ceased throughout the world, and was not re-established until the reign of Pius IX.

Benedict XV, the Sovereign Pontiff at the present time (1917), is the 260th Pope. That long line of saints, of martyrs, of learned teachers and of wise rulers has endured for nearly twenty centuries, and will endure till the end of time. Other religions have arisen and flourished and died; for they were not divine in their origin, and contained at most only a part of God's truth in their teachings. But the Catholic Church was founded by Jesus Christ Himself, and that church will be man's guide and the chief means of his salvation until that dread day when "the Son of Man shall sit in the seat of His majesty and all nations shall be gathered before Him."

Chapter II

THE CARDINALS AND THE ROMAN COURT

NEXT to the Pope, in the Church's hierarchy, come the Cardinals. They are the counselors of the Pontiff in many important matters pertaining to the government of the universal Church, and some of them exercise extensive jurisdiction in the various "Congregations" and tribunals which have been instituted for the administration of Church law. They form, so to speak, the Senate of the Church.

The word *Cardinal* is derived from the Latin "cardo," a hinge. They are, as it were, so necessary to the government and discipline of the Church that it may be said to revolve around them as a door on its hinges.

Princes of the Church. The office of Cardinal is a dignity only; the person who holds it has not received any new Order. It merely makes him higher in rank than other prelates. He is second to none but the Pope, and takes precedence of all other dignitaries in the Church. He is considered equal in rank to a prince of a reigning house, and is often spoken of as a "Prince of the Church." He is responsible to the Pope only, and may be deposed by him alone.

The Cardinals are appointed solely by the Sovereign Pontiff. By a law made in 1586, the membership of the "College of Cardinals" (or "Sacred College," as it is sometimes called) is not permitted to exceed seventy, and generally there are several vacancies. They are taken from many nations, although the number of Italian Cardinals is usually greater than all the others combined.

The Grades of Cardinals. They are of three grades: Cardinal Bishops, who are six in number, being the Bishops of certain suburban sees around Rome; Cardinal Priests, so called, although these, nearly always, are Bishops also; they may number fifty; and Cardinal Deacons, of whom there are fourteen; these are priests, or may be merely in Minor Orders.

The garb of Cardinals is scarlet, with a biretta or cap of the same color. Chief among their insignia is the "red hat," which also forms a prominent feature of their armorial bearings. A Cardinal is usually addressed as "Your Eminence."

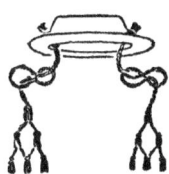

Cardinal's Hat

The Duties of Cardinals. The principal duty of the Cardinals is to assist and advise the Pope in the governing of the Church. This is done in many ways — in "Papal Consistories" (in which details of Church administration are discussed and settled, such as the appointing and transferring of bishops, the division and creation of dioceses, etc.), and in "Congregations," so called, in which are decided questions of discipline, subject to the approval of the Pope. The Cardinals have also a most important function when the Holy See becomes vacant, for, as explained in the preceding chapter, they elect the new Pope.

The Roman Congregations. The Congregations by which the Holy Father is assisted in the governing of the Church are: The Sacred Consistory, or Consistorial Congregation, composed of the Pope and the College of Cardinals, assembled to discuss the most weighty matters; the Congregation of the Sacraments; the Congregation for Extraordinary Ecclesiastical Affairs, which deals specially with the relations of the Holy See and other governments; the Congregation of the Inquisition, often called the Holy Office, which considers cases of heresy and apostasy, supervises certain classes of indulgences, and examines books; the Congregation of Bishops and Regulars; that of the Affairs of Religious; the Congregation of Studies; the Congregation of Rites, which regulates ceremonial details and also is in charge of the process for the canonization of saints; the Congregation of Ceremonies; the Congregation of the Council, which attends to matters of discipline and some matrimonial cases; the Congregation of Seminaries and Universities, recently established; and the Congregation for the Propagation of the Faith, often called the *Propaganda*, which supervises the spreading of the faith in missionary countries.

Besides these Congregations there are various tribunals. Three of these are known as "Tribunals of Justice" — the *Rota*, which means "the wheel," because its twelve officials, called auditors, are seated in a circle and by turn examine the controversies submitted to it the Apostolic *Camera* or Treasury; and the *Segnatura* or Signature of Justice, which examines petitions for justice and reports on them to the Holy See. There are also three "Tribunals of Grace," which consider favors asked from the Sovereign Pontiff. These are the *Signature of Favor*, the *Datary*, in charge of benefices, etc., and the *Sacred Penitentiary*. Through this latter Office the Holy See gives absolution from sins and censures specifically reserved to it, grants dispensations from vows, etc. The Sacred Penitentiary, under a recent decree, has all to do with indulgences (except indulgences which touch dogmatic teaching, and those attached to new prayers and devotions, which are under the care of the congregation of the Holy Office).

There are, moreover, several tribunals or offices "of Expedition," through which apostolic letters are sent and other business is done. The more important of these are the Apostolic Chancery and the Secretariate of State. The Cardinal who holds the latter office attends especially to the relations of the Holy See with other governments.

Apostolic Legates. A *Legate*, in the practice of our Church, is a person sent as a representative of the Pope to a government or to the bishops and faithful of a country. He may be a Cardinal, or a prelate of lower rank. There are several grades. The highest are Legates properly so called, who have jurisdiction in many things which otherwise would be referred to the Pope, and who act as resident ambassadors of the Holy See in capitals where the Papal Government is recognized. Next comes *Nuncios*, sent to certain European States, whose duties are much like those of the preceding. Some representatives of the Holy See bear the title of Apostolic Delegate, and of these one of the most important is the prelate who represents the Holy Father in this country. He has broad powers, and from his decision there is no appeal to the Roman See; in other words, an ecclesiastical matter may be appealed from a diocesan or metropolitan tribunal either to Rome or to the Delegate, but if the appeal is made to him his decision is final.

Other minor legates of the Holy See, sent for special purposes to various parts of the world, are entitled Apostolic Vicars and Ablegates.

CHAPTER III

THE BISHOPS AND THE DIOCESAN CLERGY

The Archbishops. After the Cardinals come the Archbishops, and of these there are several grades. Certain prelates have the rank of "Greater Patriarchs"; they are the Archbishops of Jerusalem, Constantinople, Antioch and Alexandria. Besides these there are several others to whom the honorary title of Patriarch is given, such as the Archbishops of Venice and of Lisbon. A step lower in dignity than these come the "Primates," or Archbishops to whom this honorary rank has been given; they formerly exercised authority over the dioceses of a whole country or over several provinces. A "Metropolitan" is an Archbishop who has certain rights and jurisdiction over a province, that is, a number of dioceses, and over the bishops who rule them. A "Titular Archbishop" is one who rules a single diocese only, or who has merely the title of some extinct archdiocese.

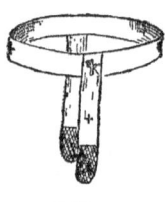
Pallium

All these grades of dignity, of course, add nothing to the sacred Order which the holder has received. He is a Bishop, whether he bear the title of Patriarch, Primate, Metropolitan, Archbishop or simple Bishop.

The Archbishop's Insignia. The heraldic arms of an Archbishop are surmounted by a double or four-armed cross, and this form of cross is carried before him in solemn processions. After his elevation to the archiepiscopal rank he receives from the Sovereign Pontiff the "pallium," a vestment consisting of a band of white wool worn on the shoulders, having two pendant ribbons hanging therefrom, and ornamented with four purple crosses.

Archiepiscopal Cross

An Archbishop is spoken of as "Most Reverend," and is addressed as "Your Grace."

The Bishops. Next come the Bishops, who preside over

the individual dioceses, and this they do by divine right, for the Episcopate of our Church, as well as the Papacy, was instituted by Jesus Christ. Bishops are divided into two classes — "Diocesan Bishops," who rule a certain allotted territory called a diocese, and "Titular Bishops," who bear the title of a diocese but have no jurisdiction over it. These latter may be commissioned by the Holy See as "Auxiliary Bishops" or "Coadjutors," to assist the Bishop of a diocese. The term "Coadjutor Bishop" is usually employed to designate one who has the right to succeed the Bishop whom he is appointed to aid. Archbishops and Bishops who are merely "Titular" receive their titles, in many cases, from ancient sees in regions that are not now Catholic; therefore they are known as Archbishops or Bishops "in partibus infidelium" — that is, in infidel lands.

In missionary countries where dioceses are not established, the government of the Church is under the direction of a "Vicar Apostolic," who is usually a titular Bishop.

The Visit "Ad Limina." Every Archbishop and Bishop in charge of a diocese is obliged at certain intervals to visit Rome and make a report to the Pope. This rendering an account of his stewardship is known as the visit "ad limina," or to the threshold, and is to be made every three years by Bishops who live near Rome; every four years by Europeans, and every five years by those who rule over more distant sees. Our American Bishops were, until lately, obliged to make their visit only every tenth year, but they have been notified to do so hereafter at intervals of five years.

The Choosing of a Bishop. In the first days of the Church, and for some time afterward, the appointing of a Bishop was a very simple matter. The Acts of the Apostles tells us of the first election to the episcopate. When the place of the traitor Judas was to be filled, the eleven Apostles selected two candidates, and then left the result to God's providence, drawing lots to see who was to be the new shepherd of the flock of Christ; "and the lot fell upon Matthias, and he was numbered with the eleven Apostles."

But in later ages it was seen that there was great need of care and deliberation in choosing these rulers in the Church of God, these guardians and leaders of His flock.

The Election of Bishops. The method of choosing bishops varies in different countries, and, by a recent decree, has been changed in regard to the United States of America. Formerly the nomination of candidates was made by a "terna," or list of three names, proposed and voted on at a meeting of the diocesan consultors and permanent rectors, presided over by the administrator of the vacant diocese, and afterward by a meeting of the bishops of the province. These proceedings necessarily entailed much delay; and hence the new method has been put into effect, as follows:

The bishop of each diocese secretly communicates with each of the consultors and permanent rectors, and (if he wishes) with other priests, and obtains from each the name of they priest who is, in the opinion of the proposer, worthy of the episcopal dignity. Every second year, about the beginning of Lent, the bishop sends the said name or names to the archbishop of the province, who adds his own candidates, arranges the list in alphabetical order, and sends it to each bishop.

After Easter, a private meeting of the bishops is summoned by the archbishop, and all are put under oath to observe the strictest secrecy. The names and qualifications of the candidates are considered, and each is voted on — the balloting being made by using balls of different colors, indicating approbation, disapprobation, or abstention from voting. In case of a tie vote, a further ballot is made. The result (usually with all obtainable information as to the qualifications of the candidate) is sent to the Sacred Consistorial Congregation through the Apostolic Delegation. And thus, when a vacancy occurs in any diocese, the Holy See is well provided with a list of candidates and with testimony as to their fitness for the place to be filled. The ultimate choice, of course, rests with the Holy See.

The garb of a Bishop and his special insignia — the mitre,

the pectoral cross, the ring, the pastoral staff, etc. — are tolerably familiar to all, and are described elsewhere in this work, in the chapter on "Vestments." A Bishop is entitled "Right Reverend," and in some countries is addressed as "My Lord." In our Republic, where temporal lords are not, it is customary to address him simply as "Bishop."

Mitre

The Monsignors. This title denotes the rank of Protonotary Apostolic. These are Prelates of a lower order than Bishops. Prelates properly so called are the Pope, the Cardinals, the Patriarchs, the Primates, Archbishops, Bishops and Abbots; but the name of "Domestic Prelate" is also given to certain officials who have received this dignity from the Pope. These are commonly called Monsignors, and they are of three grades; and the same name is given also to a fourth grade of Protonotaries who are not Domestic Prelates.

The grades are as follows: 1. Protonotaries Apostolic "de numero participantium" (of the number of the participating), of whom there are only seven, forming a College of Notaries to the Sovereign Pontiff. 2. Protonotaries Apostolic Supernumerary — Canons of certain Roman basilicas. 3. Protonotaries Apostolic "ad instar participantium" (resembling the participating), who are either the Canons of certain cathedrals or have been raised to this dignity by the Pope. The clergy who are known as Domestic Prelates in this country belong to this third class of Protonotaries. 4. Titular Protonotaries Apostolic, called also Honorary or "Black" Protonotaries. These are not members of the pontifical household, and enjoy their rank as Prelates only outside of Rome. Since 1905, Vicars General, by virtue of their office, belong to this class of Protonotaries, unless they are of a higher rank.

Pectoral Cross

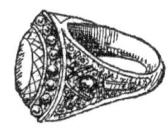
Bishop's Ring

Members of the first three classes of Protonotaries have

the right to use and wear some of the insignia of Bishops, and are addressed as "Right Reverend." Those of the fourth class wear black, without any red or purple, and are addressed as "Very Reverend." Protonotaries of all grades are addressed "Monsignor."

A Bishop, in the administration of his diocese, is assisted by priests who have various offices and duties. We shall confine our attention to the list of such officials as are found in the dioceses of the United States.

The Vicar General. Chief among the officers of any diocese is the Vicar General, who is, as canonists say, the "other self" of the Bishop. Consequently, he takes precedence over all the other clergy of the diocese. The official acts which he performs have the same force as those of the Bishop — so much so that the latter cannot receive an appeal from a decision of the Vicar General; it must be made to the higher tribunal of the Metropolitan, the Archbishop of the province.

Being a Monsignor, the Vicar General is so addressed, and is designated, according to his rank as Protonotary, by the title "Right Reverend" or "Very Reverend."

Other Officials. Each diocese has a Chancellor, whose office is the channel for nearly all diocesan business; and there is also, usually, a Bishop's Secretary. There are also the "Diocesan Consultors," six or more in number, who form an advisory board for the Bishop, and are convened for the discussion of important matters; the Diocesan Attorney, or "Procurator Fiscalis," whose duty is to act as advocate for the Bishop and as prosecutor in ecclesiastical trials; a board for the consideration of reasons for the administrative removal of pastors, consisting of Examiners and Consultors, two of each being chosen for action on each particular case; the Matrimonial Court, consisting usually of a judge, a notary and the "Defender of the Marriage Tie;" the Board of Examiners for the clergy, a similar Board for schools, and the Censor of Books, who examines all works published in the diocese and dealing with matters of faith or morals. A decree of Pope Pius X also provides for a Committee of Vigilance, to guard against the danger of "modernistic" errors.

In some dioceses there is a "Board of Deans," each of whom has supervision over a certain number of parishes and their clergy. In many there are directors of the Priests' Eucharistic League and of other devotional associations, and sometimes there are other officials, committees and boards for various purposes.

The Clergy of Parishes. Over each parish the Church places a Pastor or Rector, who is its ruler both in spiritual and temporal things, subject of course, to the authority of his Bishop and the restrictions of Church law. Each parish has a certain designed territory, and the Pastor is responsible for the care of souls within its limits as well as for its financial management. Each parish, legally considered, is generally a corporation, of which, in some States, the Bishop is the president and the Pastor the treasurer, the Vicar General and two lay members known as trustees forming the rest of the corporation.

In the dioceses of the United States a certain number of the larger parishes have "irremovable" or "permanent" rectorships. A vacancy in these is filled by a "concursus," or competitive examination. And after the Pastor, whether "permanent" or not, come the Curates, the assistant clergy of the parish, who are (theoretically at least) subject to the Pastor and act under his direction in the care of souls.

A priest who has the spiritual care of soldiers or sailors, or who officiates in a hospital or other institution, is called a Chaplain.

Our Church is a spiritual kingdom, indeed, but it is a human society as well. Even considered as a mere worldly institution, it is truly a remarkable example of efficiency and orderly development. No other society on earth is so well and thoroughly organized — so well adapted to its work. Some of the parts of the governmental system of the Catholic Church are of Divine origin; many of them are human institutions; and these are a grand monument to the wisdom of the saintly men who through twenty centuries have sat in the chair of Peter as vice-gerents of Jesus Christ.

PART II
THE RELIGIOUS STATE

Chapter IV

THE MONASTIC LIFE

WHY are certain societies, whose members live in communities and under a defined code of rules, designated as "religious orders"? Not because they have any monopoly of the religious spirit; for the virtues proper to true religion may be found flourishing abundantly throughout the length and breadth of the Catholic world — not only in monastic cloisters but in the busy life of the secular priesthood and in the lowly career of the millions of the pious laity whose fervor and sanctity are known to God alone. But it has become a custom to apply the title of "religious" to those who have given themselves entirely to God in the monastic state and have taken the three vows of poverty, chastity and obedience. Therefore the word is used to designate those who have devoted themselves to the service of God and have forsworn the things of the world, even though there are many others who are equally, though perhaps not so evidently, imbued with the spirit of religion.

The Catholic Church, through nearly all of her history, has encouraged the institution and spread of religious orders. Their value has been appreciated by Pontiffs and Councils, and their labors for the glory of God and the extension of His kingdom have deserved and received commendation in every age since they came into being.

The Desire of Perfection. The religious life, in the sense of monasticism, owes its origin to the desire that arises in the heart of a man who is striving for perfection, to withdraw himself from the excitement and allurements of worldly things, to seek companionship and surroundings that will tend to inspire him with holy thoughts and will give him an opportunity to sanctify himself by recollection, prayer and good works. In the beginning, as we shall see, companionship was not desired; the seeker after perfection became a recluse, a hermit, dwelling in solitude. But gradually it became evident that "in union there is strength," in spiritual things as in worldly; the era of the solitary hermits passed away; and as the centuries rolled on, those grand brigades of the Church's army, the Benedictines, Dominicans, Franciscans, Jesuits and many others, were the result of uniting into strong and well-governed bodies the zealous and the devout who separately might have sanctified themselves but could have been of little benefit to others.

Older than Christianity. The belief in the efficacy of bodily mortification and discipline of the senses prevailed in many religions before the advent of Christianity. Among the Jews there were the Essenes, who withdrew themselves from the luxury and corruption of the cities and formed small communities with strict rules of abstinence and mortification. In pagan lands a similar practice existed, as exemplified by the Stoics, who held that all material things were evil, and that, consequently, he was highest in the scale of perfection who held aloof as far as possible from sensual gratification.

Among the early Christians there was also a strong desire to master the lower parts of man's nature. Unlike the Stoics, they did not consider worldly things to be sinful in themselves, if rightly used; but they strove to bring themselves into more perfect communion with God by strict discipline and self-abnegation. Chastity, fasting, earnest and long-continued prayer, castigation of the body — these were the principal means which were employed, even in the first centuries, by those who sought to "mortify the flesh that the spirit might be strengthened."

The Hermits of the Desert. The ascetics of the early Church did not, at first, separate themselves from the world. They practised their austerities in the midst of their fellow-men. But after a time, about the year 250, the stern persecutions to which the Christians were subjected caused many to seek refuge in the deserts, where they would be comparatively safe from the power of imperial Rome and could serve God without molestation.

The first of these hermits, or anchorites, as they were called, did not live in communities. Even when several of them dwelt in the same neighborhood, each lived in his own cell, supporting himself by his own labor and practising his devotions alone. The life of these solitaries of the desert is not proposed for the imitation of ordinary Christians, even though their sanctity and fervor have been commended by the Church. She praises them as men who were filled with the spirit of sacrifice and desire of perfection, who devoted themselves to lifelong prayer and penance, who vanquished the weaknesses and yearnings of nature and gave up all things for God.

Tradition states that the first who entered upon this solitary life was St. Paul of the Desert, who was succeeded by the famous St. Anthony the Hermit, concerning whose long and severe conflicts with the Spirit of Evil many legends have been handed down. The fame of his sanctity caused others to gather around him, to listen to his wisdom and profit by his example; but even then, each lived in a separate hermitage and generally practised his devotions in solitude.

The First Monasteries. About the year 315 another saintly recluse, St. Pachomius, began what is considered the first monastic house, in which the religious dwelt together in a community. It was seen that there were great advantages in living in the company of others who were striving for the same end, because by mutual example and contact they could each advance more rapidly in virtue.

It was not long before the knowledge of monastic life and the appreciation of its excellence spread throughout the Christian world. St. Hilarion, a disciple of St. Anthony, introduced it into Palestine, and St. Basil established communities of monks in Greece. Others were founded in various parts of Asia Minor; and St. Athanasius, the great bishop of Alexandria, on the occasion of a journey to Rome, is said to have inspired the centre of Christian unity with a wonderful spirit of monastic fervor by preaching there on the life and austerities of St. Anthony.

As missionaries carried the light of the Gospel into the remoter parts of Europe, religious houses sprang up everywhere. St. Martin of Tours founded several monasteries in France and others were established in England, Ireland, Germany, Austria and elsewhere.

The Monastic Rule. In the earliest period of their history the communities were usually independent. Each has its own system of government; but some uniformity was soon seen to be desirable, and gradually certain codes of rulers were formulated for the guidance of these religious bodies. That known as the Augustinian Rule is attributed by some to St. Augustine, although it is very probable that he had nothing to do with its formation. However, it is undoubtedly of very ancient date.

One of the oldest and most celebrated of monastic rules is that established by St. Basil, the great light of the Eastern Church. His laws were adapted to the religious life of the West, and continued in almost universal use until the advent of the great "Father of the Religious Life," St. Benedict, who lived in the sixth century. He instituted the code known as the Benedictine Rule, and for several hundred years nearly all the monastic houses of the Christian world obeyed it and flourished under it. In the course of time several great communities branched off from the Benedictine order, still keeping much of the spirit of the old rule laid down by its saintly founder.

About the beginning of the thirteenth century St. Francis of Assisi founded the Franciscans, who have since been subdivided into many branches. He formulated an excellent rule, which has served as a model for the governing codes of many religious bodies. At almost the same time the zealous St. Dominic established the great order which bears his name, using the ancient rule of the Augustinians as the basis of its statutes.

When Protestantism was spreading devastation throughout the Christian world, a new corps of defenders was organized to aid the kingdom of God in its struggle against error. St. Ignatius of

Loyola founded the Society of Jesus; and the simple but thorough regulations which he laid down for its government may be looked upon as a new and excellent religious rule, differing much in detail from those of other orders, but eminently adapted to the work for which the Society was organized.

A brief history of the above-mentioned orders and of a few other great religious bodies will form the matter of the next chapter.

The Work of the Monks. It is difficult to see how the work of the Church could have been carried on, how her great mission could have been successful, without the help of these great communities. When volunteers have been needed for a particular work, they have always been found ready to undertake it. The nature of the work has varied from age to age. In the early days of monasticism the religious life afforded to the devout an opportunity to withdraw from the wickedness of the decadent Roman world, that they might sanctify themselves in solitude. Later on, there was a need of missionary labor for the conversion of pagan tribes. Then it was necessary to teach them the arts of civilization; and so, all over Europe, great monasteries were established, whose inmates cleared the wilderness and brought it under cultivation. When all of Christendom was in the turmoil of constant warfare, the only abodes of learning were the religious houses; and to the studious zeal of the monks of the so-called Dark Ages we are indebted for the priceless classics of Greek and Latin literature, which were preserved, copied and handed down to us by the patient scribes of countless monasteries. The writings of the early Fathers of the Church have given to later ages a treasury of doctrinal and ascetical lore; and we owe these also to the medieval houses of religion. The Sacred Scriptures themselves would possibly have been lost to the world, or at least would have reached later generations in an imperfect condition, if they had not been laboriously transcribed and multiplied into thousands of copies by the persevering labor of the monastic orders.

Thus we see that the "ignorant and lazy monks," who have long furnished to the enemies of our faith a subject for misrepresentation and deliberate falsehood, have been of considerable use in the world. They were neither ignorant nor lazy. We of this twentieth century would indeed be ignorant were it not for their industry and their love of learning. The Europe of to-day would perhaps be on a level with the Europe of the fourth century, had not these zealous pioneers opened the way to civilization and diffused not only the light of faith but the knowledge of the arts and sciences among the wild tribes of Gaul, of Germany and of Britain.

The great monastic orders have been one of the chief instruments in the spread of God's truth, in the progress of His church; and to-day, while the reasons for their continuance and the work which they are doing are different in some details from those of former times, they are assuredly not less useful than they were in earlier centuries. Their zealous missionaries are carrying the light of the Gospel into the darkness of pagan lands; no danger daunts them, for they have "given up all things to follow Christ." The work of reviving and strengthening the religious spirit in our Catholic faithful is largely entrusted to them; they preach missions to our people and retreats to our clergy with the success that comes from long training and experience. The education of Catholic youth is the work of some; in colleges and seminaries they train the student for the rank in life he is destined to fill, be it Catholic layman or Catholic priest.

We do not deny, we freely admit, that in some parts of the world certain communities have at times fallen away from their first fervor — that abuses have crept in, that unworthy men have been found in the monastic state. But the watchful eye of Mother Church did not long tolerate such laxity. Reforms were instituted, rules were enforced, and the success of her efforts may be seen from the magnitude of the work which the religious orders have accomplished since their foundation, and from their present strength and efficiency after so many centuries.

The monastic orders are assuredly a work of God. He inspired the saintly founders whose wisdom framed the laws under which these societies have achieved such marvelous and long-continued success. He has sanctified their members, imbuing them with the right spirit and intention, bestowing upon them and their work an abundance of grace, and aiding them to secure wonderful results. Long may these ancient institutions live and flourish! Long may they labor in the service of God's Holy Church! There is great work still to be done. "The fields are white with harvest, and the reapers are few" — and some of the reaping can be done with full success only by those who have "left all things" — who have vowed poverty, for they seek not earthly gain; chastity, for they wish to be free from ties of human affection; and obedience, for they know that unless the will of the commander is the law of the soldier, no army can win its battles.

Chapter V

THE GREAT RELIGIOUS ORDERS

It is not within the scope of this work to give a history of all religious orders of men. During the centuries since the monastic life began, many distinct societies have been founded, varying in their rule and in the work which they were intended to perform. We shall be able to devote a little space only to those that are best known and that are active in our own country at the present day.

The Augustinians. This is one of the oldest of the monastic orders. Legend assigns their origin to Apostolic times, and their rule is declared (though without much probability) to have been formed by St. Augustine. There is no real evidence, however, that they existed earlier than the year 816, and they were put into their present form by St. Peter Damian in 1063. They adopted the name of Augustinians, or Canons of St. Austin, because the details of their monastic rule are in conformity with the writings of the great Bishop of Hippo. They spread very rapidly throughout Europe, and were numerous in England at the time of the Reformation. An offshoot of the order, known as the Augustinian Hermits, was the monastic body to which Luther belonged before his rebellion against the Church. The Augustinians have about twenty-five religious houses in different parts of the United States.

The Benedictines. This is the oldest order which has a consecutive history — which has maintained its rule and government practically without change. It was founded by St. Benedict, at Subiaco, in Italy, in 529, and a little later in the great monastery of Monte Cassino was established and has been the centre of government for the order since that time.

Benedictine
(Ancient)

The order has a noble history. It has aided greatly in the extension of Catholicity throughout the world. One of its members, St. Augustine of Canterbury, was the apostle of England; and others in later centuries went from the English monasteries to carry the Gospel into other parts of Europe. The order was for hundreds of years the most flourishing in the Church. Up to the fourteenth century it had given to the Church twenty-four Popes and more than twenty thousand archbishops and bishops.

The order, at several periods of its history, needed reformation to restore the spirit of its saintly founder. New zeal and vigor were infused into it by St. Benedict of Anian in the ninth century, and by Peter the Venerable at Cluny in the twelfth. In England the order was brought back to its original fruitfulness by the great St. Dunstan, and at the time of the Reformation it possessed in that country nearly two hundred houses. Several of the Benedictine abbots and monks were martyred for their faith in London under Henry VIII and Elizabeth, and many others died in prison.

Franciscan

In this country the order has seventeen large abbeys and several colleges and seminaries, and it is in charge of many parishes and missions in the West.

The Franciscans. There are several great religious bodies which are distinct in government but which follow substantially the same rule — that laid down by St. Francis of Assisi. He established a community in 1209, with a most austere rule. Poverty of the severest kind, bodily discipline, untiring zeal for souls, strict fasting, unquestioning obedience — above all, gentleness toward every one — such were the features of the rule of St. Francis.

Some time after his death the order was divided into several branches — the Observants, the Reformed Franciscans, the Capuchins, etc. Some of these were reunited into one body by Pope Leo XIII.

The Franciscans have always been an energetic body of workers. They have devoted themselves to missionary labor in many parts of the world, and the spread of the Gospel in pagan lands is largely due to their zeal and fearlessness. Several of the great lights of Catholic theology were members of this order, and it has given five Popes to the Church. In the United States the various communities which are known as Franciscans possess a large number of monasteries, colleges and other institutions, and have altogether a membership of about one thousand priests and lay-brothers.

The Dominicans. The great "Order of Preachers" has existed since the thirteenth century, and has done remarkable work for the spread of religion and the saving of souls. It was founded by St. Dominic, a Spaniard, who was laboring against the Albigensian heresy, which was widespread and productive of many evils at that time. The society was rapidly extended through the countries of Europe, and when new lands had been discovered beyond the Atlantic the Dominicans took a prominent part in preaching the Gospel in Mexico and Peru.

Dominicans

In the intellectual life of Europe the order held a distinguished place for centuries. Its learned men became professors in the great universities. That most profound of theologians, St. Thomas Aquinas, whose genius has illumined the whole field of Catholic dogma, and whose "Summa Theologica" is the foundation of all succeeding works on doctrine, was a Dominican — famous not only for his incomparable intellect but also for his eminent sanctity. Others who shed luster on the order's history were John Tauler, the Blessed Henry Suso, St. Raymond of Peñafort, Vincent of Beauvais and Dominic Soto. The community has given to the Church three Popes and more than a thousand bishops.

The order is flourishing in many parts of the world, and continues successfully the great task for which it was instituted — the preaching of the word of God. Missions are given with a zeal and effectiveness which come from centuries of experience. The picturesque garb of the Dominicans is familiar to the people as the Fathers have been often employed in the giving of missions in many of our parishes. In the United States the order is divided into two provinces, comprising altogether about 250 priests.

The Trappists. In every epoch of the Church's history there have been some zealous and devout persons who have had a desire and a vocation for a more austere life than that prescribed by the ordinary monastic rule. They wish to practise sterner and more rigorous penances — to "mortify the flesh that the spirit may be strengthened"; and they carry their austerities to a degree which may seem extreme to many — possibly excessive to some.

The strictest of our present-day orders is the Reformed Cistercians, popularly known as the Trappists. This community is an offshoot from the Benedictine order. St. Robert, in the eleventh century, was dissatisfied with certain relaxations of the primitive rule of St. Benedict, and founded a separate congregation with a most rigorous rule, at Citeaux (in Latin, Cistercium), in France, in the year 1098. The aim of the order has always been the sanctification of its members through prayer and penance, and it was not intended that they should care for the souls of others. One of the great lights of this congregation was the illustrious St. Bernard, who founded the famous monastery of Clairvaux, and who is venerated as a Doctor of the Church.

Cistercian

In the course of time there was a tendency to relaxation in the rule, sanctioned in 1475 by Sixtus IV; and this in its turn led to a reform of the order by the establishing of new communities which desired to follow the primitive and rigid rule. The branch now known as the Reformed Cistercians or Trappists was instituted in 1662 at the abbey of La Trappe by Armand de Rance.

The monks of the Trappist order rise at two o'clock in the morning, and recite Matins in choir, adding the Office of the Blessed Virgin (their special patroness) to the regular office. They then make a meditation for a half hour. They celebrate or assist at Mass; the other parts of the office are recited at certain hours and

THE RELIGIOUS STATE

other spiritual exercises are performed. There is no leisure time except that spent in sleep. All the members of the community, priests and brothers, labor with their hands, in the gardens, barns, workshops or fields. There are no delicacies in their daily fare — not even much of what we would call necessaries. No meat is used; vegetables, bread and fruits are the principal articles of diet. One full meal of these is taken at midday, with a frugal collation later in the afternoon. Bedtime comes at seven o'clock in winter, at eight in summer; each retires to his straw bed and sleeps in the rough habit of the order, till the clanging bell at two a. m. summons him to another day of prayer, labor and penance.

The most trying part of the discipline is the rigorous silence. No monk is allowed to speak to another, except to the Superior, and then only about necessary things. The abbot and the guest-master are the only ones who are permitted to speak to strangers.

Truly a wonderful life, in the eyes of those who live as we do in the midst of the luxuries of the twentieth century. It shows that the spirit of zeal for personal sanctification which animated the anchorites of the desert has been handed down to a chosen few in later generations.

The Trappists have several houses in England and Ireland, the famous Mount Melleray being in the latter country. In Canada they have an old-established monastery at Oka, and in the United States their abbeys are four in number.

The Passionists. This order, the complete title of which is "the Congregation of the Discalced Clerks of the Most Holy Cross and Passion of our Lord Jesus Christ," was founded in 1720 by St. Paul of the Cross, a zealous Genoese, whose canonization took place under Pius IX in 1867

The rule of this community is one of considerable severity. In some points it resembles the austere rule of the Trappists, but without the obligation of silence. The Passionists in their monasteries observe the "canonical

Passionist

hours," rising at night for the reciting of the office; and they have frequent fasts and days of abstinence.

Their habit is a plain loose black gown, girt with a leather belt. On the breast they wear an enameled representation of the Heart of our Lord, surmounted by a cross and bearing in white letters XPI Passio — the Passion of Christ. On their feet they wear open sandals, which gives them their title of *Discalced* — that is, unshod.

The Passionists were intended by their founder to exemplify two kinds of religious spirit — contemplative and active. They have had great success in the giving of missions and retreats, due to the excellent training which they receive and to the zeal which animates them. According to the directions of their sainted founder, they are to seek nothing in their preaching but the good of souls, and are to set always before the faithful the sufferings and death of our Blessed Saviour as the greatest motive of repentance.

They have two provinces in the United States, and number altogether about three hundred, of whom nearly one-half are priests.

The Redemptorists. Another order which devotes itself mainly to the preaching of missions is the Congregation of the Most Holy Redeemer, generally known as the Redemptorists. It was founded by St. Alphonsus Liguori, in 1732. The Saint wished to form a band of apostolic men who "should preach the Gospel to the poor," as our Saviour did. The order was approved by Benedict XIV, and has always been distinctly a missionary society. Its members take the usual three vows, of poverty, chastity and obedience, and bind themselves also by a vow of perseverance — that is, to remain in the order until death.

Redemptorist

They are to be found in nearly all the countries of the Catholic world, and they are engaged in missionary labor in many pagan lands. They have met with great opposition from the infidel governments of Europe, and have been repeatedly driven out of so-called Catholic countries. In the United States they have two provinces, the total membership being more than seven hundred, of whom about one-half are priests.

The Jesuits. The promise of our Blessed Lord, "Behold, I am with you all days," has been amply fulfilled in every age of the Church's history. In the centuries when she was evangelizing Europe the need was for zealous and fearless apostles to spread the light of the Gospel among pagan nations — and God provided them. Later, when heresies were rife, the Church required men who could declare her teachings accurately and explain them clearly — and an Augustine, an Athanasius, a Chrysostom were given to the world. When the tribes of central and northern Europe were emerging from barbarism and needed to be instructed in the arts of civilization, the Church found her most effective instruments in the great monastic orders.

Jesuit

In the sixteenth century came a new danger and a new need. Protestantism arose, and spread with alarming rapidity. It spurned the authority of Christ's Vicar on earth, rejected some of the most essential of Catholic dogmas, extended its dominion over the fairest parts of Europe, and led millions into the darkness of unbelief. Then God raised up new champions of the truth, strong defenders of His Church — that admirable body of religious men known as "the Society of Jesus," or the Jesuits.

In 1521 a Spanish soldier received a severe wound in battle. It was Ignatius of Loyola, of a noble Biscayan family, and up to that time he had shown no special inclination toward religion. During his recovery from his injury he happened to read a volume of "Lives of the Saints" — and a new career was unfolded before him. He resigned his military commission, retired from the world, and formed the resolution of establishing a new religious community which should wage unceasing war on error — which should devote itself to the cause of the Gospel and of Catholic truth, and carry the light of the true faith to the heretic and the heathen.

In 1534, having been ordained a priest, he gathered around him, at Paris, six zealous companions, and bound them and himself by a solemn vow "to preach the Gospel in Palestine or elsewhere, and to offer themselves to the Sovereign Pontiff to be employed in the service of God in what manner he should judge best." In 1536 the new society was received by Pope Paul III, and was solemnly approved in 1540.

The members of the Society of Jesus take the usual three vows of the religious state — poverty, chastity and obedience; and they add to these a fourth vow which reflects clearly the spirit of the order and of its intrepid founder. They bind themselves to go without question or delay wherever the Sovereign Pontiff may send them for the salvation of souls. Their motto is "For the greater glory of God" — "Ad Majorem Dei Gloriam"; and the initial letters of these Latin words (A. M. D. G.) are a favorite symbol of the Jesuits.

The scope of their labors is indeed a wide one. Preaching, spiritual exercises, all kinds of charitable endeavor, teaching elementary and advanced science, giving retreats, missionary work among Christians and heathen — all of these are specified in their constitution. Each member of the order must undergo a long and rigorous probation, the details of which are embodied in the "Book of the Exercises," which Saint Ignatius wrote before he established his Society. Personal sanctification is ensured by mental prayer, examination of conscience, pious reading and frequent retreats. The Jesuit must be a man of learning, and his natural talents are carefully fostered. The long and discriminating training which its members receive is responsible for much of the success which the order has achieved. The novice who manifests an aptitude for any particular branch of useful learning is subjected to a thorough course of instruction in that line. If he has natural ability as an orator, he receives training which will develop that talent; if he gives evidence of a genius for sciences, or languages, or philosophy, he is urged to perfect himself in all that pertains to his speciality, without neglecting his education in other directions. Each becomes an expert in something; and, as a result, the Society has produced a multitude of preachers, professors, writers, scientists and defenders of Catholic truth who have been of incalculable benefit to the Church and have aided immeasurably in her work of diffusing Christian knowledge among men.

The saintly Loyola intended that his followers should be soldiers of Christ, ever in the forefront of the battle; and these soldiers were to be not only men of action but men of prayer. They were not to dwell in solitude, like the anchorites of early days; they were to be "in the world, but not of it"; and they were to be themselves sanctified that they might sanctify others. They were not to strive for worldly honors, nor to accept ecclesiastical dignities unless by a special command of the Holy See.

The annals of the Jesuits are a brilliant chapter of history, but any detailed account of them will not be feasible here. During the lifetime of their founder they established universities in Rome and elsewhere, and were also engaged in missionary labor in all parts of the world. Zealous and learned teachers were sent into Germany and France, and waged a vigorous and successful war against the heresies of Luther and Calvin. St. Francis Xavier journeyed to the far East and brought the faith of Jesus Christ to India and Japan. Somewhat later came the glorious epoch of Jesuit missionary enterprise in the New World. The adventurous Marquette discovered the Mississippi. French priests, filled with ardor for souls, went among the savage Indian tribes, and were put to death with fiendish tortures. Lallemant, Brebeuf, Daniel, Jogues — these are a few of the brave Jesuits who gave up all things, even life itself, that the light of God's truth might shine in the dark places of the earth. "Greater love than this no man hath."

The enemies of Christian truth and morality lost no opportunity to harm the Society of Jesus. It encountered strong opposition from its very foundation, and was subjected to many unjust accusations. Ambitious politicians in many countries sought its downfall, and the climax came when the rulers of Europe succeeded in securing the election of a Pope who was not friendly to the Jesuits. He was Clement XIV, formerly Cardinal Ganganelli, and in 1773 he issued a decree by which the Society of Jesus was suppressed in every part of the world, and its members were directed to enter the ranks of the secular clergy.

This action of the Holy See was unprecedented in the history of religious societies, and it is difficult to ascertain the true reasons for it. There seems to have been little cause for such drastic action except the hatred of freethinking despots and the prejudices of a pliant Pontiff. Lalande, the distinguished astronomer, voiced the sentiment of the best minds when he said: "They have destroyed the best work of man, unrivalled by any human institution — an army of twenty thousand men, unceasingly employed with duties most important and useful to the world."

Among those who were thus compelled to secularize themselves was the famous John Carroll, afterward the first bishop of Baltimore and the first American member of the hierarchy.

In 1814 the Jesuits were permitted to reorganize, under Pius VII, and since that time they have had an uninterrupted though troubled existence — ever in the van of battle, everywhere assailed by the forces of infidelity and revolution, always the first to feel the wrath of the enemies of God's Church.

In the United States the Society of Jesus is notably prosperous. It has five large provinces, with about 1300 priests, 1000 scholastics and 500 lay-brothers. It conducts no less than thirty-four colleges of various grades, manages many parishes, does extensive missionary work, and is especially successful in the preaching of missions for the laity and of retreats for the clergy.

The Society is ruled by a Superior-General, elected for life, whose authority is practically absolute. The garb of the order is a loose black cassock, with a white linen collar attached, and a black sash or girdle.

It is indeed a mark of God's providence that this great religious society was re-established, for without their ardent zeal and well-directed energy the condition of the Church throughout the world, and especially in our own land, would be far less prosperous than we find it to-day.

The Christian Brothers. A most essential part of the work of the Church is the education of the young. Upon the intellectual and moral training that is given to them depends the future welfare of God's kingdom on earth.

No religious body has been more successful in its allotted field of labor than the Christian Brothers, more properly known as "The Brothers of the Christian Schools." This congregation of teachers, respected and admired throughout the world, was founded by a priest, although its members are not elevated to the priesthood. St. John Baptist de la Salle was a man of grand intellect, steadfast will and ardent piety; and his life was so holy and the fruits of his zeal so wonderful that he was beatified by Pope Leo XIII in 1888 and canonized by the same Pontiff in 1900.

Christian Brother

His efforts were first directed towards the Christian education of youth by a zealous layman, M. Nyel, of Rouen, who had himself devoted much time and money to that excellent work. Having established a corps of teachers, the Abbé de la Salle, in 1684, drew up a code of rules for them and chose the title they now bear — the "Brothers of the Christian Schools." The system of instruction formulated by him has never been equaled for effectiveness; and many of the much-vaunted discoveries of modern pedagogy are mere rivals of ideas originated by the zealous French priest. The Brothers have been prominent in education work for more than two hundred years, and these have been years of constant expansion and progress. They have always been in the van; they keep pace with the development of the arts and sciences, and are always prepared to impart to their pupils the latest and the best results of the world's advance in civilization.

The new religious society was solemnly approved by Pope Benedict XIII in 1725, and was established as a "religious congregation." It has had a checkered career. The storms of persecution which have swept over France have often driven the Brothers into exile, but sooner or later they have returned and resumed their work. At the present time the Congregation is not allowed to teach there as a body; it has been despoiled of its property, and the results of its earnest labor of many years are being obliterated. In other countries it has been prosperous. Its membership at the present time is more than seventeen thousand, and in its schools are nearly 350,000 pupils, of whom about 40,000 are in the United States.

The religious rule of the Brothers is fairly strict in its requirements. A thorough course of study is necessarily demanded. A review of primary branches and a comprehensive normal course are exacted from each candidate. He takes the usual religious vows, and pledges himself to remain a layman — for the Brothers are not allowed to aspire to the priesthood.

They wear in their schools and convents a black cassock with a white collar having two square wings at the front — the clerical collar of the French Church in the seventeenth century.

Their title expresses well their purpose. They are "Brothers," not priests; merely laymen living in community, banded together for a noble work; "Brothers of the Christian Schools," for the school is their field of labor, wherein these zealous reapers garner mighty harvests. They are teachers; and the substance of their teaching is, first of all, the religion of Jesus Christ — and, secondly, the whole field of useful human knowledge, illumined by the light of His doctrine.

. . . .

There are scores of other religious bodies which deserve extended notice, and would receive it if space permitted. We shall be compelled to pass over our zealous American society, the Paulist Fathers; the Sulpicians, who devote themselves to the training of candidates for the priesthood; the Carmelites, the Fathers of the Holy Ghost, the Congregation of the Holy Cross, the Marists, the Oblates, the Vincentians, and many others. And even with this multiplicity of religious societies, "the harvest indeed is great and the laborers are few."

CHAPTER VI

RELIGIOUS LIFE FOR WOMEN

IN the work of the Catholic Church, which is the sanctifying of souls and the diffusion of the knowledge of God's truth, a very important part is taken by women. It is true that they are not eligible to Holy Orders. A woman cannot be a priest. She is not empowered to preach the Word of God officially, nor to share in the government of the Church, nor to administer sacraments — excepting, of course, the giving of Baptism privately in case of necessity. But she is permitted not only to aspire to perfection, but to assist largely in the perfecting of others; and she is provided by the Church with ample means of self-sanctification and with a broad field of effort in the domain of charity.

What would our Church be — what would be its condition throughout the world to-day, were it not for the zealous labors of those saintly women who have given up all things to follow Christ?

Called by God. At an age when the world is most attractive, when its allurements are most potent, when the natural instincts of humanity crave for affection and worldly ties, some women deliberately choose to leave the world, to sacrifice their right to its lawful pleasures, to devote themselves to arduous work, rigorous self-restraint, severe penance, strict obedience and perpetual chastity. For what reason? Because in their souls they hear the call of Jesus Christ, inviting them to become His servants, to do His work in a state of life higher and more perfect than any that the world could offer them. The life of seclusion and prayer and charitable endeavor is attractive to these holy souls. They have the desire of self-sacrifice; they perceive the vanity of earthly things; they long for the service of our Blessed Lord, and are zealous for the promotion of His glory.

Religious Women in Early Times. The religious state for women in the Catholic Church is probably as ancient as that for men. Long before the institution of nunneries, the Church recognized and recommended several classes of pious women. St. Paul speaks of the holy state of widowhood, in which devout elderly women gave themselves to works of charity; and writers of the first centuries mention other varieties of work assigned to the gentler sex. Some were known as deaconesses, who labored among the poor, hospitallers, who cared for the sick; canonesses, one of whose duties was to assist at burials; and consecrated virgins, who at first lived at home and practised their devotions in private.

When religious communities of men were established in Egypt and elsewhere, t hose for women began to be recognized as of almost equal value; and before the end of the fourth century they were common in many parts of the world. St. Augustine founded one in northern Africa, and St. Scholastica, who was St. Benedict's sister, governed a religious house for women under a rule prepared by that great "Father of the Monastic Life." And a the centuries rolled on, the Church encouraged more and more the establishing of new societies of women, until they have been multiplied almost beyond counting.

The Work of the Sisterhoods. They are engaged in manifold labors. They teach the young the principles of worldly science as well as of spiritual things. They care for the orphan, the aged, the infirm, the wayward. They journey fearlessly into distant lands, to aid in the extension of Christ's Kingdom among pagan tribes. When war fills the hospitals with wounded men — when the breath of pestilence sweeps over the land — when the leper colony needs nurses who are not afraid of disease or death, the Catholic nun takes her place and does her work, without flourish of trumpets or desire of earthly commendation. She does not fear death, for death means the attainment of a long-sought reward; and she would only regret its approach because it would end the labor that she loves.

All this heroic work in the service of her Master is done unassumingly, without ostentation or desire of praise. We are so accustomed to see it that we take it almost as a matter of course, giving little credit oftentimes to those who are doing it. We honor the brave — but generally we give the most honor to the brave who advertise themselves. When a soldier, whose profession is fighting, risks his life in some daring deed of heroism, the whole land rings with praises of his bravery. The Sister who goes to a remote Chinese mission or to a small-pox hospital or a leper settlement, is risking her life just as bravely and much more deliberately — but we seldom hear of her. The Catholic nun has been doing such work for several hundred years; but she wears no medals of honor, and is seldom mentioned in the newspapers.

The Three Vows. The woman who enters a Catholic religious order or sisterhood binds herself by a threefold vow, to which, in some cases, other solemn promises are annexed, varying according to the special work to which the order is devoted.

First of all, the Church recognizes the dangers of self-will and the advantages of perfect and harmonious cooperation; and therefore the Sister takes a vow of perpetual and complete obedience. This is the foundation upon which every religious community is erected and sustained. They pledge themselves to conquer their own inclinations; to obey in all things the wise laws laid down for the guidance and government; to look upon the rule, interpreted by their lawful superior, as the expression of God's will in their regard. And it is owing to the completeness with which this essential vow has been observed that the results of their labors are so wonderful. Each order, each separate convent, becomes a smoothly working machine, doing its appointed work with all its component parts moving in harmony; and the desire of each member is not the securing of her own comfort or the satisfying of her own ambitions, but the doing of her allotted task so that the whole work may be thereby made more perfect.

The nun also takes a vow of poverty. She says, like St. Paul: "I esteem all things as naught that I may gain Christ." She is willing that the fruits of her labor shall not be her own. She cares not for worldly luxury. Her habit, her cell, her plain but sufficient food — these are assured her. She is better fitted for her chosen work because she has few anxieties.

The Catholic nun makes also another and greater sacrifice. She dedicates her virginity to Almighty God, taking a vow of perpetual chastity, that she may "think on the things of the Lord and be holy in body and spirit." The state of matrimony is holy, and the virtues of Christian wives and mothers are worthy of all praise; but holier still, and more perfect, and more deserving of admiration is the state of those who voluntarily make a sacrifice of all worldly affections that they may be better able to serve God without being restrained by earthly ties. They enter into espousals with Christ, as is so beautifully expressed in the ritual of their profession. They put the crown on their self-sacrifice and consecration to God by a virtue which is well called the queen of all virtues.

A Striking Contrast. In proportion to the strength of the Church and of Catholic spirit in any country is the progress of the institutions which the Church fosters. When error and irreligion seek to undermine and overthrow the influence of Catholicism, they always begin by destroying these centres of Catholic effort. And with what result? When the homes of the sisterhoods have been suppressed and their members dispersed, the growth of the virtues of charity and mercy has been blighted. In Protestant and infidel lands we have schools without religion, hospitals and almshouses without charity. In Catholic countries alone, or in those in which the progress of the Church is not hampered by hostile legislation, we find the perfect manifestation of Christian charity in the grand institutions established by the handmaids of Christ, in which they give themselves body and soul to the service of their Divine Spouse.

There is not an infirmity or affliction to which our fallen nature is heir, that has not found its appropriate remedy in some department of the work of these societies of women. They instruct the ignorant, feed and clothe the poor, visit and care for the sick; they provide for the helpless infant, the orphan child and the aged; they harbor and reform the fallen. They are angels of mercy, messengers of divine charity, who vary the field of their zeal according to the needs of mankind. They are the wise virgins of the parable, bearing lighted lamps and shedding their radiance on the dark places of the world, that the Bridegroom may come and make His abode in the souls which He died to save.

PART III
THE ADMINISTRATION OF THE SACRAMENTS

Chapter VII

THE CEREMONIES OF BAPTISM

IN order to symbolize the spiritual benefits derived from the reception of the Sacraments, the Church uses for each of them (except the Sacrament of Penance) certain ceremonies which are, for the most part, of very ancient origin. They are intended to denote mystically the gifts and graces bestowed on the soul through the Sacrament which is administered.

Baptism is the first of the Sacraments. In the language of the Apostle, it "clothes us with Jesus Christ." The sacred rites with which it is given remind us of the corruption in which we were born, the trials that await us in this world, and the immortal heritage for which we are destined.

In the Early Ages. The ceremonies of Baptism, as now practised, are a survival of the solemn rites with which it was administered in the early Church. We find a complete and curious account of this in the work of St. Ambrose "On the Mysteries." In his day Baptism was given publicly to adults on Holy Saturday only, and this fact is still indicated in the Church's liturgy by the blessing of the baptismal water on that day. The minister of the Sacrament at this solemn administration was always a bishop, assisted by priests and deacons.

On those occasions Baptism was usually given by immersion — by putting the person entirely under water. This was never considered essential, but was generally practised until about the ninth century.

In ancient ceremonies, after the baptized person had been anointed with holy oil and clothed in a white garment, he immediately received the Sacrament of Confirmation, assisted at Mass and usually received Holy Communion.

In our times the Sacrament of Baptism is given to infants much more frequently than to adults. The sponsors or god-parents bring the child to the baptismal font, and the priest, clad in surplice and purple stole, asks (mentioning the name which the child is to bear): "What dost thou ask of the Church of God?" The sponsors answer: "Faith." "What does faith bring thee to?" "Life everlasting." "If therefore thou wouldst enter life, keep the commandment: Thou shalt love the Lord thy God with thy whole heart and soul and mind, and thy neighbor as thyself."

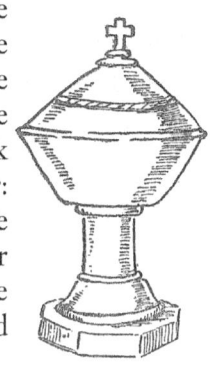

Baptismal Font

He then breathes on the face of the child, saying: "Depart from him, thou unclean spirit, and give place to the Holy Ghost, the Comforter." This ancient ceremony of breathing is always symbolical of the imparting of the Spirit of God.

The Sign of the Cross. The forehead and breast of the infant are then marked with the sign of the cross, to signify that he must be sanctified in mind and heart. An appropriate prayer is then recited, asking that the child thus marked with the cross of Christ may keep His commandments and gain everlasting life.

The priest then places his hand upon the head of the child — which ceremony is always symbolical of the giving of strength and power. He prays that this servant of God, who has been called to the light of faith, may be freed from all blindness of heart and all snares of Satan; that he may be imbued with wisdom, may joyfully serve God in His Church, and advance daily in holiness.

The Giving of the Salt. Then follows a curious ceremony. A small quantity of salt, previously blessed, is put into the mouth of the person to be baptized, with the words: "Receive the salt of wisdom. May it be unto thee a propitiation unto eternal life."

Salt, in the symbolic usage of the Church, has many meanings. It denotes wisdom, regeneration, purification, preservation from corruption — as we see in the passage of the Gospel wherein our Lord calls His Apostles "the salt of the earth." These meanings are expressed in the next prayer, in which God is besought to sanctify the person who has tasted this salt; that he may be filled with heavenly food, that he may be fervent in spirit, joyful in hope, and faithful in the service of God.

The Exorcisms. According to the teaching of the Fathers of the Church, the soul of an unbaptized person is particularly under the dominion of the spirits of darkness. Therefore a solemn adjuration is pronounced, in the name of the three Persons of the Trinity, commanding the devil to depart from the servant of God. Then the sign of the cross is again traced on his forehead, as a shield and protection against any further attacks of Satan.

With the imposing of the priest's hand on the child, another solemn prayer is offered, beseeching God the Father, the Author of light and truth, to illumine this His servant with the light of understanding — to cleanse and sanctify him — to give him true knowledge, that by the grace of Baptism he may possess firm hope, right counsel, and holy doctrine.

The priest then lays the end of his stole on the infant — a relic of the ceremony of early days, when the catechumens were conducted into the church in solemn procession. Then the sponsors, together with the priest, make a profession of faith in the name of the child, by reciting aloud the Apostles' Creed, which is followed by the Our Father.

The "Ephpheta" and the Vows. After another exorcism comes the ceremony of the "Ephpheta." The priest moistens his finger with saliva from his own mouth, and touches lightly the ears and nostrils of the child, saying: "Ephpheta, which is: Be thou opened, in the odor of sweetness; go out from him, O evil spirit; for the judgment of God will come."

The touching of the ears signifies the opening of the understanding to the Word of God; that of the nostrils denotes the sweetness of the spiritual life. The use of saliva reminds us of a ceremony used by our Lord in one of His miracles, as recorded in the Gospels.

The baptismal vows are next in order. The priest asks the child, by name: "Dost thou renounce Satan?" And the sponsors answer: "I do renounce him." "And all his works?" "I do renounce them." "And all his pomps?" "I do renounce them."

The Anointing. The first anointing is then made, with the Oil of Catechumens. The priest dips his thumb into the blessed oil and marks the sign of the cross on the breast of the infant and on the back between the shoulders saying; "I anoint thee with the oil of salvation, in Christ Jesus our Lord, that thou mayest have eternal life."

The cross on the breast means that our holy faith is a shield against temptation. That on the back signifies that to obtain salvation through Jesus Christ we must "take up our cross and follow Him."

The priest then puts on a white stole in the place of the purple one, and solemnly inquires: "Dost thou believe in God, the Father Almighty, Creator of heaven and earth?" The sponsors answer: "I do believe." "dost thou believe in Jesus Christ, His only Son, our Lord, Who was born and suffered?" "I do believe." "Dost thou believe in the Holy Ghost, the Holy Catholic Church," etc.; and the same answer is given. Then, addressing the child by name, the priest asks: "Wilt thou be baptized?" — and the sponsors answer: "I will."

Baptismal Shell

The Baptism. The sponsors hold the child over the font, and the priest takes a small vessel which he fills with the baptismal water, pouring it upon the head of the infant three times in the form of a cross, saying at the same time the sacramental words: "N——, I baptize thee in the name of the Father and of the Son and of the Holy Ghost."

The top of the child's head is immediately anointed with Holy Chrism in the form of a cross, to denote that he has been made a Christian. Then comes a ceremony which is a survival of the ancient practice of attiring the newly baptized person in white robes. The priest takes a white cloth and drapes it over the child's head, adjuring him to "receive this white robe, and carry it spotless before the judgment-seat of our Lord Jesus Christ."

A lighted candle is then placed in the hands of the sponsors, typifying the light of faith and the flame of charity; and the baptized person is urged: "Keep thy Baptism without blame; observe God's commandments; so that when the Lord cometh to the wedding-feast thou mayest meet Him with all the saints in the halls of heaven, and mayest obtain eternal life."

Then with the simple words of farewell and benediction, "Go in peace, and the Lord be with thee," the ceremonies come to an end.

Thus we see how the beautiful symbolism of our Church's rites expresses clearly the wonderful effects of Baptism on the soul of man. These ancient ceremonies are intended to illustrate the freeing of the human soul from the domination of Satan, the cleansing of it from original sin, and the strengthening of it against the world, the flesh and the devil. They denote the receiving of a new and holy character, and the adding to the flock of Christ of a new member, destined to everlasting life in God's heavenly Kingdom.

Chapter VIII

THE SPONSORS IN BAPTISM

In the administration of the Sacrament of Baptism a very prominent part is taken by the sponsors or god-parents, who present the child at the baptismal font and make a profession of faith and certain promises in his name. As this is an office which may fall to the lot of any of our readers, it may be well to explain just what the duties of sponsors are, and what are the obligations which they assume; for there is danger in undertaking these duties without due consideration and of estimating these obligations lightly.

An Ancient Practice. From the very beginning it has been the practice of the Church to have certain persons assisting at the administration of Baptism, whether of an infant or an adult — to offer the infant at the font, to answer for it, to make a profession of the Christian faith in its name, and to receive it from the hands of the priest after it is baptized; to act as witnesses of the Baptism of adults, and to attest their acceptance of the Church's teaching and their avowal of allegiance to her authority. These persons, from these various duties were called, in the Latin of the Ritual, "Sponsors," or Promisers, "Fidejussores," or Attestors of Faith, "Offerentes," or Offerers, or "Susceptores," Receivers.

In later times they have usually been called "Patrini," a medieval Latin word signifying those taking the place of parents, since they undertake the office of spiritual parents towards those whom they bring to the sacramental font. In English they are called "god-fathers" and "god-mothers," which words denote the spiritual relationship which they acquire.

The Duties of Sponsors. The Catechism of the Council of Trent directs that "all sponsors should at all times recollect that they are bound to exercise always great vigilance over their spiritual children, and to take particular care that, in those things that pertain to the Christian life, the baptized persons shall act through life as the sponsors promised for them at the solemn ceremony of Baptism." If for any reason the natural guardians of a child are unable or unwilling to attend to its religious training, this must be looked after by the god-parent. Of course, in the case of an adult there is a less likelihood that such responsibility would come upon a sponsor; but for those who assist at the Baptism of a child there is a serious obligation, and one which every god-parent should understand and appreciate — that if the child's parents do not provide for its Christian training, the burden comes upon those who have assumed a spiritual relationship with it.

The sponsor at the administration of Baptism holds the child or physically touches it while the sacrament is being conferred — or at least receives it from the priest's hands immediately after it has been baptized. The actual holding of it by both sponsors while the water is being poured is the custom with us.

It is allowed in certain cases for a person to become a sponsor "by proxy" — that is, to assume the office and obligations without being actually present, by having an agent take his place. This is the case sometimes in royal families and elsewhere, when it is desired to have as god-parent some person who cannot be present. In this case the proxy or agent contracts no obligations whatever, these being assumed by the real sponsor whom he represents.

Impediments from Sponsorship. How many sponsors are allowable? Only two at the most — a man and a woman; and only one is strictly necessary. Why is the number so restricted? Because a spiritual relationship is contracted by the sponsor with the baptized person and his parents — a relationship which would be an impediment to marriage unless a dispensation were previously obtained; that is, no person is permitted, without dispensation, to marry his or her god-parent or god-child, or the father or mother of the god-child. This spiritual relationship is looked upon by the Church as a real relationship, binding in some respects as strongly as a tie of blood.

Do sponsors contract any impediment in regard to each other? Or, in other words, if a man and a woman become god-parents of a child, is there any obstacle thereby to their subsequent marriage? No; the impediment exists only between a god-parent and a god-child, and between the god-parent and the father or mother of the god-child.

The Qualifications of Sponsors. On account of the all-important duties which sponsors may be called upon to perform, it is not surprising that the Church requires her pastors to make diligent inquiry regarding persons selected for this office, and to enforce the rule that none but those who would be suitable guardians of the child's spiritual welfare can become godparents.

The two sponsors should be of different sexes — not two men nor two women; for it is deemed proper that there should be an analogy between spiritual and natural parentage. When there is only one sponsor, it is usual (but not necessary) to select one of the same sex as the child, for thereby it is made certain that there will never be any question of marriage between the godparent and the god-child. Parents are not allowed to be sponsors for their own children, to mark more strongly the difference between spiritual and carnal parentage — for it is not deemed proper that one person should hold both relationships.

In the private administration of Baptism, whether by a priest or a layman, there are no sponsors. The person who holds the child contracts no relationship. After private Baptism the Church requires that the baptized child be presented at the font for the supplying of the other ceremonies. It is then necessary to have sponsors, and they bind themselves to look after the Christian education of the child if their intention should be needful — but they contract no impediment as regards marriage.

The Church directs that small children shall not be chosen as sponsors. They should be fourteen years or more of age, and should have received the Sacrament of Confirmation. In certain dioceses it is expressly forbidden to select god-parents who have not made their "Easter duty."

Members of religious communities, whether men or women, are not allowed to be sponsors, and in some dioceses the clergy are also forbidden to assume this obligation.

The choosing of non-Catholics is not permitted. The Church does not wish that the Christian training of her children should be entrusted tho those who are themselves in error. And, in general, all those who are unable or unwilling to discharge with fidelity the duties of a spiritual parent should not be admitted to this sacred trust.

In the chapter on "The Ceremonies of Baptism" the duties of the sponsors at the font have been sufficiently mentioned. If the father of the child is not present, the god-parents should be prepared to answer the various questions which the priest may ask — as to the names and residence of the child's parents, the date of birth, the name to be given, whether the infant has been privately baptized or not, and, if so, by whom. When it can be conveniently done, the person who has baptized privately should be present, to explain to the priest how the Baptism was administered, and thereby to enable him to ascertain whether it was valid or not.

The Name of the Child. As one of the duties of the sponsors is to tell the priest the name which is to be conferred on the child at its Baptism, it may be well to say a word about the choice of the name. The Church, in her rubrics and in the writings of her teachers, has expressed the wish that it should really be a Christian name — the name of a Saint. The use of that name will serve to stimulate the imitation of the virtues of the Saint and the attainment of holiness like to his; and the blessed one in heaven who is thus made the patron of the new member of Christ's flock on earth will, by his advocacy and intercession, become the guardian of the soul and body of the person upon whom his name has been bestowed.

Is this an obligation? It is not. The priest is merely admonished by the Church's rubric to do what he can to have every child baptized in the name of a Saint. But it may easily happen that in some special cases there are reasons for giving another name — as in the contingency that an inheritance might depend upon it, or that the memory of a loved relative might thus be perpetuated. In such cases it is recommended that another name, that of some Saint, be added or prefixed to the name desired. Outside of these exceptional instances, our Catholic parents should remember that the name of a Saint is better for their child than the name of the heroine of a novel; that our ordinary English names are finer and more appropriate than French ones, which are usually mispronounced; that the use of a "stylish" baptismal name in conjunction with a good old Celtic patronymic is incongruous, to say the least; and that it is no evidence of refinement (except the refinement of cruelty) to inflict such combinations upon their helpless offspring. To quote a caustic bit of Irish wit: "There are three hundred and sixty-five saints' days in the year, and they named their child after a nut. They called her Hazel!"

Chapter IX

THE CEREMONIES OF CONFIRMATION

In this chapter we shall examine the history and liturgy of a sacrament which we all have received, and which is of special interest because, unlike Baptism, we can remember when we received it. Confirmation was administered to us when we had come to the age of reason, and after a long and thorough preparation. The ceremonies and prayers which the Church uses in conferring it are not long nor numerous; but they express very clearly the meaning of the sacrament and the nature of the special graces given through its administration.

The Nature of the Sacrament. Confirmation is a sacrament of the Church through which grace is conferred on baptized persons, strengthening them for the duty of professing the Christian faith. As the Catechism tells us, by it we are made "strong and perfect" in our Christianity; we become "soldiers of Jesus Christ," earnest and loyal in His service, willing to wage war against His enemies and ours. It is administered ordinarily by a bishop, who makes the sign of the cross with chrism on the forehead of the recipient, while he pronounces a certain formula of words.

This sacrament not only gives us special graces to help us to live up to our faith, but also, like Baptism and Holy Orders, imprints a seal or character upon the soul — an indelible spiritual mark which remains forever, and which renders the repetition of the sacrament at any future time impossible.

A Catholic Sacrament. Confirmation is a Catholic sacrament. It is true that it exists in the schismatic churches of the East, which were originally members of the true Church and have preserved most of her teaching; but the Protestant sects have always denied the sacramental nature of Confirmation. Some reject it altogether; others, such as the Episcopalians, retain an imitation of it — a ceremony which they call Confirmation, but which they hold to be merely a rite and not a sacrament. With them it consists in the public renewing and confirming of the promises made for them by their sponsors at Baptism. But the

Catholic Church has always held that Confirmation is one of the seven sacraments, the God-given channels by which His grace is brought to our souls through the ministry of His Church. In it we have all the requisites for a true sacrament — the outward sign, the giving of grace, and the divine institution.

Confirmation in the Scriptures. This sacrament was instituted by our Blessed Lord, for it is a doctrine of our holy faith that each of the seven sacraments owes its origin not to the Church nor to the Apostles, but to Christ Himself. There is no mention in the Gospels of such institution; but according to tradition and the general opinion of the Doctors of the Church, it took place during the forty days after the Resurrection of our Savior.

The first account of it is found in the eighth chapter of the Acts of the Apostles. St. Philip, a deacon, had converted and baptized certain Samaritans, and when he announced this fact to Peter and John, these Apostles went down from Jerusalem and "laid their hands upon them, and they received the Holy Ghost." In St. Paul's Epistles allusion is also made to the same sacrament, by which Christians are made "partakers of the Holy Ghost" and are "sealed with the Holy Spirit of promise."

In the works of the early writers of the Christian Church we find Confirmation mentioned repeatedly. In the first centuries it was generally conferred immediately after Baptism. Tertullian speaks of "the imposition of hands on the baptized, which calls and invites the Holy Ghost."

The Minister of Confirmation. Who can give this sacrament? In our Catechism we are taught that "the bishop is the ordinary minister of Confirmation." In our part of the world, and, in fact, the whole Western Church, this sacrament is always administered by a bishop, except in very special cases; for example, if a missionary were going into the middle of Africa or to the remoter parts of China, he might receive permission from the Pope to carry holy chrism and to give the sacrament of Confirmation to his converts, who otherwise would never be able to receive it, since they could never have access to a bishop. In the Eastern Churches Confirmation has been for many centuries administered by priests, and in the Churches which are united to the Roman See this custom is tacitly permitted.

The Matter of Confirmation. What is strictly required in the administration of this sacrament? There has been much dispute about this. Some ancient writers held that the essence of Confirmation was the laying on of hands — that the anointing with oil is not necessary; but the great majority of authorities as well as the wording of the Church's ritual support the teaching that the real "matter" of this sacrament is the anointing with the consecrated oil which we call *chrism*.

This is olive oil with which balm or balsam of a certain kind has been mixed. This balm is a species of perfumed resin which exudes from a tree called the terebinth, which grows abundantly in Eastern lands, especially in Arabia. Similar substances are produced in the West Indies and in the tropical parts of America.

Probably in the first ages of the Church pure oil without admixture was used; but we find mention of the use of balm from about the sixth century. In many Eastern churches the chrism is highly perfumed, and rare spices of many kinds are dissolved in it; but the uniform practice of the Roman Church has been to prepare the chrism simply with olive oil and balm. The oil is symbolic of strength, for it was used by the athletes and gymnasts of classic times as an ointment, to promote bodil vigor; of light, because it can be used in lamps, to dispel darkness; of health, because it is taken internally as a food and a medicine. The balm denotes freedom from corruption and the "sweet odor of virtue."

The chrism is blessed on Holy Thursday in every cathedral church. This is an ancient custom, going back before the year 500. The beautiful ceremonies which accompany this solemn blessing are described elsewhere in this work.

The Words of Confirmation. To administer Confirmation validly, what form of words must be used? Here again there is a great diversity of opinion and of practice. Among the Greeks the form is: "The seal of the gift of the Holy Ghost," and this has been in use among them from very early times. The words used in our Latin ceremonial are: "I sign thee with the sign of the cross and I confirm thee with the chrism of salvation, in the name of the Father and of the Son and of the Holy Ghost." These date back only to the twelfth century.

Before that time a very common form was: "I confirm thee in the name of the Father," etc. In some parts of the world these words were used: "The sign of the cross with eternal life'" and elsewhere the following very expressive formula was commonly employed: "Receive the sign of the holy cross with the chrism of salvation in Christ Jesus unto eternal life."

We see from this variety of forms that it was evidently the intention of our Lord and the practice of His Church that the sacrament of Confirmation could be validly administered with any words which sufficiently indicate the graces given; but, of course, for us at the present day the form prescribed by the Church's ritual is the one to be followed.

The Age for Confirmation. This sacrament is generally administered among us when the candidate is about twelve or thirteen years of age; but this is by no means an ancient or universal practice. In the Oriental churches it is usually conferred immediately after Baptism, and this was the rule in all parts of the world until about the thirteenth century. In fact, the prompt confirming of newly baptized children was strictly enjoined, and penalties were prescribed for parents who neglected it. But gradually it was seen to be preferable to defer this sacrament (which is not necessary for salvation) to an age when it could be received "with knowledge and free will."

The Sponsors at Confirmation. At the administration of this sacrament the Church requires sponsors, as at Baptism. These must be Catholics, and must themselves have received Confirmation; and, just as in Baptism, they contract a spiritual relationship with those whose sponsors they become.

This relationship is an impediment to marriage, and it is well to remember that sponsors in either Baptism or Confirmation are subject to this impediment not only as regards the person baptized or confirmed, but also as to his parents; so that the person who acts as sponsor in either of these sacraments would be unable, without a dispensation, to marry validly the parent of the one who received the sacrament.

On account of the relationship thus contracted, it is usual to have in Confirmation one sponsor only, of the same sex as the person confirmed. In many parts of the world each candidate has his or her own sponsor; this is the custom in our Italian parishes in this country; but generally in our churches one man acts as sponsor for all the males confirmed and one woman for all the females. The sponsor has no duty at the ceremony except to place his or her hand on the soulder of the person while the sacrament is being administered.

A peculiar detail of the ceremony, no longer in vogue, was that the candidate placed his or her foot upon the right foot of the sponsor while being confirmed. Another, which has also fallen into disuse, was the binding of a white cloth around the head of the person who had received Confirmation; this was worn for seven days, to preserve, as it were, the sign of the holy chrism. In ancient times the sacrament was always received fasting, but this also is no longer deemed necessary, and is not now observed.

The Ceremonies. The bishop who confirms is vested in amice, stole and white cope, and wears his mitre. He goes to a seat before the middle of the altar, facing the people; and, after washing his hands, he begins the ceremonies of the confirmation. He first says aloud, in Latin, "May the Holy Spirit come upon you, and may the virtue of the Most High guard you from sin. Amen." Then, after making the sign of the cross, he extends his hands over those who are to be confirmed, and prays as follows:

"Almighty and eternal God, Who has deigned to regenerate these thy servants with water and the Holy Spirit, and Who hast given them the remission of all their sins, send upon them from heaven Thy sevenfold Spirit, the Paraclete. Amen. The Spirit of wisdom and understanding. Amen. The Spirit of counsel and fortitude. Amen. The Spirit of knowledge and piety. Amen. Fill them with the Spirit of Thy fear, and sign them with the sign of the cross of Christ unto everlasting life. Through the same Lord Jesus Christ," etc.

The candidates are arranged before the bishop, generally at

the altar-rail; and it is customary with us for each to hold a card bearing his baptismal name and the new name which he wishes to take at his Confirmation. This taking of a new name is not necessary, but is sanctioned by long usage.

The bishop goes to each and administers the sacrament as follows: Dipping his right thumb into the vessel containing the holy chrism, he makes the sign of the cross with the consecrated oil on the candidate's forehead, and says at the same time (addressing him by his Christian name or names), "N——, I sign thee with the sign of the cross and I confirm thee with the chrism of salvation, in the name of the Father and of the Son and of the Holy Ghost."

He then strikes the cheek of the person lightly, saying, "Peace be with thee." This ceremony is not found in ancient rituals. It symbolizes the persecutions to which we may possibly be exposed on account of our faith, and reminds us that as soldiers of Jesus Christ we may have to suffer for Him.

The chrism on the forehead of each is wiped off with cotton by one of the assisting clergy. The bishop then washes his hands, to remove all traces of the chrism, and the choir or clergy chant or recite the following words: "Confirm this, O God, which Thou hast wrought in us, from Thy holy temple which is in Jerusalem. Glory be to the Father," etc.

The Closing Prayer. The bishop then offers a prayer, preceded by certain versicles — "Show us, O Lord, Thy mercy and give us Thy salvation . . . O God, Who hast given Thy Holy Spirit to Thy Apostles, and hast willed that He should be given to the other faithful by them and their successors, regard benignantly the service of our lowliness; and grant that the same Holy Spirit, coming upon those whose foreheads we have anointed with holy chrism and marked with the sign of the cross, may make their hearts a temple of His glory . . . . So will every man be blessed who hears the Lord."

Finally the bishop gives his solemn blessing to those confirmed, making the sign of the cross over them, with the words: "May the Lord bless you from Sion, that you may see the good things of Jerusalem all the days of your life, and may have life everlasting. Amen.

It is customary for the bishop to deliver an instruction appropriate to the occasion, teaching the newly confirmed the greatness of the sacrament they have received, urging them to be "strong and perfect Christians and soldiers of Jesus Christ," steadfast in faith, loyal to their Leader; and warning them against the dangers to morals and faith to which they will be exposed through life.

At the bidding of the bishop, those who have been confirmed recite aloud (as a kind of penance) the Creed, the Our Father and the Hail Mary; and this concludes the ceremonies of Confirmation.

Chapter X

THE CONFESSION OF SINS

The telling of sins in Confession, or in other words, the receiving of the Sacrament of Penance, is something distinctively Catholic. It is true that it is found in schismatic churches but only because they have preserved it and continued it from the time when they were Catholic. When the Greek and Oriental churches separated themselves from communion with the Roman See, they retained nearly all the dogmas and practices which then prevailed in the Christian world. The Sacraments, the Mass, the priestly office and many other essentials of Catholicism are still to be found in these schismatic bodies, and the necessity of confessing sins is recognized in them just as it is in the Church of Rome.

There is hardly anything in the whole system of our religion which is so misunderstood and misrepresented as is Confession. Even learned non-Catholic writers and preachers show astounding ignorance of the true facts of the case when they treat of the "Romish" practice of confessing sins; and as for the rank and file of our separated brethren, the extent of their misinformation is appalling.

Objections Against Confession. Confession is the bugbear of Protestants. Four centuries of misstatement, of oft-repeated falsehood, have resulted, among non-Catholics, in almost universal misunderstanding of the teaching and practice of the Catholic Church regarding the forgiveness of sins. Of course, any one who wishes information about Confession may get it from even the simplest books that explain Catholic doctrine; but the average non-Catholic does not try to get it. He cheerfully and unquestioningly receives what has been handed down to him, and passes it on to others; he repeats the slanders over which his ancestors gloated, and looks upon Confession as a slavish superstition — if not as something worse.

The usual ideas of the average non-Catholic are somewhat like this: "Catholics believe that, to be forgiven, they need merely to tell their sins."

"Priests have sometimes given a license or permission to commit future sins."

"Catholic priests, through the confessional, acquire a complete and harmful domination over souls."

"Being mostly evil-minded men, they delight in hearing confessions, and revel in listening to accusations of sins, especially those of women."

"Any sin will be forgiven if the sinner pays enough."

It would hardly seem to be necessary to refute these assertions or even to notice them. Some of them are so preposterous that it is strange that they can be believed by any sensible person. However, the gullible always outnumber the sensible; and a word or two concerning the Church's real teaching may not be out of place.

The Answers. The Church does not teach, and never has taught, that "the telling of sins is enough to bring forgiveness." The telling of sins, while necessary in most cases, is by no means essential to the Sacrament of Penance; there is something far more important, something without which there can be no sacrament — namely, contrition, or sorrow for sin, with its necessary consequence, a firm purpose of amendment. Mortal sin may be forgiven without confession; it never can be without contrition.

Of course, no confessor ever gave a "license" or "permission" to commit sin. The idea is blasphemous. The Sacrament of Penance is intended and used only for the good of souls — to wash away sin, to give graces for the strengthening of the soul against future sin; and the advice, reproof and encouragement given by the priest are also potent factors in bringing about amendment. Many well-informed non-Catholics, who know nothing of the supernatural effects of the Sacrament of Penance, bear willing testimony to the good effects of Confession in promoting purity, honesty and respect for divine and civil laws.

But, say our Protestant critics, suppose that a priest is a wicked man, does not the confessional give him ample opportunity to indulge his evil propensities?

Not so much as one might think. Of course, there are

unworthy priests — not many, thank God; but the Church has safeguarded the confessional and the penitent against them. No priest could absolve one who has been his accomplice in sin. No priest would be likely to try to use the tribunal of penance for wicked ends; for the person to whom he had spoken evil could not be absolved by any other priest until the name and guilt of the unworthy confessor had been revealed to the bishop of the diocese, and the said person would be excommunicated if the accusation be not made promptly.

We can assure our readers that the average priest finds his work in the confessional the most monotonous and at the same time the most comforting part of his labors. There is no desire to remember the sins that he hears. He has no time for curiosity. The hearing of confessions is a task that would be a drudgery were it not for the consciousness which every confessor has, that he is doing God's work, and is accomplishing more good than he could do anywhere else. In the long hours spent in the confessional he can give comfort to the sorrowing, can send the sinner away purified from all stain, can guide the earnest soul to higher perfection; and oftentimes, good priest though he be, he has to confess himself inferior in sanctity to some who kneel at his feet.

What Catholics Believe. We Catholics believe that our Saviour has given to His Church a sacrament for the remission of sins committed after Baptism, this remission being affected by the absolution of the priest, joined to true supernatural sorrow, earnest purpose of amendment, and sincere confession of all grievous sin when confession is possible.

This sacrament is necessary for the salvation of those who have fallen into mortal sin after Baptism; that is, they either must receive it or must have an actual or implied desire to receive it, joined to perfect sorrow for sin.

What about baptized Protestants who are in good faith? Do we claim that these are all lost, because they do not know the efficacy of the Sacrament of Penance and therefore do not receive it? No; they may turn to God in ardent and loving contrition, and, being in good faith, this contrition implies that they earnestly desire to fulfill Christ's law as far as they know it. If they knew the Sacrament of Penance as it is, they would receive it. And so we do not deny that God may be ready to forgive the sins of those non-Catholic Christians who are in good faith and are sorry for their sins.

Our Church teaches us that her priests have real power to forgive sins, and that every person is bound by God's law to confess to the priest every remembered mortal sin committed after Baptism. There is no need of entering here into the Scriptural arguments to prove this doctrine; such is not the scope of this book; but let us see what is necessary for the practical exercise of this power of the priest, and why the obligation of confessing sins necessarily follows from the fact that the priest possesses this power.

The Priest Needs Jurisdiction. What priests have the power of forgiving sins? All priests have it, but all priests cannot use it. No priest can hear confessions unless he has jurisdiction; just as no magistrate can try a case unless it is submitted by law to his tribunal. Every Catholic priest has received this power, indeed, at his ordination; but its exercise depends altogether on the authority of the Church. For instance, if a priest who belongs to one diocese goes to another, he cannot hear confessions there unless he first obtains permission from the bishop of that diocese. He cannot even hear confessions in his own diocese unless he has received "faculties" to do so from his own bishop. In the words of the Catechism, he must be a "duly authorized priest."

Why Catholics Confess Their Sins. Why do we have to confess our sins? Would it not be a great deal more comfortable if we were merely required to manifest our sorrow and not our sins? Undoubtedly; but God has not so arranged it. Our Blessed Saviour gave His Apostles and the priests of His Church the power "to bind and to loose" — in other words, a discretionary power. They are judges, advisers and physicians — not merely absolvers.

Now, a priest is not a mind-reader, nor is he endowed with any miraculous knowledge. He cannot know your sins or mine, nor judge them, nor advise about them, nor suggest remedies for them, unless we tell them to him. Therefore we must tell them, completely and clearly, so that he will know them as we know them; so that they will be displayed before his mind as they are before our conscience.

The Form of Absolution. What does the priest say when he raises his hand over us, after bidding us to say the Act of Contrition? Or, in other words, what is the form of absolution? After reciting the last two sentences of the Confiteor, the Confessor uses these words:

"May our Lord Jesus Christ absolve, and I by His authority absolve thee from every bond of excommunication and interdict in so far as I can and as thou needest it; and so I absolve thee from they sins, in the name of the Father, and of the Son, and of the Holy Ghost. Amen. May the Passion of our Lord Jesus Christ, the merits of the Blessed Mary ever Virgin, whatever good thou hast done and whatever evil thou hast borne, be for thee unto the remission of sins, the increase of grace, and the reward of everlasting life. Amen."

Such are the impressive words which God's appointed minister uses as the sentence of pardon for God's faithful. And when these words are uttered over one who is rightly disposed, the soul that has been loathsome with the leprosy of sin becomes pure in God's sight; the wickedness that defiled it is cleansed away forever.

The Seal of Confession. Every Catholic knows, and many non-Catholics know as well, that a priest is not permitted under any circumstances or for any reason whatever, to reveal what he has heard in Confession. This obligation of secrecy is what is known as the "seal of Confession."

The Confessor is not acting as a mere man, but as one who stands in the place of God; and he is never allowed to disclose to any one the matters submitted to him in the sacred tribunal. This law admits of absolutely no exception. Unless the penitent freely gives the Confessor leave to use his knowledge, the priest must not by word or look or gesture reveal sins or weaknesses, or the names or sins of accomplices, or anything that would bring contempt or trouble on the penitent. If harm would thereby ensue, he must not even admit that a certain person has confessed to him. He must not even by change of conduct or manner remind the penitent of anything that has been told in Confession. To violate this law in any way would be a detestable sacrilege, and would entail the severest penalties for the guilty priest. And it is right that this should be so; for any revelation of matters of confession would make the Sacrament of Penance an intolerable evil instead of a ministry of mercy and reconciliation.

An Ancient Practice. The forgiveness of sins, as said above, entails the confession of them; and therefore the practice of telling one's sins to a priest goes back to the beginning of the Church. In all the ages of her history the power of absolution, of judgment of sins, has been recognized and used. St. Cyprian urges the sinner to repent "while confession may be made." St. John Chrysostom tells us that the priests of the Gospel excel those of the Jewish Church, because while these latter could merely declare a man clean of leprosy, the Christian priests "have received power to cleanse the impurity of the soul." And this is confirmed by others of the earlier writers; they do not argue for the priestly power of absolving, but assume it as unquestionable. Origen, who lived at the beginning of the third century, exhorts the sinner "to find a physician, learned and merciful," who will judge if his sickness be of such a nature that "it ought to be manifested in the meeting of the whole Church"' and he tells his hearers: "If we reveal our sins, not only to God but also to those who can heal our sins, they will be blotted out."

Confessional

In the early centuries public penance, of the greatest severity and sometimes lasting for years, was demanded in reparation for great sins — especially for murder, idolatry and adultery. This practice, however, was later abolished, because it was not of divine origin, and was often a deterrent from reconciliation with God rather than a help towards it; but sacramental confession has endured, because, as St. Leo has said, "It is enough that guilt should be manifested to the priest alone by secret confession."

The Confessional. The seat which the priest uses, or the enclosure within which the confession is ordinarily made, is known as a "confessional." In our churches it consists usually of a central box in which the confessor is seated, and side alcoves, fitted with doors or curtains, in which the penitents kneel. The partitions have openings provided with gratings or screens, separating the penitent from the priest, and these may be closed by sliding shutters. The Ritual demands that the confessional be located in a conspicuous place in the church, and it is recommended that in the part where the penitent kneels there shall be a crucifix or a picture of our Lord, to inspire devotion and contrition in the sinner.

This present form of confessional is of somewhat recent origin. In ancient times confessions were heard in the open church, the penitent kneeling before the priest or seated by his side. The division of the confessional into compartments seems to have come into use about the sixteenth century.

The priest, when hearing confessions, wears a purple stole: and, in according to the requirements of the Ritual, should also wear a surplice — which latter detail, probably for comfort's sake, is sometimes omitted by our clergy.

A Secret Sacrament. The Sacrament of Penance is the only one that is always administered in secret. The other six Sacraments are given ordinarily in a solemn manner, in the presence of witnesses or others, with lights and prayers. The Sacrament of Penance is a private affair, concerning no one but the penitent and the priest; and hence it is generally administered in the narrow space of the confessional, and always without pomp or ceremony.

Much more might be written about the sacred tribunal of Penance, but it would be rather an exposition of Catholic doctrine than of practice and would not come within the scope of this chapter. Every Catholic is familiar from childhood with the requirements for a worthy Confession, and every Catholic knows also, from his own experience, the peace and heavenly comfort that have filled his soul when he arose from his knees and went forth "with God's benediction upon him." The confessing of our sins may seem hard, but God, in reality, has made the work of reconciliation easy for us. Earnest sorrow, a real purpose of amendment, a sincere accusation — and the sins, be they few or many, no longer exist. They must be told, and the telling is hard — but it is not made to the world at large. They are whispered only to one man, who is bound by a most sacred obligation, bound by his own hope of Heaven, to preserve everlasting silence.

Chapter XI

THE CEREMONIES OF EXTREME UNCTION

The ministry of the Catholic Church is at its best in the care which it manifests towards the sick. In the sick-room and at the death-bed the Catholic priest wins the grateful love of the faithful and the admiration of those who are not of the One Fold. There is no part of his work, no service that he renders to his flock, that is better calculated to make men of all creeds respect the priest. When they see him wending his way to the homes of the poor, through darkness or rain or snow, when they know that no danger of contagion can keep him away, that no peril is worthy of notice when a soul is at stake, they realize that the priest believes what he teaches.

"The Last Anointing." In this chapter we shall take up the ceremonies of the Sacrament by which a soul is prepared for its passage to eternity. Why is this Sacrament called Extreme Unction? Because it is the last or extreme anointing which the Catholic receives. At Baptism his breast and shoulders were anointed with the Oil of Catechumens and his head with Chrism. At Confirmation he was marked on the forehead with Chrism, to show that his faith must be manifest to the world. If he has been raised to the priesthood, he has received on his hands another anointing by which these members were consecrated to God's service. And, now that he is about to cross the threshold of eternity, his various senses receive a last anointing in the Sacrament of Extreme Unction.

The Oil of the Sacrament. For this Sacrament the oil which is used is olive oil, consecrated by a bishop on Holy Thursday of each year. It is known as "Oleum Infirmorum" — the Oil of the Sick — and it is applied by the priest to the principal organs of the body through which sin may have come upon the soul.

A Symbol of Strength. The symbolism of oil can be easily understood if we remember the many uses for which it was employed among the ancients. It was a medicine, a food, a source of light, and especially a means of producing that strength and flexibility of muscle which athletes seek to acquire. The gymnast, runner, boxer, or wrestler of the old Olympic games rubbed oil into the pores of his skin, and thereby nourished and strengthened his muscular system in preparation for his contests. So it is with the sacramental oil with which the Church anoints her children to give them spiritual strength in their conflict with Satan.

Scriptural Authority. Like all the other sacraments, Extreme Unction was instituted by our Blessed Saviour; but there is no mention of it in the Gospels. We find the first account of it in the Epistle of St. James the Apostle, where the manner of administering it and the nature of its effects are clearly set forth: "Is any man sick among you? Let him bring in the priests of the church; and let them pray over him, anointing him with oil in the name of the Lord. And the prayer of faith shall save the sick man, and the Lord shall raise him up; and if he be in sins, they shall be forgiven him."

The Sacrament of Extreme Unction should, if possible, be given when the patient is in full possession of his mental faculties and realizes the importance of the Sacrament, and not when he is deprived of his senses and is in the throes of death.

In the Sick-Room. When it can be done, the Holy Viaticum is given to the sick person before Extreme Unction. It may be well to mention the various things which should be prepared. These should always be kept together and in readiness in every Catholic household, for in each the day will come (and may come suddenly) when they will be needed.

Table for Sick-Room

A table should be provided. A small firm stand, perhaps two feet square, is suitable. The articles for the administration of the sacraments should not be placed on a bureau which is partly occupied by other things. The table should be entirely covered with a clean white cloth. On this is placed a standing crucifix and two blessed candles, which should be lighted when the priest is expected; a saucer containing holy water (with a sprinkler, if possible); a glass of fresh water, a spoon, a plate with small crumbs of bread, a towel, a napkin (to be used as a Communion-cloth) and seven small balls of clean cotton.

Through mistaken devotion prayer-books, rosaries, statues, pictures, etc. are sometimes placed on the table. These should be omitted. The table is, for the time, an altar, which is a resting-place for the Blessed Sacrament when Holy Communion is to be given, and for the Holy Oil used in Extreme Unction.

The parts of the sick person which are to be anointed should be washed before the priest arrives — the face, hands and feet.

When the priest is known to be carrying the Blessed Sacrament, it is a laudable custom for one of the family to meet him at the street-door with a lighted candle, and all the others present should kneel when he enters. It is almost needless to say that at the administration of the sacraments none but blessed candles, of unbleached yellow wax, should be used.

The Prayers Before the Anointing. As the priest comes into the sick-room he says, in Latin, "Peace be unto this house and all who dwell therein." He sprinkles the sick person, the room and the other persons present with holy water, uttering the words of the Psalmist: "Thou shalt sprinkle me with hyssop, O Lord, and I shall be cleansed; Thou shalt wash me, and I shall be made whiter than snow. Have mercy on me, O God, according to Thy great mercy. Glory be to the Father," etc.

He then hears the confession of the sick person, if it has not been previously heard, and gives the Holy Viaticum, if it is to be given. He then recites three prayers. The first asks that "into this house may come eternal happiness, divine prosperity, serene joy, fruitful charity and lasting health; that the devils may flee; that the angels of peace may be present; that all evil discord may disappear." The second asks blessings from our Lord Jesus Christ on the house and all who dwell in it, that He may give them a good angel as their guardian; that He may protect them "from all the powers of darkness, from all fear and perturbation." The third asks again for the angel of God "to guard, protect, cherish, visit and defend all who dwell in this abode."

The Confiteor is then recited. It may be said in English

(or any other language) by the sick person or by those who are present. The priest says, in Latin, the concluding sentences, which are, in English: "May the Almighty God have mercy on thee," etc. As he pronounces the final words he makes the sign of the cross.

Then, before the anointing, the priest offers a prayer to the angels and saints, which opens with an invocation of the three Persons of the Holy Trinity, with a threefold sign of the cross over the patient: "In the name of the Father, and of the Son, and of the Holy Ghost, may all the power of the devil be extinguished in thee, by the imposition of our hands and by the invocation of all the holy Angels, Archangels, Patriarchs, Prophets, Apostles, Martyrs, Confessors, Virgins, and all the Saints. Amen."

The Anointings. At the anointing of the sick person, those who are in the room should kneel and pray. The Oil of the Sick is carried in a small gold-plated box, known as an oil-stock, which is enclosed in a leather case. The oil is usually soaked into cotton, to avoid danger of leakage. The priest dips his thumb into the oil and makes the sign of the cross with it on several parts of the sick person's body; first on the eyes, with the words, in Latin: "By this holy unction and His most loving mercy may the Lord pardon thee whatever thou hast sinned by sight." Then on the ears, with the same formula, except the last word, which is "hearing." He anoints the nose, mentioning the sense of smell; the lips, for taste and speech; the palms of the hands, for the sense of touch; and the feet, for sins committed by walking. Each unction is wiped away with cotton immediately after it is made.

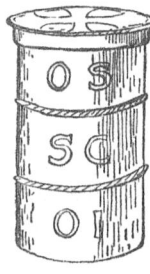
Oil Stock

When a priest receives Extreme Unction his hands are anointed not on the palms, but on the back. The reason is that his palms have been previously consecrated with oil, at his ordination.

The Final Prayers. The priest then prays, "Kyrie eleison," etc. — "Lord, have mercy" — after which the Our Father is recited secretly down to the last words, "Lead us not into temptation, but deliver us from evil," which are said aloud, in Latin. Then follow several versicles with their responses: "Make safe Thy servant, my God, who trusts in Thee. Send him, O Lord, help from Thy holy place, and defend him from Sion. Be to him, O Lord, a tower of strength from the face of the enemy. May the enemy avail naught against him, and the son of iniquity be powerless to harm him." These and the other prayers are varied according to the sex of the sick person — "Thy handmaid" instead of "Thy servant," etc.

Three prayers are then offered. The first asks for forgiveness of sin and restoration of bodily health. The second, in which the Christian name of the sick person is used, implores refreshment of soul and divine healing; and the third begs that he may be restored to Holy Church "with all desired prosperity." This concludes the ceremonies of Extreme Unction.

The Apostolic Blessing. Immediately after the administration of this Sacrament it is usual to impart the Last or Apostolic Blessing, which gives a plenary indulgence to the recipient. This indulgence is gained, not when the prayers are read, but at the moment of death — "in articulo mortis."

The priest exhorts the sick person to elicit acts of contrition, faith, hope and love, and to invoke the Sacred Name of Jesus. A prayer is offered to "the Father of mercies and the God of all consolation," to look with favor upon His servant and to grant him the pardon of all his sins. After the Confiteor has been said, the Blessing is given, as follows:

"May our Lord Jesus Christ, Son of the Living God, Who gave to Peter the power to bind and to loose, receive thy confession and restore to thee that first robe of innocence which thou didst receive in Baptism; and I, by the power given to me by the Apostolic See, grant thee a plenary indulgence and remission of all thy sins, in the name of the Father and of the Son and of the Holy Ghost.

"Through the most sacred mysteries of man's redemption may God remit unto thee the pains of the present and future life, open to the gates of heaven, and bring thee to everlasting life."

And with a solemn benediction, "May Almighty God bless thee, Father, Son and Holy Ghost," the ceremonies are concluded which prepare the Christian soul to meet its God.

CHAPTER XII

THE CEREMONIES OF HOLY ORDERS

THE rites used in the administration of Holy Orders are of great antiquity and full of meaning. They are beautiful and symbolical ceremonies, expressing well the dignity and the duties of the Orders conferred through them.

In the catechism which we all studied in childhood we find the following definition of the Sacrament of Holy Orders: "A sacrament through which bishops, priests and other ministers of the Church are ordained and receive grace and power to perform their sacred duties." We are tolerably familiar with priests and more remotely with bishops; but who are the "other ministers of the Church?" Not the Cardinals; these are not elevated to that dignity by any ordination. Not the Pope himself; he is a bishop — and if he be (as has generally been the case) a bishop before his election to the Papacy, he needs no ordination or consecration to make him Pope. The "other ministers of the Church" are those who have received Orders below that of priesthood; for a candidate for the sacred ministry passes through several steps before the priestly character is conferred upon him.

The Steps to the Priesthood. He first receives the clerical tonsure, which is not an Order — merely a ceremony. Then four Minor Orders are conferred upon him; these will be described in detail. Then come the Sacred Orders, namely, subdeaconship, deaconship and priesthood. Therefore a candidate for the priesthood, after receiving the tonsure, is ordained to six different grades of the clerical state before he is finally made a priest.

It is usual to give these various Orders on the same day and at the same Mass, but not to the same individual at one time. An ordination will sometimes include a hundred candidates or more, some for each of the above Orders. A student will generally receive the tonsure at the end of his first year in the seminary; Minor Orders during his second; subdeaconship at the end of the third year, and finally deaconship and priesthood in his fourth year of theological study.

The Clerical Tonsure. When a student has manifested

sufficient signs of a probable vocation and fitness for the clerical state, he receives a summons to the ceremony of tonsure. This is the rite by which a man is taken from the world, ceases to be a layman, and is made a member of the clergy. The tonsure has been for many centuries the special badge of those who have been elevated to the clerical state. It consists in the cutting off of some of the hair from the candidate's head. In our part of the world it has never become a custom to wear the tonsure; but in Catholic countries it is an obligation upon all clerics. Among the secular clergy (where it is worn) and in some religious communities the tonsure consists of a smoothly shaven circular spot, perhaps three inches in diameter, on top of the head towards the rear. In certain orders of monks it is much larger, the whole crown of the head being denuded of hair, leaving merely a fringe around the head, like a wreath; this may be seen in pictures of St. Anthony and some other saints.

Two kinds of Tonsure

What is the meaning of this particular practice of the Church? It signifies the putting away of useless and superfluous ornaments, the separating of one's self from vanity and worldliness. It is also considered as a symbol of the crown of thorns of our Blessed Lord, and therefore typifies the austerities which the wearer should practise in imitation of Him.

The conferring of the tonsure and of the various Orders usually takes place on one of the Ember Days; they may, however, be given on other days. So careful is the Church that her clergy shall be well qualified in every way that when the candidates appear for ordination the first ceremony is the pronouncing of a solemn sentence of excommunication on any one who presents himself to receive Orders and who is legally unfit or unworthy.

The Tonsure Ceremonies. Those who are to be tonsured stand before the Bishop, and he recites a prayer that "these servants of God who have hastened hither to lay aside the hairs of their heads for love of Him" may receive the Holy Ghost, Who will defend them against the world and earthly desires; and that, being endowed with an increase of virtue, they may receive the light of eternal grace.

Then the Bishop with a pair of scissors clips five small locks of hair in the form of a cross from the head of the young man who kneels before him — taking them from the front, back, both sides and centre of the head, while the candidate says: "The Lord is the portion of my inheritance and my chalice; it is Thou Who wilt restore my inheritance to me." Then after a prayer asking God's blessing on the new clerics and the reciting of a psalm, the Bishop invests each with a surplice, the garb of their new state, with the words: "May the Lord clothe thee with the new man who has been created according to God in justice and the holiness of truth." He then recites a beautiful prayer that these new servants of God may be freed from all slavery to worldly things; that as they carry the likeness of Christ's crown on their heads, they may be worthy of an eternal inheritance with Him. The Bishop then admonishes them "to remember that this day they are made members of the Church's court and have received the privileges of the clergy; to beware lest they lose them; and to endeavor to please God by honorable living, good morals and works."

The Minor Orders. These Orders are a necessary part of the preparation for the priesthood, and they are given only to those who have previously received the tonsure. They are four in number: The Order of Porter, of Reader, of Exorcist and of Acolyte.

In the early centuries of the Church's history, for the proper celebration of the sacred mysteries, it was deemed necessary to appoint various ministers who would attend to certain duties connected with the divine worship. Some of these were afterwards raised to the priesthood; some never advanced further than the Minor Orders, spending their lives in the exercise of these lower functions of the ministry, much like the "lay brothers" who serve in the churches of various religious orders. Gradually, however, these Minor Orders became merely a step towards the sacred office of the priesthood, and all those who received them did so with the intention of ultimately becoming priests. Thus it has come about that every man who becomes a priest first receives the four Minor Orders, although as a matter of fact he seldom or never exercises their functions. The office of Porter is filled

ADMINISTRATION OF THE SACRAMENTS

in our churches to-day not by a cleric but by a layman. Those of Reader and Exorcist are exercised only by priests. The duties of the office of Acolyte fall to the lot of the altar-boy who serves Mass.

These Orders are sometimes conferred all at one time; sometimes they are given at two or more separate ordinations.

The Order of Porter. The first Minor Order is that of Porter — the door-keeper of the house of God. The tonsured cleric comes before the Bishop clad in cassock and surplice and carrying a candle, and is instructed in the duties of his office. He is to sound the gong, to ring the bell, to open the church, to prepare the book for the preacher. He is warned not to be negligent about the care of the Church's goods; not to be tardy in his duties; and, just as he opens and closes the visible house of God, so likewise he must by word and example close the hearts of the faithful to the devil and open them to God. Such is the substance of the Latin exhortation which is read by the Bishop to the candidates. They then receive the keys of the church, and are led to the door, which is locked and unlocked by each of them; they then ring the church-bell, after which the Bishop prays over them and solemnly blesses them.

The Order of Reader. The Lector or Reader was a very important person in the ages when the Church was engaged in evangelizing Europe. He was the instructor, the catechist, the reader of the Scriptures for the semi-savage tribes which were being brought into the fold of Christ. A knowledge of reading was unusual among the common people in those days, and a book was an almost priceless treasure; and therefore, that the people might be instructed concerning sacred things and that they might know the written Word of God, a cleric was ordained to read to them in the church. He also acted as chanter at solemn ceremonies, and was permitted to bless certain articles for the faithful.

Those who receive this Order come before the Bishop with candles and receive an admonition from him regarding their new duties. They are exhorted to proclaim the sacred truths clearly and openly, and not to falsify them in any way; and as they are to be placed in an exalted position in the church so that they may be seen and heard by all, so must they hold a high place in the order of virtue, that they may lead to eternal life those who see and hear them.

The Bishop then places in the hand of each the Holy Scriptures, as a symbol of their office. He then asks God's blessing on them and prays that they may always "preach what should be done and do what they preach."

The Order of Exorcist. In the first centuries of the Church the devil undoubtedly had more power than he has now, especially in regard to material things. The greater part of the world was his dominion, for it was sunk in paganism, which was to a large extent devil-worship. The enemy of God and of mankind had extended his sway over the souls of a great portion of the human race, and God even permitted him in some cases to control the bodies of men. This is why we read in the Gospels, in the writings of the Fathers and the lives of the early saints, of many instances of demoniac possession — actual control by the Evil One of the minds and bodies of unfortunate victims, who probably had merited such severe punishment, which was therefore allowed by the Almighty.

The Exorcist is one whose office it formerly was to cast out devils; and he received the right to use the solemn formulas of the Church for that purpose. He also assisted at the administration of Baptism, imposing hands on the catechumen and thereby giving him the graces of the Holy Spirit; but in our times these duties are exercised only by those who have been elevated to the priesthood.

At the ordination of an Exorcist the Bishop admonishes him that, having the power to expel devils from others, he must keep all uncleanness and evil from his own mind and body, lest he be conquered by those whom he has driven from others. Then the Missal or the Pontifical (the Ritual used by the Bishop) is handed to him; the blessing of God is invoked upon him, and he is declared to have power and dominion over unclean spirits, and to be "an approved physician of the Church, confirmed in the grace of curing and in heavenly virtue."

The Order of Acolyte. The Order of Acolyte or Mass-Server is the last and highest of the Minor Orders which are conferred before promotion to the greater dignities of subdeaconship, deaconship and priesthood. As the candidates kneel before the Bishop they are instructed in their duties — to carry candles at the services of the Church, to light the lamps, and to serve the priest at Mass. They are warned that those whose office it is to care for lights must have nothing to do with the works of darkness. They must themselves be lights in the house of God. And as they are to present wine and water at the altar, so they should offer themselves as a sacrifice to God by a chaste life and good works.

Afterwards, the Bishop presents a candle to each of them, stating that they thereby receive the right to light the lamps of the church; then a cruet, such as is used at Mass, to express their duty of serving the wine and water. A prayer is then offered to ask a blessing upon them, and God is besought to enkindle in their minds and hearts the love of His grace, that they may faithfully serve Him in His Holy Church.

The Order of Subdeacon. The subsequent steps to and including the priesthood are known as the Sacred or Major Orders. Some time after the reception of the Minor Orders the candidate, if he be deemed worthy, is notified that he is to be raised to the subdeaconship. This decision is only arrived at after the merits of the cleric have been well examined by his superiors; for this is the important step which, once and forever, separates him from the world and devotes him to the perpetual service of God in His sanctuary.

The ordination of subdeacons is a most impressive ceremony. The young men have decided that God calls them to give up earthly things, to make a sacrifice of much that is in itself lawful and laudable. They have resolved to bind themselves by and obligation to absolute and perpetual chastity and to strict obedience — to offer their lives as an oblation before the throne of God.

In company with those on whom the deaconship and priesthood are to be conferred, the candidates for subdeaconship are arranged before the Bishop, who sits at the altar and gives them a solemn admonition in these words: "Dearly beloved sons, who are to be promoted to the Order of subdeaconship, you ought to consider again and again what kind of burden you voluntarily seek to-day. For thus far you are free, and you are allowed, if you wish, to pass to earthly vows; but if you receive this Order it will not be lawful for you any longer to turn aside from what you have proposed to do; but you will be obliged perpetually to serve God, to serve Whom is to reign; but you will be bound to preserve chastity with His aid, and to be joined forever to the ministry of His holy church. Therefore, while there is time, reflect; and if it please you to persevere in your holy resolution, in the name of God, come hither!"

The candidates take a step towards the Bishop — and that step is irrevocable. They are ministers of God's Church forever, vowed to obedience and chastity.

Together with those who are to be elevated to deaconship and priesthood, they then prostrate themselves on the floor, lying motionless on their faces while the Bishop and clergy recite the Litany of the Saints. This prostration is a most impressive ceremony. The young men who have given themselves to God fall to the earth before His altar and lie there like sacrificed victims. The world with its pleasures and ambitions is left behind; henceforth they belong to God, and are bound to His service forever.

The Bishop then instructs them as to their duties. A subdeacon is to prepare and present the water used at the altar; to sing the Epistle; to assist the deacon; to wash the sacred linens; to care for the chalice and the paten. All these external actions symbolize many spiritual obligations which are incumbent upon him. He is to assist in the instruction of the faithful, by word and example. He is to be zealous, vigilant, sober and pure.

The empty chalice and paten are then presented, and are touched with the hand; the Bishop says: "See whose ministry is entrusted to you. Henceforth, I admonish you, show yourselves so that you may please God." Then the cruets of wine and water, with the basin and towel, are also presented and are touched in like manner.

The Bishop then solemnly blesses the candidates and calls down upon them the seven gifts of the Holy Ghost. The vestments of the new subdeacons are blessed, and their mystical meaning is explained. The amice, which is worn on the neck and shoulders, signifies the restraining of speech. The maniple, which is placed on the left arm, symbolizes good works. The tunic, the large vestment worn by the subdeacon at Mass, typifies happiness and joy.

The Mass-Book is then given to each of the newly ordained, to signify their office of chanting the Epistle in solemn Masses. One of them sings the Epistle of the day, and this concludes the ordination of the subdeacons.

The Order of Deacon. The Order next below the priesthood is deaconship. The deacon is the priest's principal assistant not only at Mass but in other sacred rites. He is permitted to preach the Word of God from the pulpit of the church, and he has authority to baptize, although that faculty is seldom exercised by deacons at the present day.

The Order has a very ancient origin. We read in the Acts of the Apostles that in the very first years of the Church it was found necessary to ordain assistants, called deacons (meaning ministers or servants), to take charge of various duties to which the Apostles themselves could not attend. Among these first deacons was St. Stephen, the first Christian martyr.

The conferring of deaconship, like subdeaconship, takes place at Mass, and begins after the latter Order has been given — just after the Epistle. The candidates, clad in albs and carrying their vestments, are presented to the Bishop by one of the clergy, called the Archdeacon, who says in Latin: "Most reverend Father, our holy Mother the Catholic Church asks that you ordain these subdeacons here present to the burden of the diaconate." The Bishop inquires: "Do you know that they are worthy?" And the other answers: "As much as human frailty permits me to know, I both know and testify that they are worthy of the burden of this office." To which the Bishop responds: "Thanks be to God."

Then he calls upon any person to state any reason why these subdeacons should not receive the higher order. Afterwards follows a long instruction on the duties to which the deacons will be bound. They are to minister at the altar, to baptize and to preach. They are like the Levites of old, especially deputed to the service of the sanctuary. They are urged to be shining examples to the Church — to be pure and chaste, as befits ministers of Christ — to preach the Gospel by example as well as by word.

Next comes the prostration before the altar, unless this has been previously done with the subdeacons; for when the different Sacred Orders are conferred at the same Mass, all the candidates prostrate themselves together.

Afterwards the Bishop asks the prayers of the clergy and people for those who are to be elevated to deaconship, and then intones or recites a beautiful Preface (like that which is sung in a high Mass), in which he invokes the blessing of God upon them. In the middle of the Preface he places his hand on the head of each candidate, saying: "Receive the Holy Ghost, for strength and for resisting the devil and his temptations, in the name of the Lord."

The deacon's stole is placed on his shoulders. He wears this in a manner different from that in which a priest's stole is put on. It is placed on the left shoulder and extends diagonally to the right side, where the ends are fastened.

The dalmatic, which is the large vestment worn by deacons, is then imposed, with a prayer which expresses its symbolic meaning. It represents salvation, joy and justice.

Next comes the bestowing of the Book of the Gospels, with the words: "Receive the power of reading the Gospel in the church of God, both for the living and the dead, in the name of the Lord."

Then, after two prayers asking God to bless the newly ordained and to give them grace to persevere, the Gospel of the day is chanted by one of the new deacons, and this concludes the ceremonies of their ordination.

The Order of Priesthood. All the Orders described thus far are a preparation for the priestly dignity, which imprints on the soul of the recipient a character which endures forever. The priest possesses all the faculties of the porter, the lector, the exorcist, the acolyte, the subdeacon and the deacon, and he receives also in his ordination powers which they do not enjoy — wonderful privileges which are of so sublime a nature that human reason cannot grasp their full import or measure their magnificence. The priest, in the words used by the Bishop in the ceremonies of ordination, is "to offer, to bless, to rule, to preach, to baptize." His most august function is the offering of the Holy Sacrifice of the Mass — to call down the Almighty from heaven — to hold God in his consecrated hands. He receives power to bless, to bring God's benediction upon any one or anything. He is placed in authority, to rule over a part of Christ's flock. He is God's spokesman, appointed to preach His word, set apart to do the work of an evangelist. He is the ordinary minister of Baptism, empowered to bring souls into the fold of Christ. He, a man and a sinner, has the marvelous power of forgiving the sins of other men.

These and many other wonderful supernatural faculties are given to the priest in his ordination, and they are symbolized by the beautiful ceremonies which our Church uses when she raises a man to this exalted dignity.

The Ordination of a Priest. As at the ordination of deacons, the candidates are presented to the Bishop by the Archdeacon, with the request that they be ordained to "the burden of the priesthood." The Bishop inquires about their worthiness, and the Archdeacon testifies to it. The Bishop then solemnly asks if any one is able to give reasons why the priestly dignity should not be conferred upon any of these.

He then admonishes the candidates that they must endeavor to receive the priesthood worthily and to live holy lives. He instructs them concerning their future duties; he compares their office with that of the seventy priests who were selected from all Israel under the Old Law to minister to God, and with the seventy-two who were chosen by our Blessed Saviour to go two and two to preach His Word. He reminds them that they and the other Orders of the clergy make up the mystical Body of Christ — the Catholic Church. He exhorts them to be chaste and holy, to mortify their bodies, to make their teaching the spiritual medicine of the people of God, to build up the household of the Lord by preaching and example.

If the candidates have not taken part already in the prostration with the subdeacons, they then prostrate themselves before the altar, as previously described.

The Imposition of Hands. They kneel two and two before the Bishop, who presses both hands upon the head of each. Afterwards all the priests who are present do the same to each candidate. The imposing of hands always symbolizes the imparting of grace.

The Bishop then prays that all heavenly gifts may be bestowed on them, and invokes a blessing. He then chants or reads a long and beautiful Preface, thanking the Almighty for having instituted the priesthood and asking that all those who enter it may receive all necessary helps and graces; that those now being ordained may be filled with the spirit of holiness and may through their priesthood win an eternal reward.

The Giving of the Vestments. The Bishop moves the stole from the left shoulder of each candidate (where it is worn by the deacons) to his neck, crossing it in front as it is worn by priests, with the words; "Receive the yoke of Christ, for His yoke is sweet and His burden light."

The chasuble, the large vestment worn by a priest at Mass, is then put on his shoulders, but the rear part of it is kept folded until later. The Bishop says: "Receive the priestly vestment, by which charity is understood; for God is powerful, that He may increase charity in thee, and perfect work." The symbolic meanings of this and other vestments, as well as their history, are set forth in another chapter of this work.

He then again invokes the blessing of God on all the candidates, and prays that they may possess and practise all the virtues necessary to their exalted state.

The Anointing of the Hands. The "Veni, Creator Spiritus," or hymn to the Holy Ghost, is then intoned by the Bishop and is sung by the choir. During this hymn the Bishop anoints the hands of each of the candidates with the Oil of Catechumens. This anointing is done in the form of a cross on the palms of the hands, which are thereby specially consecrated that they may be worthy to touch and handle the Sacred Body of our Lord.

The hands are then tied together with a strip of white linen and remain bound until the Offertory of the Mass.

The Giving of the Chalice. The chalice, containing wine and water, and the paten, holding the unconsecrated Host, are placed in the hands of each, with the words: "Receive the power to offer sacrifice to God and to celebrate Masses, both for the living and the dead, in the name of the Lord. Amen."

During the remainder of the Mass the newly ordained priests utter the words of the Holy Sacrifice in unison with the Bishop, so that the Mass is really celebrated by all together.

The Power to Absolve. After all have received Holy Communion they receive the power of forgiving sins — that wonderful faculty which the priest exercises by virtue of the commission given by our Lord to the Apostles. The Bishop places his hands on the head of each, uttering the words of Jesus Christ: "Receive ye the Holy Ghost; whose sins you shall forgive, they are forgiven; whose sins you shall retain, they are retained." He then unfolds the chasuble (which up to this time has been hanging folded on the priest's shoulders) with the words: "May the Lord clothe thee with the mangle of innocence."

The Oath of Obedience. Each of the new priests goes to the Bishop, kneels before him, and places his hands in those of the prelate, who says to him: "Do you promise me and my successors reverence and obedience?" And the priest answers: "I do promise." The Bishop says devoutly: "The peace of the Lord be always with thee."

If the priest belongs to another diocese the question is asked in a different form. Then a solemn admonition is addressed to the new priests, warning them that as the sacred things which they are to use and handle are worthy of all reverence, they must be well trained in the ceremonies of the Holy Sacrifice before they attempt to offer it.

The Bishop pronounces a blessing, calling down upon them the benediction of the three Persons of the Blessed Trinity; and near the end of the Mass he gives them another solemn warning, saying: "Beloved sons, consider diligently the Order received by you and the burden imposed upon your shoulders. Study to live holy and religious lives, that you may please the Almighty and acquire His grace."

A penance is then announced for each of the Orders that have been conferred at the ordination. Those who have received tonsure and the Minor Orders are told to recite the seven penitential psalms; the subdeacons and deacons, a part of the sacred office; and the priests are directed to celebrate three Masses, one in honor of the Holy Ghost, one of the Blessed Virgin, and one for the souls in Purgatory; and all are requested to pray for the Bishop.

These ancient rites used in the conferring of Holy Orders show us the wisdom of our Holy Church. She teaches not only by word but by example. This sacrament imparts wonderful graces and privileges and powers to those who receive its various grades; and that these may be well understood by them and also by the faithful who witness the ordination, the Church has enriched and adorned with beautiful and symbolic ceremonies the administration of the sacrament of her priesthood and the steps which lead up to it. Every one of the details of an ordination is of great antiquity; little change has been made in them for centuries. Every one is intended to instruct us concerning some gift or faculty given by our holy Church to the Levite who aspires to the service of her sanctuary. Every duty and every power belonging to the various Orders is symbolized by the majestic rites with which they are administered, or are expressed in the solemn prayers offered to God and the admonitions addressed to the candidates by the ordaining Bishop.

Chapter XIII

THE CEREMONIES OF MATRIMONY

Our holy Church uses a very beautiful and appropriate ritual when she blesses the matrimonial union of two of her children. The ceremonies with which the Sacrament of Matrimony is administered express the solemnity of the contract by which the man and woman bind themselves, and the holiness of the sacrament which they receive.

The Ceremonies of a Marriage. Although the Church recommends most strongly that the Sacrament of Matrimony shall be received at Mass and shall be accompanied by the giving of the Nuptial Blessing, a marriage may be performed apart from Mass and even in some other place than a church. We shall, therefore, describe briefly the ceremonies employed in the actual administration of this sacrament, whether at Mass or note, and afterward we shall explain in detail the beautiful ritual which is used at the solemn celebration of a marriage at a Nuptial Mass.

A marriage is a very simple ceremony. It consists essentially in the expression of mutual consent by the parties to take each other as man and wife. This is followed by the blessing of their union and the ceremony of the ring.

At a marriage of two Catholics (which is the only one we shall consider), the parties, attended by the witnesses, appear before the priest, who wears a surplice and a white stole if no Mass is to be said. If the Nuptial Mass is to follow the marriage ceremony, he is vested for it, except that he does not wear the maniple during the marriage rite.

The Expressing of Consent. The priest first asks the consent of the parties. Addressing the man by name, he says, in Latin and in English: "Wilt thou take . . ., here present, for they lawful wife, according to the rite of our holy Mother the Church?" To which the answer is given aloud, "I will." The same question is put to the bride: "Wilt thou take….., here present, for thy lawful husband," etc., to which the same answer is given by her. Then, at the bidding of the priest, they join their right hands.

In many places it is the custom for the parties to pledge themselves to each other formally by repeating certain words after the priest. This is not essential, as the consent of both has been sufficiently manifested already; but the solemn repetition of the mutual obligations which they are assuming adds to the impressiveness of the ceremony. The words used for this purpose are not defined in the Church's ritual, and vary considerably in different countries and different languages. The following is the form generally used by us:

"I, N. N., take thee, N. N., for my lawful wife (or husband), to have and to hold, from this day forward, for better, for worse, for richer, for poorer, in sickness and in health, till death do us part." Indeed, these are solemn and impressive words! Very beautiful also is the formula usually employed by those speaking French: "I take you, N., for my wife (or husband) and my lawful spouse; and I swear to you that I will be a faithful husband (or wife), and that I will assist you with all my power in all your necessities, so long as it shall please God to leave us together."

Then the priest, in Latin, pronounces the words by which the marriage is blessed: "I join you together in marriage, in the name of the Father and of the Son and of the Holy Ghost" — and while saying this he makes over the couple the sign of the cross, and then sprinkles them with holy water.

The Giving of the Ring. The blessing of the wedding-ring comes next. The priest recites in Latin the following beautiful prayer: "Bless, O Lord, this ring which we bless in Thy name, that she who is to wear it, keeping true faith unto her husband, may abide in Thy peace and in obedience unto Thy will, and ever live in mutual love. Through Jesus Christ our Lord. Amen." Holy water is sprinkled over the ring, and the bridegroom then places it on the third finger of the left hand of the bride, saying in old-fashioned English, which has come down to us from past centuries: "With this ring I thee wed, and I plight unto thee my troth." In other lands and tongues the words are different. The French formula is: "My spouse, I give you this ring in token of marriage."

The priest then recites certain versicles and the Our Father;

and it is usual for the married couple to recite this latter prayer also. A final prayer is said, asking God's protection for those whose union has been sanctified by the Church. "Look down, we beseech Thee, O Lord, upon these Thy servants, and graciously protect Thy institutions whereby Thou hast provided for the propagation of mankind; that those who are joined together by Thy authority may be preserved by Thy help. Through Christ our Lord. Amen."

The Nuptial Mass. It is the desire of our Church that the Sacrament of Matrimony shall be administered, in every possible case, in connection with the Adorable Sacrifice of the Mass. The graces needed in the married state are so many that every available means should be taken to obtain them. The Church bestows these graces not only through the Sacrament of Matrimony itself, but also through the Holy Mass which is celebrated for the special benefit of the married couple, and through the solemn blessing which is pronounced over them.

As early as the second century we find traces of this practice. St. Evaristus, Pope and martyr, decreed that "in accordance with Apostolic tradition marriage should be celebrated publicly and with the blessing of the priest"; and in the third century marriage with a Mass was common.

The Nuptial Mass is filled with special prayers invoking the blessing of the Almighty on those who are entering the married state. It may be said during the greater part of the year. On the most important festivals the Mass of the feast is said instead, with a commemoration of the Nuptial Mass; and marriage at a Mass is not allowed at all during what are called the "closed times" — Advent and the following days until Epiphany inclusively; Lent and Easter week.

Why is a marriage at Mass not allowed at these times? A marriage ceremony is an occasion of joy, and it is the wish of the Church that her children should not be married with solemnity or outward pomp in penitential seasons; and on the days of joy which follow Advent and Lent she desires that there should be nothing to distract us from the proper observance of them. Therefore, although the Sacrament of Matrimony may be received at any time, the solemnizing of it with Mass and blessing cannot take place during the aforesaid seasons. Even the bishop cannot dispense from this law.

The Nuptial Mass is filled with beautiful quotations from the Scriptures, expressing the dignity and holiness of the matrimonial union. The Introit is taken partly from the Bible narrative of Tobias and his bride. The Collect or prayer of the Mass asks that "what is performed by our ministry may be abundantly filled with God's blessings." The Epistle is very appropriately taken from the teaching of St. Paul to the Ephesians: "Let women be subject to their husbands as to the Lord; because the husband is the head of the wife" — a teaching not precisely in harmony with the spirit of our twentieth century. The Gospel is that in which our Lord declared the indissoluble character of matrimony. "What God hath joined together, let no man put asunder."

And so it is through the whole Mass. All the parts which admit of change are adapted to the spirit of the ceremony, expressing the sanctity of marriage and invoking God's blessing upon those who are contracting it.

The Nuptial Blessing. After the Pater Noster of the Mass, the priest turns and faces the married couple, and imparts to them the solemn Nuptial Blessing. This is directed rather to the woman than to the man, and is given to her only once. Consequently, if it has been received by the bride at a previous marriage, it is omitted at a subsequent one; and if a marriage takes place without a Mass, it is not given.

It consists in the invoking of God's grace upon the union which has just been made; and the prayer goes on thus: "May her wedlock be to her a yoke of love and peace. May she marry in Christ, faithful and chaste, and be an imitator of holy women. May she be amiable to her husband, like Rachel; wise, like Rebecca; long-lived and faithful, like Sarah. . . . May she be fruitful in offspring, approved and innocent. May she attain to the repose of the blessed in heaven; and may they both see their children's children, even to the third and fourth generations, and arrive at their desired old age. Through Jesus Christ our Lord. Amen."

Near the end of the Mass, just before the usual blessing, the priest turns to the married couple and prays that they may enjoy fruitfulness, peace and everlasting happiness. Holy water is then sprinkled upon them, and the Mass concludes as usual.

Such is the Nuptial Mass, established as a means of grace for the Church's children who are entering into the married state. It is not necessary to have an ostentatious celebration when a marriage takes place; but the marriage in the church, with a Mass, with the Nuptial Blessing and with the reception of Holy Communion by the parties, should never be omitted except for the gravest reasons. The Catholic man and woman who wish their married life to be happy and blest by God should never be tempted to deny themselves the graces which will be obtained through the beautiful ceremonial which the Church has authorized for the solemnizing of Christian marriage.

PART IV
THE HOLY SACRIFICE OF THE MASS

CHAPTER XIV

THE MASS

IT will not be necessary, under this heading, to explain the Catholic doctrine regarding the Mass, for this book is devoted rather to practice than to doctrine. In this chapter we will confine ourselves to an explanation of the meaning of the name of the Mass, the past and present customs and rules as to the time of saying it, the applying of its fruits to souls, and the various kinds of Masses that are celebrated at the present time.

The Name of the Mass. Why is the great Sacrifice of the Altar called the Mass? The English word is from the Latin "missa," derived from the verb "mittere," to send, and signifies "a dismissal." But why is it used as the name of the Sacrifice? Because in the ancient liturgy of the Church there were two solemn dismissals; first, that of the catechumens, those partly instructed and not yet baptized, after the Gospel and the sermon; and secondly, that of the faithful at the end of the Mass — still preserved in our Masses by the announcement "Ite, missa est," — "Go, it is the dismissal" — just before the blessing and the last Gospel. The word for dismissal gradually came to denote the service from which these persons were dismissed. The French form, "Messe," was taken into England in Norman times, and was later modified into "Maesse," "Masse," and finally "Mass."

In the early centuries of the Church it was known by various names — the Breaking of Bread, the Lord's Supper, the Solemnity of the Lord, the Sacrifice, the Holy Liturgy, and the Eucharist, which means Thanksgiving.

The Frequency of Celebration. To us, who have Mass in our churches every day, and who know that priests usually offer the Holy Sacrifice daily, it may seem strange that it was not always thus. In the first centuries the bishops and priests celebrated together — one Mass, said by several. The only vestige of this practice that remains is in the Mass of Ordination, in which the newly ordained priests say Mass jointly with the bishop, though they do not partake of the same Host nor of the Precious Blood. In those early times, then, there was usually only one Mass each day in a church; and this is the custom at the present day among the Greek and Oriental schismatics. In many parts of the world, in the first centuries, Mass was only celebrated on Sundays and great feasts; but as far back as the time of St. Augustine it began to be common to have at least one daily Mass in each church.

At the present time Mass may be said in our churches every day except on Good Friday, on which day the priest merely receives Holy Communion, consuming the Host consecrated on Holy Thursday and reserved over night in the Repository.

Many centuries ago it was customary for the same celebrant to say more than one Mass if he wished to do so. Some priests said several daily. It is related that Pope Leo III, from a spirit of devotion, sometimes celebrated nine times in one day. But another Pope, Alexander II, restricted all priests to one Mass a day, although shortly afterwards it was tolerated to offer two Masses, one of the feast of the day and the other for the dead.

Others were led to devotion in quite an opposite direction. They said Mass very seldom, deeming themselves unworthy. St. Thomas of Canterbury, from a spirit of humility, did not celebrate daily. Even the seraphic St. Francis of Assisi had such a reverence for the Mass that he wished to have it celebrated only once each day in the monasteries of his Order; the other priests were to content themselves with hearing Mass.

By the present law priests are prohibited from saying Mass more than once on any day except Christmas and All Souls' Day, on which three may be said. Bishops, however, may allow their priests to "duplicate" or celebrate twice on Sunday and holydays of obligation if a considerable number of people would otherwise be unable to hear Mass; and our priests possess faculties, renewed yearly to that effect.

When is a priest obliged to say Mass? He is not required by any law to celebrate daily. The great spiritual writers of recent centuries, such as St. Ignatius Loyola and St. Francis de Sales, strongly urge priests to say Mass every day, and this may be called a common custom among our priests, at least when they are at home. A parish priest must say Mass or have it said whenever the people are bound to hear it.

The Hour of Mass. At what time in the day may Mass be said? This was subject to no special regulation down to the middle of the fifth century, although it was usually said in the morning. After a time, in monasteries, it was celebrated at nine o'clock. Later it became customary to have Mass at noon, and even at three o'clock in the afternoon. According to the present law, Mass must not be said before dawn nor after mid-day. Dawn is generally computed as five o'clock, although during a part of the year it comes later than that hour. These limits must not be transgressed unless by permission of the Holy See. Such permission is sometimes given, usually to monastic churches only, for a midnight Mass at Christmas, or to churches on the occasion of a Jubilee.

The Fruits of the Mass. The Holy Sacrifice of the Altar is a sacrifice of adoration, praise and thanksgiving. It is also a sacrifice of propitiation and of petition — a means of obtaining all graces and blessings from God. It is offered always for certain persons — for those present in the church or residing in the parish, for the relatives and friends of the celebrant, for the members of the Church in general, and for the souls in Purgatory. According to theologians and spiritual writers, there is a threefold fruit of the Holy Sacrifice: namely, the general fruit, in which all the faithful participate — the more special fruit, which belongs to those for whom the priest intends to offer the Mass — and the most special fruit, for the priest himself.

In "saying Mass" for a person, then, the priest applies to him the "more special fruit" of the Sacrifice. The "general fruit" is given always to the whole Church, and the "most special fruit" is reserved to the priest himself.

Intentions for Masses. All bishops and priests having the care of souls are obliged to say Mass expressly for the benefit and intention of their people on Sundays and holydays of obligation, and on certain other days which are now merely feasts of devotion but which were once holydays. This obligation exists, however, only in regions in which "canonical parishes" have been instituted. In the greater part of our country these parishes do not exist; and therefore those in charge of our "missionary parishes" have no obligation from justice to do this, although charity makes it fitting that they do so.

Every priest who receives an alms or stipend for a Mass incurs a strict obligation to say it or to have it said. This offering is meant as an aid to the support of the priest. The amount is fixed by diocesan rule, and the priest may not ask more, though he may accept more. If he says two Masses in one day, he is allowed to receive an offering for one only. All priests are urged not to keep on hand too many stipends for Masses, because thereby the offering of the Holy Sacrifice for the intention of the giver would be too long delayed. When they accumulate too rapidly, it is customary to give them to other priests less fortunately situated.

The Kinds of Masses. There are several kinds of Masses. The "Solemn High Mass" (in Latin "Missa Solemnis") is celebrated with incense, music and the assistance of a deacon and subdeacon; the celebrant chants several parts of the Mass, and the deacon and subdeacon intone the Gospel and the Epistle respectively. A "Pontifical Mass" is a Solemn Mass celebrated by a bishop, and a "Papal Mass" is that in which the Pope is the celebrant.

A "High Mass" (in Latin "Missa Cantata" or Chanted Mass) is one that is sung by a priest without deacon or subdeacon.

A "Low Mass" is one that is celebrated without music, the priest reading the words throughout. It was unknown in the early centuries of the Church, although now it is said more frequently than any other. It is sometimes called a "Private Mass," although that name belongs more properly to a Mass said by a priest mostly for his own devotion and not for the benefit of a parish or congregation. For a low Mass it is necessary to have a server or acolyte, but in our country, being a "missionary land," permission is given to priests to celebrate without such assistance when the services of an acolyte cannot be had.

A "Parochial Mass" is the principal Mass offered in a parish church on Sundays and great festivals. It is the "assembly of the faithful in which they offer public prayers and sacrifice by the ministry of their pastor."

A "Capitular Mass" is the High Mass on Sundays and festivals in Catholic countries in churches that are served by a "chapter" or body of canons, whose principal duty is the recitation of the Divine Office. A "Conventual Mass" is not, as the name would seem to denote, a Mass said in a convent. It is the daily Mass for the chapter of canons, taking place at a fixed hour after the chanting of a part of the Office.

A "Votive Mass" is one which does not correspond to the office of the day, but is said at the choice of the priest, and is permitted only on certain days. For instance, on many days of minor importance in the Church's calendar, the priest may omit the Mass of the day and say instead a Mass of the Holy Ghost, of the Sacred Heart, of the Blessed Virgin, or some other, according to his own devotion or the request of the giver of the offering for a Mass.

And lastly, a "Requiem Mass" is a Mass for the dead, said in black vestments. It may be a Solemn Mass, a High Mass or a Low Mass. It is called a Requiem Mass from the opening words of the Introit: "Requiem aeternam dona eis, Domine" — "Eternal rest give unto them, O Lord."

Chapter XV

THE GROWTH OF THE MASS – I

In this and the following chapters we shall see how the various parts of the Mass have been developed and modified during the nineteen centuries of the Church's history. There is not much in the New Testament to tell us of the ceremonies of the Mass among the first Christians. Nearly all of them, at first, were of the Jewish race, and at their assemblies they undoubtedly did as they had been accustomed to do in the solemn ritual of Israel. There were readings from the holy books and from the letters (or Epistles) of the Apostle Paul; sermons were preached and explanations of Christian teaching were given; psalms and hymns were sung; prayers were said publicly for "the brethren" and for others; and collections of alms were made for the poor. Thus we see that church collections are no modern innovation. The Christians of Apostolic times were required to make their offerings on Sundays, even as we of this later day. Such were the elements of what was called in those times the Communion, which we now call the Mass; and this service was usually held on Sunday, the first day of the week, instead of on Saturday, thereby distinguishing it from the Jewish worship of the Temple and synagogue.

The people prayed standing, with uplifted hands. The men had their heads uncovered, the women were veiled. There was a "kiss of peace" and a public profession of faith — details which have endured even to our day, for the kiss of peace is given at solemn Masses, and the Creed, said at many Masses, is the formula by which our faith is declared.

The First Prayers and the Introit. Let us now take up the various important parts of the great Sacrifice and indicate briefly the origin of each. The prayers said by the priest at the foot of the altar are the latest part of all. They were, in the Middle Ages, merely a private preparation for Mass, made by the priest before he approached the altar, and expressive of his trust in God and his consciousness of his own unworthiness. It became a recognized part of the Mass only when the Missal was revised by St. Pius V in 1570.

The Introit, the first matter read by the priest when he goes up to the altar, was originally a processional psalm chanted as the celebrant and his attendants entered the sanctuary. Later on, when this chanting was no longer used, the first verse only was retained and became a part of the Mass. It varies from day to day, and nearly all of the Introits of the older feasts go back to St. Gregory the Great.

The Incensing and the Kyrie. The offering of incense in sacrifices was common both in pagan and Jewish worship, and its use in Christian rites goes back almost to the beginning of the Church. It was used at the tombs in the catacombs, in processions, and (somewhat later) at the altar. St. Ambrose, writing in the year 397, speaks of it as in use at the Mass; and not long afterward suitable prayers were assigned for the incensings. The Roman rite permits it only at Solemn Masses and, in some parts of the world, at ordinary High Masses.

The "Kyrie eleison" ("Lord, have mercy") is Greek, and is the only formula in that language that is used in our Latin Mass. However, it does not go back to the time when Mass was celebrated only in Greek — namely, the first and second centuries. It came into use in the East, and is a fragment of a kind of litany which was recited by all present. The words "Kyrie eleison" are now said alternately by the priest and the server, three times in honor of God the Father; the "Christ eleison," likewise three times in honor of God the Son; and the "Kyrie eleison" again three times, to God the Holy Ghost — the whole thus forming a beautiful prayer to the Blessed Trinity.

The Gloria. This sublime canticle of praise, known also as the Angelic Hymn and as the Greater Doxology, is a translation of a very old Greek hymn. It was originally a morning prayer, addressed to the Trinity. It began to be used in church services at an early date' by some its introduction is attributed to Pope Telesphorus, about the year 130. It was at first sung on Christmas Day only, being an amplified form of the song of the angels at Bethlehem. Later it was extended to other days, to feasts of joy only. Up to the eleventh century it could be used by bishops only, except at Easter. It is said in nearly all Masses except those expressive of sorrow or penance — being omitted in votive Masses, however, except that of the Angels.

The Collects. These are the prayers said or sung immediately after the Gloria, or after the Kyrie if the Gloria has been omitted. They are called Collects because the meeting of the clergy and people was known in ancient times as a "collecta" or "collectio" — an assembly. Their history goes back many centuries; the ancient Ritual known as the Leonine Sacramentary contains many of those we now use. They express man's dependence on God, with petitions for help and security. The same prayer is used by the priest in his Office as in the Mass of the day, and is thus repeated many times. In the Mass it is said standing, with uplifted hands, the ancient attitude of prayer.

The Epistle. We use this name for the reading that takes place in our Mass shortly before the Gospel; but the word is sometimes inaccurate, for this reading is not always from the Epistles of the New Testament. Quite frequently it is taken from other parts of the Bible, such as the books of Exodus or Wisdom, the Acts of the Apostles, etc. As stated already, Epistles were read at the Mass in the days of the Apostles.

Between the Epistle and the Gospel come short readings, varying according to the day and the season of the year. These are the Gradual, Alleluia, Tract and Sequence. They were originally psalms, sung as part of the sacred service, and after a time were shortened to a few verses in most cases. The Gradual takes its name from the word "gradus," meaning an elevated step, because in the Middle Ages a chanter intoned the first verse of the psalm from a platform called the "ambo," half-way down the church.

The Sequences. The Sequences, medieval hymns, were once very numerous, but the reformers of the Missal at the time of the Council of Trent abolished all but five of them. These five are among the most perfect specimens of Latin poetry. That of Easter, "Victimae Paschali" was written by a priest named Wipo, about 1048, and was possibly at first a part of a "mystery play" depicting our Lord's Resurrection.

The great Dominican St. Thomas Aquinas, in 1274,

composed a complete Office for the new feast of Corpus Christi, including the Sequence "Lauda, Sion, Salvatorem" ("Praise the Savior, O Sion"). The "Stabat Mater Dolorosa" was probably written about 1306, by a certain Jacopene da Todi. It is used as a Sequence on the two feasts of the Seven Dolors, and has furnished the text for several great musical compositions, notably that of Rossini. The "Veni, Sancte Spiritus," used at Pentecost, is attributed to Robert, king of France, who died in 1031. And lastly, the Church has kept in her Requiem Masses the magnificent poem on the Day of Judgment, the "Dies Irae" ("Day of Wrath"), written in the thirteenth century by Thomas of Celano — the finest example of sacred poetry.

The Gospel. The selections from the Gospels, read at Mass, are very often appropriate to the feast or to the spirit of the season, although on some Sundays and festivals they would seem to have been chosen at random. Much of the present arrangement is attributed to St. Jerome.

At a Solemn Mass the Gospel is chanted by the deacon; at a low Mass it is read by the priest. Why is it read on what we call the "Gospel side" of the altar or sanctuary? Because in ancient times the right-hand side of the church (looking towards the altar) was occupied by the men of the congregation, and the Gospel was read by the deacon, facing them, from a platform called the "ambo," on the opposite side of the church. The "devout female sex" seems to have been of lesser importance in those distant days. And then, as now, all stood as a mark of respect for the sacred Word of God.

The Sermon and the Creed. The priest who preaches to his people after the Gospel on Sunday morning is following the example of his predecessors in all ages back to the Apostles, and performs what is really an element of the liturgy itself, especially if his sermon is an explanation of the Gospel. Protestantism lays great stress on preaching, for it has little else — but the Catholic Church has combined preaching with her beautiful liturgy from the earliest ages, fulfilling her divine mission of teaching all nations.

All the various liturgies of the Church now contain a Creed, often said at Mass; but this is a late addition to the ritual of the Holy Sacrifice. Originally Creeds were used only at Baptism as a profession of faith, and the one called the Apostles' Creed still keeps its place in the baptismal rite.

The Creed now used in the Mass is called the Nicene, because it was largely drawn up by the Council of Nice or Nicea, in the year 325. Its use in the Eucharistic Sacrifice began in Spain in 589, and at first it was said after the Consecration. Its use after the Gospel was ordered in 1014 by Benedict VIII.

It is not said in all Masses, being omitted on the feasts of martyrs, confessors and female saints (except the Blessed Virgin) and on vigils; also in votive Masses and in all Masses of Requiem.

CHAPTER XVI

THE GROWTH OF THE MASS – II

AFTER the Gospel or Creed the priest says: "Dominus vobiscum," and then "Oremus" ("Let us pray"), but he says no prayer. Why is this? Because in the earliest centuries the people at this part of the Mass offered prayers together, a deacon chanting a kind of litany to which all responded. This custom no longer exists.

The Offertory. Then comes the Offertory, the real beginning of the Eucharistic act. Just as our Blessed Saviour, at the Last Supper, took bread and wine, so the priest takes them and offers them to God. In many other rites this is done at the very beginning of the Mass; but the Roman liturgy has always placed the Offertory after the Gospel.

At this part of the Mass, in our parish churches, the collection is taken up — called the "offertory collection" because in early times it was customary for the people to present the bread and wine for the Sacrifice. Later the practice began of giving money instead of these. Thus we see that the Sunday collections in our churches are nothing new; for many centuries the faithful have given their offerings, even as we.

Altar Bread

The Bread and Wine. For many centuries the Roman Church has used at Mass bread that is unleavened, or made without yeast. In the East all Christians except the Armenians and the Maronites use leavened bread, and it is probable that this was done everywhere until about the eighth century. Either kind is valid, and Rome insists that each Church shall keep to the kind required by its own liturgy; thus she would not permit the Greeks who are Catholics to use unleavened bread, and would not allow us to use leavened. The unleavened kind was probably used by our Lord at the Last Supper, which was Passover of the Jews, at which such bread only was eaten.

The breads for the altar are baked between heated irons upon which is stamped some pious emblem, such as the crucifix and the letters I.H.S. The small altar-breads, intended for the

Communion of the faithful, may be plain. In the Roman rite both the large and the small Hosts are of a circular form, which rule goes back at least to the third century.

The wine must be fermented, or alcoholic — not merely grape-juice, which is not wine at all. A little water, blessed with a short prayer, is mingled with it in the chalice. Spiritual writers look upon the mixture as a symbol of the two natures of Christ. The chalice is offered with a prayer, the last words of which invoke the blessing of the Holy Ghost.

At a solemn Mass the deacon holds and offers the chalice with the celebrant, because in ancient times he had special charge of the chalice, and gave Holy Communion from it to the faithful in the days when they received the Holy Eucharist under both forms. The bread and wine and the whole altar are then incensed by the priest. This ceremony in its present form goes back to the fourteenth century.

The Washing of the Fingers. In all the various rites which our Church uses throughout the world the celebrant washes his hands before handling the offerings. He has already done so at the vesting before Mass, and formerly he repeated it twice during the Mass. While the water is being poured on his finders he recites part of the twenty-fifth Psalm: "I will wash my hands among the innocent," etc.

He then, as it were, concludes and sums up the whole offertory by the prayer "Receive, O Holy Trinity, this oblation," which is a rather recent addition to the Mass. It was not in general use until after the revision of the Missal in 1570.

The Secret Prayers. The priest then turns towards the people and asks for their prayers: "Orate, fratres" — ("Pray, brethren, that may and your sacrifice may be acceptable to God the Father Almighty") — and the response is made on their behalf: "May the Lord receive the sacrifice from thy hands to the praise and glory of His Name, and also for our benefit and that of His whole holy Church." This is a medieval addition, having been finally legalized for all Masses in the fourteenth century.

Then come the "Secreta," one or more prayers said by the priest in a low tone, and resembling those said as Collects earlier in the Mass. Many of those now in use are found in the most ancient ritual books of the Church. They usually ask God to accept the gifts offered at the altar, to sanctify them, and to give us His grace in return. The last of these prayers ends with the clause "Per omnia saecula saeculorum" ("Through all the ages of ages," or "forever and ever"), said or sung aloud.

The Preface and Sanctus. Although in our Missals the words "Canon of the Mass" stand after the Sanctus, it is important to remember that the Preface is really part of the Canon. It is so recorded in the old Sacramentaries, being the "thanksgiving prayer" which leads to the words of consecration. The name "Preface," or Introduction, is found first in the early Middle Ages.

Originally this part of the Mass was very long, containing a list of all the blessings for which man gives thanks to God. Later, especially in the Roman rite, it was shortened, and was varied according to the feast or season. In some ancient Missals there were more than a hundred different Prefaces, but the number was reduced in later centuries. We now have eleven, all very ancient except that of the Blessed Virgin, which was added by Pope Urban II at the end of the eleventh century.

The Preface begins with a dialogue. The priest says to the people: "The Lord be with you," to which the server answers for them: "And with thy spirit." "Lift up your hearts" — one of the oldest of liturgical formulas, to which the response is made: "We have lifted them up to the Lord." "Let us give thanks to the Lord our God," with the answer: "It is meet and just." The celebrant takes up these last words, saying: "Truly it is meet and just," and so begins the Eucharistic prayer, varying it, as said above, according to the occasion of the Mass. In it mention is made of the angels who praise God, and like them we are urged to say: "Holy, holy holy, Lord God of Hosts," in the beautiful prayer of adoration, the Sanctus.

This is merely a continuation of the Preface; but besides being said by the priest, it is sung in solemn Masses by the choir and recited by the assisting ministers, representing the people — who are thus enabled, as it were, to join in the chant of the angels. It is one of the oldest parts of the Church's service, being alluded to by St. Clement of Rome before the end of the first century.

The Canon of the Mass. Thus we enter into what is called the Canon of the Mass. The word "Canon" is Greek, meaning a rule or method; and the name is used for the part of the Mass before and after the Consecration because the Church requires it to be said usually without variation, according to a fixed standard to which all must conform.

The real Canon ends at the words "Per omnia saecula saeculorum," just before the Pater Noster, although the heading "Canon Missae" in the Mass-Book goes on to the end. In its first part the priest prays for the Church, the Pope, the Bishop of the place and the faithful, mentioning the Pope and the Bishop by their first names. He then makes the Commemoration of the Living, remaining silent for a few moments while he mentally prays for those who he wishes specially to commend to God. In the next prayer he brings in a list of saints, including the Blessed Mother of God, the Apostles, St. Cyprian and eleven illustrious martyrs of the Roman Church, thus emphasizing our communion with them as members of the Church of Christ. This prayer varies slightly at certain seasons of the year.

The Words of Consecration. Then follows the prayer, "Hanc igitur oblationem," beseeching God to accept the offering — at which the hands are held horizontally over the bread and wine; and this brings the celebrant to the beautiful passage which introduces the words of consecration spoken by our Blessed Saviour at the Last Supper. It reads as follows: "Who, the day before He suffered, took bread into His holy and venerable hands, and, raising His eyes to heaven, giving thanks to Thee, blessed, broke and gave to His disciples, saying: "Take and eat all of this; for this is My Body." And another introduction, "Simili modo," leads to the words of consecration said over the chalice: "For this is the chalice of My Blood of the new and eternal testament, a mystery of faith, which shall be shed for you and for many for the remission of sins." Then follows the commission to the Apostles: "As often as you shall do these things, you shall do them in memory of Me."

Let us examine these solemn words. They have not been always precisely the same, various ancient rituals giving slightly different forms. Why is the phrase "a mystery of faith" inserted, since it is not to be found in any of the Gospel accounts of the Last Supper? It is conjectured that in early times these words were an exclamation made by the deacon to announce to the people that the great Mystery of Faith was accomplished — that God was present on the altar.

The Elevation. After the priest has pronounced the words of consecration over the bread he genuflects in adoration and raises the Sacred Host so that it may be seen by all the people, and then genuflects again. This elevation is a ceremony introduced in the late Middle Ages. There was no trace of it until about the twelfth century, when it was the custom to hold the Host as high as the breast while the words of consecration were being pronounced. As done at present, it seems to have been first ordered by Eudes de Sully, Bishop of Paris, about the year 1200, and within a hundred years the practice had spread throughout the Western Church. The genuflections were ordered by the revised Missal of 1570.

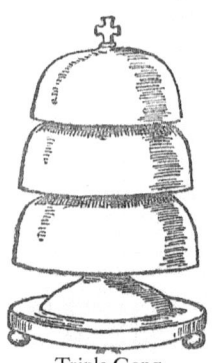
Triple Gong

The elevation of the chalice is done in like manner, and came into use a little later than that of the Host. The incensing of the Blessed Sacrament at the two elevations is a late addition to the ceremonial of the Mass. It began with the Dominicans, and was introduced at Rome about the end of the fourteenth century.

What should we do in church at the Elevation of the Mass? As the reason for the ceremony is to show the Blessed Sacrament to the people, it is right for them to look at it — an ancient practice sanctioned anew by our late Holy Father Pius X, who granted an indulgence to all who do it. However, the other practice, of bowing low in adoration, is not by any means wrong.

The Bell at Mass. The ringing of a bell has come to be a part of the ceremonies of the Mass, although, strictly speaking, it is not required at a Solemn Mass, but is merely tolerated. A peculiar and not very laudable custom existed in many parts of the world in the Middle Ages — the summoning of the people from outside the church by the sound of a bell as the time of the Consecration drew near; and after the Elevation they promptly went out again. This bell, known in England as the Sanctus or sance bell, was often hung in a small cupola over the sanctuary, and was rung by means of a role that hung down near the server's place. A small hand-bell was rung then, as now, at the Elevation; and the great church bell was tolled at the same time, that those at a distance might know the moment of consecration. At the present day the ringing at the Sanctus and at the Elevation is all that the rubrics demand. In France and in some other countries there is a great deal of bell-ringing at different parts of the Mass — which cannot be said to add anything to the dignity of the Holy Sacrifice, and is not called for by any Missal regulations. In our churches the bell is rung usually at the Sanctus three times; at the "Hanc, igitur," just before the consecration, once; at the elevation of the Host and of the chalice, three times for each; at the "Domine, non sum dignus" before the priest's Communion, three times; and the same words before the Communion of the people, three times also.

CHAPTER XVII

THE GROWTH OF THE MASS – III

FOLLOWING the recital of the words of our Lord commanding that this "be done in memory of Him," the next prayer goes on to assure us that we do remember Him always. Mention is made of His passion, resurrection and ascension, thus reminding us of the great events in His life, for which the whole Mass is an expression of thanksgiving.

Why does the priest make the sign of the cross over the Sacred Body and Blood of our Lord? Surely he cannot bless Him who is the source of all blessings. Some writers claim that these signs are not blessings — that they symbolize the Holy Trinity, the five wounds of our Savior, and so on. A more probable opinion is that the substance of these prayers was originally expressed before the consecration, and that when they were placed in their present position the ceremonies connected with them were retained. The whole Canon is one prayer, asking God to accept the offerings at the altar; and, although the consecration has changed them into the living Presence of Christ, they are still referred to as offerings. These crosses, then, are not a blessing of the Sacred Species, but may be considered as a symbol of the blessings that flow from the Holy Eucharist.

The Commemoration of the Dead. The priest then prays for the souls in Purgatory, remaining silent for a few moments to form his intention as to those souls for which he wishes particularly to pray. In ancient times this was probably before the consecration, after the Commemoration for the Living.

Then the priest prays for those present, raising his voice at the words "Nobis quoque peccatoribus" ("Also for us sinners"), that the people may know that he is praying for them. This prayer brings in a new list of saints, different from those mentioned earlier in the Mass — John the Baptist, Matthias, Barnabas and several martyr-saints, men and women. Tradition says that the female names were inserted by St. Gregory I.

The Canon proper then ends with the sublime doxology "Through Him and with Him and in Him is to Thee, God the

THE HOLY SACRIFICE OF THE MASS

Father Almighty, in the unity of the Holy Spirit, all honor and glory" — at which words the priest slightly elevates the Host and chalice. He then says aloud or chants: "Peromnia saecula saeculorum," and the answer "Amen" completes the Canon.

The Pater Noster. In ancient times, in some parts of the world the Our Father came later in the Mass, after the Communion. St. Gregory assigned it to its present place. It occurs in every liturgy, for it was always deemed proper that this most sacred of all prayers should be said at the Church's most sacred service.

It is introduced by a beautiful passage expressing, as it were, our authority for using it: "Advised by salutary precepts and instructed by divine institutions we dare to say: 'Our Father,'" etc. At the end we have a prayer which is an "embolism," an amplified form of the last phrase of the Pater Noster, asking deliverance from evil, past, present and future, through the intercession of the Blessed Virgin, Saints Peter and Paul and St. :Andrew. In former times this list of saints varied considerably in different countries.

Shortly after the Pater Noster the priest divides the Sacred Host into three parts, of which the smallest is dropped into the chalice. This is a very ancient ceremony, and has been done in every form of Mass ritual. Why is the small part of the Host put into the chalice? It may be a relic of a common way of mixing bread and wine at meals, as our Lord did at the Last Supper. In its present form the practice dates back to the fourteenth century.

The priest, while holding a small part of the Host over the chalice, says aloud: "May the peace of the Lord be always with you" — which was originally a solemn blessing pronounced by him over the people before Communion.

The Agnus Dei. This threefold petition to the Lamb of God is then said by the priest and at high Masses is sung by the choir. It re-echoes the greeting of St. John the Baptist to our Blessed Lord: "Behold the Lamb of God; behold Him Who taketh away the sins of the world." It is found in ritual books of the Middle Ages, and is said to have been introduced into the Mass by Pope Sergius I, about the year 700. It was originally sung once by the priest and once by the people; but in the twelfth century the other repetition was added, with the words: "Give us peace."

The Kiss of Peace. Just before the priest's Communion there are three prayers in the Mass (two in Requiem Masses); and after the first of these, in solemn Masses except those of Requiem, the "Kiss of Peace" is given. This, in ancient times, took place earlier in the Mass, before the beginning of the Canon. It is a sign of fellowship and unity, and is one of the oldest elements of our liturgy, being mentioned by the earliest writers. It is now given by the priest placing his hands against the deacon's shoulders with the words: "Peace be with you," while the deacon holds his hands under the arms of the celebrant. It is then transmitted to the subdeacon and to the other clergy present.

The three (or two) prayers are of recent origin. They were once merely private devotions, not included in the prayers of the Mass. After saying them the priest takes the Sacred Host into his hands, saying: "I will receive the Heavenly Bread and will invoke the name of the Lord." Then he repeats three times the beautiful words of the humble centurion of the Gospel: "Lord, I am not worthy that Thou shouldst enter under my roof; but only say the word and my soul shall be healed." These words have not always been used in the Mass, and were only authorized officially in the revised Missal of 1570.

The Communion. Then, saying reverently, "May the Body of our Lord Jesus Christ guard my soul into eternal life," the priest receives the Sacred Host. Uncovering the chalice, he says: "What shall I render to the Lord for all that He hath rendered to me? I will receive the chalice of salvation," etc. — words which were once merely a prayer of private devotion; and he then receives the Precious Blood.

Then comes the Communion of the people. It seems strange to us to learn that in early centuries the Sacred Host was put into the hand of the communicant. The placing of it on the tongue began in some places about the year 600. In those days, too, one important detail of Holy Communion was different from what we now have: the faithful received "under two kinds" — that is, drinking from the chalice as well as receiving the Sacred Host. This continued almost universally down to the twelfth century, although it was always known and taught that the reception of the Host alone was sufficient for Holy Communion.

The short prayers at the giving of Holy Communion to the people did not originally belong to the Mass at all, but were used for Communion given outside of Mass — to the sick and others. They consist in the recitation of the Confiteor, the words, "Behold the Lamb of God," etc., the "Lord I am not worthy," and the prayer "May the Body of our Lord Jesus Christ guard thy soul into eternal life," and while the Blessed Sacrament is being placed on the tongue of the communicant.

The chalice is then purified and the priest goes to the Epistle side of the altar and reads the "Communion," so called because it was formerly sung by the choir while the people communicated. This varies from day to day, as is the case with the following prayer or prayers called the "Postcommunion," which is read or chanted like the Collects earlier in the Mass.

The Dismissal and Blessing. In nearly all the liturgies of the Mass there is a formal dismissal of the people. This is done in our rite by the deacon at solemn Masses, by the priest at others. In the Roman Mass the form has always been as it is now, "Ite, missa est" ("Go, it is the dismissal") — to which the response is made: "Deo Gratias" ("Thanks to God"). In Requiem Masses the words "Requiescat in pace" ("May they rest in peace") are used instead — which custom began about the twelfth century; and in certain other Masses the priest (or deacon) says "Benedicamus Domino" ("Let us bless the Lord") instead of the "Ite, missa est."

Why do the people not leave the church immediately after the "Ite, missa est"? (Some of them do, and they should not.) Because the Church has added a few other parts to the Mass, in rather recent times. These are the short prayer "Placeat," originally a private devotion said after the Mass; the blessing, formerly given as the celebrant was passing to the sacristy; and the Last Gospel, from the first chapter of St. John, which was once merely a part of the priest's prayers after the Holy Sacrifice. All these came to be considered a part of the Mass, and this was finally authorized by St. Pius V in 1570 at the revision of the Roman Missal. On certain days other Gospels are substituted for that from St. John. And then the Mass is ended with the usual pious ejaculation at the end of a reading — "Deo gratias."

Chapter XVIII

THE REQUISITES FOR THE MASS

In order that the Holy Sacrifice may be consummated not only validly but with the proper decorum, our Church has, in the course of centuries, made many regulations concerning the ceremonies to be used at the Mass and the accessories which are to be used to increase its solemnity.

The Place. Where can a Mass be celebrated? By ordinary Church law it ought to take place only in a church, or in a chapel which has been blessed by lawful authority; but many exceptions to this rule are permitted for good reasons. The missionary in pagan lands has often no church or chapel; he must gather his flock where he can, and offer for them the Adorable Sacrifice. And even in our own land every diocese has small settlements of Catholics in which there is no special place of worship, and where the Mass must perforce be offered up in a hall or private house. Again, in public institutions, army barracks, on shipboard and elsewhere, it is often necessary to celebrate Mass in a room which is used for other purposes at other times. Therefore the bishops of this and many other lands have authority to permit their priests to offer the Holy Sacrifice in places which are not churches, when there is sufficient reason for so doing.

The Altar. It is absolutely necessary for the celebration of Mass that it shall take place on an altar; but this need not be fixed or permanent. When a priest is compelled to say Mass in a place where there is no church, he must contrive something for an altar — a table or similar construction; but in every case he must place upon it an altar-stone or "portable altar," consecrated by a bishop. This is an oblong slab of stone, usually encased in waxed cloth, and measuring perhaps twelve by ten inches — large enough to hold the Sacred Host and the greater part of the bases of the chalice and ciborium. It bears on its upper surface five crosses cut into the stone, and near its front edge a "sepulcher" or cavity containing the relics of some Saint and sealed with a cemented stone lid. A missionary priest

Altar Stone

must carry this altar-stone with him when one is not kept in the place wherein Mass is to be said.

A "fixed altar," such as we find in consecrated churches, has its entire top formed of a large altar-stone, resting upon stone sides or columns, the whole being built up from the ground on stone or brick foundations.

An altar on which the Blessed Sacrament is kept has a tabernacle — a strong locked box, usually lined and curtained on the interior with silk, and situated at the rear of the altar-table, in the centre. Before the door hangs a silken veil which is changed according to the appropriate color of the festival; at Masses of Requiem a purple veil is used. Why is the box which contains the Blessed Sacrament called a "tabernacle"? Because in early ages the altar was surmounted by a canopy with veils, forming a "tabernaculum," or tent, by which at certain parts of the service the Sacred Mysteries were concealed from the people. Traces of this remain in our present tabernacle veil, and in the chancel screen which is to be seen in many old and once-Catholic cathedrals in England.

Tabernacle Safe

Equipment of the Altar. The rules concerning the preparation of the altar on which Mass is to be said are minute and rigorous. To prevent diversity of practice and any lack of respect to our Eucharistic Lord, each detail is carefully specified in the Church's rubrics, and exact conformity with these requirements is demanded of all.

The altar must have three cloths of white linen, of which the two lower ones should be nearly of the same area as the altar-table; the upper linen is to be long enough to touch the floor at each end of the altar. The rubrics insist over and over again that these cloths shall be clean — and, in some places, there is good reason for such insistence. Sacristans are not always diligent, and pastors are sometimes given to procrastination.

The altar may have, hanging in front, an "antependium," a drapery varying in color according to the Mass celebrated. This is not strictly required, especially when the altar-front is highly decorated; and with us it is generally used only in Masses of Requiem, when the beauty and ornamentation of the altar are to be hidden as a sign of mourning.

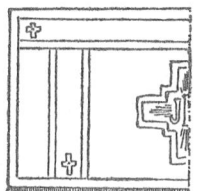

Half of an Antependium

Crucifix and Candles. Over the altar is placed a cross bearing the figure of our crucified Redeemer. This should be raised above the level of the candlesticks, and should be of such size and prominence that it can be easily seen not only by the celebrant but by the people.

When a priest says Mass he must, by strict requirement, have on the altar two lighted candles, blessed according to the formula provided for that purpose, and made of wax. Tallow, stearine and other similar substitutes are not allowed, unless, as the Roman decrees say, in distant and new missions in Oceanica or in polar regions where it is impossible to obtain wax, and where, unless other lights are permitted, the people could not hear Mass.

In Masses of more than ordinary solemnity a larger number of candles is used. A bishop's Mass, when said privately, calls for four, and when he celebrates "pontifically," in his own diocese, seven should be lighted. A high Mass sung by a priest should have six; and when the Holy Sacrifice is offered before the Blessed Sacrament exposed, at least twelve candles are used on the altar.

Speaking of candles, our readers may have noticed lately an apparent innovation in our churches which is really not an innovation at all — the lighting of a candle on the side-table or "credence" where the wine and water are kept during the Mass. This is a custom of considerable antiquity, and has been practised in nearly all parts of the world; but for some reason it did not become common in our country until recently. One candle is used when the celebrant is a priest, two when he is a bishop. The lighting is done at the Sanctus, and the extinguishing takes place after the priest has received Holy Communion; so that the candle remains lighted during all the Canon, the more solemn part of the Mass.

For holding the wine and water used in the Holy Sacrifice

Cruets

the credence table is provided with cruets or small flasks, which must be of glass, both for cleanliness and that the wine may be easily distinguished from the water. A clean towel is also provided, for the washing of the priest's fingers.

The Altar-Cards and Missal. On the altar are placed three printed cards, usually framed, containing the words of certain parts of the Mass. These are intended as an aid to the priest's memory, to obviate the necessity of turning to various parts of the Missal in case the celebrant should forget the words. The central and largest card contains usually the Gloria, the Credo, the offertory prayers for both the bread and the wine, the solemn words of consecration, and certain other parts of the Mass as well, The one at the Epistle side has two prayers which are recited at that part of the altar — that which is said when water is poured into the chalice, and the psalm "Lavabo" ("Among the innocent will I wash my hands," etc.), recited by the priest when he washes his fingers. The card on the gospel side presents the words of the first chapter of St. John which form the last Gospel of most Masses.

Altar Cards

The Missal, or Mass-Book, is an indispensable requisite for the Mass, for it contains not only the fixed parts of the wording, which the priest could learn by heart, but also the constantly changing prayers, epistles, gospels, offertories and other portions of the Mass which vary from day to day according to the festival celebrated and the season of the year. Its contents and arrangement are described in another chapter of this book. The Missal is mounted, for convenience, on a book-stand, which may be covered with a cushion or drapery of the color of the day's vestments.

Missal on Stand

Nothing is allowed on the altar except what pertains to the Holy Sacrifice; but on festival days, especially the more solemn, (except in the penitential seasons) it may be decorated very elaborately with flowers, lights and other ornaments.

THE HOLY SACRIFICE OF THE MASS

The Chalice and Paten. "And taking the chalice, He gave thanks, and gave to them, saying: Drink ye all of this, for this is My Blood of the New Testament, which shall be shed for many unto the remission of sins." (St. Matthew, xxvi.)

These words show us why the priest uses a cup or chalice — because He who gave us the adorable Sacrifice of the Mass made use of one when He instituted that wonderful mystery. When the Apostles followed His command to "do this for a commemoration of Me," they also used a cup — probably at first the ordinary drinking-goblet of those times. In the course of centuries it became customary to have the chalice formed of costly metal and often-times adorned with precious stones.

A chalice is generally from eight to eleven inches high, and consists of a wide-spreading base to insure stability, a stem which has a knob midway to facilitate handling, and a cup. The whole may be of gold or silver, or the cup only may be of precious metal; and it is even permitted, on account of poverty, to make the cup of inferior metal, such as block tin, but in every case, when any metal but gold is used for the cup, the interior must be heavily plated with gold. This is the part which comes directly in contact with the Precious Blood of our Lord, and it is proper that gold or gold-plating should be used on account of its purity and the fact that it will not easily tarnish or corrode. The best that we can supply is immeasurably unworthy of containing or coming into actual touch with the Sacred Body and Blood of Christ; and therefore gold is used in preference to other metals, in all parts of the sacred vessels which the Holy Eucharist touches or rests upon.

Chalice and Paten

A circular, slightly concave dish, resembling a saucer, and made either of gold or of silver, or other metal heavily gold-plated, is used with the chalice. This is called the paten. It is held aloft in the hands of the priest when he offers the bread which is to be consecrated in the Mass. Later on, after the Pater Noster, the celebrant blesses himself with it and places it under the Sacred Host.

The chalice and paten must be consecrated by a bishop. The

blessing of the chalice goes back many centuries, at least to the time of St. Gregory the Great, and that of the paten dates from about the eighth century. After certain prayers the paten and the whole interior of the chalice are anointed with holy Chrism, and a concluding prayer is offered, asking that they may be sanctified and made a new sepulcher of the Body and Blood of Christ.

At the beginning and the end of the Mass the chalice is shrouded in a "chalice-veil" of the same material and color as the vestments of the Mass. Upon this rests the "burse," a flat pouch of the same color, in which the corporal is kept — the square linen cloth which, during the Mass, is spread upon the altar to receive the Host and chalice. Symbolically, the corporal represents the winding-sheet in which the dead Body of Christ was wrapped for burial.

Chalice Veil and Burse

A "purificator," a folded piece of linen, is draped across the chalice, and is used for cleansing its interior, and for purifying the priest's fingers during the Mass.

The "pall" is used to cover the chalice. It is a piece of linen usually about six or seven inches square, often double and stiffened by a piece of cardboard. This part of the chalice equipment is not of ancient date. At one time a part of the corporal was brought up from the rear to cover the chalice, but about the year 1200 a separate piece began to be used.

Linen Pall

The Ciborium. When the priest is about to give Holy Communion he takes from the tabernacle the vessel in which the Blessed Eucharist is kept. This is called a ciborium, which signifies a food-vessel, from the Latin "cibus," food — being, as it is, a receptacle intended to hold the Heavenly Food which God's goodness has given to us in the adorable Sacrament of the Altar.

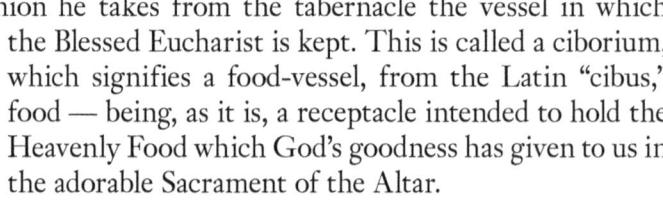
Ciborium

The ciborium is in shape somewhat like the chalice, but usually has a larger bowl, provided with a closely fitting cover surmounted by a cross. They vary greatly in size, according to the needs of the place where they are to be used — that is, the number of persons who will receive Holy Communion from them. The interior of the ciborium is heavily plated with gold, and when it contains the Blessed Sacrament the vessel is enshrouded in a silk cover or drapery, always white or gold in color and usually highly ornamented.

The Ostensorium. While treating of sacred vessels, it may be well to insert here a mention of those that are not "requisites for the Mass." The word "ostensorium" signifies an instrument for showing or displaying, and its other name, the "monstrance," has the same meaning. This sacred utensil is used in giving the Benediction of the Blessed Sacrament and in processions in which the Host is carried publicly, and is generally formed of a cluster of metallic rays radiating from a central aperture which contains a receptacle for a large Host. This receptacle is called a "luna" or "lunula" (a moon, or a little moon), and has glass on either side, so that the Host may be seen when enclosed therein. The whole is mounted on a base so that it can stand erect.

Ostensorium

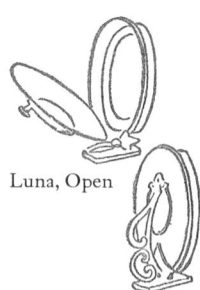
Luna, Open

Luna, Closed

The Pyx. This vessel, in which the Holy Eucharist is carried to the sick, is a very small ciborium, but is of a different shape from that used in church. It resembles a watch, being formed of two hollow cups hinged together and fastened by a spring catch operated through the stem. It also is gold-plated, unless it is made entirely of gold. It is kept with a small corporal and purificator, in a silk-lined leather case, called a burse.

Pyx

The ciborium, the pyx and the luna of the ostensorium are blessed with a simpler formula that that used for the chalice, and this blessing may be imparted, in our country, by any priest.

A "Communion paten" is often used at the giving of Holy Communion, being held beneath

Communion Paten

the chin of the communicant. It resembles the Mass-paten, but is usually provided with a handle, and does not require a blessing.

Touching the Sacred Vessels. Is it lawful for any one not a priest to touch or handle the chalice and other sacred vessels? If the vessel contains the Blessed Sacrament, it must not be touched by any one except a priest or deacon, under pain of mortal sin, unless in case of grave necessity, or to prevent profanation. For example, in time of persecution or in case of fire, it would certainly be allowable for any one to remove the Blessed Sacrament and to touch the vessel containing it.

But if the sacred vessel be empty? There is some diversity of opinion about this matter, some holding that when the vessel does not actually hold the Blessed Sacrament it may be handled by any one if there is reason for doing so; but the usual practice to-day is to restrict the touching of these vessels to clerics, even though these are not priests, and to such lay persons as have obtained permission from the bishop — for example, those whose business it is to repair or clean church goods. Any other person who may have occasion to handle or move a sacred vessel should use a cloth to prevent direct contact of the hand with it.

The chalice, the paten, the luna and the pyx are sacred things, true sacramentals, and are worthy of deepest reverence; for they are set apart for a purpose than which none can be higher and holier — to contain the Heavenly Food which the love of our Redeemer has given us. St. Augustine tells us: "I dare to say God, though He be omnipotent, is not able to give us more; though He be all-wise, knows not how to give us more; though He be all-rich, has not more to give."

. . . .

The vestments used by the priest at Mass and other services are considered in a separate chapter, in the section of this work treating of the Sacramentals.

Chapter XIX

WHY THE MASS IS SAID IN LATIN

The official language of our Church is Latin. It is used in her services in the greater part of the world. It is employed in nearly all the business correspondence of the Holy See. Encyclicals and briefs of Popes, decrees of General Councils, decisions of the Roman Congregations, acts of national and provincials councils, synodal regulations of dioceses — all these are expressed in the ancient tongue of Rome. The works of many of the great Fathers of the Church after the first three centuries and the countless tomes that treat of theology, Scripture, Church law and liturgy, all use the same majestic language.

Why Latin is Used. "Why does the Catholic Church use Latin? Why does she not conduct her services in a language which can be understood by all those who are present at them?" These are sensible questions, frequently asked; and every Catholic should be able to give a satisfactory answer.

The Church makes Latin the language of her liturgy because it was the official language of the Roman Empire, and was generally understood and spoken throughout a considerable part of the civilized world, at the time when Christianity was established. St. Peter fixed the centre of the Christian faith in Rome, the capital city of the Empire, and the Church gradually adopted the language of the Romans, and finally used it in many parts of the world over which she extended her dominion.

Latin, however, was far from being the sole language of the Roman Empire. At the time of Christ and for two or three centuries afterwards many other tongues were spoken extensively in various provinces, and Latin, as a vernacular, was confined more or less to central Italy. In northern Italy, Gaul and Spain there was a kind of Celtic; in Germany, Teutonic; but the most wide-spread language was Greek. It was spoken in Greece, Thessaly, Macedonia and Asia Minor, in Marseilles and the adjacent territories, in southern Italy and Sicily, and in parts of Africa. Moreover, Greek was everywhere the language of culture, and every educated Roman was supposed to know it.

Latin remained the language of worship, of the law, the army and the government; but Greek became the great medium of communication among the various parts of the mighty Empire. The fact that it had become common among the Jews, both in Palestine and elsewhere, led to the making of the Septuagint version of the Old Testament and the writing of nearly all the New Testament in Greek — for even the Epistle to the Romans was written in that language, although one would think that Romans would better understand Latin. The first Fathers of the Church all wrote in Greek — even those who were addressing Roman readers or the Roman Emperor; and the Popes of the first two centuries used the same language when they wrote at all.

The Official Language of Rome. All this goes to show that, contrary to the opinion usually advanced, Latin was not spoken generally throughout the Empire at the time of the establishment of Christianity, and it was not adopted by the Church because "she wished to worship in the language of the people." But, as said above, it was the language of worship, of government and of law; and the Church, which had fixed her seat of government in the imperial city, took it as her official tongue for the same purposes.

How did this come about? Because any other course would have been impracticable, and perhaps impossible.

The great centre of missionary enterprise in the west of Europe was Rome, and the priests who went to preach the Gospel were accustomed to say Mass in Latin. When they began their work in any country they had to learn the language; and when they had succeeded in doing so, they often found it too crude, too wanting in words, for the purpose of religious service. Therefore it was necessary to employ the Latin tongue for the public ceremonies of the church, and the local language or dialect was used only for the instruction of the people.

The Language of Medieval Literature. In course of time Latin became the literary language of western Christendom, because it was familiar to the clergy, who were the educated class and writers of books; because it was the only stable language in a time of chaos; because it was equally useful in any part of the world, no matter what was the native tongue of the people; and because it was a convenient means of communication between the bishops and the See of Rome.

And so everybody was content to use it, and the people of every nation in western Europe worshipped in Latin, until in the sixteenth century the so-called Reformers began their destructive work — and the people of Germany, of England and of the northern nations were led away from the old faith and were formed into national churches, each holding its services in the language of the country.

Why not Have Mass in English? "But would it not be better for the Catholic Church to conduct its worship in a language understood by the worshippers?" Yes, and no. The advantages of so doing are plausible in theory; the disadvantages render the idea difficult and even totally impracticable.

We do not intend to deny that, in the abstract, a service in the language of the country would be very useful — possibly preferable to a service in an unknown tongue; but the difficulties in the way of such action are so great that the Catholic Church has wisely persevered in offering her public worship in one language over the greater part of the world. Any other tongue than Latin is used only in certain Eastern rites — in communities which were never in close contact with Rome, and which have used Greek or Syriac or Arabic from the beginning of their history. Even in these the language employed in divine worship is not the spoken language of to-day, but an older form which is as unintelligible to the worshippers as Latin is to the average layman of our parishes.

"But why cannot the Catholic Church use English in England and French in France?" etc. Because she is a universal Church. A small sect or a "national church" can use the language of the country in its worship. But the Catholic Church is not a national church. She has been appointed to "teach all nations." She is not the church of the Italian, or the Englishman, or the Spaniard. She could, of course, translate her liturgy into any tongue, but a Mass in the language of any one nationality would be unintelligible to all the rest.

At present a priest can say Mass, privately or publicly, in almost any church in the whole world. If Mass was to be said in the language of the country only, he could celebrate only in private, and he would be forced to bring his own Mass-Book and server. Such a system (or lack of system) would be unworkable in the Catholic Church — because she is Catholic.

Although in the course of centuries the Latin of Gaul was gradually modified into French, that of Italy into Italian, and that of Iberia into Spanish and Portuguese, the Church did not attempt to follow these changes in her language of worship. Nor has she tried to translate her liturgy into the myriad tongues of the nations and tribes that have come into her fold. She has deemed it wise to retain the use of Latin in her worship and her legislation.

Unity of Speech and of Faith. How well, in the Catholic Church, her oneness of speech seems to typify her unity of faith. More than that — it not only typifies but helps to preserve it. We can readily understand that it is of the utmost importance that the dogmas of religion should be defined with great exactness, in a language that always conveys the same ideas. Latin is now what we call a "dead language" — that is, not being in daily use as a spoken tongue, it does not vary in meaning.

It is very convenient for the Church to have Latin as her official language, as a means of communication between her members and her Head. To legislate for the Church's good it is necessary from time to time to hold a General Council, at which the bishops of all the world assemble. They all understand Latin; no interpreter is required. Every bishop writes often to Rome, and goes at intervals to visit the Holy Father; and if there were no common language used in the Church, the Vicar of Christ would need to be familiar with more than the tongues of Pentecost if he would understand the German, the Spaniard, the Slav, the Japanese, or the countless others of many races to whom he would be obliged to listen.

"But do not the people suffer by this method?" No; they are instructed in religion in their own native tongue, whatever it may be — and we venture to say that, on the average, taking them as they are all over the world, our Catholic people know their religion at least as well as the Anglican or the Baptist. But the ceremonial of the Church is carried out in the grand old language of imperial Rome, where the Prince of the Apostles established the central government of Christ's kingdom upon earth — a government which has endured while other kingdoms have risen and decayed and died — from which the light of God's truth has shone farther and farther, century after century, into the dark places of the earth.

PART V
THE ECCLESIASTICAL YEAR

Chapter XX

THE CHURCH'S CALENDAR

THE first day of the Church's year is the first Sunday of Advent. This may come as early as November 27, or as late as December 3; for Advent, as at present observed, includes the four Sundays before Christmas. Therefore the year, in the Church's calendar, varies slightly in length, according to the date on which the first Sunday of Advent falls.

Fixed and Movable Feasts. The various days which the Church observes from Advent to Advent are of two kinds. Some of them are fixed feasts, having a certain day of a certain month assigned to them. Others are movable, occurring earlier or later in different years, according to a system which we shall describe.

The variable part of the calendar of the church depends principally upon the date on which Easter Sunday falls; it is always the first Sunday after the first full moon after the vernal equinox, the opening day of Spring, or March 21. This has been inherited, as it were, from the Jewish religion. In the earliest days of Catholicity the vast majority of the members of the infant Church were Jews, who had been accustomed to keep the Passover, and who therefore continued to observe it, making it serve as a commemoration of the Resurrection, the greatest event in the history of their new faith.

From this great festival day the whole year of the Church's calendar is computed, so far as movable feasts are concerned. Forty days after Easter she celebrates the Ascension of our Lord. Ten days later comes Whitsunday, the birthday of the Church, the anniversary of the coming of the Holy Ghost upon the Apostles — taking the place of the Jewish feast of Pentecost.

Before Easter the Church observes the penitential season of Lent, which has varied in length at different epochs (for at one time it extended from Quinquagesima Sunday to Easter), but which is always a time of preparation for the great solemnity of our Lord's Resurrection and ends on the eve of that festival.

In like manner the Sundays and movable feasts after Easter vary in date according to the early or late occurrence of that day, which in some years may be as early as March 22, and in some as late as April 25. Owing to this fact, it is possible that the preceding and subsequent Sundays and the movable feasts may also occur earlier or later by more than a month, from year to year.

The Fixed Festivals. Besides these movable days, there are many festivals which are fixed — that is, which usually occur year after year on the same date. The observance of some of these follows naturally from the date of Christmas, which has been celebrated on the twenty-fifth of December for many centuries.

The Circumcision. The first day of January is the feast of our Lord's Circumcision, for the Jewish law exacted the administration of that solemn rite on the eighth day after birth; and, happening to fall on the first day of the new year, it was developed into a great Christian festival, partly because it helped to wean newly converted nations from various idolatrous and pagan practices which were observed in many countries on that day.

The Epiphany. The feast of the Epiphany, the beginning of the manifestation of the newly born Messias to the nations of the world, has been observed on the sixth of January from a very early date, being probably the oldest of the distinctively Christian festivals. The birth of our Lord was commemorated on this day in some parts of the world in early centuries, as will be explained later; which fact perhaps accounts for its title of "Little Christmas," which it bears in parts of Ireland and possibly elsewhere.

The Purification. The Jewish law demanded the presentation of a male child in the Temple and the rite of purification for the m other, forty days after the child's birth. Consequently our Church observes the feast of the Purification of the Blessed Virgin on the second day of February. On that day the solemn blessing of candles takes place in our churches, as is described elsewhere in this work.

The Annunciation. Also, the fact that Christmas is

celebrated on the twenty-fifth of December has led to the institution of the feast of the Annunciation on the twenty-fifth of March, nine months before — to honor the day when Mary consented to become the Mother of the Redeemer and He became incarnate in her virgin womb.

Other Fixed Festivals. All through the year, in the Church's calendar, there are fixed festivals of greater or lesser importance on almost every day — feasts of our Lord, of His Blessed Mother and of the saints. Some of these are observed universally; others have a local or limited celebration only. Many are of very ancient origin, but some have been established in recent times. And as the work of canonization goes on, as new names are enrolled in the catalogue of the Church's saints, the list of these festivals is being constantly modified, either for the whole world or for certain countries, dioceses or religious bodies. Many of the latter have their own calendars of saints' days. In like manner many countries have local festivals, honoring patron saints or others towards whom the faithful of those places have special devotion.

The Gregorian Calendar. Each fixed festival has its own date during the year. In some cases the day assigned is that of the saint's death — the beginning of his heavenly glory; in others it is fixed merely according to the will of the Church. Hence the Church's calendar depends considerably upon the calendar in ordinary use at the present time, which is called the Gregorian, from Pope Gregory XIII, who brought it to its present form. The arrangement of the year devised by this great Pontiff is so admirable that it may be well to give a brief explanation of it and of the reasons why it was made. To do this we shall be obliged to lead our readers a little way into the paths of astronomical science.

The sun is the centre of our planetary system, and the earth travels around it in what we call a year, turning at the same time on its own axis, each complete turn constituting what we call a day. But the journey of the earth around the sun does not happen to be completed in an exact number of days. If it leaves a certain point in its track or orbit on January first, for instance, it is not at that precise point at the same hour on the following January first. Hence arises the necessity of having "leap-years," so that our calendar may be brought into close agreement with the real year of the earth traveling around the sun. Otherwise the difference between the real year and the year of 365 days would gradually cause the seasons to shift — until Christmas Day, for example, would occur in midsummer in our part of the world.

Leap-years were invented by Julius Caesar, who estimated the length of the solar year as 365 days and six hours; and to provide for these extra six hours he inserted an additional day into each fourth year. But his estimate of the year's length was not precise; the year is really less than the above figures by eleven minutes and fourteen seconds. The result was that there was an error of a full day in about 134 years.

Pope Gregory's Reform. In 1582 Gregory XIII brought the calendar to its present form by the simple plan of dropping ten days, from October 5 to 14 inclusively, for the error had increased to that extent since Caesar's time. The Pontiff provided for the future by ordering that the leap-year should not be observed in 1700, 1800 and 1900, but should be retained in the year 2000 and in every century thereafter that is divisible by 400. This ingenious method gives such a close approach to exactness that only after thirty-five centuries will there be an error of one day — and that is too remote to be of much concern to you or me..

But this was a Roman decree — and therefore it was bitterly opposed by the Protestant countries of Europe. Nearly all of them, however, adopted it in the year 1700. England, with true British obstinacy, held on to the old style until 1752, when she was eleven days "behind schedule." Russia still adheres to the Julian calendar, and is now thirteen days behind the rest of the world.

Such is a brief history of the Gregorian calendar. As the years roll on — those secular years which the wisdom of one of the Church's rulers has brought into close accord with the unvarying movements of God's universe — day by day the Church keeps her own calendar. She celebrates the great events in the history of the world's redemption. She honors the Mother of God and the faithful ones who have served their Master well. She has her seasons of penance and her festivals of joy. And so shall her years be kept while this earth endures — until the day shall come when "the heavens shall be folded together like a scroll" and time shall be no more.

CHAPTER XXI

FESTIVALS

SAINTS' days and other festivals have not been imposed upon us by any law of God. In the Jewish religion certain days were set apart for the commemoration of great events, such as the Passover, or for devotional and penitential observances, such as the Feast of Expiation. These were directly commanded by God Himself, in the laws which He gave to His chosen people through Moses. But in the Christian Church festival days are not of divine institution. They were all established by the Church herself, being begun at different times and in different parts of the world. Some few of them go back to Apostolic times, while others are of very recent origin.

The Reasons for Feast Days. Why has our Church established these festivals? Because she desires that the great truths of religion and the important events in its history shall be impressed on the minds of her children. Moreover, for the guiding of our lives, she wishes us to take as an example the virtues of those who have been faithful servants of God, that we may ever remember, in the words of St. Paul, that "we are the children of the saints." Therefore she has wisely instituted a great number of festivals, coming at certain determined times during the year, and varying in importance and solemnity according to what event they commemorate or what saint they honor.

The Kinds of Feasts. They are divided, first, into holydays of obligation and ordinary feasts. On the former, the faithful are obliged to hear Mass and abstain from unnecessary servile work; on the latter, the Church observes the feasts in her Office and Mass without imposing any obligation upon her children.

Also, the festivals and other days of the year are arranged liturgically in three classes, known as "doubles," "semi-doubles" and "simples." Of the "double" feasts (a division which dates back to the thirteenth century), the most solemn are known as "doubles of the first class" — for example, Christmas and

Epiphany. Next come "doubles of the second class," such as the feasts of some of the Apostles and the lesser feasts of the Blessed Virgin. Then "doubles major," then ordinary "doubles." A festival of lesser importance is known as a "semi-double," and one of still simpler form is called a "simple" feast. Again, certain great festivals have octaves, which extend the solemnity of the feast through eight days, although a recent decree has considerably reduced the observance of some of these.

Our Holydays of Obligation. In our country the "feasts of precept," or holydays of obligation, are now six — the number having been reduced after the third Plenary Council of Baltimore. The bishops of that Council wished to have four only, but Rome insisted that six should be retained. Therefore we American Catholics observe the following days as of obligation: Three feasts of our Lord — namely, Christmas Day, the Circumcision and the Ascension; two of the Blessed Virgin — the Assumption and the Immaculate Conception; and the feast of All Saints.

A History of Some Feasts. For at least two centuries Easter and Pentecost (with the weekly Lord's Day) were probably the only festivals celebrated. Then the feast of the Epiphany was instituted, to honor the first manifestation of our Blessed Saviour to the Gentile nations of the world.

On the first Sunday in January the Church celebrates the feast of the Holy Name of Jesus. This is of rather recent origin. It was approved at first only for Franciscan churches; but in the year 1721 it was made universal by Pope Innocent XIII. Until recently it was celebrated on the second Sunday after Epiphany.

The Purification of the Blessed Virgin, on the second of February, was first observed in Eastern countries about the year 520. It was introduced into the Western Church about the year 700.

In March comes another great festival of our Blessed Mother, the Annunciation. There is no certain record of this feast before 692, although in the opinion of some writers it was one of the festivals of the early Church, and may go back almost to the days of the Apostles.

On the nineteenth of March occurs the feast of St. Joseph,

which is not ancient. It was first kept on that day by several of the religious orders in the fourteenth century, and its establishment as a universal feast-day is largely due to St. Francis de Sales. In 1621 it was made a holyday of obligation, and has been so observed in many countries since that time.

The feast of the Ascension is one of our oldest holydays. St. Augustine speaks of it as "kept from time immemorial," and attributes it to the Apostles; however, there is no certainty that they observed it.

Trinity Sunday was observed locally as far back as the tenth century, but the date varied in different countries. It was introduced into England by the martyr-saint Thomas à Becket, Archbishop of Canterbury. It was made universal for the Church in 1334 by John XXII, who assigned it to the Sunday after Pentecost. The feast of Corpus Christi was established by the same Pope, and at about the same time.

In June the Church celebrates two festivals of great importance — that of St. John the Baptist, on the twenty-fourth, and of Sts. Peter and Paul on the twenty-ninth. The former is probably the oldest feast in honor of a saint. That of the two great Apostles dates back to the fifth century. In many parts of the world these two festivals have long been observed as holydays of obligation.

The Assumption, on August 15, is one of the holydays of obligation for the United States. It is a pious belief in our Church, though not an article of faith, that Mary's body was preserved from corruption and was reunited to her soul in heaven; and while the Church does not assert this as a part of her doctrine, she approves of it by the lessons of her Office during the octave of this great feast.

The festival of All Saints, on the first of November, Is also one of obligation. It has been celebrated on that day since the time of Gregory III, in 731. Previously it had been observed earlier in the year in various localities. All Souls' Day came somewhat later, in 998, having been established in France by a certain Abbot Odilo for monastic churches. To give greater help to the suffering souls, a recent decree permits every priest to celebrate three Masses on that day.

The great festival of the Immaculate Conception, which is the patronal feast of the United States and a holyday of obligation, was observed under the name of "the Blessed Virgin's Conception" for several centuries, having become universal about 1350. When the doctrine of Mary's Immaculate Conception was defined by Pius IX in 1854, the title of the feast was correspondingly changed, and it was made one of the greatest festivals of the Church.

Minor Feasts of Mary. As late as the twelfth century only four feasts of the Blessed Virgin were universally observed — her Nativity, her Purification, the Annunciation and the Assumption. At present, owing to the devotion of various Pontiffs, the number has increased to about twenty.

A feast is observed in some parts of the world on January 23, commemorating the Espousal of the Blessed Virgin. It is of comparatively recent origin, having been established by the Franciscans with the approval of Pope Paul III, in the sixteenth century.

There are two feasts of the Seven Dolors or Sorrows of Mary. One comes on the Friday after Passion Sunday, and was instituted by Benedict XIII in 1725. The other is kept at present on September 15, and was established by Pius VII in 1814.[1]

The title of "Help of Christians" was given to the Blessed Virgin by St. Pius V after the great naval victory of the Christians over the Turks at Lepanto. The feast was established by Pius VII, after he had been released from captivity, and had returned to Rome, in 1815.

On the second of July the Church celebrates the festival of the Visitation, commemorating the journey of Mary to her cousin Elizabeth. The origin of this feast is obscure. It became

---

1 What are the seven dolors of the Blessed Virgin? According to many spiritual writers they are: The prophecy of Simeon; the flight into Egypt; the loss of Jesus for three days in Jerusalem; seeing her Son carrying His Cross; the Crucifixion; the descent from the Cross; and the entombment. Thus were fulfilled the prophetic words of holy Simeon: "Thine own soul a sword shall pierce."

universal only in the fourteenth century, under Pope Urban VI.

The feast of Our Lady of Mount Carmel is celebrated on the sixteenth of July. It honors the intercessory power of Mary as manifested in the benefits granted to wearers of her scapular, and was approved for the Carmelite order by Sixtus V in 1587, being made a feast for the entire Church at a later date.

The festival of "Our Lady of the Snows" comes on August 5. It is based on an ancient legend which states that the site of the great Church of St. Mary Major in Rome was determined by a miraculous fall of snow in mid-summer; and therefore it commemorates the dedication of that church.

The month of September is especially rich in the minor feasts of Mary. Her Nativity is celebrated on the eighth, although there is nothing to show that she was born on that day. This festival was established about the year 870.

The feast of the Holy Name of Mary is now commemorated on the twelfth of September, and was originally a Spanish holiday. It was extended to the whole Church by Innocent XI in 1684. On the twenty-fourth of the same month comes the festival of Our Lady of Ransom, the patronal feast of the Order for the Redemption of Captives.

October is the month of the Holy Rosary, and on the seventh of that month occurs the feast which honors Mary as the "Queen of the Most Holy Rosary." The victory of Lepanto, mentioned above, took place on that day in the year 1571, at the very hour when all over the Catholic world the Rosary was being recited by order of St. Pius V for the success of the Christian arms.

A tradition of very doubtful value states that Mary, at the age of three years, was presented in the Temple, and remained there until she had attained womanhood. A feast commemorative of this has been observed in various parts of the world since about the twelfth century. It was suppressed by Pius V, but was later permitted by Sixtus V in 1585, and has been generally kept since the seventeenth century.

One of the lesser feasts of the Mother of God was formerly celebrated in many parts of the world a week before Christmas — the "Expectation of the Blessed Virgin," meaning the expecting of her delivery, the birth of our Saviour being near at hand. This was originally a Spanish feast, and was approved for other countries by Benedict XIII in 1725.

. . . .

A special chapter will be devoted to the history of Christmas Day. Besides these greater feasts, our Church celebrates many others during the year, each of which has its own interesting history — an annual cycle of glory to God and veneration towards God's servants who have fought the good fight, have kept the faith, and have gained their immortal crowns.

CHAPTER XXII

ADVENT

It has always been the aim of our holy Church to cause her children to reflect. She sets apart during the year two seasons, in which she tries to imbue the faithful with a spirit of penitential fervor. One of these seasons, which is called Advent, from the Latin word "adventus," a coming to, embraces four Sundays, beginning with that which is nearest to the feast of St. Andrew, the thirtieth of November. The first Sunday of Advent, in our part of the Church, is always the beginning of the ecclesiastical year — the Church's New Year's Day.

The spirit of the church during this time is symbolized by the purple vestments, emblematic of penance, worn at her services on each of these Sundays and on some other days, in preparation for the great festival of our Lord's Nativity.

The History of Advent. The origin of the Observance of Advent is very obscure. Unlike Lent, which goes back nearly to Apostolic times, it was not known in the first centuries of the Church; in fact, the feast of Christmas was not celebrated in those earliest days of Christianity.

About the end of the fourth century the practice was established of having a few days of preparation for the proper observance of that great festival, and in some countries a regulation was put into force requiring the presence of the faithful at Mass each day from the seventeenth of December to the feast of the Epiphany. And some of us are tempted to complain because we are commanded to assist at Mass on six week-days during the whole year!

These days of devotion before and after Christmas seem to have been the beginning of the observance of Advent. However, no general law regarding it existed for some centuries later. But the practice of the Church, of setting apart several weeks of penance and prayer before the feast of our Lord's Resurrection, led in time to the establishing, in many parts of the world, of a similar but shorter season as a preparation for the other greatest festival of our faith, the day of the Saviour's birth.

In the year 650 Advent was observed in Spain, and was longer than it is at present, for it included five Sundays. A little later the prohibition of the solemnization of marriages during this season was put into force, and various local laws were enacted by diocesan and national synods, regarding fasting and abstinence; for the season of Advent has always been looked upon as a time not only for prayer but for penance, though not to the extent that the Church requires during the season of Lent. By some of these regulations abstinence and fasting were enjoined from early in November to Christmas, and even from the date of the September equinox and the beginning of Autumn. But about the ninth century the time of Advent was arranged as we have it now — taking in four Sundays only. Thus the present practice of our Church in observing this holy season is of a very respectable antiquity; it has lasted more than a thousand years.

Advent Penances. The law of the Church requires a certain amount of fasting and abstinence during the time of Advent, but in regard to this her practice has varied greatly. In the earlier ages, after the establishment of this season, the regulations were very strict, and Advent was observed almost as rigorously as Lent. Later on, the strictness was considerably relaxed. At the present day, the Fridays of Advent are kept as fasting-days in this and other English-speaking countries; but in France and other parts of continental Europe the practice of observing them has died out except in religious communities. The special dispensations recently granted by the Holy See in favor of working people and their families have made this fasting no longer obligatory for many of the faithful. The idea of the Church has nearly always been that Advent, while a penitential season, is not to be observed as strictly as Lent; and therefore, at the present day, she has restricted the physical mortification to Fridays only, and even that penance binds only a comparatively small portion of the faithful.

The Advent Liturgy. Advent, then, is a time for devout and penitential preparation of the soul for the proper and worthy celebration of the great feast of Christmas; and the Church wishes us also during that season to prepare for the judgment which we all must undergo, both at death and at the second coming of our

Blessed Saviour. The whole of the Church's practice and liturgy during Advent is filled with this spirit — with the praises of the Redeemer of the world, and with exhortations to the faithful to receive Him worthily into their souls.

In the Divine Office recited by the clergy during Advent the *Te Deum*, the hymn of joy and thanksgiving, is omitted. In the Mass, the exultant *Gloria in Excelsis*, the angels' song at Bethlehem, is not said or sung. The solemn celebration of marriage (that is, with Mass and nuptial blessing) is prohibited from the beginning of Advent to the feast of the Epiphany inclusively. In the Advent Masses the Church uses purple vestments, the color of which always symbolizes penance. Flowers are not placed on the altar, except on the third Sunday, on which, as it were, a slight gleam of joy is permitted to shine through the gloom of this penitential season. This day is known as "Gaudete Sunday," from the opening words of the Introit of the Mass: "Gaudete in Domino . . ."—"Rejoice in the Lord; again I say, rejoice! Let your modesty be known unto all men; for the Lord is near."

The whole liturgy, in the Office and in the Mass, is arranged to manifest the prevailing spirit of penance mingled with hope. There is a marvelous beauty in the language which the Church uses in all her services during this season. The Breviary is filled with expressions of longing and of adoration for "the Lord, the King that is to come." The lessons read in Matins are taken from the book of the great prophet of the Incarnation, Isaias, who tells of the Man of Sorrows, suffering for the sins of His people — who describes the passion and death of the coming Redeemer and foretells His final glory. In the hymns of the Office the Church expresses her praise for the coming Christ, and prays that He may enlighten the world and prepare it for His second coming. On the last seven days before the vigil of Christmas a series of sublime antiphons is used, in which the Church calls upon the Divine Wisdom to teach us the way of prudence; on the Key of David to liberate us from bondage; on the Rising Sun to illumine those who sit in darkness, etc.

The Advent Masses. The various parts of the Mass are also appropriately chosen to express the spirit of our holy Church during the Advent season. The Epistles exhort the faithful to "put off the works of darkness and put on the armor of light, because the Redeemer is near." The Gospels speak of the Saviour coming in glory, and describe the ministry of St. John the Baptist, who "prepared the way of the Lord and made straight His paths."

Thus does the Church's liturgy take us back in spirit to the days when the Messias had not yet come; and it shows us that the same spirit of preparation, of hope and prayer and penance, is as necessary now as it was then, if we are to profit by the Incarnation of our Blessed Lord. We are exhorted to prepare ourselves for His coming into our hearts by His grace, and for that other coming also, when He shall appear again among men — not obscure, helpless and lowly, as at His birth in Bethlehem, but "coming in the clouds of heaven with great power and majesty" — when He shall come not as a Saviour, but as a Judge.

Chapter XXIII

CHRISTMAS DAY

Year after year the Christmas season brings to the minds of all Christians the wondrous story of the Child in the manger, the shepherds on the Judean hills, the celestial song "Glory to God in the highest," and the Angel's message, telling that the Long-Expected One had come: "Fear not, for behold, I bring you tidings of great joy; for this day is born to you a Saviour."

On that great day the altars gleam with myriad lights; the notes of joyful hymns resound in God's temples. The faithful kneel in homage before the Christmas crib, wherein is depicted the mystery of Bethlehem. Throng after throng, in their thousands, they adore, at the Masses of that day, Him who is mystically born again in that Adorable Sacrifice. Reverently they receive Him in the Sacrament of His love. And it is not only for us Catholics that this is a day of joy. Others celebrate it as well as we, though hardly with the same spirit. All of mankind to whom even a part of the Christian faith h as been given look upon Christmas as the greatest and most joyful of the festivals of the year.

A Catholic Feast. Christmas has, indeed, come to be a festival day for all; and the universal observance of this Catholic feast is the more remarkable when we remember how this "Papist" custom was frowned upon only a few years ago in this Christian land of ours. Perhaps some of us can recall when there was little respect for Christmas, either in a religious way or otherwise, among non-Catholics in this country. It was only when the narrow-minded sects had ceased to be in a majority, and when European immigration had infused new vigor and new ideals into the life of America, that the anniversary of the Saviour's birth began to be a religious and social festival.

Not in the Early Church. How old is Christmas Day? When we see with what unanimity that great festival is celebrated at the present time, it is surprising to learn that it was probably not observed at all in the first three centuries, and came gradually into existence in the fourth. One would naturally think that the anniversary of so great an event as the birth of the Son of God would have been a day of religious joy from the earliest years of the Church; but it is clear that this was not the case. There is no mention of it in any of the oldest lists of Church festivals. Much more attention was given in the first centuries to the Epiphany, the beginning of the manifestations of our Lord to the world; and the commemoration of His birth, if observed at all, was combined in those times with that feast.

On What Day Was Christ Born? There was a great diversity of opinion among ancient authorities as to the birthday of our Blessed Saviour. Many writers, especially of the Eastern Church, assigned an entirely different season of the year from that observed at present. St. Clement of Alexandria quotes some who placed it on the twentieth of April or the twentieth of May, and a very common belief in the Orient was that our Lord was born on the sixth of January.

In the part of the Church which follows the Latin rite the celebration of Christmas on the twenty-fifth of December was begun probably about the middle of the fourth century. An ancient tradition assigned that day as the probable date of the great mystery of the Nativity. St. Augustine mentions it as well established in his day, and about the year 380 the Oriental Churches began to celebrate our Saviour's birth on the same date.

The Vigil of Christmas. What is a *vigil*? The word signifies "a watching." In ancient times nearly all the greater feasts were celebrated with much solemnity, and the ceremonies included the reciting of the Divine Office at stated hours. Parts of it were chanted late at night, the evening before the festival, and were followed by a Mass. The faithful were encouraged to be present at these services, and as a further preparation for the worthy observance of the feast they were required to fast on the day before. The practice of "watching" or attending the night services in the church is almost entirely abolished, except for religious communities, and the vigil has come to mean to the laity a day on which some of them at least are obliged to observe certain laws of fasting and abstinence. The vigil of Christmas is one of the few days on which the dispensation granted in favor of working people and their families to use meat is not in force. It is a day of fasting for some and of abstinence for all, unless excused for some real and urgent reason — not merely on account of the ordinary needs of a working life.

The Name of Christmas. Why is this day called Christmas? This word, which we of English-speaking race use as its name, shows the Catholic origin of the festival. Christmas is "Christ's Mass" — the Mass offered in honor of the birth of Christ. Probably few of our non-Catholic friends advert to the fact that the day which they celebrate so universally is a feast of the Catholic Church, taking its very name from the supreme act of Catholic worship.

This name seems to have come into use about the year 1038, and, in the early English language of that time, was written "Christes Maesse"' about a century later it had been modified to "Crist-messe" — and, as the English tongue developed into its present form, it finally became "Christmas." Nearly all the other languages of Europe use a word signifying "birthday" — in Latin, Dies Natalis; in Italian, Il Natale; and the French have softened the Latin form to Noël.

In English books and accounts of old English customs we often find the day mentioned under the name of Yuletide, "the time of the Feast" — the word Yule being a modification of the Anglo-Saxon "Geol," a feast.

How Our Church Keeps Christmas. Christmas is everywhere a day of joy and gladness, and all the riches of the Church's liturgy are employed to express these sentiments. Rich vestments and the glow of countless candles, costly decorations and the strains of sweet music — all these are used to signify that she celebrates the earthly coming of our Redeemer as a festival, a day of happiness.

Christmas is in every part of the world a holyday of obligation — a day on which all the faithful are commanded to be present at Mass; and on account of the Church's desire to enrich both priests and people with an abundance of spiritual blessings, every priest enjoys on that day a special favor and privilege. He is permitted to celebrate three Masses. Ordinarily, on any other day, he can say Mass only once. When there is a real necessity, in order that on Sundays and holydays the people may conveniently assist at the Holy Sacrifice, the priests of our country (and of many others as well) are allowed by special permission of their bishops, renewed each year, to celebrate Mass twice in one day. On Christmas Day, whether there is need or not, every priest is permitted, though not obliged, to offer the Adorable Sacrifice three times.

This is a custom of considerable antiquity, although it was originally practised by the Pope only. It was later permitted to bishops, and finally to priests. In very early times the Sovereign Pontiff was accustomed to say three Masses on Christmas Day — one at midnight in the Liberian basilica (in which, according to legend, the manger of Bethlehem is preserved), as a conclusion to the nocturnal service or vigil; the second at the tomb of St. Anastasia, whose martyrdom is commemorated on December 25; and the last in the Vatican as the principal Mass of the day. This practice is said to date back to the fourth century.

This Roman custom was introduced into France, for bishops only, in the time of Charlemagne, and was later permitted to priests. Thence it gradually spread throughout the world.

Mystical writers give an explanation of the three Masses, stating that they symbolize the three births of our Blessed Lord — namely, His birth from the Father before all ages, His birth from Mary at Bethlehem, and His spiritual birth in the hearts of the faithful by sanctifying grace; but the real reason for the three Masses was, as stated above, that the Pope wished to observe the vigil by the first, to give a commemoration to the Roman virgin-martyr Anastasia in the second, and to celebrate the third as the solemn Mass of the festival in his own basilica.

The Christmas Crib. An interesting feature of our church decorations on Christmas Day is the "crib," or representation of the stable of Bethlehem. It is oftentimes artistic, sometimes commonplace, occasionally grotesque; but in every case it gives evidence of the commendable practice of our Church, to "teach by showing" — to set before us some visible sign which will impress upon us, more forcibly than would mere words, some point of her doctrine or some event in the history of religion.

It is probable that the real stable of Bethlehem was a cave. At the present day a small hollow or grotto is shown as the place where our Divine Lord was born and was "wrapped in swaddling-clothes and laid in a manger." We are told by tradition or legend that the cave was dug in the rear of a humble shed which served as a shelter for beasts of burden; and so the usual representation of the birthplace of our Redeemer as a thatched stable may not be very inaccurate..

This custom of erecting a crib in our churches at the Christmas time, with figures representing the Divine Infant, His Blessed Mother, St. Joseph, the shepherds, the Magi, etc., goes back to about the year 1260, and was introduced by the Franciscan Fathers in some of their Italian churches. It was evidently looked upon as a happy idea, for within a comparatively short time the practice had come into vogue in other parts of the world.

In our churches, on Christmas Day, the crib is always an object of interest and devotion. It brings before us, perhaps more vividly than would a sermon or a reading, the loving humility of our Blessed Saviour and the lowly beginning of that life which was from its very inception a life of suffering. Our holy Church urges us to kneel and meditate before it in the spirit with which the shepherds were filled on that first Christmas Day — with simple minds and firm faith making an offering of our hearts and souls to our Infant Saviour.

Some Christmas Customs. When we give or receive Christmas gifts, and hang green wreaths in our homes and churches, how many of us know that we are probably observing pagan customs? We do not wish to assert that they are not good customs; but they undoubtedly prevailed long before Christian times. The Romans gave presents on New Year's Day, and our bestowing of gifts at Christmas is a survival of that practice, as well as a commemoration of the offerings of the Magi at Bethlehem. The Yule-log, a feature of Christmas in old England, goes back to the days of the pirate Norsemen. Holly and mistletoe and wreaths of evergreen have been handed down to us by the Druids. And even our good old friend Santa Claus, that mysterious benefactor of our childhood days, existed in one form or another long before Christianity had attributed his virtues to St. Nicholas; for the god Woden, in Norse mythology, descended upon the earth yearly between December 25 and January 6 to bless mankind.

But, pagan though they be, they are beautiful customs. They help to inspire us with the spirit of "good will to men," even as the sublime services of our Church remind us of the "peace on earth" which the Babe of Bethlehem came to bestow. May that spirit fill the heart of each of us on every Christmas Day!

Chapter XXIV

LENT AND HOLY WEEK

The penitential season of Lent consists of forty fasting-days, being the week-days of the six and one-half weeks preceding the great feast of Easter. The Sundays during this time are also a part of Lent, but are not observed as days of fasting. As explained elsewhere, the date of the beginning of this season varies from year to year, according to the date of Easter. The Church has instituted it as a remembrance of the forty days' fast of our Blessed Lord in the desert, and as a means of sanctification for her children — for she has always taught the necessity of penance for justification.

Lent is called by various names in various languages. In Latin it is Quadragesima (fortieth), from which are taken the Italian Quaresima and the French Carême. The English name, Lent, is from the Anglo-Saxon *Lencten*, meaning "Spring."

The History of Lent. The duration of this penitential season has not always been the same in the different ages of the Church's history. We cannot assert positively that Lent can be traced back to the Apostles, but we know that some sort of fasting time has been observed before the Easter festival from very early days. It is mentioned by Tertullian and St. Irenæus, and especially by St. Athanasius, bishop of Alexandria, who defined that it was to be a fast of forty days; and rules concerning it were made by early Councils, prescribing fasting as a strict obligation. From about the fourth century it became a fast of forty days in many parts of the world, although the Greeks began it earlier than we do, ruling that there should be no fasting on the Saturdays of Lent (except Holy Saturday) and on the feast of the Annunciation. For some time the Roman Church observed the fast only for thirty-six days, beginning after the first Sunday of Lent; and it was not until the year 846 that a Council held at Meaux, in France, added four days before that Sunday. This practice, even then, was not generally followed, for as late as the eleventh century the Lenten season included only thirty-six fasting days in some parts of Europe, and this is still the case in the diocese of Milan, in Italy.

It is said that in very early times there were so-called Renunciants, who subsisted only on two meals a week for no less than eight weeks preceding Easter — fasting strictly from the breakfast of Sunday until after Holy Communion on the following Saturday. This, however, was never an obligation, but merely a voluntary penance.

Nevertheless, the Lenten regulations of our Church were very severe, especially in the early Middle Ages. All flesh meat was forbidden, and also, for the most part, what were called "lacticinia" — milk, butter, cheese, eggs, etc. — and this prohibition extended originally to Sundays. On all the fasting-days only one meal was allowed, and this was to be taken in the evening. However, this extreme rigor was, after a time, somewhat relaxed; the meal could be taken at three o'clock, the hour of None in the Divine Office, and this was gradually advanced to midday — which, indeed, derives its English name of noon from that part of the Office. More details are given of the Church's ancient law in the chapter on "Fasting and Abstinence."

The Lenten Masses. At Masses during the Lenten season (except those celebrated in honor of saints or on festivals) the whole tone of the Church's ritual is penitential. The Gloria, the joyful hymn of the angels at Bethlehem, is omitted. The Alleluias which are said or sung at other times are replaced by the "Tract," which is used in nearly all the Masses after Septuagesima Sunday. Near the end of the Mass is inserted a "Prayer over the People," which was originally intended for those who had not received Holy Communion at the Mass, just as the Postcommunion was intended for those who had.

Laetare Sunday. On the fourth Sunday of Lent the Church has a note of joy in her liturgy. That day is called *Laetare Sunday*, from the opening words of the Introit of the Mass, "Laetare, Jerusalem. . . ." — "Rejoice, O Jerusalem, and meet together, all ye who love her; rejoice exceedingly, ye who have been in sorrow," etc. It is, as it were, a relaxation in the midst of penance, a gleam of light in the gloom of the Lenten time. The rubrics of the Church (not always observed) call for rose-colored vestments on this day, being probably a sort of compromise between the penitential purple and the lighter colors used on feasts of joy.

Passion Sunday. This is the fifth Sunday of Lent, and is so called because on it the more solemn part of the penitential season begins and the liturgy of the Church deals more and more with the sufferings of our Blessed Lord. To typify her increasing sorrow, the images in our churches are veiled in wrappings of purple, the color of penance, and remain thus covered until the end of the services on Holy Saturday.

The Tenebrae. In cathedrals and many of our larger churches the solemn service of Tenebrae takes place on the Wednesday, Thursday and Friday of Holy Week, being the "anticipated" Matins of the Divine Office of Holy Thursday, Good Friday and Holy Saturday. With its chanting of penitential psalms, the mournful strains of the "Lamentations" and the symbolic ceremony of the extinguishing lights, it well expresses the spirit of our Church on these days of sorrow.

Tenebrae Candlestick

The lessons of the first Nocturne of the Matins are taken from the Lamentations of the Prophet Jeremias. They are sung to a tune which has been universally recognized as one of the most beautiful specimens of the Church's chant. Nothing could convey more perfectly the spirit of sorrow with which the Prophet describes the desolation of Jerusalem, and nothing can better express the grief of our Church mourning over the sufferings and death of her Saviour. It is "the saddest melody within the whole range of music."

The service is called *Tenebrae* (darkness) from a very remarkable ceremony — the gradual extinguishing of candles in a triangular candlestick standing in the sanctuary. This, in the Middle Ages, was called the Tenebrae "hearse," which means a harrow — from its shape and the points to which the candles were affixed. The number of candles used has varied at different times. Fifteen are now required, the reason for this being that fourteen are extinguished one by one at the conclusion of the fourteen psalms of Matins and Lauds. The six candles on the altar and the lights in the church are likewise put out, during the chanting of the Benedictus. The fifteenth candle, the uppermost in the Tenebrae candlestick, is then removed and hidden behind the altar.

As the sanctuary grows darker and darker, the desolation of the Church seems to increase. After the Benedictus comes the mournful chanting of the words "Christus factus est . . . " — "Christ was made obedient for us, even unto death," and then all is hushed into absolute stillness. The psalm "Miserere" is recited in a low tone, followed by a prayer; and then comes a noise, made by the clergy with their books, symbolizing, it may be, the earthquake at the death of our Blessed Lord. The hidden candle is brought forth and replaced on the candlestick, as an emblem of the Risen Saviour.

Holy Thursday. The earlier portion of the Mass of this day resembles that of a joyful festival. When the Gloria is intoned, the organ peals forth triumphantly, the bells of the church are rung, and the whole service seems full of gladness. Suddenly there comes a change. The bells and the organ are silent, and the deepest sorrow and desolation are expressed by the remainder of the liturgy.

At this Mass a second Host is consecrated, to be consumed at the service on Good Friday. This is carried in a solemn procession to another altar, preferably in a separate chapel, and is there honored by the use of lights and flowers, and by relays of adorers.

When the Mass is finished and the Blessed Sacrament has been removed to the altar of repose, the sense of desolation returns with redoubled force. The altars, symbolic of the body of Christ, are stripped of their linens, and the clergy, while thus engaged, recite the antiphon, "They have parted my garments among them, and upon my vesturs they have cast lots," with an appropriate psalm.

This day is sometimes called Maundy Thursday, from the word "mandatum," a command, or from "mundare," to cleanse — reminding us of the precept of our Blessed Lord: "you ought to wash one another's feet" — a ceremony which is seldom or never observed in our country.

On this day, as described elsewhere, the solemn blessing of the holy oils takes place in cathedral churches.

Good Friday. The altar is bare, the crucifix is veiled, the priests wear black vestments. They suddenly prostrate themselves before the empty tabernacle, in sorrow and self-abasement. When they rise, the service begins. Two lessons are read, followed by St. John's narrative of the Passion of our Lord. Then comes the ceremony of the "Adoration of the Cross" — a name which is sanctioned by long usage, but which is, of course, inaccurate; for we Catholics do not adore crosses, but simply venerate them. The veiled crucifix is taken down from the altar and is gradually uncovered, with the threefold chanting of the "Ecce lignum crucis" — "Behold the wood of the cross, on which hung the salvation of the world." The clergy then remove their shoes — an ancient sign of reverence — and, kneeling and bowing profoundly three times, kiss the crucifix, which is placed on the altar-steps. In our churches the laity then come to the sanctuary rail and venerate the crucifix by devoutly kissing it.

The so-called Mass of the Pre-Sanctified on Good Friday is not really a Mass. It is simply the priest's Communion. He receives the Sacred Host which was consecrated the previous day and reserved on the "altar of repose." While It is being brought to the main altar, a beautiful hymn is sung, the "Vexilla Regis," — ("The Banners of the Cross Advance") — dating back to the beginning of the seventh century, and composed by a certain Venantius Fortunatus. The Sacred Host is incensed, wine and water are put into the chalice, the Pater Noster is said, one more prayer is recited, and then the priest receives Holy Communion. The chalice is purified, and then, abruptly, the service ceases and all leave the sanctuary.

Holy Saturday. There are many parts to the service of this day. Originally these took place in the evening — not in the morning, as we have them now. They were the ceremonial portion of the "vigil" of Easter. At these night-services the Church wished to anticipate the celebration of the Resurrection of our Lord, and also to administer Baptism to the catechumens who had been prepared for it. And so we have in our present Holy Saturday liturgy the blessing of the new fire and of the paschal candle (both types of the Saviour's Resurrection), the reading of the prophecies, the blessing of the baptismal font, the chanting of the litany, and the Mass.

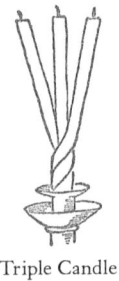

Triple Candle

The blessing of the new fire takes place at the door of the church. Why? Probably because in early times, when flint and steel were used to ignite charcoal, the door furnished a convenient exit for the smoke; or because, in come countries, the fire was obtained by means of a lens or burning-glass. Appropriate prayers are used, and the grains of incense to be inserted in the paschal candle are also blessed. A procession brings the new fire into the church, and a triple candle is lighted, one branch at a time, the deacon chanting three times in ascending tones "Lumen Christi" — ("The light of Christ"). This ceremony goes back to about the twelfth century.

The blessing of the paschal candle opens with the singing of the magnificent Eucharistic prayer, the "Exsultet" — one of the most beautiful chants in all the Church's liturgy. During it, the five grains of incense are fixed into the candle — symbolical of the five wounds in our Saviour's glorified body.

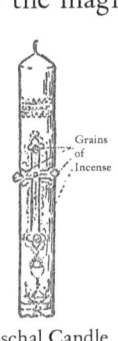

Paschal Candle

The blessing of the font — that is, of the baptismal water to be used during the ensuing year, —begins with a sort of Preface, expressing the regeneration which the waters of Baptism bring to mankind. The paschal candle is plunged into the water three times, and the Oil of Catechumens and the Chrism are poured into it, to sanctify it. Before this is done, the people are sprinkled with the water, and a portion of it is set aside to be used for the blessing of their homes.

Why is the Mass of Holy Saturday a joyful Mass? Lent is not over; and it would seem, at first sight, that all manifestations of joy should be deferred until the morrow. The explanation is this:

The Mass of Holy Saturday was originally the midnight

Mass of Easter Sunday, the conclusion of the long ceremonies of the vigil. Hence it is that at the Gloria the bells are rung, the organ peals, the statues and pictures are unveiled, and the glad Alleluias are heard again — all intended to express the Church's joy on the happy day of our Lord's Resurrection. Century after century the time of the ceremonies, and consequently of the Mass, was put earlier, until it came to pass that the nocturnal Mass of Easter Sunday became the morning Mass of Holy Saturday.

Clapper for Holy Week

Such are the solemn ceremonies and the beautiful symbolism of the liturgy of Holy Week. The rites are, for the most part, ancient — developed during many centuries, when the ritual of the Church was carried out in its fullness in great cathedrals and in monastic chapels. Well do they express the feelings with which she wishes to inspire us, her children — penance and sorrow during the Lenten time, reaching its climax on Good Friday, because our Blessed Saviour suffered for our sins — and triumph and exultation on the glorious feast of our Lord's Resurrection, because "He hath risen from the dead, to die no more."

PART VI
THE SACRAMENTALS

Chapter XXV

THE SIGN OF THE CROSS

THE most important sacramental of our Church, and the one most frequently used, is the sign of the cross. The sacramentals are intended, as the Catechism tells us, "to excite good thoughts and to increase devotion," and these results are accomplished most effectively by this holy sign, for whenever we use it we are reminded of the sufferings and death of our Blessed Savior, and thereby we are filled with more fervent love, more profound gratitude and more earnest contrition. The sign of the cross is the symbol of our deliverance and the emblem of the mercy of God giving redemption to sinful man.

A Summary of Our Faith. The form of the words which we use in making this sign, together with the action performed, manifests our belief in the principal truths of our religion. We say: "In the name" — not "names" — and thereby express our faith in the unity of God. We mention the three Persons, the Father, the Son and the Holy Ghost, and thus show our belief in the Adorable Trinity. The cross itself, made with the hand, manifests our faith in the incarnation, death and resurrection of our Blessed Saviour, and shows that we regard Him not only as God but as man — for that He might be able to die on the cross it was necessary that He should possess a human nature. Thus we have in this brief formula a summary of the most important articles of our faith. And the sign of the cross is more than this. It is a prayer to God, made in the name of our Mediator Jesus Christ, Who has declared: "If you ask the Father anything in My name, He will give it unto you."

How the Sign is Made. The making of the sign of the cross is a very ancient practice. It probably goes back to Apostolic times, and was in common use in the second century. Among the early Christians it was usually made very small, by a slight movement of the finger or thumb, on the forehead or breast. In the days of persecution the faith of the Christian had to be concealed, and any more conspicuous sign would have put him in danger of death.

The devotion to the sign of the cross in those distant days is attested by many writers. They tell us that it was used by the more devout on every occasion. No work was begun without invoking God's blessing by this holy sign. The triple sign of the cross was employed very commonly in the early centuries of the Church and in the Middle Ages. It is not used at present except at the beginning of the Gospels at Mass. It is made by marking the forehead, the lips and the breast with a small cross, using the thumb, and is intended to remind us that our intellect must be attentive to the Word of God, our lips ready to announce His truths, and our hearts filled with love toward Him.

The ordinary method of making the sign of the cross is that which every Catholic learns in early childhood — the putting of the right hand to the forehead, to the breast and to the left and the right shoulder, with the words: "In the name of the Father, and of the Son and of the Holy Ghost. Amen." In past centuries the formula varied greatly. "The sign of Christ." — "The seal of the living God." — "In the name of Jesus." "In the name of the Holy Trinity." — "Our help is in the name of the Lord," etc, were used. One of these old forms, "Oh God, come to my assistance," is still in use at the beginning of Vespers and in other parts of the Divine Office.

As we shall see further on, important indulgences are to be gained by the sign of the cross, but only when it is made correctly and devoutly.

In the Church's Liturgy. This is not only the greatest but the most frequently used of all the sacramentals. No ceremony is performed without it. When a priest is ordained, his hands are anointed with holy oil to give them the power to confer blessings by the sign of the cross. In the administration of all the sacraments this holy sign is used at least once, and in some of them it is employed many times. In the ceremonies of Baptism it is made fourteen times; in Extreme Unction, seventeen times.

When holy water is blessed, the sign of the cross is made over it twelve times. In the reciting of the Office by the clergy it is prescribed a great number of times. And especially in the Holy Mass we have all noticed that the celebrant makes the sign of the cross very frequently, but it may not be generally known that he does so no less than fifty-one times — signing himself, the book the altar, the bread and wine, and even the Sacred Host and the Precious Blood after the consecration.

The Indulgences. Has the Church granted any indulgences for the sign of the cross? She has. In 1863 Pope Pius IX gave an indulgence of fifty days to all who make that sacred sign and say "In the name of the Father, and of the Son, and of the Holy Ghost. Amen." An indulgence of one hundred days is given if holy water is used when the sign of the cross is made.

This holy symbol of our salvation, then, should be frequently used by us. It teaches us our true dignity. It reminds us that we are the brethren of Jesus Christ. In making the sign of the cross we become partakers in the wonderful history of our faith, and companions of the glorious saints of our Church. We are soldiers, and this is our weapon. The cross of our Redeemer has vanquished death, has overthrown the dominion of Satan. Let us, then, re-echo the words of St. Paul: "God forbid that I should glory save in the Cross of our Lord Jesus Christ."

Chapter XXVI

THE CROSS AND THE CRUCIFIX

THE cross is one of the most important of Christian emblems. It is the distinguishing mark of every edifice that is set apart for Catholic worship, education and charity. Bearing the image of our crucified Saviour, it stands upon the altar on which the Sacrifice of Calvary is continued throughout the ages; because He ennobled and sanctified it when He died on it for the salvation of mankind.

It may be well to state that there is a difference between a cross and a crucifix. A cross is a crucifix only when it bears the image of our Lord's sacred Body. A cross without an image is simply a cross; a cross with an image is a crucifix.

The Cross Among Pagans. Among many nations the cross was in use for the execution of criminals. The most ancient practice was to hang the condemned person on a tree, either by nails or ropes; and this led to the employing of two pieces of timber for the same purpose. Our Blessed Redeemer was put to death in the cruel manner that was customary among the Romans for the execution of slaves and degraded criminals — namely, by being fastened to the cross with large nails driven through the hands and feet, the arms being extended on the transverse beam of the cross. The barbarity of scourging before the crucifixion, and the compelling of the condemned sufferer to carry his cross were all in keeping with the cruel Roman character.

It is remarkable that the cross, although an instrument of torture, was held in religions honor among pagan nations and was regarded as possessing extraordinary sanctity. The most ancient form was the "swastika," emblematic of the revolutions of the sun and consequently a symbol of life. In Egypt and Assyria the cross typified creative power, and many of the pictures and statues of the gods of those countries represent them carrying in their hands the "crux ansata," or cross with a handle, which was possibly a symbol of the productive powers of

Swastika

Ansated Egyptian

Nature.

The Buddhist sects of India regarded the cross as an emblem of immortality, a sign of the life to come. The early explorers of Mexico and Peru found numerous crosses among the carvings in the heathen temples of those newly-discovered lands. The crosses found in these pagan regions are all modifications of the symbol referred to above, emblematic of Nature and her forces. Although there is no real connection between these pagan crosses and the sacred Christian symbol, it is curious that among these heathen the same sign should typify earthly life which among Christians denotes spiritual and eternal life.

When Christianity had spread throughout the Roman world, the cross became everywhere an emblem of faith, an object of religious veneration, and one of the most common ornaments. The church made both the cross and the crucifix sacramentals, by establishing formulas for blessing them — thus setting them apart as objects intended to inspire us with faith and devotion.

The True Cross. What became of the cross on which our Saviour died? The legend of the Finding of the True Cross is of great antiquity, and the event is commemorated by the Church on the third of May. The details may possibly have been added to in later ages, but the important facts rest on very good authority, namely, that of Saints Ambrose, Chrysostom and Cyril of Jerusalem

The story is as follows: The pious Empress Helena, the mother of Constantine the Great, in the year 326 made a pilgrimage to Jerusalem. She was then seventy-nine years of age. When she reached the Holy City she caused excavations to be made on Mount Calvary, and at a considerable depth found three crosses, and, lying apart, the tablet bearing the inscription placed by Pilate's command on the cross of Christ. There seemed to be no means of knowing the cross on which our Saviour died; but at the suggestion of Macarius, bishop of Jerusalem, the three crosses were applied in turn to a sick woman, and at the touch of one of them she was immediately and miraculously cured.

The upright beam of the cross was kept in Jerusalem, and the other was carried to Constantinople; and a large portion of this was afterwards sent to Rome, where it was preserved in the Church of Santa Croce. Tradition states that the portion left at Constantinople was taken to Paris in the thirteenth century, by St. Louis, king of France. The part left at Jerusalem was carried away by the Persians under Chosroes II, after they had captured that city. It was recovered by the Emperor Heraclius in 628, but only nine years later the Saracens took Jerusalem, and since that time there is no further mention of that portion of the True Cross.

The Nails. There is considerable difference of opinion as to whether three or four nails were used in the crucifixion of our Blessed Saviour. Various representations show sometimes two nails in His feet, sometimes only one. In certain pictures the feet are supported on a block of wood, a "suppedaneum," or foot-rest. It is chiefly in the later pictures that the feet of our Lord are shown crossed and fastened with one nail.

These nails have legendary history of their own. One is said to have been cast into the Adriatic Sea by the Empress Helena when she was returning from Palestine, whereby a storm was quelled that had menaced the ship with destruction. A second nail was placed among the jewels of the royal crown of Constantine; another is said to be preserved in the cathedral of Milan, and a fourth at Treves.

It is hardly necessary to say, that these and many other poetic legends concerning holy things and persons are not articles of faith. We may believe them; we are not obliged to do so. They may be wholly or partly true, or they may be wholly or partly the product of the fervid imagination of some medieval romancer. We recognize their beauty, but we do not thereby oblige ourselves to believe them.

It is possible, however, that many of the "fragments of the True Cross" which are preserved and venerated in various places are genuine, as its discovery is probably a historical event, being fairly well authenticated, and it is likely that so great a relic would be kept and guarded with considerable care.

Some Varieties of Crosses. The form of crosses has been modified in different countries, and there are several distinct varieties. In some places the cross used for executions was in the form of the letter T — sometimes called the Tau cross, from the Greek letter. The ordinary cross, such as generally shown in representations of our Saviour's crucifixion is the "crux capitata," or headed cross, also known as a Latin cross, and tradition tells us that this was the form used on that momentous occasion. When the four limbs of the cross are of equal length we have a Greek cross, so called because it was largely used in medieval Greek architecture. A cross in the form of the letter X is known as St. Andrew's, that Apostle having been crucified on one of that description. A cross with four equal limbs of spreading or triangular form is a Maltese cross, so called because it was the badge of the military and religious order of the Knights of Malta. If the arms of a cross are connected by a circle it forms the well-known Celtic cross, of which many ancient specimens may be seen in Ireland. A cross with two cross-bars is variously known as an archiepiscopal or patriarchal cross, because it is used in the heraldic arms of these higher prelates. There are also other variations, due to the ingenuity of artists and architects.

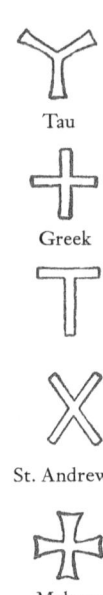

The Cross in Christian Art. Throughout the whole range of religious art, particularly in the Middle Ages, the cross has exercised a most powerful influence. The ground upon which the grandest churches were erected was made to assume a cross-shaped form, so that the very walls from their foundations upward might show that sacred sign. Crosses, exhibiting an endless variety of form and ornament, surmounted the lofty spires and gables of cathedrals and churches, and were used profusely for the interior adornment of these temples of God.

When Protestantism arose, the fury of its leaders was oftentimes directed against the crosses which they regarded as a symbol of Popery, and they accordingly

Processional Cross

THE SACRAMENTALS

tore them down from the Catholic Churches which they seized and devoted to their own worship — placing over them, instead, a weather-vane, fitting emblem of that inconstancy and uncertainty which are "blown about with every wind of doctrine." In recent years a better spirit is manifesting itself towards the sacred symbol of our salvation, and crosses are appearing on and in some Protestant churches.

But among Catholics the cross has always been held in honor. It appears on the lofty gable of the church and on the summit of the tapering spire rising far into the sky, as if to announce to all that "this is none other than the house of God and the gate of heaven." Crosses are cut into the masonry and corner-stone to attest the consecration of the edifice to Christian worship. They are graven in the altar-stone, five in number, to symbolize the five wounds of our Blessed Lord, to bear witness to the sacrificial purpose to which the altar is dedicated. They are placed over the tombs of all, noble and lowly, to proclaim that each of the dead has died in the faith of Christ.

The Crucifix. The representation of our Saviour nailed to the cross is one of the important sacramentals of our holy religion. The Church requires the crucifix to be placed over the altar where Mass is to be offered, and during the Holy Sacrifice the priest bows his head toward it several times. It is also used in solemn ceremonies in the form of a processional cross, being carried at the head of the line of the clergy. As explained elsewhere in the account of the ceremonies of Holy Week, the crucifixes in our churches are veiled from Passion Sunday to Good Friday as a sign of sorrow; and after the unveiling the clergy and laity devoutly kiss the feet of our Blessed Lord, to express their gratitude for His infinite mercy and love.

Crucifix

The faithful are urged to keep prominently before them in their homes the figure of their crucified Lord, and the same blessed symbol is generally attached to the rosary which every fervent Catholic possesses and uses.

A very special indulgence has been granted to all who, after a worthy Communion, recite on their knees before a crucifix or a picture of our crucified Lord the prayer beginning "O good and most sweet Jesus, before Thy face I kneel," which may be found in prayer-books of recent date. This is a plenary indulgence, applicable to the souls in Purgatory, and is about the easiest to obtain of all those granted by the Church.

Above the head of the figure of our Saviour a scroll or board is attached to every crucifix, bearing the letters I. N. R. I. This is called the "title," and represents the inscription affixed to the cross of our Lord by order of Pilate. What is the meaning of the letters? They are the initials of the words "Iesus Nazarenus, Rex Iudaecorum" — "Jesus of Nazareth, King of the Jews." Sometimes a skull and bones are shown at the bottom — the Hebrew name of Calvary (Golgotha) meaning "the place of the skull," probably because it was a burial-ground for those who were put to death there.

Chapter XXVII

HOLY WATER

It is interesting to note how often our Church has availed herself of practices which were in common use among pagans, and which owed their origin to their appropriateness for expressing something spiritual by material means. The Church and her clergy are "all things to all men, that they may gain all for Christ," and she has often found that it was well to take what was praiseworthy in other forms of worship and adapt it to her own purposes, for the sanctification of her children. Thus it is true, in a certain sense, that some Catholic rites and ceremonies are a reproduction of those of pagan creeds; but they are the taking of what was best from paganism, the keeping of symbolical practices which express the religious instinct that is common to all races and times.

Holy water, as our catechisms taught us, is "water blessed by the priest with solemn prayer, to beg God's blessing on those who use it, and protection from the powers of darkness."

A Symbol of Interior Cleansing. Water is the natural element for cleansing, and hence its use was common in almost every ancient faith, to denote interior purification. Among the Greeks and Romans the sprinkling of water, or "lustration," was an important feature of religious ceremonies. Cities were purified by its use, in solemn processions. Fields were prepared for planting by being blessed with water. Armies setting out for war were put under the protection of the gods by being sprinkled in a similar manner. Among the Egyptians the use of holy water was even more common, the priests being required to bathe in it twice every day and twice every night, that they might thereby be sanctified for their religious duties. The Brahmins and others of the far Orient, and even the Indians of our own continent, have always attached great importance to ceremonial purification by means of water.

Among the Jews the sprinkling of the people, the sacrifices, the sacred vessels, etc., was enjoined by the regulations laid down by Moses in the books of Exodus and Leviticus; and it was undoubtedly from these practices of the Mosaic law that our

Church took many of the details of her ritual in regard to holy water.

When Was It Introduced? The use of holy water in Catholic churches goes back possibly to Apostolic times. There is a tradition that St. Matthew recommended it in order thereby to attract converts from Judaism by using a rite with which they were familiar in their former faith. However, we have no certainty that he introduced it, but we know that it can be traced back nearly to the beginning of our religion. It is mentioned in a letter ascribed by some to Pope Alexander I, and supposed to have been written in the year 117; but the genuineness of this letter is very doubtful. We find a detailed account of its use, however, in the "Pontifical of Serapion," in the fourth century, and the formula of blessing mentioned therein has considerable resemblance to that used at the present day.

Sprinkler

Holy Water Vessel

The Asperges. The blessing of water before the High Mass on Sunday and the sprinkling of the congregation with it, which ceremony is called the "Asperges," goes back to the time of Pope Leo IV, in the ninth century, and possibly even further. The word Asperges is the opening word of a verse of Psalm 50, which is recited by the priest as follows: "Thou shalt sprinkle me with hyssop, O Lord, and I shall be cleansed; Thou shalt wash me, and I shall be made whiter than snow."

The custom of placing holy water at the door of the church for the use of the faithful is still more ancient. Among the Jews a ceremony of purification was required before entering the Temple to assist at the sacrifices, and this undoubtedly suggested the Catholic practice of using holy water at the church door. It is said to have been in vogue in the second century, and we know that it is at least of very ancient date.

Holy Water Font

In the Middle Ages it was customary to use holy water when entering the church, but not when leaving it —

the idea being that purification was necessary before entering the house of God, but that after assisting at the Holy Sacrifice it was no longer needed. However, the general practice now is to take it both on entering and departing, and this is to be recommended for the reason that the Church has attached indulgences to its use, and these may be gained every time it is taken.

The Kinds of Holy Water. Often a priest is asked: "Is Easter water the same as the other holy water?" The answer is that it has the same uses, but is blessed in a different manner and at a different time. There are four distinct kinds of holy water. The first kind is baptismal water, which is blessed on Holy Saturday, and may also be blessed on the eve of Pentecost. This water receives a special and solemn blessing, and the holy oils consecrated on Holy Thursday are mingled with it. It is used only for the administration of Baptism. Water which has been thus blessed is the only licit matter for solemn Baptism. However, the Sacrament is valid if merely ordinary water is used, and in "private Baptism" the latter is lawful as well as valid.

The second kind is "water of consecration," or "Gregorian water," so called because its use was ordered by Pope Gregory IX. It is used by bishops in consecrating churches, and in its blessing it has wine, ashes and salt mingled with it.

The third kind is the so-called Easter water, which is distributed to the people on Holy Saturday. A part of this water is used for the filling of the baptismal font, to be blessed as baptismal water and to receive the holy oils; and the remainder is given to the faithful to be taken to their homes. In Catholic countries, and in some parishes in our own, this water is used by the clergy for the solemn blessing of houses on Holy Saturday.

The fourth and most common kind is the holy water which is blessed by the priest for the sprinkling of the people before Mass, and is placed at the doors of the church. This also may be taken home and used for the blessing of persons and things.

Thus the only varieties of holy water that directly concern the faithful are the water blessed on Holy Saturday for them, and that obtainable at any time at the church. They have the same value and the same uses, although the formula of blessing is different.

The Blessing of Holy Water. When holy water is blessed, the priest reads several prayers, which include an exorcism of the salt and the water. An exorcism is the banishing of evil spirits. The Fathers of the Church teach us that when Satan caused the fall of our first parents he also obtained an influence over inanimate things intended for the use of man; and therefore, when any material object is to be devoted to the service of God, the Church often prescribes for it a form of exorcism, to free it from the power of the Evil One.

The prayers used in this ceremony are very beautiful, and express well the reasons for the use of holy water. Those said over the salt invoke the power of "the living God, the true God, the holy God," that whosoever uses it may have health of soul and body; that the devil may depart from any place in which it is sprinkled; that whoever is touched by it shall be sanctified, and freed from all uncleanness and all attacks of the powers of darkness. The prayers said over the water are addressed to the Father, the Son and the Holy Ghost, that through the power of the Blessed Trinity the spirits of evil may be utterly expelled from this world and lose all influence over mankind. Then God is besought to bless the water, that it may be effective in driving out devils and in curing diseases; that wherever it is sprinkled there may be freedom from pestilence and from the snares of Satan.

Then the priest puts the salt into the water in the form of a threefold cross, saying: "May this mingling of salt and water be made in the name of the Father and of the Son and of the Holy Ghost" — after which another prayer is recited, in which God is asked to sanctify this salt and water, that wherever it shall be sprinkled all evil spirits shall be driven away and the Holy Spirit shall be present.

The Meaning of the Salt. Why does the Church use salt in holy water? Because it was a Jewish custom, and because of the symbolical meaning of salt. Just as water is used for cleansing and for quenching fire, so salt is used to preserve from decay. Therefore the Church combines them in this sacramental, to express the various reasons why it is used — to help to wash away the stains of sin, to quench the fire of our passions, to preserve us from relapses into sin. Moreover, salt is regarded as a symbol of wisdom. Our Lord called His Apostles "the salt of the earth," because by them the knowledge of the Gospel was to be spread over the world. The custom of using salt is a very ancient one, and is traced by some to the second or third century.

The Liturgical Uses of Holy Water. Holy Water is used in the blessing of nearly everything which the Church wishes to sanctify. The Ritual contains hundreds of distinct benedictions in which it is used. Besides the pouring of baptismal water which forms the "matter" of the Sacrament of Baptism, the sprinkling with holy water is a part of the ceremonies of Matrimony, of Extreme Unction and of the administration of the Holy Eucharist to the sick; and it is employed also in services for the dead.

The *Asperges*, or sprinkling of the congregation on Sunday, has a mystical meaning of its own. It renews every Sunday the memory of Baptism, by which we have been sanctified and purified from sin; and it is intended also to drive away all distractions which might hinder us from the proper hearing of Mass. It is well to remember that the holy water need not actually touch every person in the congregation. The whole assembled body of the faithful is blessed together, and all receive the benefit of the blessing, even though the holy water may not reach such individual.

How We Should Use It. Holy water should be used frequently. There is an indulgence of one hundred days every time it is taken. This indulgence was renewed by Pius IX in 1876, and in order to gain it there are three requirements: The sign of the cross must be made with the holy water, the person must have contrition for his sins, and he must say the words: "In the name of the Father and of the Son and of the Holy Ghost."

Stand at the door of any church and watch the people who enter. Do many of them gain the indulgence? They dip their fingers into the water, make a mysterious motion in the air, and pass along. There is no recollection, no audible words, no recognizable sign of the cross — merely an action performed through habit and in a very slovenly manner. None of the above requirements are fulfilled. Bear in mind that while the use of holy water in any way may be beneficial, to gain the indulgence it is necessary to make the sign of the cross, to say the usual words, and to have in our hearts a spirit of true contrition.

Chapter XXVIII

VESTMENTS

Man's nature is such that he needs external helps to assist him in fixing his attention on sacred things. We are all impressed to a remarkable degree by "pomp and circumstance." A king on his throne, clad in his royal robes, holding his scepter and wearing his jeweled crown, is an imposing sight; all these accessories indicate his dignity and help us to realize his greatness. The same king without these trappings of royalty would possibly be a very insignificant object.

For this reason it has been customary in every age and country to invest those holding any position of dignity or practising certain avocations with some uniform or badge, by which their rank and duties are designated. The soldier wears his uniform, by which he is distinguished from the ordinary citizen. The policeman, the fireman, the railway employee, each has his special garb, marking him as set apart for some definite work.

This is done for a twofold purpose — that others may respect and obey him as far as is necessary, and that he may respect himself and be more conscious of his duties and more attentive to them, on account of the uniform he wears. This is even more true of the religious garb. The priest wears it that he may be thereby distinguished form other men, and that he himself may be always reminded by it that he is "taken from among men to offer sacrifices and holocausts for them" — to be a mediator between the Almighty and His creatures.

In every religion since the world began, the practice has been in vogue of wearing some form of vestment. The priest has had a distinctive dress, whether he was an uncouth "medicine-man" of some barbarous tribe, an augur of pagan Rome, or a priest of the Hebrew Jehovah. Here, as in many other cases, our Church has shown her wisdom by making use of a meritorious feature of other religions.

A Sacramental of the Church. The word "vestment" is from the Latin, and signifies simply clothing, but it is now used generally to denote the garments worn by the ministers of religion in the performance of their sacred duties.

Vestments are a sacramental — that is, they are set apart and blessed by the Church to excite good thoughts and to increase devotion in those who see and those who use them. They are the uniform of the priest when he is "on duty," while he is exercising the functions of his ministry and using the sacred powers which he received at his ordination.

Among the Jews. Under the Jewish law every detail of the vestments used in the worship of God was provided by divine command. The garb of the highpriest and his assistants was specified most minutely as to material and form, and observance of these rules was enjoined under the severest penalties. The veneration of the Jewish people for the vestments of the highpriest was so great that they kept a lamp constantly burning before the repository of the sacred robes, just as we do now before the Blessed Sacrament.

When Christianity arose, no divine command was given concerning the dress to be worn by the priests of God. This was left to the judgment of the heads of the Church, and in the different ages of her history many changes have been made in the number and form and material of the priestly vestments.

There is no record of any special form of them during the first four centuries. It is probable that the garb of the clergy in those times was the common dress of laymen.. The outer garments worn by men of those days were long and flowing, a modified form of the old Roman toga; and consequently the vestments used in the divine service took the same general form. Gradually the custom was introduced of making them of rich and costly materials, to add greater beauty thereby to the rites of religion. When the hardy barbarians of the North had overwhelmed the luxurious nations of southern Europe and had brought in their own fashions of dress, the Church did not see fit to change the garb of her ministers as worn at the services of her ritual, but she permitted them to change their ordinary dress to some extent, and forbade them to wear their vestments except while officiating at sacred rites.

Colors of the Vestments. The Church ordinarily permits the use of five colors in the sacred vestments — white, red, green, violet and black. Rose-colored vestments are prescribed (when obtainable) at the solemn Mass on the third Sunday in Advent and the fourth in Lent. Gold may be used as a substitute for white, red or green.

Each of these colors has its own meaning. The Sacrifice of the Mass is offered for many purposes and in honor of many classes of saints; and these various purposes are all designated and symbolized by the color of the vestments which the Church prescribes for each Mass.

When are these colors used? When the Church wishes to denote purity, innocence or glory, she uses white; that is, on the feasts of our Lord and of the Blessed Virgin, on the festivals of angels and of all saints who were not martyrs. Red is the color of fire and of blood; it is used in Masses of the Holy Ghost, such as on Pentecost, to remind us of the tongues of fire — and on the feasts of all saints who shed their blood for their faith. The purple or violet is expressive of penance; it is used during Lent and Advent (except on Saints' days), and also on the sorrowful festival of the Holy Innocents. Black is the color of mourning for the dead; it is worn at all Masses of Requiem for the departed, and also on Good Friday. Green is the color which denotes the growth and increase of our holy Church, and is also symbolic of hope; it is used at various times of the year, on days that are not saints' days.

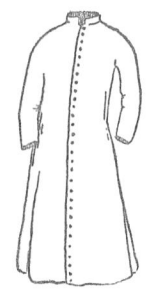
Cassock

The Priest's Vestments. The black gown of the priest, called a cassock or soutane, is not a vestment. It is simply the ordinary outer garb of a cleric, and in Catholic countries it is worn on the street as well as indoors.

The biretta, or cap, is also not a part of the vestments, although it must be worn when the priest is going to and coming from the altar, and while he is seated at certain parts of the service. This peculiarly shaped head-covering has a history of its own. It was originally a brimless soft cap of medium height. In putting this on and taking it off it became

Biretta

indented into folds by the fingers; after a time these folds were so sewn that they made a convenient wing or handle. As the right hand is used mostly for removing one's hat, the biretta often has no fold on the left side — although in some parts of Europe four-winged birettas are commonly used. The top is often ornamented with a "pompon" or a tassel.

The vestments worn by the priest at Mass are as follows: The amice, the alb, the cincture, the maniple, the stole and the chasuble; and at certain other services he uses the cope, the humeral veil and the surplice. Each of these has its own history and its own symbolical meaning, expressed in the prayers which the priest recites when he is putting on the vestments.

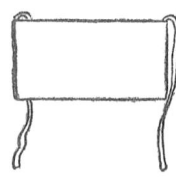
Amice

The Amice. When a priest begins to "vest" for Mass, he first puts on an amice. This is an oblong piece of white linen, with strings attached by which it is fastened into place around the shoulders. It has been worn in the Mass since about the year 800, and takes its name form the Latin *amictus*, a wrapper. It was formerly worn covering the head, and certain religious orders still use it in this manner until the beginning of the Mass. It is looked upon as a symbol of a helmet, by which the priest is protected against the assaults of Satan.

Alb

The Alb. The long linen gown worn by the priest is called the *alb*, meaning simply the white garment. The lower part of it is frequently made of lace. It is a survival of the white Roman toga. As the vesting prayers tell us, its white color denotes the necessity of purity, both of soul and body, in him who offers the Immaculate Lamb of God it the Eternal Father.

Cincture

The Cincture. This is the proper name for the girdle worn around the waist to bind the alb closely to the body. In some countries it is of the same color as the vestments used, but among us it is generally white. It is made of braided linen, or sometimes of wool, and is symbolic of continence, according to the prayer which the priest says while putting it on: "Gird me, O Lord, with the girdle of purity, and extinguish in me all concupiscence."

The Maniple. We now come to the vestments which vary in color from day to day, according to the object for which the Mass is offered or the saint who is honored in it.

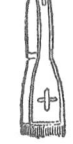
Maniple

A small vestment of peculiar shape is worn by the priest on his left arm. This is the *maniple*, and it was originally nothing more nor less than a handkerchief; but it has been so changed in form that it is now merely an ornament.

The word *maniple* is from the Latin "manipulum," which has various meanings — something carried in the hand, a small bundle, a handkerchief, a sheaf of grain; and therefore this vestment is considered as symbolical of good works. It is the special badge of the order of subdeaconship, and is not used by those in lower orders.

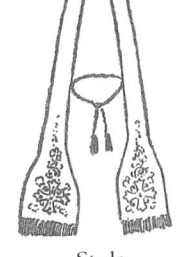
Stole

The Stole. At Mass, and also in nearly every other religious function, the priest wears around his neck a long narrow vestment, the ends hanging down in front. When used at Mass, these ends are crossed. The deacon at a solemn Mass wears a similar vestment, but in a different manner — diagonally from his left shoulder to his right side. The stole came unto use about the fourth century, and was originally a sort of robe or cloak; but its form was gradually modified until it became a narrow strip of cloth. It is said by some to have been the court uniform of Roman judges, and to have been adopted by the Church to denote the authority of her ministers. According to the vesting prayer, it symbolizes immortality, and also the yoke of obedience under which the priest exercises his office.

Chasuble

The Chasuble. The most conspicuous part of the costume of the priest at Mass is the *chasuble*, the large vestment worn on the shoulders and hanging down in front and behind. The rear portion is often, though not always, ornamented with a large cross.

The word *chasuble* is from the late Latin "casula," a little house, because it is, as it were, a shelter for the priest. It is considered as a symbol of protection, of preservation from evil — a spiritual suit of armor.

The vestment has been greatly altered during the centuries of its history. It was originally a large mantle or cloak, with an opening for the head in the centre, and had to be raised at the sides to allow the hands to be extended outside the cloak. The assistants at the Mass were obliged to help the priest by holding up the sides of the chasuble, and a trace of this practice may be noticed still in the solemn Masses, where the deacon and subdeacon ceremoniously hold the edges of the priest's chasuble, although there is no longer any need of their assistance.

Cope

The Cope and Veil. The *cope*, used at the *Asperges* before a high Mass and at many solemn functions of the Church, was originally worn only in outdoor processions, and was considered merely as a rain-cloak, as is shown by its Latin name, *pluviale*, a protection against rain. The cape attached to it, which now has no use whatever, is a reminder of the large hood formerly used to cover the head in stormy weather. Our English name, *cope*, is from the Latin "cappa," a cape.

The *humeral veil* is worn on the shoulders of the priest at the Benediction of the Blessed Sacrament when he holds the Sacred Host for the blessing of the people, and also when he carries the Blessed Sacrament in procession. This veil is also used by the subdeacon in solemn Masses.

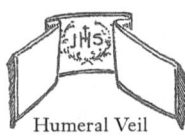
Humeral Veil

The Surplice. It may be well also to say a word about this vestment, which is worn over the cassock at the administration of the Sacraments and at various services of the Church. It is the special garb of clerics not in sacred orders, and its use is

THE SACRAMENTALS

tolerated for lay altar-boys, or acolytes, in our churches.

In its present form it is one of the most modern of vestments. The word surplice is from the Latin "superpellicium" — a dress worn over furs. In the Middle Ages it was allowed to the monks in cold countries to have fur garments, and over these a linen gown was worn in choir. It was later considered practically as an alb, and in the twelfth century it was usually so long that it reached the feet. Gradually it was made shorter, and about the seventeenth century the custom began of ornamenting it with lace.

Surplice

The Tunic and the Dalmatic. The *tunic* is the vestment of subdeacons, the *dalmatic* of deacons. They are usually exactly alike, although, strictly speaking, the tunic should be of smaller size than the dalmatic. Each is of about the same length as the chasuble of the priest. These vestments hang from the shoulders, which are covered by projecting flaps; these are sometimes connected under the arms, so as to resemble short sleeves. The color, of course, varies according to the Mass, and on the back are usually two ornamental vertical stripes, but no cross.

A *tunic* signifies simply an outer garment. The *dalmatic* gets its name from a Roman garment made of wool from the province of Dalmatia, worn under the outer clothing in ancient times.

The tunic, according to the words used in conferring it at an ordination, signifies joy, while the dalmatic is looked upon as an emblem of righteousness and charity.

Dalmatic

The Broad Stole. During the Lenten season, at High Masses, the deacon is directed by the rubrics to wear a broad stole, covering his other stole, instead of the usual dalmatic. This broad stole was not originally a stole at all; it was a folded chasuble — for some centuries ago, the deacon wore a chasuble at Lenten Masses instead of a dalmatic, and was directed to take it off and fold it early in the Mass, putting it on again over his shoulder and wearing it thus during the chanting of the Gospel. For convenience, this folded chasuble was later replaced by a stole-like vestment, as we have it now.

The Vestments of a Bishop. These are numerous, and each has its own interesting history and its own symbolic meaning. The bishops are the links in the Apostolic chain, the pastors of Christ's flock, the principal laborers in His vineyard. All the dignity which a bishop has by virtue of his office, and all the qualities which he should have to be worthy of his exalted position, are symbolized by the chief insignia which he is privileged to use.

The Mitre. This is the distinguishing mark of the episcopal office — a tall double-pointed cap, probably of Oriental origin, which can be traced back to pagan times; at least, something very similar was worn by kings in Persia and Assyria long before the Christian era. As an ecclesiastical vestment it came into general use about the year 1100, although some form of tall and dignified headdress was worn considerably earlier. The present double or cleft form was evolved gradually; it was at first low and concave, and was subsequently increased in height and more richly ornamented. Its two points or horns symbolize the Old and New Testaments, which the bishop is supposed to explain to his people.

The Crosier. This, the bishop's pastoral staff, is, of course, not a vestment, but may be mentioned here. It typifies his duties as shepherd of the flock. It is a copy of the shepherd's crook, used for the guidance and restraining of the sheep, and has been looked upon as the special badge of the episcopal office since the fifth century at least, and is so mentioned in the ritual of a bishop's consecration. It signifies his power to sustain the weak, to confirm the wavering, and to lead back the erring. The upper part is often very beautifully moulded and enriched with images and symbolic ornaments.

Crosier

THE SACRAMENTALS

The Ring. On the third finger of a bishop's right hand he wears a large ring — a custom traceable to about the year 600. It was a signet ring originally, but is now considered as a symbol of faith or fidelity.

The Rochet. A vestment somewhat like a surplice, but with closely fitting sleeves, is worn by the bishop at certain functions. This is called a *rochet*, from a late Latin word meaning a coat. It is made of white linen, and is usually ornamented with lace.

Rochet

When a bishop is celebrating a pontifical Mass, he is attired in three vestments — the chasuble of the priest, the dalmatic of the deacon and the tunic of the subdeacon, to signify that in his episcopal office all the various orders find their culmination and perfection. The last two vestments are necessarily made of thin material, so as not to be cumbersome.

The Cappa Magna. A long cope with a hood, the latter being lined with silk or fur, may be worn by the bishop at solemn functions. This is called the *cappa magna* — a large cope.

Cappa Magna

The Pectoral Cross. Attached to a chain which he wears around his neck is a cross of precious metal, which hangs on his breast, and thence derives its name, from the Latin *pectus*, the breast. This badge of the episcopacy came into use about the twelfth century.

Gloves, Sandals, etc. At a bishop's consecration, gloves are blessed for him and placed on his hands. The practice of wearing them as a part of his vestments began probably about the eleventh century. They are worn only at a pontifical Mass, and then only to the washing of the hands. They are made of knitted silk, and are ornamented on the backs with crosses. They vary in color according to the Mass celebrated, but are not used in Requiem Masses.

Bishop's Glove

At a pontifical Mass the bishop also wears stockings which

are of woven silk and conform in color to the vestments, and low-heeled shoes called sandals, likewise of the liturgical color.

When he is seated during a Mass, or when he is conferring sacred orders, a sort of apron, called a *gremiale*, is laid upon his lap. Its original purpose was to keep his garments from being soiled; but after a time it became a vestment and is often adorned with gold lace and other ornaments.

Gremiale

A bishop's cassock varies in color according to the occasion. On penitential days it is black with purple silk trimmings; but on other days he wears a purple cassock, called a *choir cassock*, with crimson trimmings, at church functions, and an *ordinary cassock*, of black with red trimmings and without train, on other occasions.

Over his cassock he wears a short cape, bearing the Italian name of *mozzetta*, buttoned over the breast and provided with a small hood.

Such, then, is a brief account of many of the ecclesiastical vestments which our Church prescribes for her prelates and other clergy in the functions of her liturgy, and of the garb which, at other times, points them out as "set apart." We should reverence these things, for many of them are true sacramentals of our Church; and when we see them, we should endeavor to remember the dignity which God has given to their wearers, and the symbolism by which these consecrated garments set before us the virtues which He wishes His bishops and priests to manifest in fulfilling the duties of their holy and exalted state.

Mozzetta

Chapter XXIX

THE STATIONS OF THE CROSS

In every Catholic church there are pictured representations of various events in the Passion of our Blessed Lord. These enable the faithful to accompany our Redeemer, as it were, on that sorrowful journey which began at the house of Pilate and ended at the sepulcher. The whole devotion is replete with sorrow, with penitential love towards Him who gave His life on the cross of Calvary for our salvation.

The Origin of the Stations. In the early days of the Church, when the spirit of faith was strong in the souls of Christians, no hardship was deemed too great when spiritual advantages were to be gained. Vast multitudes of pilgrims undertook the arduous journey to the Holy Land that they might visit the places that had been sanctified by our Saviour's sufferings. Tradition had preserved a very accurate knowledge of these localities, and the devout pilgrims were accustomed to make what we now call the Way of the Cross, at the places which were the actual scenes of our Lord's Passion.

But Jerusalem became a Mohammedan city, under the sway of the Sultans; and even when the perilous journey had been made, there was always danger from the despotic government and from the savage fanaticism of the Moslem people. The idea, therefore, occurred to several devout persons who had accomplished the pilgrimage, that it would be well to have some means of performing the same devotion in a safer way and of giving its benefits to those who were unable to make the journey to Palestine. The Blessed Alvarez, a Dominican of Cordova, in Spain, is said to have constructed several small chapels, each containing a representation of some part of our Lord's sufferings. A similar practice was adopted about 1350 by the Franciscan Minorities, who had been permitted by the Sultan to take charge of the Sepulchre of our Blessed Lord at Jerusalem, and who erected Stations in many of their European churches, so that all the faithful who could not become pilgrims might make the journey in spirit. It was immediately seen that this was a most excellent devotion, well adapted to arouse in the hearts of Christians a fervent spirit of contrition and love of God; and it was, consequently, soon approved and recommended by the Holy See.

Pope Innocent XII, in 1694, reaffirming the decrees of his predecessors, declared that the indulgences granted for visiting certain places in Palestine could be gained by all Franciscans and all affiliated to that Order, by making the Way of the Cross devoutly. Later, in 1726, Benedict XIII extended these indulgences to all the faithful. For some time afterwards the Franciscan Fathers had the sole faculty of erecting Stations in churches, but this power is now given to all bishops, and they may delegate it to their priests.

Station of the Cross

What are the Stations? It is a common but erroneous belief that the Stations of the Cross are the pictures or reliefs or groups of statuary representing our Saviour on His journey to Calvary. These are not the Stations. They are merely aids to devotion. The Stations, to which the indulgences are attached, are the crosses, which must be of wood, and which are generally placed over the pictures. The latter are not essential, and are only used that we may more vividly realize our Saviour's anguish and the greatness of our debt to Him.

The Stations are fourteen in number. For some hundreds of years there was a diversity of practice in this regard, the number varying from eleven to sixteen in different places; but the Church finally ruled that they must not be more nor less than fourteen.

Some of the scenes depicted in the Way of the Cross are described in the Gospels; others are transmitted to us by tradition. Thus we have no Scriptural authority for the falls of Jesus under the cross, nor for the beautiful story of Veronica. These are based on pious beliefs which have probably been handed down from the times of the Apostles.

The Stations are generally affixed to the interior walls of the church, although in Catholic countries it is not unusual to see beautiful Stations erected in the open air, in the grounds of religious institutions and also in cemeteries, where it is an edifying sight to witness the public devotion of the Way of the Cross for the benefit of the departed ones whose bodies are buried there.

The reader may have noticed that the Stations do not everywhere begin on the same side of the church. There is no fixed rule in regard to this; but they are always so arranged that our Saviour is represented as moving forward; so that the place of beginning and ending depends on the manner in which He has been depicted by the artist. Therefore in some churches you will find the first Station on the Gospel side, in others on the Epistle side of the main altar.

The Indulgences of the Stations. What are the indulgences granted to those who perform the Way of the Cross? Strange to say, we do not know. While we are assured that no other devotion is so highly indulgenced, there is considerable uncertainty as to just what indulgences we gain when we "go around the Stations." For many other devotions we have an exact list of the indulgences; but we can only say, in regard to the Stations, that the person who devoutly performs this devotion and is in the state of grace gains the same indulgences as if he had visited the actual Way of the Cross in Jerusalem. The precise number or amount of these indulgences is not specified in any extant decree of the Church; and all that we know is that no other practice of our holy religion is so earnestly recommended or so plentifully indulgenced for us and for the souls in Purgatory.

How to Gain the Indulgences. We are not bound to read a meditation at each Station. We are not obliged to recite any prayers. Those that are customarily said, such as the Our Father, the Hail Mary, etc., are commendable and meritorious, but are not necessary. We must merely go around from the first Station to the fourteenth, stopping at each for a short time, and meditating on the Passion of our Lord in general or on the particular event which the Station represents. If we cannot go around, on account of the crowded condition of the church, or if the Stations are being performed publicly, it is sufficient merely to turn towards each Station. The two essential points of the devotion are the making of a journey, as it were, in company with our Blessed Lord from His trial to His tomb, and the meditation on His sufferings while the journey is being made.

For those who cannot go to the church, it is sometimes permitted to gain the same spiritual benefits by using an indulgenced crucifix, which is to be held in the hands while the Our Father, Hail Mary and Glory be to the Father are recited fourteen times, followed by the same prayers repeated six times — the last being for the intention of the Holy Father.

The Stations of the Cross must be lawfully erected that indulgences may be gained from them. The priest who blesses them must be specially delegated for that work by the bishop of the diocese. It may be well to mention, then, that pictures of the Stations, such as are found in prayer-books, or printed so as to form a sheet or chart, cannot be used for gaining these indulgences. Many of the faithful, with sincere but mistaken devotion, pay great reverence to such representations of our Lord's sufferings, and imagine that by praying before them they are "making the Stations." There is a specially objectionable device which has been widely sold and is proudly displayed in many Catholic homes, consisting of a series of gaudy pictures mounted on rollers so that they can be successively exposed to view; the purchaser is assured that this can be used "to make the Stations at home" — which is absolutely untrue. The Way of the Cross cannot be made except by visiting the Stations which have been lawfully erected and meditating on the Passion of our Lord.

For Ourselves and for the Souls. We see, then, how our holy Church has made it easy for us to gain great spiritual benefits, for our own souls and for the souls in Purgatory. She does not exact from us the rigorous penances of former ages. She does not require that we shall make a long and perilous journey. She tempers her laws to the weakness of her children, and permits us to gain in a very easy manner the favors which we would obtain if, like the pious pilgrims of old, we traversed land and sea to the Holy Places where our Blessed Saviour wrought the redemption of mankind.

CHAPTER XXX

THE HOLY OILS

A SERVICE of great solemnity and beauty takes place in every cathedral church on Holy Thursday of each year. The Bishop blesses the oils which are to be used during the ensuing year in the administration of the Sacraments, as well as in various consecrations and blessings of persons and things.

The ceremony of the Blessing of the Oils is full of significant symbolism. It requires the presence of a large number of the clergy, for the sacred oils are considered by the Church to be of such importance as to call for extraordinary pomp and imposing ceremonial. Few inanimate things receive more homage and honor than the oils which are to be used so often during the year in the imparting of God's grace through Sacraments and blessings.

Each of us Catholics has received already some of the benefits given through these holy oils, namely, in the ceremonies of Baptism and in the conferring of the Sacrament of Confirmation; and we hope some day to obtain further graces through them in Extreme Unction; and yet it may be that we know little about them. Moreover, few of us are able to be present when the solemn blessing of them takes place in a cathedral church. Therefore this chapter will be devoted to a description of the nature, the uses, the history and the blessing of the Holy Oils.

The Symbolism of Oil. In the countries of the Orient and in southern Europe, olive oil has always been a necessity of daily life, much more than with us. It enters into the preparation of food; it is used as a remedy, internally and externally; in past centuries it was the chief means of furnishing light, being consumed in lamps; it was employed in ancient times by the athletes of the Olympic games, to give suppleness to their muscles. Hence we see the various symbolic meanings of which the Church takes cognizance when she uses it to give us spiritual nourishment, to cure our spiritual ailments, to diffuse the light of grace in our souls, and to render us strong and active in the never-ending conflict with the Spirit of Evil. The use of oil to express the imparting of spiritual strength is so appropriate that the Church employs it not only for the anointing of living beings but also for bells and chalices and other lifeless things which are to be used as aids in the sanctification of her children.

The oils blessed on Holy Thursday are of three kinds — the Oil of Catechumens, the Chrism and the Oil of the Sick. Each of them is oil extracted from olives, but the Chrism is distinguished from the others by having balm or balsam mixed with it.

Each of these is blessed by the Bishop with a special form of prayer, expressing the purpose for which it is to be used and its mystical signification as well.

The Oil of Catechumens. This kind of sacred oil is used in the ceremonies of Baptism, and derives its name from that fact — a *catechumen* being an instructed convert who is about to receive the Sacrament of Baptism. As described in the chapter on the administration of that Sacrament, the priest makes with this oil the sign of the cross on the person who is to be baptized, on the breast and on the back between the shoulders, with the solemn words: "I anoint thee with the oil of salvation, in Christ Jesus our Lord, that thou mayest have everlasting life."

Why are these unctions used? Because the catechumens are considered to be to some extent under the power of the Evil One until they have been united to Christ's mystical body, the Church, by Baptism.

This oil is also employed for other purposes — in the ceremony of the "blessing of the font" or the baptismal water on Holy Saturday, in the consecration of a church, in the blessing of altars and altar-stones, in the ordination of priests, and in the coronation of Catholic kings and queens.

The Holy Chrism. The Chrism is generally held to be the "matter" or essential substance for the administration of the Sacrament of Confirmation. It is applied by the Bishop in the form of a cross on the forehead of the person confirmed. It is used also in the ceremonies of Baptism, an unction being made with it on the crown of the head immediately after the pouring of the water. Its use is required also in the consecration of a Bishop, and of a church, as well as in the blessing of chalices, patens, baptismal water and church bells.

The use of balsam in the Chrism dates from about the sixth century. Balsam is a resinous substance which is procured from terebinth trees, which grow in Judea and Arabia; and similar substances of even greater excellence are obtained from various plants in the West Indies and tropical countries. In some Oriental rites, a great variety of sweet-smelling spices and perfumes are used in addition to the balsam.

The mixing of this fragrant material with the sacred oil gives the latter the name of Chrism, which signifies a scented ointment. As oil typifies the fullness of grace imparted through the Sacrament, so balsam expresses freedom from corruption and the sweet odor of virtue.

The Oil of the Sick. This sacred oil, called in Latin "Oleum Infirmorum," is the "matter" or necessary substance for the Sacrament of Extreme Unction, and is also used in the blessing of bells. In the Churches which follow the Latin rite this oil is always pure, without admixture; but in some Eastern Churches it contains a little wine or ashes.

As regards the use of this oil in Extreme Unction, we know that it was employed in Apostolic times practically in the same manner as now. St. James, in his Epistle, thus instructs the faithful of the early Church: "Is any man sick among you? Let him bring in the priests of the Church; and let them pray over him, anointing him with oil in the name of the Lord. And the prayer of faith shall save the sick man, and the Lord shall raise him up. And if he be in sins, they shall be forgiven him."

The use of oil as the "matter" of this Sacrament is undoubtedly of divine institution, entering as it does into the very nature of the Sacrament, which has been given to us by our Blessed Saviour and not by the Church.

Ancient Practices. The liturgical use of oil for other purposes, as in the ceremonies of Baptism and Holy Orders and in other blessings and consecrations mentioned above, is, in nearly every case, of very ancient origin, being often traceable nearly to the times of the Apostles. In this, as in many other practices, our Church has retained and made use of something which had been employed in the ritual of Judaism; for in the Old Testament we find mention of the anointing with oil in several religious functions, such as the consecration of priests and kings, as well as in sacrifices, legal purifications and the consecration of altars.

The use of oil in the "blessing of the font" or baptismal water probably does not go back to very early times. The practice of giving a special blessing to the water is indeed very ancient, dating from about the second century, but we have no evidence that at that period oil was mingled with it. It is therefore probable that the present mode of imparting the Church's blessing to it is of more recent origin.

When our Church wishes to use any material object for sacred functions she usually sets it apart from other things by giving it a special blessing; thus it is distinguished from substances intended only for ordinary purposes. As regards oil, such blessings are recorded in the rituals of very early times, and do not differ greatly from those given at the present day. Even as far back as the fourth century two kinds of oil were solemnly blessed on Holy Thursday for sacramental uses, one being pure and the other mixed with balsam; the first was what we now call the Oil of Catechumens, and the other was the Chrism. The third kind, the Oil of the Sick, was consecrated by a more simple formula either on that day or at other times, and in some parts of the world it was customary to have this oil blessed as needed, by priests. This custom has persevered to the present day in some Eastern rites, although among us, by Church law, the blessing by a Bishop is always necessary.

The Blessing of the Oils. The grand ceremony of Holy Thursday requires the presence of a large number of the clergy. Besides the Bishop and his immediate attendants, there are twelve priests wearing priests' vestments, seven who are vested as deacons, and seven others in the garb of subdeacons. The Bishop is robed in white vestments, and is the celebrant of the pontifical Mass, and he proceeds with the Mass in the usual manner until just before the Pater Noster. At this point the Oil of the Sick is called for by him and is solemnly brought in, contained in a large vessel of silver, by a subdeacon accompanied by two acolytes. The Bishop pronounces over it an exorcism to banish from it all influences of the Evil One. He then prays that the Holy Spirit, the Paraclete, may come upon it, for the refreshing of mind and body, that it may be a remedy for all pains, infirmities and weaknesses.

The Mass then continues until after the Communion, when the solemn consecration of the Chrism and the Oil of Catechumens takes place. The oils are brought out from the sacristy by a procession made up of a censer-bearer, a subdeacon carrying a cross, two acolytes with lighted candles, two chanters, and all the priests, deacons and subdeacons enumerated above; two of the deacons carry the oils in large silver urns shrouded in veils, and a subdeacon bears a vessel containing the balsam; the chanters intone several beautiful verses, which are repeated by the choir.

The Bishop then blesses, with appropriate prayers, the balsam which is to be mixed with the oil to form the Chrism — the "fragrant tear of dry bark," as the ancient and beautiful language of the Pontifical expresses it. He then mixes it with a little of the oil, and recites another prayer, that "whosoever is outwardly anointed with this oil may be so anointed inwardly that he may be made a partaker of the Heavenly Kingdom." He then breathes three times on the Chrism, and this is done also by the twelve priests. An exorcism is then recited over the oil, and a beautiful Preface is intoned by the Bishop, enumerating the sacred uses of oil in the Old Law, and invoking God's blessing on this holy oil which is to be used as a chrism of salvation for those who "have been born again of water and the Holy Spirit."

He then pours the mixed oil and balsam into the Chrism-vessel, and, bowing to the consecrated oil, he chants three times, in Latin, "Hail, Holy Chrism," and reverently kisses the vessel — which salutation and homage are repeated a like number of times by each of the twelve priests.

Next comes the consecration of the Oil of Catechumens, which consists of an exorcism and a prayer of benediction. The Bishop then chants three times "Hail, Holy Oil," and kisses the vessel containing it, all of which is repeated by each of the twelve priests. To the accompaniment of verses intoned by the choir the sacred oils are then solemnly borne back to the sacristy.

The Holy Oils in Our Churches. The priests of the various parishes, later in the day, obtain a sufficient quantity of the three Oils for the needs of their churches and people. In each parish church these consecrated Oils are kept with great care and reverence, being enclosed in suitable metallic bottles, which are preserved in an *ambry* or locked box (old English "aumery," from the French "armoire," a safe or arms-chest), affixed to the wall of the sanctuary. The Oil of Catechumens is usually labeled O. C. or O. S. ("Oleum Catechumenorum" or "Oleum Sanctum"); the Chrism is distinguished by the letters S. C. ("Sanctum Chrisma"); and the Oil of the Sick ("Oleum Infirmorum") bears the initials O. I.

Ambry

The unused oils which may be left over from the preceding year are not to be used for any Sacrament or any liturgical purpose. They are poured into the sanctuary lamp, and are consumed as ordinary oil.

This necessarily incomplete account of the beautiful ceremonies of Holy Thursday will show us the value which the Church attaches to these Holy Oils. She requires for their consecration a wealth of ritual which testifies to her appreciation of their importance in her liturgy; and she offers them a degree of homage which should teach us how holy and how efficacious for our salvation is this lifeless substance which she, inspired by her Divine Founder, consecrates for the benefit of us, her children, that through its use in Sacrament and in blessing we may receive graces which we need for the saving of our souls.

Chapter XXXI

CANDLES

The use of lights as an adjunct to worship goes back to the beginning of the Church, and even farther. Among the Jews and in many pagan rites the use of lights had long been looked upon as appropriate in connection with public homage to their God or gods. It is probable that among Christians they were first employed simply to dispel darkness, when the sacred mysteries were celebrated before dawn, as was the custom, or in the gloom of the catacombs; but the beautiful symbolism of their use was soon recognized by the writers of the early Church.

The Symbolism of Candles. Light is pure; it penetrates darkness; it moves with incredible velocity; it nourishes life; it illumines all that comes under its influence. Therefore it is a fitting symbol of God, the All-Pure, the Omnipresent, the Vivifier of all things, the Source of all grace and enlightenment. It represents also our Blessed Saviour and His mission. He was "the Light of the world," to enlighten "them that sit in darkness and in the shadow of death."

Even the use of wax has its symbolic meaning. The earlier Fathers of the Church endeavored always to seek out the mystical significance of Christian practices, and one of them thus explains the reason for the Church's law requiring candles to be of wax: "The wax, being spotless, represents Christ's most spotless Body; the wick enclosed in it is an image of His Soul, while the glowing flame typifies the Divine Nature united with the human in one Divine Person."

The Blessing of Candles. On the second of February the Church celebrates the festival of the Purification of the Blessed Virgin, which may be considered as the conclusion of the series of feasts that centre around the stable of Bethlehem. Christmas Day presents to us the birth of the Redeemer; the Epiphany commemorates His manifestation to the Gentiles; and the Purification reminds us of the offering of our Saviour in the Temple by His Blessed Mother, as the Victim who should reconcile God and man. This day has been chosen by the Church for a very important ceremony, the solemn blessing of candles, whence the day is often called Candlemas — the Mass of the candles.

Why is this ceremony performed on the feast of the Purification? Probably because on or about that day the Roman people, when pagan, had been accustomed to carry lights in processions in honor of one of their deities; and the Church, instead of trying to blot out entirely the memory of this pagan festival, changed it into a Christian solemnity — thereby honoring the Blessed Mother of God by assigning to one of her feast-days the solemn blessing of candles for Christian services.

The prayers which are used in this blessing are quaint and beautiful, and express well the mind of the Church and the symbolic meaning of the candles. God, the Creator of all things, Who by the labor of the bees has produced this wax, and Who on this day fulfilled His promise to blessed Simeon, is besought to bless and sanctify these candles, that they may be beneficial to His people, for the health of their bodies and souls; that the faithful may be inflamed with His sweetest charity and may deserve to be presented in the Temple of His eternal glory as He was in the temple of Sion; and that the light of His grace may dispel the darkness of sin in our souls.

The Uses of Blessed Candles. Candles are used at the administration of all the sacraments except Penance — for all the others are usually given solemnly, while Penance is administered privately. They are lighted at Mass and other church services, at the imparting of certain blessings, in processions and on various other occasions.

The custom of placing lighted candles on our altars goes back, probably, only to about the eleventh century — before which time they were left standing in tall candlesticks on the floor of the sanctuary, or in brackets affixed to the walls.

At Masses, candles are used as follows: At a solemn Mass six are lighted on the altar. At a "Missa Cantata," sung by one priest, four are sufficient. At a Pontifical Mass, sung by a bishop in his own diocese, seven are lighted. Four are used at a bishop's private Mass, and two at all other Masses. These rules, however, do not prohibit the use of more candles on occasions of special solemnity. Bishops and certain other prelates have the right to use a reading-candle, called a "bugia," at their Masses.

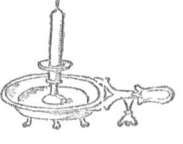
Bugia

At Vespers, six candles are lighted on the more solemn feasts; four only will suffice on other days. In the processions to the sanctuary before solemn services two candles are borne by acolytes, and these are also carried to do honor to the chanting of the Gospel and to the singing of certain parts of Vespers, etc.

Votive Candles. The use of votive candles has become very general in our churches, especially during the last few years. They are usually not blessed candles, and are, therefore, not sacramentals. It is customary to use for this purpose "stearic" candles, which are made of other material than wax. They are commonly placed in large numbers in a candle-holder of special form, before some statue or shrine, and are lighted by the people themselves, who give a suitable donation for the privilege.

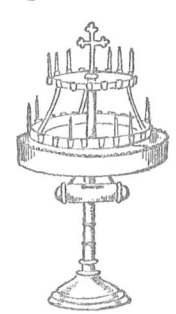
Votive Candlestick

A "votive" candle signifies literally that the lighting is done in fulfillment of a vow (Latin, "votum"), although in most cases the intention is merely to give honor and to manifest devotion to the saint before whose images the candle is lighted.

Such is the spirit of our Church in regard to blessed candles. The faithful in general have come to look upon them as among the most efficacious of the sacramentals. Every Catholic home should have one or more, to be used when the sacraments are to be administered; and when death approaches, it is a beautiful and pious custom to place in the hand of the dying Catholic a blessed candle, the light of which is an image of the faith which he has professed before the world, the grace which God has given to his soul, and the eternal glory to which he is destined.

Lamps in Our Churches. It may be well to mention here the use of lamps as an adjunct to Catholic worship — for, though they are not sacramentals, they have had from very early times a sacred character. In the catacombs they were used not only to give light but to honor the remains of martyrs, being burned constantly before their tombs.

It is an ancient and universal rule that a lamp shall be kept burning always before the Blessed Sacrament, wherever It is reserved. This is known as the sanctuary lamp. The oil used in it must be olive oil; but if this cannot be easily obtained, the bishop may permit the use of other oils; these, however, must be vegetable oils, except in case of absolute necessity, when, by a very recent decree, other substitutes may be used. In our country the use of cotton-seed oil is common, either pure or mixed with olive and other oils.

Sanctuary Lamp

Sanctuary lamps are often of very beautiful and costly design, and are usually suspended before the altar on which the Blessed Sacrament is kept. They are arranged, in most cases, with a counterweight device, so that they may be easily lowered for convenience in filling.

It is a pious custom to keep lamps burning elsewhere in our churches — before altars and images of saints and before their relics. In many European churches such lights are found in great profusion; and the shrines of favorite saints are often illumined with hundreds of them, while in many cases the altar of the Blessed Sacrament has only the one lamp which the Church's law requires, although He Who dwells thereon is infinitely greater, infinitely more worthy of honor and love than even the holiest of His servants.

Chapter XXXII

THE ROSARY

Repetition in prayer is a very ancient custom. It would seem to be natural for man to recite his prayers over and over, especially when he is inspired by a spirit of earnest devotion. Whether he is returning thanks for favors received or offering petitions to God, he finds that the repeating of his prayers satisfies his religious instincts. This usually leads to a resolution to say a certain number of prayers daily; and then the utility of having some counting device suggests itself at once. Hence comes the string of beads which we call a Rosary.

The use of some means of counting prayers is not restricted to Catholics. The Brahmin of India or Thibet has his long rosary which he uses to measure his eternal repetitions of the praises of Buddha. The Mohammedan votary has his chaplet of ninety-nine beads, to count his fervent invocations to Allah.

Who Gave Us the Rosary? The devotion takes its name from the Latin "rosarium," a garden of roses, or a wreath of the same beautiful and symbolic flowers; or, according to some, more directly from the title "Mystical Rose," given to Mary in her Litany. It was established by St. Dominic, the famous founder of the Order of Preachers; and he testifies in his writings that he acted under the direction of the Blessed Mother of God. However, there are traces of somewhat similar methods of praying before his time, although they did not include any part of the Hail Mary, at least until about the twelfth century, when the first part of that beautiful prayer came into use. It seems strange to us Catholics who recite it so frequently, to learn that for more than eleven centuries our forefathers in the faith knew nothing of the Hail Mary, and that the latter part of that prayer was not added until some centuries later. Therefore, when the Rosary was invented, it was composed of the Our Father and the first part of the Hail Mary only, repeated probably much as we use them at the present day.

How Beads Came Into Use. As said above, devices for counting prayers were not new, even in St. Dominic's time. Many of the faithful in earlier ages could not read, and books were scarce and dear; and so they were accustomed to say repeatedly the few prayers they knew, especially the Our Father. We are told that the great Apostle of Ireland recited it a hundred times at intervals of a few hours during each day and night and he probably used some device to count these numerous prayers. The early hermits said it many times daily, and kept an account by passing small pebbles from one hand to the other. It soon occurred to some one that it would be well to fasten these pebbles together — and so came the beads. The soldiers of the Middle Ages, illiterate but often pious men, wore a heavy belt studded with rivets, and this formed a convenient means of counting prayers.

St. Dominic's Work. St. Dominic gave us the Rosary, although not precisely as we have it now; and his illustrious Order has always been full of zeal in the spreading of this devotion. He was a Spaniard, and about the year 1205 entered on the mission of preaching for the conversion of the Albigenses, a heretical sect which had arisen in southern France and northern Italy. Holy and eloquent as he was, he had little success, until he was instructed by the Blessed Virgin herself to cease his argumentative discourses, to teach the people to pray, and especially to propagate the devotion of the Rosary. Then a wave of faith and piety swept over these heretical provinces; and, before Dominic's death, hardly a vestige of the sect remained.

The devotion spread with great rapidity throughout the world, and has always been highly esteemed by the faithful in every walk of life. Many of the saints have had a wonderful love for this beautiful prayer. St. Alphonsus Liguori was most devoted to it. St. Francis de Sales recited it for an hour each day. All the spiritual writers have sounded its praises, and many indulgences have been granted to it by successive Pontiffs. St. Dominic called it "the rampart of the Church of God," "the Book of Life." In various papal briefs it has been described as "the salvation of Christians," "the dispeller of heresies," "the scourge of Satan" and "the promoter of God's glory."

The Rules about Beads. The Rosary is counted on beads, which are arranged in "decades," each consisting of an Our Father and ten Hail Marys — indicated by a large bead and ten smaller ones. These beads may be of any suitable substance not easily broken. Formerly glass beads were forbidden, but they may now be used and indulgenced if they are solid; hollow ones are not allowed, being too fragile. They must be provided with a crucifix or with a medal stamped with a cross, and they must have the proper number of beads, divided into decades. It is recommended that they should not be too elaborate in design, or too expensive in quality; devotion, and not vanity, should be the reason for using them.

Rosary

How to Say Them. The manner of reciting the Rosary varies somewhat in different countries. Among us it is customary to begin with the Apostles' Creed, an Our Father, three Hail Marys and a Glory be to the Father, followed by the five decades in order, with their mysteries (either mentioned or mentally considered) and with the "Hail, Holy Queen" at the end. But some of these prayers are not essential to the Rosary, nor necessary for the gaining of the indulgences. The Rosary, strictly speaking, consists of fifteen decades, of which five only need be said on any one day. Each decade is composed of one Our Father and ten Hail Marys, and should be recited orally while the corresponding mystery is meditated on, in order to gain the indulgences. Therefore the Creed, the preliminary Our Father and Hail Marys, all the repetitions of the "Glory be to the Father," and the "Hail, Holy Queen" are not necessary parts of the Rosary.

The Mysteries. The Incarnation of our Blessed Lord is the central point in the world's history. The Son of God became man that He might redeem us; and the meditations connected with the Rosary are made on the principal events in that work of redemption, in order that honor may be paid to Him as our Saviour, and to His Blessed Mother as the most important auxiliary in affecting our salvation.

The meditations on the fifteen decades are divided into three classes. The joyful mysteries comprise the events from the Annunciation to the Finding in the Temple. The sorrowful mysteries recall the sufferings and death of our Saviour. The glorious mysteries extend from His Resurrection to the Coronation of Mary in Heaven.

The mysteries should be taken in turn, according to the days of the week — the joyful on Monday and Thursday; the sorrowful on Tuesday and Friday; the glorious on Wednesday and Saturday. On Sundays the mysteries assigned will depend upon the season of the year. During Advent and after Christmas the joyful should be meditated upon; during Lent, the sorrowful; during the rest of the year, the glorious.

"I cannot say the Rosary devoutly. It is so long that I become distracted." This is a common complaint, and arises from the fact that many try to recite it without meditation on the mysteries. The mere repetition of the prayers is likely to become monotonous — and it does not gain the special indulgences which are attached to the beads. For these the meditation is strictly required.

The Indulgences of the Rosary. The spiritual benefits of the Rosary are very numerous, and are different in some respects from those granted to other devotions. They are attached directly to the beads themselves, and are gained only by those for whose use the beads were blessed. The forms of blessing by which they are imparted are of three kinds — the Dominican, the Brigittine and the Apostolic, of which the last is the one most generally given. All the priests of this in this country have faculties for bestowing the Apostolic indulgences, which are as follows:

Every time that the Rosary is recited on one's own blessed beads (provided that it be done at least once a week) an indulgence of one hundred days is gained. A person who is in the habit of reciting the beads once a week or oftener may, by a good Confession and worthy Communion and by praying for the intention of the Holy Father, gain a plenary indulgence on any of the principal feasts of our Lord, of the Blessed Virgin and of the Apostles; also on Trinity Sunday, Pentecost and All Saints' Day. Complying with the same conditions on any other day, he may gain a partial indulgence, varying form one hundred days to seven years, according to the feast celebrated on that day. All these indulgences are applicable to the souls in Purgatory.

THE SACRAMENTALS

Assuredly it is profitable to say the Rosary. Well may we resolve to be faithful to this devotion. Well may we do our part in that chorus of praise — sending up daily that beautiful homage which consists not only in the repetition of prayers, but in salutary meditation on the great events in the lives of Jesus our Saviour and of Mary, His Mother and ours.

NOTE. — Many other forms of beads for the counting of prayers have come into use through the devotion of the faithful, and have been approved by the Church. Space will not permit going into details concerning them. Among the better known are the Brigittine beads, consisting of seven Our Fathers in honor of the sorrows and joys of the Blessed Virgin, and sixty-three Hail Marys to commemorate the years of her life; a similar rosary in use amount the Franciscans, with seventy-two Hail Marys, based on another tradition of Mary's age; the Crown of our Saviour, with thirty-three Our Fathers in honor of the years of our Lord's life; and five Hail Marys in honor of His sacred Wounds; the beads of the Five Wounds, established by the Passionist Fathers, approved in 1823 and 1851, consisting of five divisions, each having five Glories in honor of Christ's Wounds, and one Hail Mary in commemoration of the Sorrowful Mother; the beads of the Immaculate Conception and the Crosier beads.

Chapter XXXIII

SCAPULARS – I

THIS chapter will be devoted to the history and description of a sacramental which, in its different forms, is in very general use among Catholics, and which is a channel of great graces and spiritual benefits, inasmuch as it gives its users a share in the merits and prayers of great associations of holy men and women.

Monk with Scapular

The word *scapular* is from a Latin word which means literally the shoulder-blade. In many of the religious orders, such as the Carmelites and Benedictines, a garment is worn called a scapular, which forms a part of the monastic habit. It is a long piece of cloth, varying in color according to the order, with an opening for the head, and hanging down in front and at the back from the shoulders almost to the ground. It is worn over the monk's gown, and is open at the sides. In some religious orders the sides are fastened together under the arms; in others, formerly, there were hanging flaps which covered the shoulders, thus making the whole somewhat like a cross; and sometimes a cowl was attached, which could be drawn over the head.

A Symbolic Yoke. It is a curious fact that the original scapular of the monks undoubtedly was developed from a working garment or apron, such as was worn in those days by laborers. The monks found such a covering useful in their toil in the fields, to protect their monastic habit; and it was only about the eleventh century that it was recognized as a part of the religious garb and was blessed and imposed at the reception of a candidate. Then its use became a symbol of the burden of the monastic life. It was called, in the language of the Ritual, "the yoke of Christ," "the cross" and "the shield"; and as the obligations of the religious life were never to be laid aside, so (in many religious communities) the scapular was never to be removed, but was to be worn at night as well as during the day.

The Scapulars of the Third Orders. In the pious times which we call the Middle Ages, many devout lay persons were permitted to join the religious orders as "oblates" — that is, they remained in the world, but assisted regularly or frequently at the monastic services, united their prayers with those of the monks, and partook of the spiritual benefits of the devotions and good works of the order. These often received the religious garb, which some of them wore constantly; but gradually the custom prevailed of wearing it only at divine service. It was looked upon as a great privilege to die in the monastic habit and to be buried in it; and frequently it was given to those who were dying or was placed upon the bodies of the dead.

In later times it was found to be more convenient to dispense with the rest of the religious garb and to wear the scapular, much reduced in size, under the clothing. Thus it has come to pass that the associations of the laity known as "Third Orders," such as those connected with the Franciscans and Dominicans, wear to-day as their badge a so-called "large scapular" made of woolen cloth and measuring about 5 by 2½ inches. That of the Franciscans, often called simply the Scapular of St. Francis, is brown, gray or black in color, and has usually a picture of the Saint and one of the church of Portiuncula, where he was favored with a vision. Those who belong to these Third Orders must wear the scapular constantly in order to partake of the indulgences and privileges.

The Small Scapulars. Like the "large scapulars" for the laity, the first small scapulars were derived from the monastic habit. Many pious laymen associated themselves with various religious communities, that thereby they might participate in the good works and consequent merits of those who had consecrated themselves to God. It was deemed proper to form these devout persons into societies whose badge was a miniature of the scapular of the order. These societies or confraternities became sources of great good, and were rapidly extended throughout the Catholic world.

There are now eighteen small scapulars in use among Catholics. The early history of some of them is, to a great extent, obscure; but it is likely that the oldest of them is the Scapular of Mount Carmel. Each of the small scapulars consists of two pieces of woolen cloth, about two inches wide and a little longer, connected by two strings or bands so that when these rest on the shoulders one piece hangs ant the breast and the other at the back. The bands need not be of the same color as the two pieces, except in the case of the Red Scapular. On each half of the scapular pictures or emblems are usually sewn or painted, and for some scapulars they are essential. While the two parts of the scapular must be of woolen cloth, these decorations may be of other material, such as silk or linen. Some of the faithful may imagine that the picture is the scapular, or at least adds to its efficacy. This is a mistaken idea. While a picture or emblem is necessary in some cases, the scapular is the woolen cloth, and richness of ornament does not enhance its religious value in any way.

The Scapular of Mount Carmel. In describing the various kinds of scapulars we shall first consider that which is best known — the "brown scapular" of our Lady of Mount Carmel. A beautiful story is told of its origin. In the thirteenth century there lived at Cambridge, in England, a holy man named Simon Stock, the Superior-General of the Carmelite order. He was a man of such sanctity, wisdom and prudence that he was afterwards canonized by the Church. He is said to have declared that on the sixteenth of July, 1251, the Blessed Virgin appeared to him and presented him with a scapular, telling him that it was a special sign of her favor; that he who dies clothed with it shall be preserved from eternal punishment; that it is a badge of salvation, a shield against danger and a pledge of her protection.

Scapular of Mt. Carmel

Do we Catholics believe that this vision was vouchsafed to the holy Carmelite? We may — but we are not obliged to do so. There is little or no historical evidence that the small scapular was known so far back as the thirteenth century; in its present form, at least, it is probably of much later origin. Nevertheless, the account of St. Simon's vision remains a pious and praiseworthy tradition; that is, it is quite credible that the Saint was supernaturally assured of the protection of the Blessed Virgin for all who should wear this badge. This vision has been accepted as genuine by several Pontiffs, and has been cited by them as a reason for the granting of indulgences to those who wear the scapular.

The Scapular Privileges. The above promise is what is known as the "first privilege" of the Carmelite order, and it amounts to this: That all who out of true love and veneration for the Blessed Virgin constantly wear the scapular in a spirit of faith after they have been properly invested in it, shall enjoy the protection of the Mother of God, especially as regards their eternal welfare. If even a sinner wears this badge through life, not presumptuously relying on it as a miraculous charm, but trusting in the power and goodness of Mary, he may hope that through her intercession he will obtain the graces necessary for true conversion and for perseverance.

The Sabbatine Indulgence. The second privilege of the scapular is what is called the Sabbatine (Saturday) Indulgence. There has been much discussion concerning it, and its existence has been denied by many. According to those who uphold the genuineness of this indulgence, the Blessed Virgin assured Pope John XXII that any wearer of the scapular who shall have complied regularly with certain conditions will be released promptly from Purgatory, especially on the first Saturday after his death. Concerning this privilege, as stated, there is considerable doubt. Several Pontiffs seem to have been in favor of it. Benedict XIV and Paul V granted permission to the Carmelite Fathers to preach it to the people, and thereby would seem to have indirectly sanctioned it. "The faithful can believe that the Blessed Virgin will help by her continued assistance and her merits, particularly on Saturdays, the souls of the members of the Scapular Confraternity who have died in the grace of God, if in life they wore the scapular, observed chastity according to their state of life, and recited the Office of the Blessed Virgin or observed the fasts of the Church, practising abstinence on Wednesdays and Saturdays.

About this supposed privilege, then, we cannot speak decisively. It may be true, or it may not be. It is one of the pious beliefs which have not been expressly confirmed by the Church, even though a qualified or partial approval may have been given by individual Pontiffs. We may readily believe that our Blessed Mother consoles with special affection those who have worn the scapular, her livery, while on earth, and are now in Purgatory — especially if they have been chaste and devout — and that she will endeavor to bring them speedily to Heaven. But whether this will take place on the Saturday after death is another question.

Investing in the Brown Scapular. Among us, the investing in this scapular often takes place at the time of First Communion or Confirmation, but there is no rule to at effect. The investiture may be performed for infants; and after they have come to the use of reason they do not need a renewal of it.

Who can perform the investing? This was originally restricted to the priests of the Carmelite Order; but for many years our bishops have had the power of giving this faculty to all their priests. Therefore to-day, in our country, any priest having ordinary faculties in a diocese can vest in this scapular.

The form to be used is that prescribed by Pope Leo XIII in 1888, which is shorter than the one formerly in use. After a few introductory versicles and responses a prayer is offered to our Blessed Lord, asking him to bless this habit which is to be worn for love of Him and of His Mother. The scapular is then placed on the shoulders of the recipient with an appropriate formula, as follows: "Receive this blessed habit, imploring the most holy Virgin, that through her merits thou mayest wear it without stain, and that she may defend thee from all adversity and lead thee to everlasting life. Amen."

The priest then declares that, by virtue of the power granted to him, the person invested is received into the Scapular Confraternity and is entitled to share in the spiritual benefits of the Order of Mount Carmel. And after another prayer to God asking a blessing on the new member and praying that he may receive the aid of our Mother Mary at the hour of death, he is sprinkled with holy water — which concludes the ceremony of investiture in this scapular.

Scapular Rules. The scapular may be given in any place — not necessarily in church; thus the sick may receive it in their beds. It must be worn so that one part hangs on the breast, the other on the back, with a band on each shoulder. If worn or carried otherwise, no indulgences are granted. It may be worn under all the clothing or over some of it; that is, inside or outside of the undergarments.

After having been once invested, it is never necessary to have a scapular blessed. When one is worn out or is lost, the wearer simply puts on another without ceremony.

On any except the Red Scapular any suitable ornaments or emblems may be sewn or embroidered in another material than wool; these neither add to nor take away from the value of the scapular. In the case of some scapulars, the investment means reception into a confraternity; the blessing of the scapular and its imposition must then take place at the same time as the enrollment.

The scapular is intended to give its wearer a share in certain spiritual benefits and privileges. It must, therefore, be worn constantly. Laying it aside for a short time — an hour or a day — probably does not deprive one of these advantages; but if the wearing of it has been neglected for a long time, no indulgences are gained during that time. As soon, however, as the scapular is resumed, the spiritual benefits begin again for the wearer.

The "Five Scapulars." It is permitted to attach several scapulars to the same pair of strings or bands, provided that the scapulars be different from one another and that both parts of each be used. It has long been customary with certain devout persons to combine five of the best-known scapulars. Those generally used are: The scapular of the Most Blessed Trinity, which is white, blue and red; the brown scapular of the Carmelites; that of the Servites, called the Seven Dolors, which is black; the blue scapular of the Immaculate Conception, and the red scapular of the Passion. Each of these will be described briefly in our next chapter.

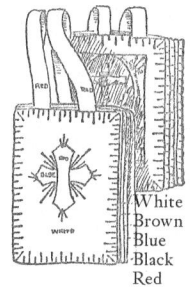

The Five Scapulars

When these are used together, it is necessary that the bands should be red — because that color is strictly required for the last-mentioned, the red scapular of the Passion; and it is customary to wear this scapular uppermost, so that the images prescribed for it may be visible, and that of the Blessed Trinity undermost, so that the red and blue cross may not be hidden by the other scapulars.

As five scapulars worn together make rather a bulky appendage, the use of them has become less common of late, especially since the approval of the scapular medal as a substitute for any one or all of them, provided that it be lawfully blessed for that purpose — as will be explained later on.

Benefits of the Brown Scapular. To come back to the Scapular of Mount Carmel — what are the advantages and privileges which we gain by using it? All those who have been invested in this scapular become sharers in all the fruits of the good works of the great religious order of the Carmelites — their prayers, meditations, Masses, penances, charitable works, etc. More than this — by a special decree of the Holy See they partake in a special manner in all the good works performed in the whole Catholic Church by clergy and religions and laity. After death they share in all prayers of the Carmelites and in the weekly Mass which every priest of that order offers for the deceased members of the Scapular Confraternity.

Many indulgences may be gained — a plenary one on the day of receiving the scapular, under the usual conditions; another at the hour of death; and all Masses said for deceased wearers of the scapular have the advantage of a "privileged altar" — that is, a plenary indulgence is gained for the person for whom the Mass is offered. Besides these, there are many partial indulgences.

Many of the other scapulars, also, give to their wearers a share in the good works of some religious order, and in the merits gained by the members of the confraternity of that scapular.

Scapular Medal

The Scapular Medal. By a regulation made by Pope Pius X in 1910, it is permitted to wear a medal instead of one or more of the small scapulars. There is a story — which may be true or may not be — that the attention of the kindly Pontiff was first called to this matter by an African missionary who told how his naked negro Catholics found the wearing of the scapular difficult in the thorny jungles of the Congo. The permission intended at first for these dusky children of the Church, to use a medal as a substitute, was finally given to all Catholics. The wearing of several scapulars is inconvenient and possibly unsanitary, and this medal can replace any or all of them; that is, all persons who have been validly invested with a blessed woolen scapular may use the scapular medal instead — and if they have been invested with several, the medal will take the place of all if properly blessed. This refers only to the small scapulars, for the medal is not a substitute for the so-called "large scapulars."

As said above, a new scapular may replace an old one without a blessing — but this is not the case with the medal. It must be blessed; and this can be done only by a priest, who has faculties to bless and invest with the corresponding scapular. If the medal is to be used instead of several scapulars, a blessing must be given to it for each scapular which it is intended to replace. For each blessing the Church requires merely the sign of the cross.

The scapular medal must have on one side a representation of our Lord with His Sacred Heart, and on the other an image of the Blessed Virgin. It may be made of any kind of hard metal.

How is it to be worn? There is no rule about this. It may be hung from the neck, carried in the pocket or purse, or worn in any desired manner. If worn or carried constantly, it gives a share in all the spiritual privileges that would come from the wearing of the scapular or scapulars which it replaces.

Chapter XXXIV

SCAPULARS – II

Having considered the origin and use of the Scapular of Mount Carmel and the regulations concerning it, we shall now give a brief history and description of each of the other scapulars which have received the approval of the Church.

The Scapular of the Most Blessed Trinity. This scapular is of white woolen cloth, bearing a blue and red cross, usually only on the front portion. It is the special badge of the confraternity of the same name. When Pope Innocent II, in 1198, was considering the matter of approving the Order of the Trinitarians, an angel is said to have appeared to him, clothed in a white robe and bearing on his breast a cross of red and blue. This was accordingly assigned to the new community as their habit. Later, when the faithful sought to associate themselves with this order, a confraternity was established with this scapular as its badge of membership. Many indulgences have been granted to those who wear it, and these were reaffirmed by Pope Leo XIII in 1899.

The Scapular of Our Lady of Ransom. The "Order of our Lady of Mercy for the Redemption of Captives" was founded by St. Peter Nolasco about 1240. The members of a confraternity which has been affiliated to it are invested with a scapular of white cloth, bearing on its front half a picture of Our Lady of Ransom. The General of the order can give to other priests the faculty of investing with this scapular, and those who wear it receive the benefit of many indulgences, which were renewed and approved by the Holy See in 1868.

The Scapular of the Seven Dolors. One of the great religious orders founded in the thirteenth century was that of the Servites; and soon after its institution many of the faithful sought a share in its good works and prayers. A confraternity was established in honor of the Seven Dolors or Sorrows of Mary. Their scapular is black, and often bears on the front portion a picture of the Mother of Sorrows. To those who wear it constantly many indulgences have been given, which were reaffirmed by Pope Leo XIII in 1888.

The Black Scapular of the Passion. This is the emblem of the confraternity associated with the Passionist Fathers, who were founded by St. Paul of the Cross nearly two hundred years ago. It is related that he, in a vision, received the black habit of the order with its badge, which consists of a heart bearing the inscription "Jesu XPI Passio," and below, "sit semper in cordibus nostris" which is, in English, "May the Passion of Jesus Christ be always in our hearts." The letters XPI are Greek, of which the Latin equivalent is CHRI, an abbreviation of "Christi." This device is used on the black scapular of the Passion, on the front half only. At various times indulgences have been granted to the faithful who wear it, and these were last approved by Pius IX in 1877.

The Scapular of "The Help of the Sick." A community founded by St. Camillus, the patron of hospitals, has long venerated a picture of the Blessed Virgin which is preserved in the church of St. Mary Magdalen at Rome. This painting is said to be the work of Fra Angelico, and before it St. Pius V prayed for the victory of the Christian fleet at Lepanto, when Europe was threatened with a great Moslem invasion. A confraternity, founded in 1860, has taken this picture as the distinguishing mark of its scapular, which is of black woolen cloth, the front part bearing a copy of the picture and the other half having a small cross of red cloth sewn on. Indulgences were granted to the confraternity by Popes Pius IX and Leo XIII.

The Scapular of St. Benedict. This is also black, and one of the parts has a picture of St. Benedict, although this is not essential. The confraternity of St. Benedict is of English origin, and was founded about fifty years ago, with the object of giving the members a share in the good works of the great Benedictine order. It received a grant of indulgences from Pope Leo XIII in 1883.

The Scapular of the Immaculate Conception. The order of Theatine nuns was founded by a saintly woman, Ursula Benicasa, who has been declared Blessed by the Church. She affirmed that the habit which she and her community were to wear was revealed to her in a vision by our Blessed Lord. She besought Him that the graces promised to the new order might be extended also to all who would wear a scapular of the Immaculate Conception. The use of this scapular was approved by Clement X and by succeeding Popes, and the various indulgences granted for it were renewed by Gregory XVI in 1845. It is of blue woolen cloth; on one of the parts is a picture of the Immaculate Conception, and on the other is the name of Mary.

The Scapular of the Precious Blood. Members of the Confraternity of the Precious Blood can wear either a red girdle which is blessed by the priest who enrolls them, or a special scapular of red woolen cloth; but there is no indulgence granted for so doing. For this scapular it is merely defined that it shall be red; but usually on one part of it there is a representation of a chalice containing the Precious Blood of our Lord and adored by angels. The other half is without symbol or picture.

The Red Scapular of the Passion. This owes its origin to a vision which our Lord vouchsafed to a member of the Sisters of Charity of St. Vincent de Paul, in 1846. To her it was promised that all who would wear this scapular would receive every Friday a great increase in the virtues of faith, hope and charity. The faculty of blessing it belongs to the order of men founded by St. Vincent, known as the Priests of the Mission, or the Lazarists. Their Superior-General, however, can give this faculty to other priests. Several indulgences were granted to the wearers of this scapular by Pius IX in 1847. Both the scapular and the bands are of red woolen material. On one half is a picture of our Lord on the cross, with the implements of the passion and the words "Holy Passion of our Lord Jesus Christ, save us." On the other are shown the Hearts of Jesus and Mary, a cross and the inscription "Sacred Hearts of Jesus and Mary, protect us."

The Scapular of the Immaculate Heart of Mary. This scapular was sanctioned and endowed with indulgences by Pius IX in 1877, and further indulgences were granted for its use under Pius X in 1907. It is the special badge of the religious congregation known as the Sons of the Immaculate Heart of Mary. It is of white woolen cloth, one part being ornamented with a picture of the burning heart of Mary, out of which grows a lily; the heart is encircled by a wealth of roses and pierced by a sword.

The Scapular of St. Michael, Archangel. This is the only scapular which is not oblong in shape. Each half of it has the form of a small shield. One of these is of blue cloth, the other black; and the connecting bands are also one blue, one black. On each part is a picture of St. Michael slaying the dragon, with the words "Quis ut Deus?" ("Who is like to God?"), which is the meaning of the name Michael. It is the special habit of the Archconfraternity of the Scapular of St. Michael, which was founded in 1878 and received various indulgences from Leo XIII.

The Scapular of the Mother of Good Counsel. This is one of the newest scapulars. Its use is promoted chiefly by the Augustinian Fathers, and the faculty of blessing it belongs to them, though their Superior can give this privilege to other priests. It was approved by Leo XIII in 1893, and indulgences were granted by him to those who wear it. This is a white scapular, of the usual form, having on one half a picture of the Mother of Good Counsel (after a well-known painting in an Augustinian church at Genazzano, Italy), and on the other the papal crown and keys.

The Scapular of St. Joseph. This is the scapular of the Capuchin Fathers, who received faculties for blessing it and investing the faithful in it in the year 1898; but previously, since about 1880, it had been used and approved in certain dioceses. It is made of two pieces of woolen cloth, violet in color, connected by white bands; to each of these pieces is sewn a square of gold-colored cloth, which may be linen, silk, or cotton. On the front half a picture is shown on the gold cloth, representing St. Joseph with the Child Jesus and the staff of lilies, with the inscription "St. Joseph, Patron of the Church, pray for us." On the other part is the papal crown, with the dove, symbolic of the Holy Ghost; under these is a cross and the keys of Peter, with the words "Spiritus Domini doctor ejus" — ("The Spirit of the Lord is his guide").

The Scapular of the Sacred Heart of Jesus. Many Catholics wear the well-known badge of the Sacred Heart on an oval piece of woolen cloth, and some have a mistaken idea that this is a scapular. It is merely a pious emblem, the wearing of which was recommended by the Blessed Margaret Mary Alacoque. There is, however, a real scapular of the Sacred Heart, which was introduced in France about 1870 and was approved in 1900. It is of the usual form and material, white in color. One part bears a picture of the Heart of our Blessed Lord, the other that of the Blessed Virgin under the title of Mother of Mercy. Leo XIII granted indulgences to those who wear it.

The Scapular of the Hearts of Jesus and Mary. This somewhat resembles the red scapular of the Passion, described above, except in color. It was approved in 1900, and owes its origin to the Daughters of the Sacred Heart, a religious community founded at Antwerp in 1873. Indulgences for the wearers were granted by Popes Leo XIII and Pius X. The scapular is of white woolen material, having on one half a picture of the Sacred Hearts of Jesus and Mary with the implements of the Passion. On the other part is sewn a red cross.

The Scapular of St. Dominic. The use of this scapular is fostered by the Dominican Order, but the General of that society can give other priests the faculty of blessing it. It was approved in 1903 by Pius X, who granted an indulgence of three hundred days to wearers every time that they devoutly kiss it. White wool is the material; no ornaments are required, but it usually bears on one part an image of St. Dominic kneeling before a crucifix, and on the other that of Blessed Reginald receiving the Dominican habit from the hands of the Blessed Virgin.

The Scapular of the Holy Face. This, the last of the scapulars, is of white cloth, with the well-known picture of the Face of our Lord which is connected with the tradition of Veronica. It is worn by the members of the Archconfraternity of the Holy Face — who, however, can wear instead a medal or cross with the same emblem. It is simply recommended to the members of the society, and there is no indulgence for its use.

We see, then, how many means our Church has granted to her children for partaking of the merits of great religious orders and confraternities. She has multiplied the scapulars so that each individual may find one or more that appeal to his devotional spirit; and she has enriched nearly all of them with indulgences for the wearers. They are uniforms of great societies, the members of which are banded together for the same ends — to glorify

God, to honor His Mother, and to benefit one another mutually by the gaining of merits which are shared by all.

Chapter XXXV

THE AGNUS DEI

In every form of religion, even in the grossest paganism, it has been customary to consider certain objects as holy, and to use them as means of supposed protection from evil. Among the ancient Romans such objects were employed for children, to guard them from all malign influences. These charms were of various kinds — images of the gods, herbs, acrostics formed of letters arranged in mystic fashion, and many others.

Now, to put one's trust in things of this sort, to imagine that inanimate objects such as these could protect against disease or other evil, was undoubtedly nothing but gross superstition. How is it, then, that we Catholics are permitted by our Church to have amulets of many kinds, such as crosses, scapulars, medals and the Agnus Dei? Is this superstition? No; because the Catholic, unlike the pagan, does not trust in them on account of any inherent virtue which he imagines them to have, or any supposed magical power. He puts his trust only in the living God, Who, through the prayers of His Church, blesses these material things and bids her children to keep and use them as memorials of Him, as symbols of His merciful providence. Through the Church's benediction these objects become vehicles of grace; they bring the divine protection upon such of the faithful as use them with earnest faith, ardent charity and firm confidence in God.

What is the Agnus Dei? The sacramental of our Church which is called an Agnus Dei, a "Lamb of God," is a small flat piece of wax impressed with the figure of a lamb. These are blessed at stated seasons by the Pope, and never by any other person. They are sometimes round, sometimes oval or oblong, and of varying diameters. The lamb generally bears a cross or a banner, and often the figure of some saint or the name and coat-of-arms of the Pope are stamped on the other side. The Agnus Dei is usually enclosed in a small leather cover, round or heart-shaped, so that it may be preserved, and is intended to be

Agnus Dei Wax

worn suspended from the neck.

History of the Agnus Dei. The origin of this sacramental is a matter of great obscurity. When the people of Italy and other countries had been converted from idolatry, they retained some of their belief in charms and amulets; and it is possible that the Agnus Dei was devised as a substitute for these relics of paganism. Instead of attempting to repress totally a practice which was misguided indeed, but which showed an instinctive reliance on higher powers, the Church in many instances took the religious customs with which the people were familiar, and made these customs Christian. She eliminated all that savored of idolatry, and substituted for the superstitious charms of paganism the emblem of our Saviour, the Lamb of God.

They were first used in Rome, and it is possible that they go back as far as the final overthrow of pagan worship in that city, about the fifth century. Indeed, there is some evidence that they were in use even a little earlier; for in the tomb of Maria Augusta, wife of the Emperor Honorius, who died in the fourth century, was found an object made of wax and much like our Agnus Deis of the present time. And we know, moreover, that it was customary in those days for the people to obtain fragments of the paschal candle after it had been extinguished on Ascension Day, and to keep them as a safeguard against tempest and pestilence. From this pious custom the use of waxen Agnus Deis probably arose. They began to come into common use at the beginning of the ninth century, and from that time we find frequent mention of them. They were often sent by Popes as presents to sovereigns or distinguished personages. The use of them spread widely, and up to the time of the Reformation they were everywhere regarded as an important sacramental of the Church. In the penal laws against Catholics in England, in the reign of Queen Elizabeth, they were specified as a "popish trumpery," and the possession of them or the importation of them into the country was a felony.

Blessed by the Pope. Centuries ago, at Rome, the Agnus Deis were made by the archdeacon of St. Peter's of clean wax mingled with chrism, on the morning of Holy Saturday; and on the following Saturday they were distributed to the people. After a time it became customary for the Pope himself to attend to this, and at the present day the blessing is always imparted by him. What is called the "great consecration" of Agnus Deis takes place only in the first year of each Pontiff's reign and every seventh year thereafter. The pieces of wax are now prepared beforehand by certain monks, without the use of chrism. On the Wednesday of Easter week these are brought to the Holy Father, who dips them into water mingled with chrism and balsam, with certain appropriate prayers. On the following Saturday the distribution takes place with great solemnity, when the Pope, after the "Agnus Dei" of the Mass, puts a packet of them into the inverted mitre of each cardinal and bishop present, and the remaining ones are sent to prelates and religious communities in all parts of the world.

A Symbol of Our Lord. The meaning of the Agnus Dei is best understood from the prayers used in the solemn blessing by the Holy Father. The wax, white and pure, typifies the virgin flesh of Christ. The lamb suggests the idea of a victim offered in sacrifice. The banner signifies the victory of our Lord over sin and death. As the blood of the paschal lamb protected the Israelites from the destroying angel, so shall this emblem of the Lamb of God protect him who wears it from many kinds of evil. The mercy of God is implored for the faithful who piously use and reverence the Agnus Dei; and He is besought to give His blessing to it, so that the sight or touch of the lamb impressed on it may guard us against the spirits of evil, against sickness and pestilence, against tempest, fire and flood; that it may strengthen us against temptations; that those who use it may be preserved from a sudden and unprovided death. Also in the prayers it is especially recommended to women who are expecting motherhood.

The Agnus Dei, then, represents our Blessed Lord; and he who would derive full benefit from its use must imitate Him in His lamblike virtues — innocence, meekness, indifference to the world. The angelic virtue of innocence — spotless purity of soul and body — is symbolized both by the wax and the lamb. He who wears it should be sinless. The lamb is meek, and the Lamb of God has told us to learn of Him, because He is meek and humble of heart. The lamb is "dumb before the shearer," teaching us contempt for the world, silence under its persecutions, and indifference to its judgments and its vanities.

How it is Worn. There is no obligation to use the Agnus Dei. There is no special manner in which it must be worn, such as we have for the scapular. The Agnus Dei may be attached to the latter, or otherwise suspended from the neck, or it may be carried in any other way about the person. Though it is an important sacramental, there are no indulgences attached to its use. Its efficacy comes from the fact that it is a symbol of our Lord, blessed by His Vicar upon earth. And we would do well to remember that it does not derive its value from the beauty of its outside covering. Whether this be plain or elaborate is of no importance whatever. Nor should any attempt be made to "have it blessed." All Agnus Deis are blessed; they would not be Agnus Deis if they had not received the benediction of the Holy Father.

The solemnity with which this beautiful sacramental is blessed and distributed by the Sovereign Pontiff, the graces which are besought in the prayers by which it is consecrated, the benefits derived from its pious use, and the symbolical meaning which it possesses — all these show us that in the Agnus Dei we have a very efficacious means of grace and a powerful protection against the evils that threaten our bodies and souls.

Chapter XXXVI

PALMS

The beautiful ceremony of the blessing and distributing of palms on Palm Sunday is a remembrance of our Saviour's entrance into Jerusalem a few days before His death. As He approached the city a great throng came forth to meet Him — some, perhaps, in a spirit of mere curiosity, to see the far-famed prophet and wonder-worker; others because they hoped to see some evidence of His miraculous power; and some because they believed in Him and recognized Him as the long-expected Redeemer.

The Gospels tell us that the people conducted Jesus in triumph through the city gate, spreading their garments before Him as a mark of homage, and that they went before Him in a joyful procession, carrying palms and chanting hosannas of praise.

The Eastern palm which they used is the date-tree, which forms a distinctive feature of every Oriental scene; and it must have been a graceful and inspiring sight to see the vast throng waving the beautiful palm branches as they marched towards the Holy City.

A Symbol of Victory. The palm is emblematic of victory, just as the olive-branch is of peace; and the custom of using it to denote triumph and joy seems to have been widespread. Among the pagan nations victorious generals and conquering armies decked themselves with the spreading branches of the palm-tree in their triumphal processions; and among the Jews the palm was used to express rejoicing, especially for the celebration of the harvest festival known as the Feast of Tabernacles. In Christian art the palm-branch is often introduced in pictures of martyr-saints, to signify the victory which they have gained and the triumph they are enjoying. And as the palm-tree is a shade tree and produces fruit, it symbolizes well the protection of Divine Providence and the giving of grace.

The genuine Oriental date-palm is, of course, the most suitable for the ceremony of Palm Sunday, but as this is practically unobtainable in many parts of the world, the Church allows the use of other kinds of branches. She states in the rules of the Missal that they may be of "palm or olive or other trees." Some of our readers will remember when spruce or hemlock was used commonly in our churches, and it is only of late years that the Southern palmetto has come into vogue. It is more suitable, because it considerably resembles the real palm.

The History of the Blessing. Palms are blessed and distributed to the faithful on only one day of the year — Palm Sunday. This, of course, changes in date from year to year, according to the date of Easter.

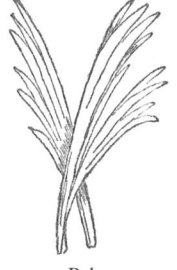
Palm

It is uncertain just when this beautiful custom began. In old Church calendars and other books there are various references which would lead us to suppose that it was practised early in the fifth century, but there is nothing very definite about it until the time of the English saint, the Venerable Bede, about the year 700. It is likely that the use of palms began in the "Miracle-Plays," or reproductions of the Passion of our Lord, which were common in the early Middle Ages. Just as at the Passion Play of Oberammergau at the present day, the actors in these earlier religious dramas endeavored to represent all the details of our Saviour's life and sufferings, and it is probable that the triumphal entry into Jerusalem was shown on the stage with the use of palms. Then, following her usual custom of blessing anything intended for religious purposes, the Church began to give a solemn benediction to the palms and made them a sacramental.

The Prayers of the Blessing. The prayers used by the priest in the blessing of the palms are full of beautiful sentiment and expressiveness. The ceremony takes place before the High Mass. The celebrant wears a cope of purple color, denoting penance, and reads from the Old Testament the account of the journey of the Children of Israel through the desert to Mount Sinai, where they found twelve springs of water and seventy palm-trees, and where God promised them manna from heaven. Then comes a Gospel, taken from St. Matthew, describing the entry of our

Blessed Lord into Jerusalem, followed by a prayer that we may gain the palm of victory. Then a beautiful Preface is said or sung, asking a blessing on the palms and on those who take and keep them in a spirit of devotion, and referring to the olive-branch brought by the dove to Noah in the ark and to the palm as an emblem of triumph.

In past centuries the procession on Palm Sunday was a real procession — not merely around the church, but to some distant church, or "station," where a Mass was said. The blessing of the palms, as we have it now, shows the skeleton of this stational Mass, for it contains many parts of a Mass — an Introit, a Collect, an Epistle, a Gospel, a Preface, a Sanctus, etc. — and still it is no longer a Mass.

The proper way for distributing the palms, as prescribed by the Church, is at the altar-railing; but on account of the large congregations in many of our churches it is usual to have them given to the people in the pews. They should be held in the hand during the reading of the Passion of our Lord in the Mass of Palm Sunday.

The palms which have not been distributed are preserved until the following year, and, being then dry, are burned to obtain the ashes for the ceremony of Ash Wednesday, when they are placed on our foreheads with the solemn admonition to remember that we are dust and shall return to dust — impressing upon us the stern truth that only by keeping ever in mind our last end and preparing for it may we hope to win the palm of final victory.

Chapter XXXVII

INCENSE

Our Holy Church has always recognized the value of rites and ceremonial observances, not only for increasing the solemnity of her services but for arousing a spirit of devotion in those who minister at them and those who attend them.

And because a religious practice happened to be of Jewish origin or had been used in the rites of paganism, the Church does not therefore look upon it as something to be necessarily condemned or forbidden. She has taken some of the details of her liturgy not only from the ceremonial law of Moses, but even from pagan worship. On account of this, some of her more biased critics have asserted that "Romanism is nothing but Christianized paganism" — an accusation which reveals the inbred prejudices of those who can find no word of praise for aught that is taught or done by "the benighted Church of Rome."

Expressing Homage to the Deity. The Catholic Church knows that in every form of worship, in every effort of man to do homage to his concept of the Deity, there are many practices that are commendable, inasmuch as they are a good expression of religious sentiment, and she has adapted the best of these to the requirements of her ritual. Thus, for instance, we find in Catholic worship the use of holy water, which was not only a Jewish but a pagan practice; the wearing of medals and amulets, common to all religions of antiquity; and the use of incense at religious functions. It is concerning the last of these that we shall treat in this chapter.

The Incense and the Censer. What is incense? It is a granulated aromatic resin, obtained from certain trees in Eastern and tropical countries, especially from those of the terebinth family. When sprinkled upon a glowing coal in the "censer," it burns freely and emits an abundant white smoke of very fragrant odor. Various spices are sometimes mixed with the resin to increase its fragrance.

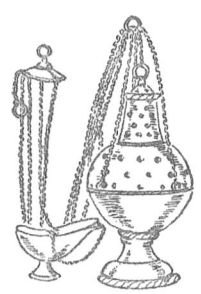

Censer and Boat

The censer is a vessel in the form of a bowl, provided with a cover, the whole being generally adorned with gilding and ornaments and suspended from chains, so that it may be swung to and fro for the better diffusion of the sweet odor. It is held in both hands when being used, elevated to the height of the eyes, while the left hand holds the ends of the chains against the breast. The censer is swung forward toward the person or thing to be incensed, once or oftener, according to the requirements of the rubrics.

The incense is kept in a vessel known as a "boat," from its peculiar shape, and is transferred to the censer by means of a small spoon.

Of Ancient Origin. What is the history of incense? First of all, we find in the Scriptures many references to its use in Jewish worship. In the sanctuary of the Tabernacle of God an altar was provided for the burning of incense, morning and night. It is thus described in the ritual which Moses gave to the Israelites, in the book of Exodus: "Take unto thee spices . . . of sweet savor and the clearest frankincense . . . and when thou hast beaten all into very small powder, thou shalt set of it before the Tabernacle. Most holy shall this incense be unto you." It is also mentioned in the Psalms and by the prophets Isaias, Jeremias and Malachias, as well as in the Gospel account of the vision of Zacharias, the aged priest, who was "offering incense in the temple of the Lord" when he received the promise of God that a son would be given to him.

In the ceremonies of pagan creeds incense had an important part. Its use is mentioned by Ovid and Virgil as a feature of the rites of Roman worship, being probably adopted from the Eastern nations with whom the Romans had come into contact. Among these, especially the Assyrians and Egyptians, it has been known almost from the dawn of history. The carvings of the tombs and temples of Egypt represent kings offering homage to the gods by burning incense in censers much like those used in our Catholic churches at the present day.

In Catholic Worship. When did the Church begin to use it? We do not know exactly. There is no evidence that it was employed in Christian worship until about the fifth century, although when we consider to what an extend it was used in the rites of Judaism and how many times it is mentioned in the Scriptures, it seems probable that incensing, as a part of the Catholic ceremonial, goes back to an earlier day. It came into use in the East before the Western or Latin Church adopted it, for the Orientals in the early centuries had a much more elaborate ritual than did the Roman Church. Incense was used at first at the Gospel of the Mass only, but in succeeding centuries other incensations were introduced, not only at the Mass but at other services of the Church.

At the present day the use of incense forms a rather prominent feature of the more solemn services of our Church. In our Latin rite it is not employed in private or "low" Masses, but in the so-called "solemn" Mass incensings take place at several parts of the services. A brief description of the prayers used will show clearly the meaning of the ceremony and the beautiful figurativeness of incense as a symbol of the prayers of God's faithful ascending before His throne.

Incense at Mass. Incense is used in solemn Masses at the Introit, the Gospel, the Offertory and the Elevation; but in Masses for the dead the first two incensings are omitted. At each of the times when the censer is to be used, fresh incense is put into it and is blessed, usually by the celebrant. At the Introit and the Gospel the blessing is simple: "Mayest thou be blessed by Him in Whose honor thou shalt be consumed. Amen." At the Offertory a more elaborate ceremonial is carried out. The blessing is given thus: "May the Lord, through the intercession of blessed Michael the Archangel standing at the right hand of the altar of incense, and of all His elect, deign to bless this incense and to accept it as an odor of sweetness. Through Christ our Lord. Amen." The celebrant then incenses the bread and wine which are upon the altar, with the words: "May this incense, blessed by Thee, ascend to Thee, O Lord; and may Thy mercy descend upon us." He next incenses the crucifix and the altar, saying, in the words of the 140th Psalm: "Let my prayer, O Lord, be directed as incense in Thy sight; the raising up of my hands as an evening sacrifice. Set a watch, O Lord, on my mouth and a door around my lips. Incline not my heart to evil words to make excuses in sins." And finally: "May the Lord kindle in us the fire of His love, and the flame of everlasting charity. Amen."

The censer is swung as a mark of respect before the celebrant, ministers and assisting clergy at a solemn Mass, and incense is used also in many of the public services of the Church — in processions, blessings and other functions, and in the "absolution" or obsequies for the dead. Not only persons but inanimate things are thus honored — things which are in themselves sacred, such as relics; things which have been previously blessed, such as crucifixes, altars and the book of the Gospels; and things to which a blessing is being given, such as bodies of the dead and sepulchers.

On Holy Saturday, when the paschal candle is solemnly blessed in each parish church, five grains of incense are inserted into it, each being encased usually in a piece of wax resembling a nail. These are fixed in the wax of the candle in the form of a cross.

When an altar or altar-stone is consecrated, grains of incense are burned upon it, and other grains are put into the "sepulchre," that is, the cavity containing the relics, thus symbolizing the prayers and intercession which will be offered in Heaven by the Saint whose sacred relics are enclosed within the altar on which the Holy Sacrifice of the Mass will be offered.

The Symbolism of Incense. The mystical meaning of incense is not difficult to comprehend. By its burning it symbolizes the zeal with which the faithful should be animated; by its sweet fragrance, the odor of Christian virtue; by its rising smoke, the ascent of prayer before the throne of the Almighty. As St. John tells us in the Apocalypse, or Book of Revelations: "The smoke of the incense of the prayers of the saints ascended before God from the hand of the Angel."

The use of incense, then, is a beautiful example of the wisdom of our Church, which adapts to our own purposes all that is good in every creed, all that will typify the spirit with which she wished her children to be animated, all that will aid them to attain to true fervor, all that will add solemnity to the worship which she offers to God.

Chapter XXXVIII

CHURCH BELLS

The sweet music of bells has given occasion to two of the most melodious poems in our English language — the weird and the beautiful "Bells" of Edgar Allan Poe, and the somewhat less inspired but very musical "Bells of Shandon," in which the Rev. Francis Mahoney, who wrote under the name of "Father Proud," immortalized the sweet chimes

> *That sound so grand on*
> *The pleasant waters of the River Lee.*

Bells in Ancient Times. The use of bells for general and even for religious purposes is of very ancient origin, although it is likely that in early ages they were of very rude form and imperfect sound, and that they were gradually developed into their present perfection.

They are said to have been used by the ancient Egyptians in the worship of their god Osiris; but these bells were small, and rather in the form of a flat gong. Moses, who had been educated in the priestly class of Egypt, introduced them into the ceremonial of the Jewish religion.

Among the Romans there is no trace of their employment for religious purposes, apart from the processions of rejoicing after victories. In these triumphal events, which were partly of a religious character, expressing gratitude to the gods for success in battle, bells were sometimes mounted in chariots and joyfully rung during the progress of the procession.

In Christian Churches. Bells came into use in our churches as early as the year 400, and their introduction is ascribed to Paulinus, bishop of Nola, a town of Campania, in Italy. Their use spread rapidly, as in those unsettled times the church-bell was useful not only for summoning the faithful to religious services, but also for giving an alarm when danger threatened. Their use was sanctioned in 604 by Pope Sabinian, and a ceremony for blessing them was established a little later. Very large bells, for church towers, were probably not in common use until the eleventh century.

In various museums of Europe many curious old bells are preserved, and particularly in Scotland and Ireland fine specimens may be seen of the ancient monastic bells of the Celtic abbeys. These are sometimes square in shape, and are made of bronze or iron sheets riveted together. Their sound, consequently, must have been discordant and far less powerful than that of our modern bells.

Bells were introduced into the Eastern churches about the ninth century and some of the largest in the world are to be found in the great cathedrals of Russia. The most enormous of these is the famous "Bell of Moscow," which, however, is not in condition to be rung, as a large piece is broken out of its side. It is about nineteen feet in height, and of nearly the same diameter. Moscow also boasts another gigantic bell, which weighs eighty tons and is nearly fourteen feet in diameter.

The largest bell on this side of the Atlantic is said to be that in the tower of the Church of Notre Dame in Montreal. It weighs nearly fifteen tons.

Chimes and Peals. In many European churches and in some of our own, beautiful chimes of bells have been installed, varying in number from eight to twelve or fourteen, and so arranged that the notes of the musical scale may be sounded upon them. In the old parish churches of England it is customary to ring the bells in a harmonious peal, in which all are rung at the same time, the volume of sound thus produced being enormous and the effect very beautiful, particularly at a distance.

Many of the bells used in churches are engraved with appropriate inscriptions, telling the various uses to which they are put. Some bear the title "Ave Maria," and are used especially for the Angelus; others have an invocation to St. Gabriel, the archangel of the Annunciation. On many of the bells in the old churches in England quaint verses were used, such as:

Men's death I tell by doleful knell;
Lightning and thunder I break asunder;

THE SACRAMENTALS

On Sabbath all to church I call;
The sleepy head I rouse from bed;
The tempest's rage I do assuage;
When cometh harm, I sound alarm.

An idea which was common some centuries ago was that the sound of church bells was a sure safeguard against lightning and violent tempests; and therefore the bells were rung vigorously during storms.

The "Passing Bell." A beautiful and pious custom which prevailed in many Catholic countries was the "passing bell," which was rung slowly when a death was imminent in the parish. When the sick person was near his end the solemn tones of the bell reminded the faithful of their Christian duty of praying for his happy death and for his eternal repose; and after his spirit had departed, the bell tolled out his age — one short stroke for each year.

In rural England this custom of Catholic days has been kept up, although those who ring the bells and those who hear them have no faith in the efficacy of prayers for a departed soul.

The Angelus. One of the most important uses to which church bells are devoted is the ringing of the Angelus. This practice is distinctively Catholic. There was nothing resembling it in Jewish and pagan rites. All religions, it is true, have had certain times for prayer; but they have had nothing at all like our Angelus, which consists essentially in the reciting of certain prayers at the sound of a bell at fixed hours.

The Angelus is a short practice of devotion in honor of the Incarnation of our Blessed Lord, and it is recited three times a day — at morning, noon and evening — at the sound of a bell. It consists in the triple repetition of the Hail Mary with certain versicles, responses and a prayer. It takes its name from the opening words of the Latin form, "Angelus Domini nuntiavit Mariae" ("the Angel of the Lord declared unto Mary.")

The history of this beautiful devotion is extremely vague. The Angelus possibly owed its origin to a practice which was not at all religious — namely, the Curfew, or sounding of an evening bell as a signal that all must extinguish fires and lights and retire to rest. This was done principally as a precaution against conspiracy, especially in conquered countries. For example, when the Normans had invaded England and had overthrown the Saxon power, they imposed many strict and cruel regulations upon the people, among which was the curfew law, prescribing that all must be in their homes and with lights extinguished when the sound of the warning bell was heard; for thus did the dominant race prevent the unlawful assembling of the discontented serfs whom it desired to keep in bondage.

Morning, Noon and Night. Now, among a people who were Christian, it was natural that this bell should become a signal for nightly prayers. But the question may be asked, how did the custom arise of reciting prayers in the morning and at noon at the sound of a bell, and why were these prayers in honor of the Blessed Virgin? A rather vague tradition assigns these practices to St. Bernard, but there is no certainty regarding them. The prayers to Mary probably came into use gradually, and in this manner: In the monasteries it was customary on certain days to recite the Office of the Blessed Virgin in addition to the regular Office of the day; and this included the repetition of the salutation of the Archangel to Mary, with the other versicles, much as we have them now. The people began to use these as ejaculatory prayers, and recited them as a part of their evening devotions at the sound of the bell.

The earliest custom resembling our morning Angelus is traced back to Parma, in Italy, in the year 1318, when three Our Fathers and three Hail Marys were ordered to be recited, to obtain the blessing of peace; and the bell which gave the signal for these prayers was known as the "Peace Bell." A similar practice was prescribed in England by Archbishop Arundel in 1399.

The bell at noon was originally intended to summon the faithful to meditate on the Passion of Christ, and was rung only on Fridays; but after a time it was sounded also on other days, and the same prayers were recited as at morning and evening. This was ordered in the year 1456, by Pope Calixtus III.

The Prayers of the Angelus. At first the Angelus consisted only of the first part of the Hail Mary, repeated three times. This was prescribed for the success of the Crusades and the recovery of the Holy Sepulchre.

The Gospel narrative which is summarized so beautifully in this devotion is found in the first chapter of St. Luke, from which two of the versicles and responses are taken, the third being from the Gospel of St. John. Thus, by reciting it, we are reminded at morning, noon and night of Him Whose Name is "the only one under heaven given to men whereby they may be saved," and of her who is well entitled "our life, our sweetness and our hope."

The Legend of the Regina Coeli. During the season after Easter the Church substitutes the "Regina Coeli" for the usual prayers of the Angelus. The following legend, beautiful indeed but somewhat fanciful, is handed down concerning its origin:

"During the reign of St. Gregory, about the year 596, a severe pestilence raged in Rome. At the Paschal season the Pontiff was taking part in a great religious procession, to implore God's mercy on the stricken city. He was carrying in his hands a picture of our Blessed Lady, which was said to have been painted by St. Luke, and was reputed to be miraculous. Suddenly the sound of angels' voices was heard in the air, chanting the Regina Coeli. The Pope and people listened, amazed and filled with awe, until they had learned the words. The plague ceased from that moment."

Of course, there is no obligation to believe that such an occurrence ever happened. The legend is probably only the product of the fertile imagination of some medieval story-teller. It is far more likely that the beautiful words of this anthem owe their origin to the genius and piety of some devout religious of the early Middle Ages. We know that it is at least of very ancient date.

The Indulgences of the Angelus. Nearly two hundred years ago, in 1724, Pope Benedict XIII granted an indulgence once a month for those who recite it habitually. Leo XIII, in 1884, modified the requirements for gaining these indulgences. It is no longer strictly necessary that the Angelus shall be said kneeling, although that posture is the proper one on every day except Sunday and Saturday evening, when the rubrics prescribe that it be said standing. Owing to this change, the Angelus may be said easily in a public place, where kneeling would attract undue attention. Nor is it necessary now that it be recited at the sound of the bell, provided that it is said approximately at the proper hours — in the early morning, about the hour of noon, and toward evening. This enables one who is not within sound of an Angelus-bell to gain the partial indulgence daily and the plenary indulgence monthly, simply by reciting the required prayers at nearly the proper time, and performing the other things requisite for obtaining the plenary indulgence.

But what is to be done by one who does not know the prayers of the Angelus? How can he gain the indulgences? He must recite five Hail Marys in place of the three which, with the versicles and prayer, form the regular Angelus devotion. The same is to be said concerning the Regina Coeli, which is substituted for the Angelus during the Paschal time.

The manner of ringing the Angelus seems to have varied very little since the beginning of the devotion. Old monastic records, going back to the fifteenth century, show that the bell-ringer was directed "to toll the Ave-bell nine strokes at three times, keeping the space of one Pater and Ave between each of the three tollings." In those days the concluding prayer was not in use; but when it began to be recited, the further ringing of the bell came into vogue, as we have it at the present day.

The Tower-Bell at the Elevation. The practice of elevating the Sacred Host and the Chalice at Mass, immediately after the consecration of each, was introduced in the Latin churches about the beginning of the thirteenth century. It was then deemed fitting that those who were not present at Mass should also be invited to adore their Eucharistic Lord. And so the practice was begun of ringing one of the great bells of the church, to give notice to all the people, that they might kneel for a moment and make an act of adoration.

No bells, large or small, are rung between the end of the Gloria of the Mass on Holy Thursday and the beginning of the Gloria on Holy Saturday, when the Church begins to anticipate joyfully the Resurrection of our Lord. Then both the sanctuary-gongs and the tower-bells peal forth triumphantly, to announce that Christ has risen from the dead, to die no more.

The Blessing of Bells. The ceremony of the blessing of a church bell is one of the most elaborate and impressive in the whole liturgy of our Church; and this is not surprising when we consider the many and how important uses to which bells are devoted in Catholic worship.

This blessing is given only by a bishop or by a priest who has special faculties from the bishop, empowering him to administer it. The bell is placed at the head of the main aisle of the church or in some other prominent place, and is so situated that the clergy may pass around it conveniently and that the interior may be reached without difficulty.

The bishop and clergy go to the bell in solemn procession, and recite aloud seven psalms, invoking the mercy of God on the Church and its members. Then the water which is to be used in the ceremony is blessed by the bishop in the same manner as ordinary holy water, except that an additional prayer is recited, asking that God's benediction be given to it, so that the bell which is to be blessed with it may have the power of overcoming the deceits of the wicked, and of preventing lightning, whirlwind and tempest; that when the faithful shall hear the bell, their devotion may increase and the services of the Church be rightly be performed by them.

The bishop then begins to wash the bell with this water, and his attendants continue the washing over all the surface of the bell, inside and outside. In the meantime, six other lengthy psalms are recited by the bishop and clergy. Then a quaint and beautiful prayer is intoned by the bishop, asking God to give His grace to His people, that at the sound of this bell their faith and devotion may be increased, that the snares of the Evil One may be ineffectual, that the elements may be calmed, that the air may be healthful, that the demons may flee when they hear the sweet tones of the bell.

After the recitation of another prayer the bell is anointed with the Oil of the Sick in seven places on the outside, with the words: "May this bell, O Lord, be sanctified and consecrated, in the name of the Father and of the Son and of the Holy Ghost. Amen."

Another prayer is chanted, and four crosses are made on the inner surface of the bell with the Holy Chrism. After still other prayers and a psalm, a Gospel is sung by a deacon just as at a solemn Mass. The Gospel selected is from St. Luke, describing the visit of our Blessed Lord to Martha and Mary. "Mary hath chosen the better part, which shall not be taken from her."

Such, then, is the history of bells and the liturgy of their blessing. They are assuredly a great help to us in the worship of God. They summon us to the services of the Church. They peal forth joyfully on the wedding day, as if to prophesy happiness and prosperity to the young people who are beginning their life-long union. They toll mournfully as the corpse is borne to receive the Church's last blessing, to remind us of the duty of praying for the departed soul. And as our holy Church knows the value of frequent prayer, she has given us the Angelus, which raises our hearts to God three times a day — and, by reminding us of the Incarnation of our Blessed Saviour, thereby enlivens our faith, strengthens our hope, and increases our love of God.

Chapter XXXIX

RELIGIOUS MEDALS

A RELIGIOUS medal is a piece of metal, usually resembling a coin, struck or cast for a commemorative purpose or to increase devotion, and adorned with some appropriate device or inscription. The varieties of these medals are almost beyond counting. They have been produced in honor of persons, such as our Divine Saviour, His Blessed Mother and the saints; of places, such as famous shrines; and of historical events, for example, definitions of Church doctrines, jubilees, miracles, dedications, etc. They are made to commemorate events in the life of the wearer, such as First Communion. They often recall mysteries of our faith; and some of them are specially blessed to serve as badges of pious associations, or to consecrate and protect the wearer. Many medals thus blessed are enriched with indulgences for the user.

The History of Medals. It is very likely that the use of medals among Christians came about because similar ornaments were common among many pagan races. There was in every form of paganism a constant endeavor to propitiate the deities who were adored and to secure their protection. Amulets, talismans and charms of various kinds were used, being generally worn suspended from the neck, as a supposed means of warding off danger, disease and other evils. Even after Christianity had become the prevailing religion, it seemed to be impossible to root out the practice of using some of these ancient pagan charms.

The Church, therefore, instead of trying to prevent it, endeavored to turn it to good ends by suggesting or tolerating the use of similar devices with Christian symbols. Our holy Church has shown her wisdom in this manner in regard to many pagan customs, purifying them and adapting them to her own purposes. What more natural than that the early Christian converts should wear symbols of their religion, just as in paganism they had worn amulets to secure the protection of their gods?

We find traces of the use of medals at a very early date, when the Roman Church was hiding in the catacombs. Some of these ancient medals are preserved in various museums, and are often marked with the "chrisma," that is, the Greek monogram of the name of Christ. Others have portraits of the Apostles Peter and Paul, or representations of the martyrdom of certain saints.

In the Middle Ages. Later on it became customary to coin money with crosses and other religious emblems stamped on it, and such coins were often suspended from the neck and used as medals. About the twelfth century the great era of pilgrimages began, and at the famous shrines of Europe and Palestine the custom arose of making metal tokens or medals, to be used by the pilgrim as souvenirs of his pious journey, and also to attest the fact that he had really visited the shrine. These badges or "pilgrims' signs," as they were called, were generally worn conspicuously on the hat or breast. They were usually of lead, or circular or cross-shaped form, and were known by various names — the "tokens" of Assisi, the "crouches" or crosses signifying a pilgrimage to the Holy Land, scallop-shells reproduced in metal, from the shrine of St. James of Compostella in Spain, crossed keys denoting a journey to the tomb of St. Peter, etc.

The use of religious medals, however, was not common in the Middle Ages. Somewhat later, about the fifteenth century, artistic bronze and silver medals were substituted for the rude pilgrim-tokens. About 1475, and possibly earlier, the custom arose of making medals commemorative of the papal jubilees, and these were carried to all parts of the world by pilgrims who visited Rome to gain the jubilee indulgence.

In the sixteenth century the practice arose of giving a papal blessing to medals, and even of enriching them with indulgences for the wearers. And so the use of devotional medals spread rapidly throughout Europe, and celebrated artists and engravers occupied themselves with the designing of them.

Varieties of Religious Medals. To enumerate all the medals that have been issued or that are now in use would be an endless task. Specimens have been preserved of "plague medals" of the Middle Ages, used at times when pestilence was rife, as a protection against it. These often bore the picture of St. Roch or St. Sebastian, and, more often still, that of the Blessed Virgin or of some one of her shrines. When comets were objects of dread, medals were made in Germany to shield mankind from the calamities that were supposed to follow these direful portents. Others commemorated legendary miracles and important historical events.

Among the religious medals in most general use in our country are the scapular medals, which are described elsewhere in this book; the various sodality badges, differing in design according to the nature of the societies using them; many varieties of medals of the Blessed Virgin under her various titles, such as the Mater Dolorosa, Our Lady of Victory, Queen of Heaven, Our Lady of Lourdes, of Perpetual Help, of Good Counsel, of Mount Carmel, etc. There are also the medals given to children at the time of First Communion and Confirmation, with appropriate devices; others in honor of our Blessed Lord, such as the "Salvator Mundi" ("Saviour of the world"), the Holy Childhood and the Infant of Prague. Then come the innumerable medals of the saints — those of St. Joseph, popular especially among German Catholics; the St. Rita medals, bearing an image of this recently canonized saint; and others commemorating St. Dominic, St. Aloysius, St. Francis of Assisi, St. Anthony, St. Ignatius Loyola, St. Alphonsus, St. Patrick, St. Ann, St. Agnes, the Guardian Angels, etc. A medal of St. Christopher is one of the most recent, and is claimed to secure the protection of that saint for travelers and especially for automobilists — who assuredly need some such protection.

The Medal of St. Benedict. This highly indulgenced medal bears a likeness of the great "Father of the Monastic Life." In his right hand is a cross, beside which are the words "Crux Patris Benedicti" ("The Cross of the Father Benedict"); in his left hand is the book of the Benedictine rule. At his feet are represented a

Medal of St. Benedict

chalice and a raven, symbols of the priesthood and of hermit life. Around the edge are the words "Ejus in Obitu Nostro Praesentia Muniamur" ("At our death may we be fortified by his presence"). On the reverse side is a cross, on the vertical bar of which are the initial letters of the words "Crux Sacra Sit Mihi Lux" ("The holy

Cross be my light"); on the horizontal bar are the initials of "Non Draco Sit Mihi Dux" ("Let not the Dragon be my guide"); and around are other letters signifying other Latin mottoes. At the top is usually the word "Pax" ("Peace") or the monogram I H S.

This form of the Benedictine medal commemorates the 1400th anniversary of the birth of St. Benedict, celebrated in 1880. The right to make them is reserved exclusively to the Great Arch-abbey of Monte Cassino, in Italy. There are many indulgences for the wearers, including a plenary one on All Souls' Day, obtained by visiting a church on that day or on its eve, and praying there for the intention of the Holy Father.

The medal of St. Benedict was first approved by Benedict XIV in 1741, and further indulgences were granted by Pius IX in 1877 and by Pius X in 1907.

The "Miraculous Medal." There is a widely used medal known by this title because it takes its origin from a vision. It is a medal of the Blessed Virgin, and is used as a badge by our sodalities of the Children of Mary and of the Immaculate Conception. It bears on one side an image of our Blessed Mother standing on a globe. Around the picture are words "O Mary Conceived without Sin, Pray for Us Who Have Recourse to Thee." On the reverse side is the letter M surmounted by a cross and surrounded by twelve stars, and beneath are the Hearts of Jesus and Mary, the one with a crown of thorns, the other pierced by a sword.

This beautiful medal has a remarkable history. It was given to the world through a vision which was vouchsafed to a holy servant of God, Sister Catherine, a French Sister of Charity, known in the world as Zoe Labouré. On November 27, 1830, and on several other occasions, the Blessed Virgin appeared to her as depicted on the medal, and commanded the saintly nun to cause the medal to be made. This was done, with the sanction of the Archbishop of Paris, within two years; and the use of this medal of the Immaculate Conception spread rapidly throughout the world.

Many and great indulgences have been given to its wearers, and it has been an important factor in increasing devotion to the Blessed Mother of God, particularly among our young girls, the members of our parish sodalities.

Chapter XL

ASHES

On Ash Wednesday the Church begins the penitential season of Lent, the forty days of mortification during which her children are called upon to remember that they must chastise their bodies and bring them into subjection; that he who neglects to do penance is in danger of perishing; and that at all times the Christian must remember his last end and his return to the dust from which he was taken.

As we are all conscious that by nature we are "children of wrath," we are urged to appease the offended majesty of God by the practice of penance and mortification; and the Church teaches us this solemn duty by the impressive ceremony of the imposition of ashes on Ash Wednesday.

An Ancient Practice. Like many of the other symbolic practices of our Church, the use of ashes to express humiliation and sorrow is something which was common in other religions. Many references to it are found in the Old Testament. When David repented for his sins he cried out: "I did eat ashes like bread, and mingled my drink with weeping." When the people of Nineveh were aroused to penance by the preaching of the prophet Jonas, they "proclaimed a fast and put on sackcloth and sat in ashes." It is probable, therefore, that the use of ashes was introduced in the early Church by converts from Judaism because it was an observance with which they had been familiar in their former faith.

The Lenten fast, according to the ancient practice of our Church, began on the Monday after the first Sunday of Lent. Consequently the penitential season was then somewhat shorter than it is now; deducting the Sundays, there were originally only thirty-six fasting days. But about the year 700 it was seen to be fitting that the fast of the faithful should be of the same duration as that which our Blessed Lord had undergone; and the beginning of the season of penance was fixed on what we now call Ash Wednesday.

Originally a Public Penance. At first the ashes were

imposed only on public penitents. In those austere days of ecclesiastical discipline, public expiation was always exacted as a reparation for public scandal. Those who sought reconciliation with God after grievous sin were required to appear at the door of the church in penitential garb on Ash Wednesday morning. They were then clad in sackcloth and sprinkled with ashes, and were debarred from the church services until Holy Thursday.

But there were always among the faithful certain devout souls who were not public sinners, but who wished to be sharers in the humiliation of Ash Wednesday. And so, gradually, it became the custom for all Catholics, including the clergy, to receive the ashes on that day. The earliest legislation decreeing this is found about the year 1090, and within a century from that time it had become a universal practice.

The Source of Blessed Ashes. The ashes used for this ceremony are obtained by the burning of the blessed palms of the previous Palm Sunday. In this the mystical writers of the Church have found a symbolic meaning. The palm typifies victory; and the ashes show us that we cannot gain the victory over sin and Satan unless by the practice of humility and mortification.

The Prayers of the Blessing. The language of the blessing is very beautiful, and it is regrettable that our people are not made more familiar with these and other petitions which are used in the liturgy of our Church. In these prayers God is besought to spare us sinners; to send His holy Angel to bless these ashes, that they may become a salutary remedy; that all upon whom they are sprinkled may have health of body and soul. He is implored to bestow His mercy upon us, who are but dust and ashes; and, just as He spared the Ninevites, whom He had doomed to destruction, so the Church begs Him to spare us, because, like them, we wish to do penance and obtain forgiveness.

Such is the substance of the blessing, and then comes the solemn imposition. Rich and poor, cleric and layman, the tottering old man and the little child, all throng to the altar of God; and with the impressive words: "Remember, man, that thou art dust, and unto dust thou shalt return," the priest places upon the head of each those ashes which are such a striking symbol of our frail mortality. As a spiritual writer has said: "He mingles the ashes that are dead with the ashes yet alive," that the lifeless dust may impress upon us the solemn truth that we too are but dust, and that unto dust we shall return.

PART VII
THE LITURGICAL BOOKS

Chapter XLI

THE MISSAL

WHEN a priest goes to the altar to begin the celebration of Mass he opens a large book, and the people know that the prayers which he recites vary from day to day, as they see him arrange the markers or ribbons with which the volume is provided. This book is called the Missal, that is, the Mass-Book, and it contains all that is read or recited in the offering of the Adorable Sacrifice, and very complete "rubrics" or directions for the proper reading of each Mass.

As the Missal is in the Latin language, and as translations of it have not been generally accessible to the faithful until rather recently, its contents are more or less of a mystery even to well-instructed Catholics, although some of the more modern prayer-books contain parts of it rendered into English, and even complete Missals in Latin and English are now published for the use of the faithful.

A lack of knowledge regarding this and other sacred things used by our Church in divine worship tends to render our people incapable of appreciating the value and beauty of sacred rites. Therefore it may be useful to describe briefly the contents of the book from which the priest reads the solemn and beautiful prayers which the Church has incorporated into the holy Sacrifice of the Mass. The Missal is a book which treats of matters in which all we Catholics should be interested; and some knowledge of which will be useful to us because we will thereby better appreciate the grandeur and harmony of the daily Oblation which is offered before the throne of God by the appointed ministers of His Church on earth.

The Liturgy of the Jews. Among the "people of God" in Old Testament times, in the religion which was a foreshadowing of the Christian faith, a special ritual was in use, based on direct revelation from God, in which the ceremonial rules were prescribed in the most minute details, and the observance of them was enjoined under the severest penalties. This liturgy was put into form by Moses, the great lawgiver of the Jews, and it continued in use in the worship of God down to the time when it was abrogated by the institution of the Christian Church.

The Church's Liturgy. As the essence of the Christian religion is contained in the Mass and the Sacraments, which were unknown in the Jewish faith, it was necessary to create a new liturgy. This was done by the Church, and was done very slowly. Our Blessed Lord Himself instituted the Holy Sacrifice and the seven Sacraments, but He did not make any rules about their administration. The authority for arranging all these details is contained in the power "to bind and to loose," given to the teaching body of the Church; and she also has the power to establish from time to time such sacramentals and other aids to devotion as may be conducive to the spiritual welfare of the faithful.

The Growth of the Missal. The Missal, in its present form, is the result of centuries of development. From the earliest times the essential parts of it were in use in the Church, but they were not always arranged as at present. The changes that have come in the arrangement of the parts of the Mass are described elsewhere in this book, in the chapter on "The Growth of the Mass." In the early Middle Ages a portion of the prayers was found in one book, another portion in another; and these different books, copied by hand before the invention of printing, caused considerable inconvenience and confusion. A uniform ritual was seen to be advisable in a Church which has a uniform Creed, and in the sixteenth century the Missal was reduced to substantially its present form.

The Reformer of the Missal. This action was recommended by the Council of Trent, and was put into effect by Pope St. Pius V, who thoroughly revised the Missal, making his edition the standard to which all others must conform.

An exception was made for some churches and religious orders which had a liturgy of their own going back over two hundred years, and they were allowed to continue the use of their own peculiar rite on account of its antiquity. Some of our readers may have noticed the differences in the Mass as said by members of the Dominican order from that celebrated by secular priests; and some, possibly, may have assisted at the Holy Sacrifice when it was offered by a priest of some Oriental Catholic rite, with strange ceremonies and weird chanting. The decree of St. Pius V prescribing the use of the revisal Missal was issued in 1570; and, as it was not thoroughly obeyed in some parts of the world, a stricter law was made by Clement VIII in 1604 and by Urban VIII in 1634. These three decrees are placed at the beginning of every Missal.

The Missal in use in all churches having the Latin rite is printed entirely in the Latin language. The reasons for this have been very fully set forth in another chapter of this book.

The Arrangement of the Book. It contains, at the beginning, a list of the feasts of the Church, movable and immovable. Next come the rubrics, or rules for the guidance of the priest, and these are continued all through the book. The word "rubric" means "red," on account of the ancient practice among the Romans, of writing in that color the important and explanatory parts of their legal documents. This practice is still continued in all the liturgical books of the Church, which are always in two colors — red for the explanations and rules, black for the text itself.

What we may call the Missal proper begins with the Mass of the first Sunday of Advent, the beginning of the Church's year. Then, one after another, we find the Masses assigned to all the Sundays and festivals and saints' days. In these the entire wording of the Mass is not given — merely the parts that are "proper" to the day.

In the middle of the book is inserted the "Ordinary of the Mass," that is, the parts in which there is little change from day to day. In this portion of the Missal are the Prefaces, those sublime expressions of homage and thanksgiving to God, which are sung to the music of an ancient and beautiful chant in high Masses and recited in low Masses. There are eleven in number, varying according to the season and sometimes according to the feast.

The Canon of the Mass. Then comes the Canon of the Mass, which is practically unchanged from day to day. It includes the "Te igitur," in which God's blessing is invoked upon the Church, the Pope, the Bishops and all the faithful; the "Memento for the Living"; the "Communicantes," which brings in the names and asks the intercession of the Apostles and other Saints; and the solemn words of consecration, by which the bread and wine are changed into the living Body and Blood of Christ. Later on there is the Memento for the Dead, a prayer "also for us sinners," the Pater Noster, three prayers before Communion, and many other beautiful petitions.

The Masses of the Saints. As is well known, nearly every day of the year is dedicated by our Church to the honoring of some saint or the celebration of some festival. The saints are arranged in several classes — Apostles, martyrs, Doctors of the Church, confessor bishops, confessors, virgin-martyrs, virgins and widows; and for each class a special Mass is provided, while many of the individual Saints have Masses of their own — that is, some of the prayers and other parts are composed or selected especially in honor of that Saint.

The Requiem Masses. Further on in the Missal are the Masses for the dead. Special prayers are given for deceased Popes, Cardinals, Bishops and priests, for the celebrant's father and mother or both, for relatives, benefactors, etc. It should be understood that the saying of Requiem Masses is restricted to certain days. On festivals, except of the lower classes, low Masses in black vestments are not allowed, and on some of the most important feasts even funeral Masses are forbidden.

The Missal has a supplement which contains Masses in honor of certain saints whose festivals are not celebrated everywhere; for it is permitted to some countries or certain religious orders to honor saints of their own, whose veneration is not prescribed for the whole world.

The Value of the Missal. Our religion teaches us that in the Mass we have an inestimable treasure of grace. The great variety of prayers contained in the Missal enhances the value of this treasure, because those that are appropriate can be selected, in some cases at least, according to the particular needs for which the Mass is offered. In order to have a better knowledge of the beauties of our Church's liturgy, every member of our Catholic faithful should possess and use a prayer-book which contains an accurate translation of at least a part of the Mass, instead of the "Devotions for Mass," oftentimes inane and insipid, that are provided in some of our manuals of prayer.

Chapter XLII

THE BREVIARY

"Why do your priests spend so much time in reading from a little black book?" Every priest has heard this question from his non-Catholic friends. The Catholic has a general idea that the priest is under an obligation to recite his Office every day, but few Catholics have any very clear notion as to what the Office is or why it is said.

The Church's Public Prayer. The Office is a prayer, and the most efficacious prayer ever composed. It is the one great public prayer of the Church, as the Mass is her one great sacrifice. This does not mean that the Office is said necessarily in public, but that the priest who offers it is not acting in his own name but in the name of the Church, even though he may recite it alone and almost silently. It is a prayer offered by ministers of God, who have been raised to the most exalted dignity on earth, that they may praise God in the name of all mankind and ask for grace for all the Church's children. It is said in the name of the Church and by her authority; hence it is the expression of her homage to her heavenly King.

When you see a priest reading his Breviary, did it ever occur to you that you have a share in that prayer, that you derive benefit from the recitation of that Office by him? He is taking part in the public prayer of the Church of which you are a member. Reflect that in this country alone there are nearly twenty thousand priests, who daily spend more than an hour in offering this public prayer to God for the Church and for all her members — and the clergy of the United States form a very small fraction of those of the universal Church. All over the world, in monasteries and in cathedrals, the Divine Office is solemnly recited at stated hours, and every priest in every land lays aside his other duties at some time each day to raise his heart to God and to join in offering to Him the public homage of His Church on earth.

The Priest Is a Mediator. In every form of religion the priest has been considered as a mediator — one who is to stand, as it were, between God and man, who was not only to offer sacrifices, which is always the greatest act of divine worship, but also to pray for the people, to present their petitions to the Deity, and to solicit His favors for them. This was true not only of the Jewish faith but of every pagan creed. Everywhere the priest was the appointed man of prayer, selected to propitiate the powers of the unseen world.

The priests of the Church of Christ are "the dispensers of the mysteries of God," as St. Paul calls them. "Every high-priest taken from among men is ordained for men in the things that pertain to God." This is the essence of the priestly character — that he is appointed to that dignity not for himself but for mankind.

The Catholic priest who says his Office, then, is not praying for himself alone. He is acting as a representative of all the members of the Church. He is your substitute, doing in your name what you and the generality of mankind have neither the time nor the inclination to do. He is uniting his prayers with those of the blessed in heaven in honoring the Creator of all things.

What is the Breviary? The book which a priest uses for the reciting of his Office is known as a Breviary. Why is it so called? The word "Breviary" (from the Latin word "Brevis," short or brief) would seem to indicate that the contents are not lengthy— and many an overworked priest on a busy Sunday may well wonder why that word is used. For his consolation it may be well to state that the whole Office is really much shorter than it was centuries ago. About the year 1100 a considerable abbreviation was made in it throughout the Church, and the new office-book brought into use at that time was called a "Breviarium," or abridgment. A further shortening of some Offices and a rearrangement of nearly all went into effect by direction of Pope Pius X, in 1912.

The Breviary contains the Office which all priests and all clerics in Sacred Orders are obliged to recite daily under pain of mortal sin unless they are exempted by a grave reason. It is made up of four volumes, adapted to the four seasons of the year, since all the Office in one volume would be too unwieldy for use.

These Offices are in Latin, and are made up of psalms,

canticles, hymns, extracts from the Scriptures, brief lives of the saints, parts of sermons by the great Fathers of the Church (such as Gregory, Augustine and Chrysostom), many short prayers, versicles, responses, and the frequent repetition of the Lord's Prayer, the Hail Mary and the Apostles' Creed.

The Parts of the Office. It is divided into seven parts known as the Canonical Hours, and in the Middle Ages it was the general practice to recite each part at its own hour; but the secular clergy of our day and many of the religious communities are not bound now to observe this practice strictly. Each priest is obliged to say the whole Office of the day within the twenty-four hours of the day, but at any hour or hours that may be convenient, saying as much at a time as he may be able or willing to recite. Moreover, he has the privilege of "anticipating," or saying a part of the Office after two o'clock of the preceding day if he sees fit to do so. Thus, he may, for example, say a part of Tuesday's Office on Monday.

The first of the Canonical Hours is "Matins," or the morning office, which was recited originally before dawn; it is followed by "Lauds," or praises of God. The next division is "Prime," or the first, because it was said at the "first hour," or sunrise. Then "Terce," or third, recited at the third hour, nine o'clock; "Sext," or sixth, at noon; and "None," or ninth, at three o'clock. "Vespers" is next, signifying the evening service, and then comes "Compline," or the completion, which was said at bedtime.

The Office varies from day to day. It may be a Sunday Office or a week-day Office or the Office of a saint. In the latter case it is different according to the saint who is honored, the hymns, prayers, etc., being modified by the class to which he or she belongs—an apostle, martyr, confessor or virgin.

Suppose, for instance, that the Church is celebrating to-day the festival of a saint who was a martyr. Every priest all over the world recites thirty-three psalms, three canticles, eight hymns, nine prayers, the Our Father fourteen times, the Hail Mary seven times, the Creed three times and the Confiteor once. He reads three extracts from the Scriptures, three short chapters on the life of the saint, and three from a sermon by a Father of the Church, besides eight "capitula" ("little chapters") of a few lines each, the "Te Deum" once, and a great number of short verses and responses taken mostly from the Bible.

The History of the Office. According to the best authorities, the Office, in some form at least, goes back to Apostolic times. In the beginning it was made up almost entirely of the Psalms of David, and they are the groundwork of the Breviary at the present day. In later centuries various prayers and "Lessons" were added, and a great number of new festivals was established; every religious order had its own mode of reciting the Office, and there was little attempt at uniformity. The Council of Trent revised the whole Office, and the Breviary authorized by that Council was published in 1602. This became practically universal, although some of the older monastic orders have been permitted to keep their ancient Offices, and a considerable diversity regarding the observance of festivals is allowed in different parts of the world.

Pope Pius X, of blessed memory, authorized a complete revision of the Breviary, as already mentioned The new arrangement is such that all the Psalms of the Bible, 150 in number, are usually recited within each week, thus going back to the ancient idea of emphasizing the divine psalmody as the substance of the Office.

We see, then the excellence of the Divine Office of our Church, recited daily by her priests. That public prayer has been offered up for many centuries. The greater part of it is the inspired Word of God, taken from the Old and New Testaments. It treats of the lives of the most illustrious saints of God in every age; it contains eloquent discourses by the great Fathers of the Church, and hymns as notable for their literary merit as for their pious sentiments. Except the Holy Sacrifice of the Mass and the Sacraments, the Church possesses no treasure of grace so abundant as the Divine Office which her priests offer to God every day at her command.

Chapter XLIII

THE RITUAL

Our Holy Church considers that all earthly things need sanctification, inasmuch as by the fall of our first parents the world became subject to the power of the Evil one; and so, from the earliest times, she has observed the practice of bestowing blessings on various objects. She wishes that not only the things employed in her services but also those that her children use in their daily life should be "sanctified by the Word of God and by prayer."

History of the Ritual. The Roman Ritual is a book which every priest has occasion to use frequently. The Ritual means the "Book of Rites," just as the Missal signifies the "Book of the Mass," and the Pontifical the "Book of the Pontiff" or Bishop. It has taken centuries to bring the Ritual to its present form. In early times all the forms of blessing were not comprised in one book;; some were contained in the "Sacramentary," some in the Missal, some elsewhere. The first book resembling our Ritual was entitled a "Sacerdotale," or Priest's Book, and was published at Rome in 1537. In those days nearly every diocese had its own Ritual and its own list of authorized blessings; and, to promote uniformity, the Council of Trent recommended that a new and complete Ritual should be issued and should be used all over the world, at least where the Latin rite prevailed. In 1614 the learned Pontiff Paul V authorized a revised Ritual which was put into form by a commission headed by Cardinal Julius d'Antonio, a man of remarkable zeal and ability. It has not been altered to any considerable extent since that time, although it was re-edited by Benedict XIV in 1753, and many new blessings have been added to it at various times.

The Parts of the Ritual. The complete Ritual is made up of several parts. It opens with the rites of the Sacraments that can be administered by a priest — Baptism, of a child or an adult; Penance, with the form of absolving from censures; the giving of Holy Communion outside of Mass or to the sick; Extreme Unction, with an appendix of psalms and the Litany of the Saints, which may recited when the last Sacraments are administered to the sick; and Matrimony, after which is placed (very appropriately) the prayers of "churching," or the blessing of a woman after childbirth.

A chapter for the visitation of the sick contains some beautiful prayers and selections from the Gospels, which may be read over the sick person. These are worthy of special notice, on account of the consoling nature of the passages chosen from the sacred text.

The first is the touching account of the faith of the pagan centurion — "Lord, I am not worthy that Thou shouldst enter under my roof. Say only the word, and my servant shall be healed." Another gives us the divine commission bestowed on the Apostles: "Going into the whole world, preach the Gospel to every creature. . . . They shall place their hands on the sick, and these shall be made well." A third tells of the curing of the mother-in-law of St. Peter, who was "seized with great fevers." Another, the healing of the man at the pool of Bethsaida. Each of these is followed by an appropriate prayer, asking for restoration of health for the afflicted one; and at the end is a special blessing imparted by the placing of the priest's hands on the head of the sick person and by a prayer asking health for him "through the intercession of the Apostles Peter and Paul and all the Saints." And the series of prayers is concluded with the opening verses of the sublime Gospel of St. John: "In the beginning was the Word."

The Various Blessings. Further on in the book come the details of the ceremonies of Candlemas Day, Palm Sunday, and other feasts on which special blessings are imparted. But the part which is most interesting is that which contains the many blessings which the Church authorizes and uses for the sanctification of persons, places and things.

These are altogether about 140 in number. The prayers used in them generally ask that the thing blessed may tend to the spiritual and temporal welfare of the faithful.

First come the blessings of persons. There is the well-known "Blessing of St. Blaise," which is administered in some of our churches on his festival, the third of February, and which is commemorative of the legend which makes that saint the preserver from diseases of the throat. There is a blessing for sick persons, distinct from those already mentioned; and a special form of prayer and benediction for a woman who expects to become a mother.

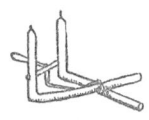
St. Blaise Candle

There are several blessings for children. One is for infants, that they may "grow in holiness"; one for a child, that it may increase, as our Saviour did, "in wisdom and age and grace with God and men"; another for an assembly or sodality of children, and a special blessing for sick children.

Blessings for Religious Articles. A blessing is given to nearly everything which the Church uses in her rites and ceremonies or offers to the veneration of her children. There is a form for a new cross, for religious statues, for banners, organs, crucifixes, rosaries of various kinds, medals, and many other articles. Some of these receive what is called the "Papal Indulgence" through the form of blessing which is recited over them.

Then there are the blessings for buildings. There is a special form for schools — for the Church is always the zealous promoter of Christian education and all varieties of useful knowledge. Several blessings are provided for dwellings. One of these is assigned to Holy Saturday, when the priest (in many countries) goes from house to house, sprinkling holy water and praying that "as the blood of the paschal lamb protected the Israelites from the destroying angel, so may the Blood of Jesus Christ protect the inmates of this house from all evil."

It is a laudable custom, when a new house is completed to have the priest visit it and invoke the mercy of God upon it and those who shall dwell in it. A blessing is given in the Ritual for that purpose — that the edifice itself may be preserved from danger of destruction, and that spiritual and worldly blessings may come abundantly upon those who shall call it their home.

Blessings for Living Things. The tiller of the soil, the herdsman and the shepherd are the primary producers of wealth;

and the prosperity — even the existence — of the human race depends upon the success of their labor. The piety of the faithful in every age has sought for the blessing of God and His Church upon flocks and herds and the products of the soil. And so we find many quaint blessings in the Ritual, for nearly every animal that is useful to man — cows, oxen, horses, sheep, fowl, bees; also a different form of blessing when any of the larger animals is sick. There are blessings, too, for the protection of the farmers' crops and granaries against harmful animals — mice, locusts, etc. The Church has always believed and taught that "every best gift, every perfect gift, is from above, coming down from the Father of Light"; that all things, even the lowliest, are directly subject to His providence.

Blessings for Eatables. This spirit of the Church leads her to extend her solemn blessings even to the things that are to be used for food and drink. "The earth is the Lord's and the fullness thereof" — and even the food which God provides for the nourishment of our bodies tends to some extent to the promotion of His glory. And so she gives her blessings for vines, fruits, eggs, oil, bread, cakes, cheese, butter — and even wine and beer. Our Church advocates temperance, indeed; but she knows, as we know, that the abuse, not the use, of these latter things is to be reprehended.

Blessings for Other Things. To permit the giving of God's blessing to the things which we use in our daily occupations, the Church has provided forms of benediction for many different objects — for the launching of a ship, for bridges, for wells and springs, for furnaces and limekilns; for granaries, bakeries, stables; for seeds and for a field after sowing; for medicines and surgical appliances. And that she may demonstrate that she appreciates modern inventions, she has added formulas for the blessing of steam engines, railroads, telegraphs, telephones — and, very recently, for the apparatus for wireless telegraphy.

All these blessings show us that the Church wishes us to recognize our dependence upon God, Who bestows His gifts upon us so abundantly; and, that these may be useful to us spiritually and otherwise, the Church bestows her solemn blessing upon the things which we, the children of God, have received from our Heavenly Father.

PART VIII
DEVOTIONS

Chapter XLIV

THE DEVOTION TO THE SACRED HEART

IT is not within the scope of this book to discuss the spiritual side of the devotion to the Sacred Heart of our Blessed Lord. There are scores of volumes that treat of the benefits of this special worship which we pay to our Divine Redeemer, and of the various ways in which it can be profitable to the souls of the faithful. The aim of this work is merely to give the history of Catholic practices and to explain their nature, their reasonableness and their use.

Each of the twelve months of the year has its special devotion. Some of these have been merely advocated by spiritual writers, with the intention of providing, throughout the year, a series of religious exercises for the devout. Others are authorized and approved by the Church, and those who practise them receive certain indulgences.

The month of June, as all Catholics know, is the month of the Sacred Heart. During it the Church urges the faithful to special zeal in the worship of the Heart of our Saviour, considered as a part of His sacred Humanity and as the emblem of His infinite love.

The devotion to the Sacred Heart is one which has become widely known only since the seventeenth century; and it was not sanctioned by the Church for general use until the latter part of the eighteenth. Though it is now recognized as an important element in Catholic worship, it met with strenuous opposition when it was first introduced — not only from the Jansenists (who had fallen into error regarding many doctrines of the Church) but from earnest Catholics who object to the new doctrine because they misunderstood it.

The Blessed Margaret Mary. Homage paid to the Heart of Jesus is mentioned by spiritual writers as early as the twelfth century; but it was practised to a very limited extent until a little more than two hundred years ago. A humble and holy French nun, the Blessed Margaret Mary Alacoque, within the space of a religious life of only nineteen years, instituted a devotion which bids fair to last forever. She became the apostle of the beautiful and now universal worship of the loving Heart of our Blessed Saviour.

She was born in the village of Lauthecort, in France, in the year 1647, and lived until 1690. After a childhood remarkable for sanctity, she entered the community of the Visitation nuns at Paray-le-Monial in 1671. Here she lived a life of mortification and prayer, and in return for her fidelity and fervor our Divine Lord is said to have vouchsafed her a privilege which He has frequently given to other holy souls. He appeared to her on several occasions; and in one of these visions He showed her His Heart, pierced with a wound, encircled with a crown of thorns, surrounded by flames and surmounted by a cross — as we see it usually represented in pictures and statues at the present day. He commanded her to practise and to teach others the devotion to His Sacred Heart, because of His ardent desire to be loved by men and His wish to give to all mankind the treasures of His love and mercy.

The pious nun sought the counsel of her superiors, and the account of her visions was received at first with incredulity. All her actions and her teachings were subjected to a most severe examination, and it was long before any approval was given to the devotion which she was endeavoring to establish. But the will of God cannot be opposed. The devotion spread rapidly through France, and was gradually established in other parts of the world. It did not at first receive the approbation of the Holy See, for our Church is cautious in giving her sanctions to anything that savors of novelty in religion, and makes a long and careful scrutiny before she recommends a new devotion to her children. In 1794, however, Pius VI issued a decree approving the devotion to the Sacred Heart and granting indulgences to those who practise it.

The Feast of the Sacred Heart. Attempts had been made, in 1697 and in 1729, to have a day set apart in honor of the Sacred Heart, but on both occasions the proposal was rejected by the Roman Congregation of Rites. In 1765, however, a number of churches were permitted to celebrate this feast, and in 1856 this permission was extended to the whole world, and all mankind was solemnly consecrated to the Sacred Heart of Jesus. On account of the importance of this great June festival, the whole month of June is considered as being specially devoted to the worship of the Sacred Heart.

Margaret Mary Alacoque was pronounced Venerable by Leo XII in 1824, and was honored with the title of Blessed by Pius IX in 1864. Through her intercession many miracles have been performed, especially at the place of her burial, and it is very probable that in this humble French nun we have one of God's chosen servants, whose name will some day be placed on the list of the Church's Saints, and whose virtues will be venerated by Catholics throughout the world.

Why We Adore the Sacred Heart. Let us examine into the reasonableness of this devotion. Are we obliged to believe the account of the visions of Margaret Mary? No. We are not obliged to believe anything supernatural except the truths that God has revealed to be accepted by all. This is a point that is nearly always misunderstood by non-Catholics. Because we Catholics practise a devotion which was established by a woman who claimed to have had a vision, they regard us as votaries of superstition and our church as a promoter of fanciful ideas, not reflecting that, even though the vision might be false, the devotion might be true. The Catholic Church does not assert that the French nun really saw our Blessed Lord; neither does she oblige us to believe it. She merely declares that the devotion to the Sacred Heart of Jesus is not only not opposed tin any way to divine revelation, but that it is an excellent form of worship; and she recommends it to her children, urges them to make use of it, and grants spiritual favors to those who do so.

We shall state briefly the Catholic doctrine regarding the worship of the Sacred Heart. It is not a mere relative homage, such as we give to holy things or to holy persons. It is not the higher form of religious veneration, such as we pay to the Blessed Mother of God. It is supreme adoration, because it is paid to the physical Heart of Christ, considered not as mere flesh, but as united to the Divinity. We Catholics adore that Heart as the

Heart of Christ, an inseparable part of Him. All the members of Christ are or may be the object of divine worship, because they are a part of His human nature and are thereby united to the Divine Nature of the Second Person of the Blessed Trinity.

But why is the Heart of Jesus selected as the object of this special adoration? Because His real and physical Heart is a natural symbol of the infinite charity of the Saviour and of His interior and spiritual life. The heart is a vital organ which, as it throbs within us, is part of our existence. It has always been looked upon as an emblem, sometimes of courage, sometimes of one's whole interior nature, but oftener of love. How often we hear such expressions as "Be of good heart," meaning "Have courage"; "He opened his heart to me," meaning "He told me all his secrets"; and our Lord Jesus, in asking our love, made the request in these words, "Son, give me thy heart." We see, then the reasonableness of taking the Sacred Heart of our Saviour as an object of our worship, not only because it is a part of Him, but because it symbolizes His love for all mankind.

From early times the Five Wounds of our Lord were venerated as the symbol of His Passion, and this devotion received the approbation of the Church. In like manner, in these later days, she has seen fit to sanction and recommend the worship of the Sacred Heart of Jesus and to urge her children to offer their homage to that symbol of our Saviour's love, wherewith "He has loved us even to the end."

A Symbol of Love. We must remember, then, that while this devotion is directed to the material Heart of our Blessed Lord, it does not stop there. It includes also a spiritual element — namely, the infinite love of Jesus for us, which is recalled and symbolized by His Sacred Heart.

Sacred Heart League Badge

There is no devotion that has been extended throughout the Catholic world in so short a time. This means of realizing and honoring the all-embracing love of our Blessed Saviour would seem to have filled a long-felt want in the hearts of the devout faithful. Religious communities of men and women have been established under the title of the Sacred Heart of Jesus, and many societies have been formed among the laity with the special object of offering united worship to that adorable Heart. Among these the League of the Sacred Heart is the best known and the most flourishing in our country as well as throughout the Christian world.

The First Fridays. One of the greatest factors not only in making the worship of the Sacred Heart known but in distributing its spiritual benefits is the "Devotion of the First Fridays." The faithful are exhorted to receive Holy Communion on the first Friday of each month for nine months in succession, by which they may gain a plenary indulgence; and in many churches and chapels the exposition of the Blessed Sacrament takes place, either during the whole day or in the evening, and special services are held in honor of our Eucharistic Lord and especially of His Sacred Heart, the symbol of His unutterable love for us whom He died to save.

CHAPTER XLV

THE INVOCATION OF SAINTS

Those who are hostile to our religion, whether through prejudice or ignorance, have several allegations which they bring up regularly concerning the "superstitions of Romanism" and the "idolatrous practices" with which Papists have overlaid the true doctrines of Christianity.

It avails little to answer these charges — to set forth the Catholic teaching and to refute the untruthful exposition of it. Those who make the statements, either do not see the refutation or do not care to notice it. Catholic writers will painstakingly explain the doctrines of the Church and will give a thorough and logical answer to the unjust charges of those who criticize her — and the next "learned author" will blandly reiterate the calumny as if it never had been or could be refuted.

The dogmas and practices of our Church are not hidden things. They may be found clearly set forth in hundreds of easily accessible books — in the elementary catechism and in the popular explanations of Catholic belief as well as in the works of learned theologians. Why is it, then, we wonder, that the literary genius who contributes to our current magazines does not prepare himself for his task by trying to ascertain precisely what the Catholic Church teaches before he attempts to criticize her teachings or to write a description of her rites and ceremonies? Why is it that the great minds that are called upon, as infallible authorities, to explain matters Catholic for certain encyclopedias do not first acquire a definite and accurate idea of their subject? Why is it, again, that hardly a minister of religion can be found in the churches of our separated brethren who can give a clear and truthful statement of the Catholic beliefs and practices which he unsparingly condemns in his Sunday sermon? It would seem reasonable to expect that a man who poses as an expert in any particular line would not fall into gross errors every time that he writes or speaks about his specialty.

Do Catholics Adore Saints? In hardly any one point have Catholics been so persistently misrepresented as in the matter of the invocation of saints. The "benighted adherents of Rome adore the Virgin," they "pay divine homage to creatures," they "pray for mercy to mere men and women, and give them the adoration which should be given to God alone." From the time of Julian the Apostate the same old calumnies have been repeated, and refuted, and repeated again. How strange is it that we, who are "adherents of Rome," are so utterly "benighted" that we have never realized that we were taking part in this false worship! How strange that there is no mention of it in the writings of our Catholic authors for nineteen centuries!

The Church and the Saints. What does the Catholic Church believe and teach and practise concerning the Saints?

That Church has been in existence nearly nineteen hundred years. It has on its list of known saints many thousands of names — men and women whom it honors, to whom, indeed, it pays real religious homage. But never in its history has it adored any one but God. It does not adore, and never can or will adore the Blessed Virgin, for it recognizes and has always taught that she is a creature of God, and nothing more than a creature. She is a glorified human soul, more perfect and more lovable than any other save the human soul of her Son; she is worthy of the highest place and the most exalted honor that a creature can attain to in heaven, for through God's choosing of her for the destiny of being His Mother, through the abundance of graces which He bestowed upon her, and through her fidelity in corresponding with these graces, she has reached a degree of glory which places her higher than God's angels or His other saints — but she remains a creature. She is not divine. She is not in any sense a goddess. She is infinitely inferior to God. The honor which the Catholic Church pays to her is altogether of a different nature from that which is rendered to God. He is adored as the Creator and Supreme Ruler of all things; she is venerated as a Saint of God and the greatest of Saints — as our most powerful intercessor before His throne.

And what the Church holds and teaches concerning her is precisely what she holds and teaches concerning the saints of lesser degree. They are chosen friends of God; they are souls which have served Him well and have thereby won their heavenly reward. They are deserving of our homage because of their holiness; and, as they are still members of God's Church, they are united to us in what we call the "Communion of Saints." We honor them, and they pray for us; but neither they nor the Blessed Virgin Mary can give us any grace or show us any mercy. They can simply present our prayers to the Almighty and unite them to their own; and we honor them with religious homage, that thereby we may obtain the assistance of those friends of God who stand before His throne.

Adoration to God, Veneration to Saints. The Catholic Church, then, makes a complete and clear distinction between the supreme worship which we give to God alone and the relative and inferior homage which we pay to the Saints. Some of the confusion in the minds of non-Catholics may arise from the fact that the Catholic authors who wrote in Latin used the word "cultus" to denote both kinds of religious homage, and that we have no one word in English which will express the meaning of this word except "worship." But these Catholic authors always distinguished emphatically between the "cultus duliæ," which we may translate "the homage of veneration," and the "cultus latriæ," which signifies "the worship of adoration."

Veneration is paid to the Saints; a higher form of it, called "hyperdulia," is given to the Queen of Saints; but adoration is given to no one but God. Any attempt to give it to a creature would certainly be false worship — but the Catholic Church has never given it. She adores God and God only. She venerates His Saints with religious homage.

The Communion of Saints. Is it reasonable to suppose that the Saints can aid us? Why not? We who are here upon earth in the membership of Christ's Church are urged to pray for one another. We are told that we should go to God with the wants of others as well as with our own. Now, it is hard to see a reason why souls that are with God, that are enjoying everlasting happiness, should cease to exercise Christian charity, and should be unable or unwilling to intercede for their brethren.

What do the Scriptures teach us — the Sacred Word of God to which our separated brethren appeal so constantly as the one "rule of faith"? In St. John's Apocalyptic vision, he saw the elders "prostrate before the Lamb, having each . . . golden vials, which are the prayers of the saints." It matters not whether the "Saints" were on earth or in heaven; in either case their prayers are offered to God by those before His throne.

An Ancient Belief. The belief in the intercessory power of the Saints is as old as the Church. It is alluded to in authentic writings, such as the "Acts of the Martyrs," in the second and third centuries. They are represented as interceding after death for the faithful upon earth. "In heaven," said the martyr Theodotus before his torments began, "I will pray for you to God."

And this Catholic doctrine is clearly set forth in the writings of the earlier Fathers of the Church. Origen, among others, tells us that "all the Saints that have departed this life care for the salvation of those who are in the world and help them by their prayers and mediation."

How the Saints Hear Us. If the Saints of God have the power of interceding for us, it is certain that we must have communication with them, that they may be able to know our needs. We may be sure that God makes the "Communion of Saints" perfect on both sides — that we, members of His Church on earth, are able to speak to the members of that Church in Heaven, so that they may speak for us to Him. How is this effected? We do not know. Catholic theologians and spiritual writers have speculated about it, but we have not certainty as to the exact means which God provides for this communication. Some have supposed that the Almighty allows those who are in His presence to see in Him "as in a mirror" all that concerns them about earthly things. At any rate, the knowledge which they have and the petitions which they may receive from us depend entirely upon God's goodness — and beyond that fact our weak human intellect cannot go.

Our Faith Regarding the Saints. We Catholics, then, adore God alone. He is our Creator, our Redeemer, our hope her and hereafter. We believe that in heaven we have a host of friends. We believe that these friends are also friends of our

Blessed Lord — that one of them is His Mother, loved by Him so dearly that He will grant her every prayer — that one is His foster-father, whom He reverenced upon earth and loves in heaven — that the others are His loyal servants who possess Him now and forever. We believe that all this "great multitude which no man can number" is a component part of God's Church, and is united in bonds of charity with the other parts of that Church on earth and in Purgatory. We believe, therefore, that we should honor them because God has honored them; that we should pay religious veneration to them collectively and separately. And we believe also that they can and do intercede for us, that they hear our prayers and present them to Him Who loves them and us. When we offer homage to them, when we build churches and institute festival days in their honor, are we depriving God of adoration? No; we are adoring Him all the more, because we are honoring the results of His infinite graces, which have been the sole means of making these men and women Saints of God.

Chapter XLVI

THE VENERATION OF IMAGES

Even in this enlightened twentieth century and in this highly civilized land the average non-Catholic has a very hazy and sometimes a very erroneous idea of what Catholics believe. The prejudiced notions of a hundred years ago persist to-day in the minds of many. For them the Catholic is a "worshiper of idols," a senseless dolt who bows down before lifeless things; who offers adoration to statues of dead men and women, and has almost lost sight of his Creator and Saviour. The inbred bigotry of generations of narrow-minded ancestors has been inherited in its fullness by many of those "native Americans" whose religion consists, for the most part, in an unwavering hatred of "Popery," whose minds are filled with a constant dread lest the machinations of Rome shall overthrow the free institutions of our Protestant land, and who seem to have derived from their daily intercourse with Catholics no more knowledge of Catholic truths than their ignorant forefathers had in the days when Papists were few and far between.

The Catholic Doctrine. What is the teaching and practice of our Church with regard to images? Let us first set forth again the Catholic doctrine about worship. First of all, Catholics adore no one but God. Absolute and supreme worship is paid to Him alone, for He is the source of all good and of all graces, and no other being has any power whatever to forgive or sanctify or reward us.

Our Church honors and venerates the Saints and Angels, with a relative and inferior homage, as friends of God, as having the power of interceding for us; but she has never held that even the most exalted Saint is to be adored. A Saint in heaven is simply a saved soul made illustrious by exceptional virtue.

Now the church has maintained for many centuries that the representation of our Blessed Saviour or of a Saint are worthy of honor; but she has never taught nor permitted that they shall be adored. A statue or a picture is, as it were, a portrait of that Redeemer or of a holy servant of God. It brings before our mind a vivid idea of the one whom it portrays. If the image be of our Lord Jesus Christ, He, of course, is entitled to the supreme worship of adoration, being God; but His image is not God, and is to be honored merely with reverence, not with adoration. If the statue or picture represents a Saint, he or she is not to be adored, for a Saint is not God. A relative homage only is to be rendered, even though the Saint be the most exalted and holiest of creatures, the Blessed Virgin herself; and the image or portrait of the person thus venerated is to be honored only as a means for directing and increasing our homage and veneration toward that person.

Therefore Catholics do not adore images, any more than they adore Saints. They give adoration to God. They pay religious veneration or relative worship to God's Saints. They show reverential respect to images of God or of His Saints.

The Church's Decrees. This matter was settled, once and for all, more than eleven hundred years ago in the second Council of Nice, in 787. "We define with all certainty and care that both the figure of the Sacred Cross and the venerable and holy images are to be placed suitably in the churches of God and in houses; that is to say, the images of our Lord and Saviour Jesus Christ, of our Immaculate Lady the Holy Mother of God, and of the Angels and Saints. For as often as they are seen in these representations, those who look at them are ardently lifted up to the memory and love of the originals and are induced to give them respect and worshipful honor. So that offerings of incense and lights are to be given to these images, to the figure of the life-giving Cross, to the holy books of the Gospels and to other sacred objects, in order to do them honor. For honor paid to an image passes on to the one represented by it; he who venerates an image venerates the reality of him portrayed in it."

The year 787 is a long while ago; but the above is still the standpoint and teaching of the Catholic Church. The customs by which we show our "respect and worshipful honor" towards holy images have varied in different countries and at different times; but in no country and at no time has the Church permitted adoration or idolatrous worship of images. She has been obliged on many occasions to forbid excesses of reverence or such signs of veneration as might be misunderstood. In the decrees of the Council of Trent she states: "Images of Christ, the Virgin Mother of God and other Saints are to be held and kept especially in churches. Due honor and veneration are to be paid to them, not that any divinity or power is in them to entitle them to be worshipped, or that anything can be asked of them, or that any trust may be put in them, because the honor shown to them is referred to those whom they represent; so that by kissing, uncovering to, or kneeling before images we adore Christ and honor the Saints."

The History of Images. When the persecuted Christians of the first centuries were forced to hide themselves and their worship in the catacombs of Rome, they began to enrich and ornament these gloomy caverns with representations of our Saviour's life and miracles. And when they were able to practise their faith openly they took the abandoned temples of paganism and Christianized them with statues and crosses. In later ages, when the mighty cathedrals of Europe were built, the use of images for their adorning and for the inspiring of devotion became the universal rule, and the genius of the world's greatest artists was employed to carve and to paint these ornaments of the house of God.

All through those centuries Catholics understood, as they understand now, that an image or a painting has no share in the adoration due to God alone. From the earliest days the representation of Christ or of the Saints was treated with respect, and gradually a tradition and practice arose of venerating these images with a ceremonial of religious honor.

In some Eastern Churches this honor was undoubtedly increased to an excessive degree. Prostrations, incensings, litanies and long prayers were offered before images. In Greek and Russian temples the walls are fairly covered with icons or tablets depicting a multitude of Saints. After a time a natural revulsion came from this excess. A reformation was begun by certain Byzantine emperors and others, but, like many so-called reformations, it was ill-advised and was carried too far in the opposite direction. It resulted in the heresy of the Iconoclasts, or image-breakers, who sought to root out all use and veneration of images in Christina churches. There were several outbreaks of this rebellion against the Church's discipline, and bitter persecutions were waged against those who continued to venerate images. Gradually the heresy died out, and the Eastern Churches of to-day, whether united to Rome or separated from it, make far more use of images than we of the Western rite.

When Protestantism arose, the zealous "reformers" were filled with a wild hatred toward anything which reminded them of the faith they had abandoned. Many of the priceless carvings, statues and painted windows of the ancient churches of Europe were ruthlessly destroyed, and the followers of the new religion offered their "pure worship" in bare conventicles or in once-Catholic temples that had been denuded of everything that savored of Catholicity. In later times, in some Protestant denominations, there is a return to the æsthetic in worship; and carven altars, glowing windows, crosses and even pictures and statues, give testimony to the fact that the human mind feels the need of such outward helps for the furthering of religious devotion.

Abuses Are Possible. In some parts of the world — perhaps even among us — the veneration of images may be said to need watchfulness to-day. Extravagances are possible; and excessive devotion to an image, perhaps on account of some miraculous power which is claimed for it, may lead to a considerable neglect of more essential things. It is not edifying, nor is it an evidence of deep religious spirit, at a Forty Hours' Devotion, for instance, to see some to see some of our people (in all good faith, doubtless, and with the best intentions) lighting scores of candles before the statue of good St. Anthony, while upon the main altar is enthroned the God Who created St. Anthony — Jesus Christ, in the Sacrament of His love, exposed for adoration.

A Reasonable Practice. Is the veneration of images a reasonable practice? Why not? We render respect to other lifeless things simply because they symbolize something which we love or reverence. A loyal Englishman rises when he hears the strains of "God Save the King," because he respects the constitutional monarchy which rules his land; and he would rightly resent an insult offered not only to his king but to a royal statue or portrait.

An American citizen salutes the flag of his country, and bares his head when the national hymn rings forth in honor of that beautiful emblem of liberty. He would shed his blood to avenge an indignity offered to his country's flag. Now if it be reasonable to show such respect to a piece of music, or a statue, or a square of colored bunting, why is it unreasonable to manifest it towards a portrait of our Saviour or of a holy Saint of God?

Is the use of pictures and images helpful for the attaining of fervor in prayer and the increasing of devotion towards God? Undoubtedly. If you or I were in a distant land, separated from one whom we love, would it not aid us to remember that loved one, if we had a portrait constantly before us? Images are aids to devotion, helping us to fix our attention on our prayers, to avoid distractions, to increase the fervor of our adoration of God and our veneration of the Saints.

Chapter XLVII

THE VENERATION OF RELICS

THERE is a point of Catholic doctrine which is generally misunderstood and nearly always misrepresented by those outside the Church. The veneration which Catholics show to relics is usually classed as "a superstition," "a form of idolatry," "a survival of paganism" — simply because our non-Catholic and anti-Catholic critics have no accurate idea as to what our Church believes and teaches concerning relics; because they seem to be incapable of distinguishing between adoration and veneration; and because they take it for granted that anything that ever existed in pagan religions must necessarily be false and wrong and un-Christian.

Not a Superstition. Catholics are not superstitious when they give to relics the religious veneration which the Church permits. Catholics are not idolaters at any time, for they give adoration to none but God. Catholics are not guilty of paganism when they use a form of devotion which happens to resemble something that was found useful in pagan worship — for we must remember that paganism was not all false. It was the result of the instinct of worship which God has implanted in the nature of man. It was false inasmuch as it led man to worship false divinities; it was true inasmuch as it caused him to worship at all.

The veneration of relics is a primitive instinct. Even apart from religion, how common the practice has always been of preserving all that has had any connection with one who has been loved or reverenced! A lock of hair, a portrait, a little child's shoe — anything that has belonged to the object of our love — is treasured as if it were of inestimable worth. And in religion the same holds true; for the honoring of relics is found in many other forms of religion besides Christianity. The Greeks honored the supposed remains of heroes, sages and demigods; the pious Buddhists still preserve and venerate the relics of Gautama. And these pagan examples were commendable in so far as they showed religious faith, even though the object of that faith was false.

What are Relics? What do we Catholics mean when we

speak of relics? They are the bodies of departed saints, fragments of their bodies, or articles which they have used, such as clothing, vestments, and the like — or, in the case of relics of our Lord, they are objects which are reputed to have been connected with His life or sufferings, such as the manger of Bethlehem, the crown of thorns, the nails, fragments of the cross, etc.

What does our Church teach concerning them? That teaching is clearly set forth in a decree of the Council of Trent: "The bodies of holy martyrs and of others now living with Christ (which bodies were the living members of Christ and the temple of the Holy Ghost, and which are to be raised by Him to eternal life and to be glorified) are to be venerated by the faithful, for through these bodies many benefits are bestowed by God on men; so that they who now affirm that veneration and honor are not due to the relics of the saints, that these are uselessly honored by the faithful, and that the places dedicated to the memories of the saints are visited in vain, are wholly to be condemned."

Why Do We Honor Them? The Catholic devotion to relics is founded upon two great principles of the Church's teaching regarding the saints. First, she honors the saints; and when they were living on earth they, like all men, were composed each of a body and a soul. The virtues which a saint practised were not virtues of the soul only; they were proper to the whole individual, to his body as well as his soul, for body and soul labored and suffered together. The soul of a saint is in heaven. Now the bodies of those who are in heaven are certain to rise again to a glorious immortality. The Church, then, joyfully anticipates the glory which God will give to these bodies at the last day. She pays religious homage to them — even to small fragments of them; and she gives similar honor even to things that were closely connected with the earthly life of those servants of God.

Secondly, Catholics believe that god is sometimes pleased to honor the relics of the saints by making them instruments of healing and other miracles, and that He bestows graces and favors on those who keep and venerate them — for the honor that is paid to such relics is really veneration of the saint himself, which gives glory to God and secures for us the intercession of those who stand before God's throne in heaven.

A Few Objections. "Is it not superstitious to suppose that there is a physical efficacy in a relic which will cause it to work a miracle? Probably it would be superstitious if we supposed it; but we do not. We believe that the relics of the saints are the occasion of the working of a miracle by God, through the intercession of the saint who is honored when the relic is honored. Far from believing that a relic can work a miracle by any power of its own, we Catholics do not believe that a saint, or even the Blessed Virgin, can do so. The power of God is the only power that can effect a miracle. The saint can merely, by intercession, obtain the exercise of that power of God in our behalf.

"But does it not border on idolatry, or at least does it not detract from the worship of God, when honor is paid to relics?" St. Jerome was a good Christian. Let us hear what he says. "We do not worship, we do not adore, for fear that we should bow down to the creature rather than to the Creator; but we venerate the relics of the martyrs, in order the better to adore Him whose martyrs they are." Could the Catholic teaching be set forth more clearly?

As Old as the Church. The Catholic practice of honoring relics goes back to the beginning of Christianity. When the brave martyrs gave their souls to God in the arena or at the fiery stake, there were always found equally brave Christians who gathered together the dismembered remains, the blood or the ashes, and preserved them as a priceless treasure. Burial near the tomb of a martyr was especially desired by the pious faithful. Objects that had merely touched the remains of a saint were thereafter treated as relics. When the wood of the True Cross was discovered by the Empress Helena, it was soon divided into minute fragments, so that within a few years, in the words of St. Cyril of Jerusalem, it "had filled the whole world." And as the number of the Church's saints increased in the course of centuries, so also the number of venerated relics was multiplied. The people of every parish naturally desired to have a relic of the saint to whom their church was dedicated; and on account of the difficulty or impossibility of obtaining bodies or parts thereof, it became customary to venerate clothing, vestments and other things which were reputed to have been used by the saint.

The Question of Abuses. "But have there not been many abuses and deceptions regarding alleged relics?" Undoubtedly — hundreds of them. They were almost unavoidable in a matter which lent itself so easily to error and greed of gain. The demand for relics caused frauds to be perpetrated by unscrupulous men. Many of the writers of the Middle Ages tell us of grave abuses, of a regular trade in reputed objects of devotion which were, no doubt, mostly fraudulent. Popular enthusiasm and the rivalry among religious houses, each seeking to be known as the possessor of some great relic, caused many deceptions to be practised, intentionally or otherwise. Copies or models of relics were made, and in some cases there were afterwards confused with the originals. Objects which at first were venerated because they had touched a relic, were later considered to be relics themselves.

Against all these abuses the Church has constantly striven, by requiring the approval of the Holy See for newly found relics, by forbidding the sale of any such articles, and by restricting in every feasible way the veneration of those which have not at least a probable authenticity. It is true that she has allowed the honoring of certain doubtful relics to continue. But we must remember that the passing of a final opinion upon many of these is no easy task. In some cases, veneration has been paid to them for many centuries — and devotions of an ancient date cannot be swept aside at a moment's notice without disturbance and scandal. Therefore, unless the evidence of spuriousness is so great as to amount to practical certainty, the Church usually lets them alone.

Reliquary

Relics in Altar-Stones. The relics of two canonized martyrs are placed within every altar-stone, and with them are sometimes included the relics of the saint in whose memory the altar is erected. In a fixed altar these relics are contained in a metal box or reliquary of oblong shape, which fits a cavity in the altar-stone and is covered by a stone lid. When relics are exposed for public veneration in a church, they are usually contained in an elaborate reliquary, somewhat resembling the ostensorium used at Benediction of the Blessed Sacrament. Many of the great churches of Europe have large collections of relics — some undoubtedly genuine, some very probably spurious. Among the most famous are those of Rome, Aix-la-Chapelle, Cologne, Naples and Antwerp; and in the Church of St. Anthony, at Padua, are many relics of its titular Saint and of other servants of God.

Chapter XLVIII

THE FORTY HOURS' ADORATION

The central object of Catholic devotion is the adorable Sacrament of the Eucharist. The great principle of the Church's worship here on earth is to copy the homage paid to our Blessed Redeemer by the Church in heaven. We are the Church Militant, and we are one with the Church Triumphant; and just as the Saints and Angels render unceasing adoration to God in heaven, so the members of the Church on earth must strive to do the same. The Church, moreover, wishes that all her children shall have their share in this continuous homage. She has decreed that in each diocese throughout the world there shall be a cycle of adoration in which all the faithful may participate, each in his own parish on some Sunday of the year. Therefore in each of the parishes of this and of every other diocese, at some designated time, occurs the impressive ceremony known as the Forty Hours' Adoration.

Not an Old Devotion. This devotion is comparatively new. Unlike some of the other ceremonies of the Church, its history goes back only a few centuries. It seems to have been gradually evolved from the solemn ceremonies of the Blessed Sacrament which were held each year on the feast of Corpus Christi, which festival was established by Pope Urban IV in the year 1264. In these public celebrations the Sacred Host was borne through the streets, but was at first entirely concealed. About a century later the custom was introduced of exposing It in a suitable vessel, very similar to the ostensorium used at the present day.

These processions aroused in clergy and people an earnest devotion to the Blessed Sacrament, and soon gave rise to the practice of leaving the Sacred Host on the altar for public adoration. This was found to be particularly useful at the Carnival time, the two days immediately before Lent, when in many countries great excesses were committed and the people gave themselves up to unbridled license and dissipation. The bishops of the Church sought to awaken the faithful to better and holier things, to prepare them for the penitential season of

Lent, and to make reparation to God for the insults everywhere offered to His majesty. For this purpose, on these two days, they adopted the plan of exposing the Blessed Sacrament solemnly in the churches for forty hours, in memory of the time during which the Sacred Body of Jesus was in the sepulchre.

Introduced at Milan. As nearly as can be ascertained, the modern practice of having the Adoration in various churches on successive Sundays originated at Milan, in Italy, and was probably introduced by the Capuchin Order about the year 1537, when a severe visitation of the plague afflicted that city. Some investigators have attributed the devotion to Joseph da Fermo, of the above Order; others maintain that the honor belongs to a certain Father Bellotto, while still others urge the claims of a Dominican named Thomas Nieto, of St. Anthony Zaccaria and of a Barnabite, Brother Buono. All that we can be sure of is that the occasional exposition of the Blessed Sacrament goes back nearly to the year 1500, and that the making of the adoration practically continuous by holding it in different churches successively originated in Milan in or about the year 1537.

In 1539 the first indulgences for this devotion were granted by Pope Paul III. The practice spread to other cities, being especially promoted by Juvenal Ancina, an Oratorian Father who had been made Bishop of Saluzzo, and who wrote many instructions relative to the Adoration of the Forty Hours. St. Charles Borromeo, that great saint and reformer, whose name is inseparably connected with the Milanese Church, also urged the devotion upon his priests and people. In those days, when European civilization was menaced by Moslem invasion, the prayers enjoined at the Forty Hours were usually for protection from the enemies and for the peace of Christendom. It was soon adopted in Rome, through the efforts and zeal of St. Philip Neri, and was finally established and regulated, substantially as we have it now, by Pope Clement VIII in 1592, "in order that the public trials of the Church may be lessened, and that the faithful may continuously appease their Lord by prayer before the Blessed Sacrament."

The Clementine Instruction. In 1731 Pope Clement XII

issued a very complete code of regulations for the Forty Hours; and this, known as the "Clementine Instruction," has been in force with few alterations since that date, and is still the law of the Church.

The devotion was not introduced into the United States until about 1854, probably by Archbishop Kenrick of Baltimore, and did not become common until much later. Many of our older readers can remember when the Forty Hours' Adoration was a novelty, and its regular observance is of comparatively recent date.

The Rubrics and Ceremonies. During the devotion, all the Church's homage centers around the altar of exposition, which is always the high altar of the church. At least twenty candles must be kept burning day and night. There must be continual relays of watchers before the Blessed Sacrament, but only priests and clerics (or in our country the altar-boys who act in the place of clerics) are allowed to kneel in the sanctuary. All who enter or leave the church should go down on both knees and bow low in adoration; and all should remain kneeling while in the church.

No Masses are allowed at the altar on which the Blessed Sacrament is enthroned, except at the opening and closing of the Adoration. The opening Mass is called the "Mass of Exposition." On the second day a "Missa pro Pace" (Mass for Peace) is said on another altar, reminding us of the original purpose of the Forty Hours' Adoration. The closing of the devotion takes place at the "Mass of Reposition." At both the opening and closing the Litany of the Saints is chanted, and a procession of the Blessed Sacrament is held. No Masses of Requiem are allowed in the church during the Adoration.

Although originally planned to continue for forty hours, the devotion does not generally last so long, at least in our part of the world, for the reason that a sufficient number of worshippers could hardly be provided during the night. Hence in our dioceses the exposition usually lasts on the opening day till about nine o'clock in the evening; on the second day, from the Mass for Peace till the same hour; and on the closing day from an early Mass till the end of the Mass of Reposition — altogether a little more or less than thirty hours.

The Indulgences. Several of the Popes have enriched the devotion with indulgences. A partial indulgence of seven years and as many "quarantines" (forty days) is gained each day that a visit is made to the church where the Blessed Sacrament is exposed. A plenary indulgence, applicable to the souls in Purgatory, is obtained by one visit with Confession and Holy Communion and the usual prayer for the intention of our Holy Father the Pope.

One of the great leaders of the Catholic Church in England — namely, Cardinal Wiseman — wrote these beautiful words concerning the Forty Hours' Adoration: "In no other time or place is the sublimity of our religion so touchingly felt. No ceremony is going on in the sanctuary, no sound of song is issuing from the choir, no voice of exhortation proceeds from the pulpit, no prayer is uttered aloud at the altar. There are hundreds there, and yet they are engaged in no congregational act of worship. Each heart and soul is alone in the midst of a multitude — each uttering its own thoughts, each feeling its own grace. Yet are you overpowered, subdued, quelled into a reverential mood, softened into a devotional spirit, forced to meditate, to feel, to pray."

CHAPTER XLIX

OUR DAILY PRAYERS

By including this chapter we do not wish to insinuate that daily prayers are something distinctively Catholic. In every form of religious belief frequent prayer is urged and practised; and in every Christian denomination there may be found, doubtless, an abiding faith in the efficacy of prayer and in the promises of our Blessed Lord.

Every Christian feels the necessity of frequent communion with his God. He knows that the Almighty wishes each of us to present our homage and petitions to Him, so that we may acknowledge His power and mercy, and may recognize our dependence upon Him. And as we receive favors from God every day, so our gratitude and homage should be offered to Him daily.

Thus the practice has arisen of praying to the Almighty each day — especially in the morning, when the toil an dangers of the day are before us, and in the evening, when we can appreciate the providence and watchful care which He has shown towards us during the day.

The Lord's Prayer. The greatest of all prayers is the Our Father. It is the only prayer that is entirely of divine origin. It was taught by our Lord to His disciples, and has been used by the Church since the very beginning of her history. The fifth, sixth, and seventh chapters of the Gospel of St. Matthew contain the "Sermon on the Mount," and the sixth is largely an instruction on prayer. Our Blessed Lord gave to His hearers a model prayer addressed to His Heavenly Father, expressing adoration, recognition of God's attributes, and petitions for the graces, temporal favors, forgiveness and protection needed by mankind — and expressing all of these in a few sentences and in simple words.

The wording of the prayer, as given by St. Matthew, is slightly different from that now used by us. It reads as follows: "Our Father, who art in heaven, hallowed be Thy name. Thy kingdom come. Thy will be done on earth as it is in heaven. Give us this day our supersubstantial bread, and forgive us our debts as we also forgive our debtors, and lead us not into temptation, but deliver us from evil. Amen."

In the Gospels of St. Mark and St. John the prayer is not recorded at all. In that of St. Luke it is found in a shorter form: "Father, hallowed beThy name. Thy kingdom come. Give us this day our daily bread, and forgive us our sins, for we also forgive everyone that is indebted to us. And lead us not into temptation."

The prayer, then, as used by the Church from the earliest times and as found in the most ancient liturgies, is a composite product, being formed by combining the versions given by these two Evangelists.

The Meaning of the Lord's Prayer. The Our Father is the greatest of all prayers, and the most perfect. It is addressed to God Himself, the Omnipotent, the Creator of all things, the Being to Whom we must look for all that we need in this world and in the next. Every word of it is pregnant with meaning, and, unfortunately, we too often recite it so hurriedly that our appreciation of that meaning is very vague. Let us analyze it.

We address God by the name of Father, because we know His infinite love for us, because He has made us His children. We say "Our" Father, because we know that He loves each of us, and because we pray not only for ourselves but for all mankind. We use the words "Who art in heaven," to show that it is God to Whom we pray. We say "Hallowed)that is, Blessed) be Thy name," to express our desire for the promotion of His glory; and by the next words we pray that His love and His truth may be made known to all men, that all may learn to do His holy will. Then follow the petitions — that through His providence we may obtain all that we need for soul and body; that our sins may be forgiven through His infinite charity, if we deserve forgiveness by showing charity to others; and that we may be preserved from temptation and from every evil. And, like nearly every other prayer, the Our Father is concluded with the Hebrew word "Amen," which signifies "truly," or "so be it."

The Concluding Words. "For thine is the kingdom, the

power and the glory, for ever and ever. Amen." Our Protestant friends (at least those of some denominations), use this sentence at the end of the Our Father. Are they right in doing so, or is there any authority for this addition to the Lord's Prayer? It is not found in the most authentic manuscripts of the Gospels, although it occurs in some of the old liturgical books of Eastern rites. In these books, however, it was not considered as an essential part of the Our Father, but as an "embolism," or added prayer, intended to increase the fervor and direct the intention of the faithful — a practice which was very common in the Oriental churches. We find an example of another embolism in the prayer which immediately follows the Our Father in our Mass, consisting of a repetition in another form of the request, "Deliver us from evil." It begins as follows: "Deliver us, we beseech, O Lord, from all evils, past, present and to come," and asks for peace and forgiveness through the intercession of the Blessed Virgin, the Apostles and the Saints.

Therefore, when non-Catholics ask us why we make the Our Father shorter than their form, we should tell them that the added words which they use are not a part of the prayer as given by our Blessed Lord, but a pious addition which is ancient indeed, but which the Roman Church has not seen fit to adopt in her ritual.

The Hail Mary. There is a prayer which Catholics recite more often than any other. It is the most familiar of all the prayers used by the Church to honor the Blessed Virgin. It forms the greatest part of the Rosary, a devotion that is practised at least occasionally by all Catholics and very frequently by the more fervent among them. It is recited at morning, noon and night, in the Angelus.

It is a prayer which owes its origin to inspiration from God, manifested through one of His Angels, one of His Saints, and His holy Church. It is one of the most complete and perfect of all prayers, expressing in a few words salutation, praise, congratulation, thanksgiving, and petition. This prayer is the Hail Mary.

It consists of three parts. The first is the salutation of the

Archangel Gabriel to Mary into which the Church has inserted her name: "Hail (Mary), full of grace, the Lord is with thee; blessed art thou amongst women." The second part is composed of the words of Elizabeth to our Lady: "Blessed is the fruit of thy womb," to which is annexed the sacred name of Jesus. And the third part is a beautiful petition added by the Church of God, giving expression the feeling with which we Catholics regard the Mother of God and declaring our confidence in her intercession: "Holy Mary, Mother of God, pray for us sinners, now and at the hour of our death. Amen."

The Origin of the "Hail Mary." What is the history of this beautiful prayer? For many centuries it was unknown — a circumstance which seems remarkable to us, who use it so frequently. We may well wonder how Catholics ever prayed without it; but it is a historical fact that the Hail Mary did not exist at all until the eleventh century, and even then only a part of it was used as a prayer.

Its origin was as follows: The monastic orders were accustomed to recite lengthy offices each day; and on certain feasts, especially those of the Blessed Virgin, these services were supplemented by the "Little Office" of Mary. In this the words of the Archangel and of St. Elizabeth were used repeatedly in the form of versicles and responses. Gradually it became a pious practice, not only for the monks but for the laity, to use these sentences as a prayer. In the year 1196 the Bishop of Paris ordered his clergy to teach these words to their flocks, and within a short time the prayer became well known throughout the Catholic world.

A little later the holy name of Jesus was added, probably by Pope Urban IV, and the last part, "Holy Mary, Mother of God," etc., was introduced about the year 1500, as it was felt that this beautiful expression of devotion to our Mother would be more complete if it included a petition to obtain her powerful intercession.

The Apostles' Creed. In our daily devotions, after offering to our Heavenly Father the prayer taught to us by His Divine Son, and after having saluted her who is "full of grace," we are counselled to make a declaration of our faith, to express in words what we believe to be God's revelation to man. Each of us in early childhood learned a compendium of our Catholic faith, a formula which contains the most important truths of our Church's doctrine. This is known as the Apostles' Creed.

It is called a "Creed" from its first word — in Latin, "Credo," I believe. Why do we call it the "Apostles'" Creed? Because throughout the Middle Ages there was a widespread belief that the Apostles composed it on the day of Pentecost. An ancient legend, dating back to the sixth century and perhaps further, tells us that when the Apostles were assembled at Jerusalem and had just received the Holy Ghost in the form of tongues of fire, each of them, inspired by the Spirit of God, contributed one of the articles of the Creed. According to the story, when the Holy Spirit had filled the souls of the Apostles with knowledge and zeal, St. Peter arose and cried out, "I believe in God, the Father Almighty, Creator of heaven and earth." St. Andrew continued, "And in Jesus Christ, His only Son, our Lord." St. James added "Who was conceived by the Holy Ghost," etc. And so on for the others.

Bear in mind, however, that all this is a legend, of uncertain origin and of very slight probability. There is no allusion to it in the Scriptural account of the events of Pentecost, and the whole story is probably the product of the vivid imagination of some Oriental or Latin romancer. Spiritual writers of those early days, like some of later times, were prone to enrich their pages with details that would have been wonderful if they had been true.

A Profession of Faith. The Apostles' Creed is, very likely, an amplified form of the "profession of faith" required in the early centuries from converts. In Apostolic times, as at the present day, those who desired Baptism were obliged to make a statement of their belief; and it is probable that the Creed was brought to its present form gradually, being developed from the declaration exacted from those converted to the faith.

The Creed is supposed to be a summary of Christian dogmas. Why is it only a partial summary? Why does it not contain all the articles of Catholic belief? There is no mention in it of the Sacraments, except the "Forgiveness of sin"; there is no allusion to the Holy Eucharist, the central object of our Catholic worship. The reason is that, in the early centuries of Catholicity, the faith in its entirety was not taught to converts until after they had been received into the Church. The knowledge of the "Divine Mysteries," that is, the nature of the Mass and the adoration of the living presence of our Lord in the Eucharist, was not imparted to them until after Baptism. When they learned the Creed, they learned only what the Church wished to teach them; and therefore the things which they were not to know were not included in it.

The Confiteor. This is a prayer which is used not only in daily devotions but on many other occasions — in the Sacrament of Penance, in the Divine Office, and especially by the priest at the beginning of the Mass.

Like the Creed, it takes its name from its first word. "Confiteor," in Latin, means "I confess." The Confiteor is a general confession of sin, an acknowledgment of guilt, made in the presence of God and His Saints, and a prayer that the Saints may intercede for the sinner.

The Confiteor was originally a part of the private prayers offered by the priest in preparation for Mass, expressing his unworthiness and asking for grace and forgiveness. After a time, about the tenth century, it became customary for the priest to say this prayer at the foot of the altar, and gradually it came to be regarded as a part of the Mass.

The Confiteor is used also at the administration of Holy Communion, publicly or privately; at Extreme Unction, and at the giving of the Apostolic blessing and indulgence to the dying.

Until quite recently it was usual to recite the first part of the Confiteor in the confessional before making the accusation of sins; but at the present time, for the sake of expediting the confession, it is recommended that it be said before entering, and that only the words "I confess to Almighty God and to you, Father," be used in the confessional.

Asking the Intercession of Saints. Why do we say the Confiteor? Why should one confess his sins to the Blessed Virgin and to the Saints, none of whom have any power to absolve from sin? This objection may be found in some Protestant works. We answer that it is reasonable to make a general acknowledgment of our weakness and guilt before these as well as before God, because we wish their prayers in order to secure His pardon. Therefore we declare that we "have sinned exceedingly, in thought, word and deed." We state the reasons why we wish them "to pray to the Lord our God" for us, but we know full well that forgiveness cannot come from them; and so we conclude the prayer with the words: "May the Almighty God forgive me my sins, and bring me to everlasting life. May the Almighty and merciful Lord grant me pardon, absolution, and remission of all my sins. Amen."

The Acts. The purpose of the Acts of Faith, Hope and Love is to testify that we possess these three great "theological virtues"; and the Act of Contrition puts into words the sorrow for sin which is necessary for forgiveness.

For the Acts a different wording is to be found in nearly every manual of prayers, and the Church has not declared that any one form must be used. The version with is taught in our later catechisms is clear and concise.

The Act of Faith declares our firm belief in one God and three Divine persons; in the Incarnation of our Lord, and the redemption accomplished by Him; and in all the other truths that God's Church teaches.

An Act of Hope expresses our trust in God's mercy and our reliance on the merits of our Blessed Redeemer.

An Act of Love manifests our love of God for His own sake, because he is the Supreme Good, and love of our neighbor for the sake of God; for our Lord has declared that the love of God is "the first and greatest commandment," and that "the second is like unto this: Thou shalt love thy neighbor as thyself."

The Act of Contrition is the declaration in words of that sorrow for sin which is absolutely required for its forgiveness. This also can be found in various forms, and the one now generally taught is perhaps better than some of the older versions, as it expresses clearly the motives of contrition and is fairly simple in wording.

Prayers at Meals. Our catechisms, after the daily prayers, insert a short form of prayer to be used before and after meals. The prayer before meals is known as a "blessing," for it consists in the invoking of God's blessing upon us and upon what we are about to receive; and that after meals is called a "grace," from the Latin word "gratiae," meaning "thanks," because it expresses our gratitude for our food and all other favors which God has given us.

There is no strict rule about the wording of these prayers. In convents and religious houses the blessing and grace are somewhat long, being made up of several verses, responses and prayers. For the use of the laity the brief form in our catechism is sufficient.

Such, then, is the history and the analysis of the prayers which our Holy Church recommends to us for daily use. Every Catholic should recite them at morning and night — the Our Father, to give homage to the Almighty and to invoke His protection; the Hail Mary, to honor our Blessed Mother and to obtain her intercession; the Creed, to profess our holy faith; the Confiteor, to acknowledge our unworthiness; and the Acts, to animate us with faith, hope, love and contrition.

Chapter L

THE LITANIES

In his devotions and prayers it seems to be natural for man to invent and multiply terms of praise. In many forms of worship the practice has existed of joining in one prayer the various titles of the deity adored and the various terms of salutation addressed to him; and here, as in many other pious practices, the Catholic Church has adapted to her own purposes something which was in common use in other religions. She has taken advantage of many commendable features of the Jewish and even of pagan rituals; and she has done this because in her wisdom she wishes to make use of everything which seems to promise good results in the exciting of devotion among her children.

A Jewish Litany. To illustrate the manner in which the Jews used what we now call a litany, we have only to refer to the 135th Psalm. This was used in the public worship of the Temple, being recited alternately by priest and people, and was also employed in private devotions. It enumerates the attributes of God, and consists of twenty-seven verses, each ending with the words "For His mercy endureth forever." This repetition gives the whole psalm the effect of a litany, such as is recited in our Church. In like manner we find in the Book of Daniel the canticle of the three youths in the fiery furnace; each verse ends with the words "Praise and exalt Him above all for ever."

How Catholic Litanies Began. In the early centuries of our Church's history it was customary to have prayers with responses, resembling our present litanies, in the Mass itself. The only trace of this practice that now remains is the repetition of the Greek words "Kyrie eleison, Christe eleison, Kyrie eleison" (Lord, have mercy; Christ, have mercy; Lord, have mercy"), which originally formed a part of these Mass litanies.

When peace was granted to the Church after three centuries of persecution, public devotions and processions became common. These processions were called "litanies," from the Greek word "lite," meaning a prayer or supplication; and they were frequently held on days which had been religious festivals among the heathen.

From this comes the practice which has endured to the present time, of reciting the Litany of the Saints in the Divine Office on the feast of St. Mark, April 25 — a day which was in pagan times a great festival, celebrated with religious processions, to bring a blessing upon the newly planted fields.

This Litany is recited also on the Rogation Days — the Monday, Tuesday and Wednesday before the feast of the Ascension. The word Rogation means a petitioning, and the practice of saying the Litany on those days goes back to the year 477, when it was prescribed by St. Mamertus, the bishop of Vienne, in France, on account of many calamities which had afflicted that country — earthquakes, tempests and the ravages of wild beasts. This was repeated year after year; the practice gradually spread throughout the world, and was finally approved by St. Leo III in thee year 816. The object of these days of devotion is to beg of god, the Giver of all good, that He will preserve the fruits of the earth and bestow upon His creatures all necessary blessings.

The Approved Litanies. For the public services of the Church only five litanies are authorized. These are the Litany of the Saints, of the Blessed Virgin, of the Holy Name of Jesus, of the Sacred Heart and of St. Joseph. In former centuries many litanies were in vogue; at one time they numbered about eighty. In 1601 Clement VIII prohibited the public recitation of any of these, except the Litany of the Saints and that of the Blessed Virgin. Somewhat later, despite this ruling, various other litanies cane more or less into use, owing to the zeal and devotion (sometimes misguided) of the religiously inclined. Some of these litanies may be found in the older prayer-books; but with the exception of the five mentioned above, they are not approved by the Church for her public services, even though some of them may be tolerated for private devotion. Certain litanies which have been published are almost heretical, imputing to the saints powers and attributes which belong to God alone, and changing the veneration proper to them into something very closely resembling the supreme homage which is due to the Almighty. Therefore in 1821 the Church issued a decree forbidding the public recitation of any except the approved litanies, and prohibiting any addition or modification of these unless by the especial sanction of the Holy

See. As we shall see further on, the Church's approval has been given to three more litanies than were permitted by the above papal decrees.

The Litany of the Saints. This is the model of all other litanies, being much more ancient than the others which the Church uses. It is called the Litany of the Saints because it is made up of petitions addressed to various saints of different classes — apostles, martyrs, confessors and virgins, as well as to Mary, the Queen of Saints. It was prescribed by Pope Gregory the Great in 590 for a public procession of thanksgiving which took place on the cessation of the plague which had devastated Rome. In a somehow different form it was in use at a much earlier date, for it is mentioned by St. Basil in the fourth century and by others in the third — although it was probably much shorter then than it is now, for the reason that prior to the fourth century only martyr-saints were publicly honored by the Church. This can be seen in the Canon of the Mass, which owes its present form largely to St. Gregory, and in which no saints are mentioned except martyrs.

The Church at the present day makes use of three forms of the Litany of the Saints. One, which is the most common, is used in many ceremonies — at the laying of the cornerstone of a church, at the blessing of a church or cemetery, on the Rogation Days, at the Devotion of the Forty Hours, and on some other occasions. Another form, somewhat shorter, is employed on Holy Saturday and the vigil of Pentecost. The third is that which is called the Litany of the Dying, or the "Commendation of a Soul Departing," and the invocations and petitions are all offered to obtain God's mercy on the soul that is about to appear before Him. The first or usual form is recommended for private devotion, but there is no indulgence granted for its recital.

The Litany of the Holy Name. This litany is made up of our Blessed Lord, with a petition for His mercy annexed to each of them. Its authorship is not known, but it has been ascribed to St. Bernadine of Siena and St. John Capistran, zealous preachers of the devotion to the Holy Name at the beginning of the fifteenth century. In the year 1588 Pope Sixtus V granted an indulgence of three hundred days for its recitation, and for many years it was used in various countries but not approved by the Church for public services, applications for such approval being rejected at various times. In fact, the prohibition by Clement VIII of any other litanies except those of the Saints and of the Blessed Virgin rendered the public recitation of this litany unlawful, but it continued to be used privately in many parts of the world.

In 1862, however, Pius IX gave his approval to one form of it, and granted an indulgence of three hundred days to the faithful of any diocese whose bishop had applied for it. Finally, in 1886, urged by the wonderful spread of the devotion to the Sacred Name of Jesus and the growth of the great society of men who honor that Holy Name, Leo XIII extended this indulgence to all the world and thereby gave the Church's full approbation to this beautiful prayer.

The Litany of the Blessed Virgin. "Behold, from henceforth all generations shall call me blessed." This sublime prophecy of Mary herself has been verified in all the ages of the Church's history. Even in early centuries the devout faithful found in Mary the fulfillment of many of the prophecies of the Old Testament, and discovered in the inspired verses of the Psalmist many beautiful figures and symbols of the Blessed Mother of God. These were soon used as pious ejaculations, and new titles were invented from time to time; and all these were gradually woven into litanies of various forms. Thus after a time the Litany of the Blessed Virgin was moulded into shape, very much as we have it now.

Among the five litanies approved by the Church, this one is used perhaps more commonly than the others. It is often called the "Litany of Loreto," because it came into use about four centuries ago at the famous Italian shrine which, according to tradition or legend, contains the little house of Nazareth in which our Saviour dwelt in childhood. This litany is a series of beautiful invocations of our Blessed Mother, addressing her by various titles and beseeching her intercession.

Its origin is obscure and its authorship unknown. There is a legend that it was composed by the Apostles, after the Assumption of Mary into heaven — but it is only a legend; it has no historical foundation whatever. By some writers it is said to have been composed at Loreto in the thirteenth century; by others it is attributed to Pope Sergius I, in 687, or to St. Gregory the Great; but there is no real evidence that (in anything like its present form) it goes back beyond the latter years of the fifteenth century. Before that time, indeed, there were litanies of Mary — one in Gaelic, probably of the eighth century, and others of later date, in which the invocations were much longer than those in the Litany of Loreto. It was seen, after a time, that a litany composed of short ejaculations was more effective and devotional and better adapted to public recitation; and so the Litany of Loreto was gradually developed until it became substantially as we have it now. At the shrine it was recited daily by thousands of pilgrims who gathered there, and in the year 1587 it was approved by Pope Sixtus V, who urged preachers throughout the world to promote its use among the faithful.

New petitions have been inserted into it from time to time. For instance, the title "Help of Christians," though used occasionally at an earlier date, was approved by the Holy See in commemoration of a great event in the history of the Church and of Christian civilization — the great naval battle of Lepanto, on October 7, 1571, when the Moslem hordes were frustrated in their attempt to conquer Europe. On the day of the battle prayers were being offered up, by order of the Sovereign Pontiff St. Pius V, in the churches of the world. The infidels were utterly defeated and their great fleet destroyed, and the nations of Europe were saved from the yoke of Islam through the intercession of the Blessed Mother of God.

The invocation "Queen of All Saints" was added by Pope Pius VII when he returned to Rome after his long imprisonment by order of Napoleon. The title "Queen Conceived without Original Sin" dates from 1846, although the solemn definition of the dogma of the Immaculate Conception was not made until eight years later. The words "Queen of the Most Holy Rosary," used by Rosary societies for more than two hundred years, were not sanctioned for the whole Church until 1883. The invocation "Mother of Good Counsel" was approved by Leo XIII in 1903; and the latest addition, "Queen of Peace, pray for us," was ordered by Benedict XV in 1917.

What indulgences are annexed to the Litany of the Blessed Virgin? There are two, a partial and a plenary indulgence. Pius VII granted one of three hundred days every time it is said; and anyone who recites it every day may obtain a plenary indulgence, under the usual conditions, on the five principal feasts of the Blessed Virgin — the Immaculate Conception, Nativity, Annunciation, Purification and Assumption.

The usual mode of reciting this litany is to say before it the beautiful prayer "We fly to thy patronage," and to conclude it with the "Hail, holy Queen," followed by the prayer "Pour forth, we beseech Thee, O Lord" — but while all these are to be recommended, they are not necessary for the gaining of the indulgences. The litany itself is all that is required.

The Litany of the Sacred Heart. The fourth among the litanies approved by the Church is that of the Sacred Heart of Jesus. Its approval is the latest event in the history of a wonderful devotion. Homage to the Sacred Heart of our Lord has become widely known only since the seventeenth century; and it was not until near the end of the eighteenth (in 1794) that the devotion was approved and indulgences were granted to those who practised it. The feast of the Sacred Heart had been previously observed in certain places, beginning about 1765; and in 1856 this festival was extended to the whole world. In 1889 it was raised to a higher rank in the Church's calendar by Leo XIII, and finally, in 1899, the same Pontiff authorized the beautiful Litany of the Sacred Heart.

It begins, as do the other litanies, with petitions to the Persons of the Trinity, and contains thirty-three invocations to the Heart of Jesus, which is entitled "sacred temple of God," "burning furnace of charity," "fountain of life and holiness," and so on. The litany closes with the usual threefold prayer to the Lamb of God, with the versicle and response: "Jesus, meek and humble of heart: Make our hearts like to Thine," followed by a prayer to God the Father, asking for mercy in the name of God the Son.

The Litany of St. Joseph. The most recent of the litanies approved by our Church is that of St. Joseph. A spirit of devotion to the great Saint who was the foster-father of our Divine Lord and the spouse and protector of the Blessed Virgin, has been constantly increasing among Catholics. In the earliest days of our Church it was customary to give religious homage only to saints who were martyrs; but even then the virtues of the holy St. Joseph were recognized and lauded. About the fourth century a festival in his honor was observed in some Eastern churches, but he was not venerated publicly in the churches of the Roman rite until the twelfth century, and his feast on March 19 was not established until the Pontificate of Sixtus IV, about the year 1480. Another feast, that of the Patronage of St. Joseph, which originated with the Carmelite nuns, was extended to the whole Church in 1847 by Pius IX, who, in 1870, solemnly proclaimed St. Joseph the Patron of the Universal Church.

The Litany of St. Joseph was sanctioned by Pius X on March 18, 1909, and, being of such recent origin, is not yet to be found in many prayer books. It is very beautiful in its wording, and is not unduly long. After the usual petitions to the Holy Trinity and one addressed to the Blessed Virgin, the litany is composed of twenty-five invocations expressing the virtues and dignities of St. Joseph. An indulgence of three hundred days may be gained once a day by reciting it.

PART IX
MISCELLANEOUS

Chapter LI

SERVICES FOR THE DEAD

Love of the departed and a desire to perpetuate their memory is to be found in every race and tribe, whether barbarous or civilized. Thee ancient countries of Asia are noted for their sepulchral monuments. The mighty pyramids of Egypt have been found to be tombs of dead monarchs. In distant India may still be seen the fairy-like Taj Mahal, perhaps the most beautiful edifice in the world, erected by a Hindoo king as a memorial and sepulchre for his beloved queen. Outside the walls of Jerusalem are the tombs of the great ones of Israel. Along the roads that radiate from the gates of Rome are the ruins of the final resting-places of patricians and of emperors.

All nations honor their dead. Whether enlightened by faith or groping in error, all strive to keep alive the memory of those whom death has taken away; all endeavor to manifest their undying love for those who have gone before. But the Catholic Church does more than this. She is a true mother to her children, and her solicitude extends not only to their perishable bodies, not only to their memory, which will endure but for a time, but to their immortal souls. Her faith teaches that the soul, when it has been separated from the body and has received its sentence from its Maker, may need help from its friends who remain on earth. Its time for meriting is over, but it may obtain merit through the prayers and good works of those who are still able to acquire merit, and particularly through the petitions of the Church in the Holy Sacrifice of the Mass.

Why the Church Honors Dead Bodies. But why does the Church pay so much attention to the perishable body, the lifeless clay, soon to be the food of worms? We can easily understand that she would be solicitous for the soul of the departed; but why should she pay honor to the body after the soul has left it?

Because the Church's faith teaches that the body has been the temple of the Holy Ghost, and is to be reunited to the soul on the day of general judgment, to share its external destiny. The body is the instrument which the soul has used for God's service. Without it the soul could not have attained to its happiness; and so the body, in the designs of God, is destined to participate in the bliss which He will give to the faithful soul. "I know that my Redeemer liveth, and that in the last day I shall rise out of the earth, and I shall be clothed again with my skin, and in my flesh I shall see my God, Whom I myself shall see and my eyes shall behold, and not another."

A Tabernacle of God. The body has received the waters of Baptism, the chrism of Confirmation, the holy oil of Extreme Unction — and hundreds of times during its life it has been a living tabernacle of the Body and Blood of Jesus Christ. And so, when death has come to the Catholic, the Church not only endeavors to help his soul, but she gives the last honors to his body. It is brought into the house of God in solemn procession, the adorable Sacrifice of the Mass is offered in its presence, the odor of sweet incense arises around it, holy water is sprinkled on it, and it is then laid away in ground that has been consecrated by the prayers of the Church.

Supplications for Mercy. How often we read in our daily papers the funeral orations delivered over those who are not Catholics — always laudatory, sometimes fulsome in their praises of the departed. There is never a word to indicate that he may have been a sinner, or that he may be in dire need of prayer by which the mercy of God may be implored in his behalf. Such is not the spirit of the Church in her services for her dead. She looks upon death as a punishment for sin; she remembers that nothing defiled can enter heaven; and so she treats the dead as souls in which some stain of sin may have been found by the all-seeing eye of God, or which may not have fully satisfied the debt of temporal punishment due for sins forgiven. She takes the salvation of no one as certain, be he Pope or king or peasant. Her funeral services are always a supplication for God's mercy on the departed soul.

The Ceremonies before Mass. In our country it is not customary to carry out all the rules of the ritual concerning obsequies. We are not living in a Catholic land, and circumstances will not permit the doing of many things that are beautiful and instructive indeed, but are not essential to the Church's ceremonial. In some parts of the world the custom is in vogue of beginning the funeral rites at the house where the death took place, and of continuing them in a solemn procession to the church; but among us these ceremonies are shortened, and generally take place at the church only.

It is the rule in some churches to have the clergy meet the body at the door and accompany it to the altar, where it is placed just outside the sanctuary. If the deceased was a lay person, his feet are pointed towards the altar, so that he is, as it were, facing it. If he were a priest, the body is turned the opposite way, the face towards the congregation, to signify that his work during life was to instruct the people from the altar.

Masses of Requiem. It is the wish of the Church that, whenever it is possible, her children should be buried with a Mass. This is not only the most solemn way in which they may receive her final blessing, but also the most efficacious for their soul's salvation. The Mass which is celebrated on that occasion is full of touching symbolism and expressive prayer. The priest is garbed in sombre black, the color of death, and all ornaments are removed from the altar or shrouded in penitential wrappings. The veil before the tabernacle door is purple, the color of penance, for it would not be fitting to put black on the dwelling-place of our Saviour living in the Holy Eucharist. Around the coffin are black candlesticks, usually six in number.

Masses for the dead are much shorter than those said on other occasions. All parts expressive of joy are omitted; the whole intention of the Church is to pray for the departed one, that God's judgment upon him may be merciful. And so there is no opening psalm of confidence and hope ("I will go unto the altar of God, of God Who rejoiceth my youth," etc.). There is no Gloria, the joyful canticle of the angels. There are no Alleluias, such as we find in other Masses at most seasons of the year. There is no Credo, such as is said or sung in the Masses of Sundays and many festivals. When the words of the Agnus Dei are said, the priest does not ask the Lamb of God to "have mercy on us," but to "give eternal rest" to the faithful departed. Instead of the parting "Ite, missa est" ("Go, the Mass is over"), the priest prays "Requiescat in pace" ("May they rest in peace"). In these Masses there is no mention of any festival or saint's day — nothing but the expression of the Church's sorrow and hope, and the presenting of her fervent petitions for the eternal welfare of the departed.

The "Dies Irae." The Beautiful "Dies Irae" ("Day of Wrath"), one of the oldest of the rhyming metrical hymns of the Church, forms a part of the Mass for the dead. It has exercised the talents of the greatest musical composers and of translators in almost all languages. It is said to have been composed by Thomas of Celano, a companion of St. Francis of Assisi, about the year 1200, and it sets before us a vivid picture of the Last Judgment — the coming of the Judge, the opening of the books, the anguish and remorse of the reprobates; and it concludes with a fervent prayer for the souls of the faithful: "Loving Lord Jesus, grant them rest. Amen." All Masses for the dead which are said in black vestments are known as Requiem Masses, from the opening words of the Introit: "Requiem æternam dona eis, Domine" — "Rest eternal grant unto them, O Lord."

Kinds of Requiem Masses. Besides the Mass on the day of burial the Church has authorized Masses for the third and seventh day after death (although these are not generally celebrated in this country), and for the thirtieth day — usually called the "Month's Mind." All of these are very similar to the funeral Mass, except in the wording of some of the prayers. There is also an anniversary Mass, differing from the others, chiefly in the Epistle and Gospel read in it. On other occasions a Mass is used called the "Missa Quotidiana," the "Daily Mass" of Requiem.

The Catafalque. Why does the Church use "an imitation of a coffin" at the commemorative Masses which are sung at certain times after the funeral? It seems peculiar to witness the incensing and the

Catafalque

sprinkling of a pall-covered frame — to behold the solemn ritual of the Church carried out over it as though it contained a human body.

This catafalque, as it is called, has an interesting history. It originated at the time of the Crusades, or perhaps a little earlier. In those centuries it happened sometimes that a pious Christian knight went on a pilgrimage to the Holy Land, or buckled on his armour to win back the Sepulchre of our Lord from the hated Saracens; and it happened also that in many instances the pious Christian knight did not come back. Pestilence or shipwreck or the Moslem scimitar put an end to his life, and it was not usually possible to bring his earthly remains back to his native land. But the Church wished to pay honor to his memory, and to celebrate for him the final rites of her liturgy; and so it became customary to erect in the church a huge funeral pile, decorated with emblems of mourning an sometimes bearing the armorial shield, knightly sword, helmet, spurs and other insignia of his rank.

Such was the origin of the catafalque; and when for any reason, at the present day, the body cannot be present at a funeral service, or at the celebration of anniversary or other solemn Masses, the same practice is adhered to. A representation of a coffin, suitably enshrouded in a sable pall, is placed before the alter, to typify the body of the deceased; and over it the Church performs the various ceremonies which would ordinarily take place over the remains of the departed one.

After the Mass. When the Mass is finished the celebrant lays aside the chasuble and maniple, puts on a black cope, and turns to the place where the body lies. The ensuing services are known as the "Absolution." He reads a prayer: "Enter not into judgment with Thy servant, O Lord," asking the divine mercy on him who during his life was signed with the seal of the Most Holy Trinity. The choir then chants the "Libera" — "Deliver me, O Lord, from everlasting death on that dread day"; a most touching appeal of the soul trembling with fear before the tribunal of God. "I am made to tremble, and I fear, at the thought of judgment and the wrath to come."

Then while the Pater Noster is being recited, the priest

sprinkles the coffin with holy water, typifying the preservation of body and soul from the dominion of Satan; and he then incenses it on all sides, to express the honor that is due to the former temple of the Holy Ghost and tabernacle of Jesus Christ.

A prayer is then chanted, which is the same as that said in the early part of the Mass: "O God, to Whom it belongeth always to show mercy and to spare, we humbly beseech Thee for the soul of Thy departed servant N., whom Thou hast this day called out of the world, that Thou deliver it not into the hands of the enemy nor forget it forever, but command that it be received by Thy holy angels and taken to Paradise, its true country; that, as it has believed and hoped in Thee, it may not suffer the pains of hell, but have joy everlasting. Through Christ our Lord. Amen."

Going to the Grave. When the priest or priests accompany the body to the cemetery, as is done in some Catholic countries, a beautiful prayer is read while the procession is wending its way thither. "May the angels lead thee into Paradise; at they coming may the martyrs receive thee and bring thee to Jerusalem the holy city. May the choirs of angels receive thee, and, with Lazarus once a beggar, mayest thou have eternal rest."

The Benedictus, or Canticle of Zachary ("Blessed be the Lord God of Israel") is then said or sung, with an antiphon formed of the consoling words of our Blessed Saviour to the sorrowing sisters of Lazarus: "I am the Resurrection and the Life. He that believeth in Me, although he be dead, shall life; and every one that liveth and believeth in Me shall not die forever." This is followed by a prayer in which the divine mercy is besought for the deceased because he has had the desire of doing God's will, although he may have deserved punishment for his misdeeds.

Such is the closing ceremony of the earthly career of a Catholic. We have all been present at it many times, and we all hope that it will be performed over us. The infidel would have us believe that he expects total annihilation when this life is over; the non-Catholic Christian, though he may imitate some of the rites of our Church, has no belief in any intercessory prayer for the dead, and generally contents himself with an indiscriminate laudation of the departed. The Catholic Church acts differently.

She knows that the immortal soul, still a member of the Church of Christ, may be in suffering which can be relieved and shortened by the prayers of the other members of that Church. And so she offers her public prayers and urges her children to pray in private for the souls of the faithful who have passed through the gates of death, teaching us that, although separation has come, it is but for a time, and that even while it continues there is a bond of union, the "Communion of Saints," between us who are still on earth and our loved ones who "have gone before."

Chapter LII

THE CHURCHING OF WOMEN

THE Church has instituted a ceremony of thanksgiving by which mothers may express their gratitude to God for the blessing conferred upon them in their motherhood, and may receive the solemn benediction of the Church when they enter God's temple for the first time after that blessing has been given to them.

This ceremony is generally known as "churching," but the Ritual calls it "the blessing of a woman after childbirth." "Churching" would seem to imply that permission is given to the woman to enter the church — whereas no such permission is necessary; and the longer title is really the more correct.

Different from the Jewish Rite. While this blessing was undoubtedly suggested by the rite of legal purification prescribed by the Jewish law, it differs essentially from the latter. The Jewish rite was based on the idea of legal defilement. The sufferings of motherhood were looked upon as a part of the penalty imposed on Eve and all her daughters. "I will multiply the sorrows and thy conceptions; in sorrow shalt thou bring forth children." And so, during the centuries from Eve to Mary, the noble function of motherhood was considered as necessarily associated with guilt. On this account, when the liturgical law of the Jews was formulated by Moses, a solemn ceremony was prescribed for the removing of the "legal defilement" resulting from the bearing of a child.

It must be understood, however, that the Jews did not consider that there was any stain of sin on the mother. Legal defilement was not sin. It was merely a restriction imposed by law, requiring the woman to comply with certain conditions before she would be allowed to take part in the public worship of God, on account of the fact that she had been subjected to the penalty inflicted don our mother Eve.

But with the coming of our second mother, Mary, womankind was elevated and ennobled. Sin had entered into the world through a woman; redemption from sin came through a woman also; and motherhood, although still a painful ordeal, was no longer looked upon as a penalty. It became truly honorable, calling for thanksgiving instead of purification.

The Origin of the Blessing. Our Blessed Mother Mary, in her humility and her obedience to the laws of her religion, submitted to the Jewish rite of purification after she had given birth to the Redeemer of the world. In imitation of her it became customary in early Christian times for women to abstain from entering the church for a certain time after God had blessed them with offspring. They then sought the blessing of the priest at the door of the church before entering, and made their first visit as an act of thanksgiving for their safe delivery. The exact time when this pious custom originated is not known; but it is of very ancient date, and has been traced back to the fourth century, shortly after the Council of Nice.

Who Should Receive It? The Church does not wish that this beautiful blessing should be given to all mothers indiscriminately. It is for honorable motherhood only. The bearing of an illegitimate child is not an occasion for thanksgiving, and therefore only those mothers whose children are born in lawful wedlock can claim this benediction of the Church. It may be given to a mother whose child has died without Baptism, because even then she has great reason for thanking God for her own preservation.

It must be distinctly understood that there is no obligation to receive this blessing. It would not be even a venial sin to omit it. On one or two occasions certain bishops and provincial councils tried to impose an obligation regarding "churching," but the Holy See refused to sanction the innovation.

How the Blessing is Given. The ceremony must take place at a church, although it need not be the parish church to which the woman belongs; but there is a certain propriety in receiving this blessing in one's own church, with the pastor or his representative as the officiating priest, in the presence of the congregation of which she is a member.

This blessing is never given outside the church. Even in the case of a mother who is in danger of death, it would be allowable to infringe on this rule, because since there is no obligation to receive it there can be no sin in omitting it. But when Mass is said in a building which is not a church, as may be the case in country missions, the blessing may be given there.

The Ceremonies and Prayers. The Ritual directs that the ceremony should begin at the door of the church, where the woman kneels, holding in her hand a lighted candle; but it has become customary to perform this part of it at the altar-rail. The priest, vested in a surplice and white stole and accompanied by an acolyte, sprinkles the woman with holy water and recites the twenty-third Psalm: "The Lord's is the earth and the fullness thereof," with the antiphon: "She shall receive a blessing from the Lord, and mercy from God her salvation; because this is the generation of those who seek the Lord."

The priest then extends the end of his stole, which the woman takes in her hand, to denote that she is being led into the church by him to offer thanks to God. The priest says: "Enter into the temple of God, and adore the Son of the Blessed Virgin Mary, Who has given thee fruitfulness"; and it is customary for the woman to kiss the priest's stole. Then, while she prays silently in thanksgiving for God's blessings, the "Kyrie eleison" and the "Our Father" are said by the priest, followed by several short verses. And finally a beautiful prayer is recited as follows: "Almighty, eternal God, Who through the delivery of the Blessed Virgin Mary hast turned the childbirth pains of Thy faithful into joy, look kindly on this Thy handmaid, who has come to Thy temple joyfully for thanksgiving; and grant that after this life, by the merits and intercession of the same Blessed Mary, she and her offspring may deserve to attain to the joys of eternal blessedness. Through Christ our Lord, Amen."

The woman is then sprinkled with holy water and is solemnly blessed with the words: "May peace and the blessing of God Almighty, the Father and Son and Holy Ghost, descend upon thee and remain forever. Amen."

It is customary to make an offering on the occasion of receiving this blessing. The ceremony is in imitation of the Jewish rite to which Mary submitted, at which she made the sacrificial offering of a pair of doves. It is therefore proper that when a Catholic woman wishes to express her gratitude for the favor which Almighty God has bestowed on her, she should make a suitable gift for religious purposes, according to her means — that thereby she may manifest her dependence on God's bounty and her thankfulness for all the favors which have been conferred upon her.

CHAPTER LIII

FASTING AND ABSTINENCE

THE penitential practices of fasting and abstinence are of very ancient origin. The Church, in her earliest days, recognized the necessity for her children to "chastise the body and bring it under subjection," as St. Paul advises. "I see a law in my members fighting against the law of my mind and making me captive to sin . . . The wisdom of the flesh is death, but the wisdom of the spirit is life. If I live according to the flesh, I shall die; but if by the spirit I mortify the works of the flesh, I shall live."

The doctrine of St. Paul has been repeated by every writer in the whole list of the Church's teachers. Century after century those who have written of spiritual things have sought to impress upon us that we human beings are composed of a human body which is perishable and a soul which is immortal; that the body is striving ever for mastery over the spirit; and that, therefore, besides the external sources of temptation which we summarize as "the world" and "the devil," we have always with us another, even more dangerous, which we cannot shun, for it is a part of our very nature. This is the reason for mortification. Besides rendering the assaults of our bodily passions less dangerous for us, the practice of self-denial in things that are lawful will enable us to turn with greater earnestness to spiritual things.

Fasting in the Jewish Law. The Catholic Church took the practice of fasting from the law of the Old Testament, and has modified and adapted it to the necessities of her children. We find in the rules imposed by Moses on the Israelites that on the Day of Atonement a strict fast was to be observed by all; and the great lawgiver of the Jews himself fasted for forty days, as did the prophet Elias at a later date. In the warnings of the other prophets to the people of Israel there are many urgings to fasting as a means of reconciliation with God.

In the New Testament. The practice of fasting was sanctioned by our Blessed Lord, by example and by word. To prepare Himself for His public ministry, He retired into the desert and spent forty days in fasting and prayer. In one of His instructions to the Apostles He said — "When ye fast, be not as the hypocrites, sad. . . . Appear not to men to fast, but to thy Father, Who is in secret, and thy Father, who seeth in secret, will repay thee." In many passages of the New Testament we find how faithful the early Christians were to this practice. "As they were ministering to the Lord and fasting." (Acts, XIII). — "Let us exhibit ourselves as ministers of God, in much patience, in fastings." (II Cor., VI.)

History of the Church's Law. Fasting, as a precept of the Church, goes back to very early times. We do not know precisely when it was enjoined upon the faithful as a command instead of a counsel, but it is mentioned as a long-established practice by Tertullian and other writers of his time. Among certain heretical sects of the first centuries of the rigors of fasting and bodily mortification were greater even than among Catholics; but the austerities of the latter were far in excess of anything which we, living in these degenerate times, would deem possible.

Up to the eighth century, during the Lenten season and on certain other occasions, the faithful kept an absolute fast until sunset; and the meal taken then consisted of bread and vegetables. In some parts of the world even water was not used during the day. Eating at noon was not permitted at all. It was customary to have Mass celebrated in the evening, and many of the congregation received Holy Communion at that time, as both clergy and faithful were still fasting. The people usually assembled in their churches at three o'clock for the Divine Office of None, which was followed by Mass and Vespers, after which the single meal of the day was allowed. How would we Catholics of the twentieth century bear up under the rigorous régime of those early days?

The Collation. About the tenth century the breaking of the fast at noonday was generally introduced, and, a little later, the taking of a "collation" was permitted in addition to the daily meal.

The word "collation" is one which has changed considerably in meaning. The laws of the Benedictine Order required the monks to assemble in the evening for a spiritual reading, generally taken from the Lives of the Saints or other edifying books. These readings were called "collations," or conferences. On account of the long offices which they had previously recited, they were allowed on certain days to partake of some light repast or luncheon, just before the reading; and thus the name of the spiritual exercise was gradually applied, not to the reading, but to the refreshment.

This taking of a collation by the faithful in addition to the regular meal is traceable back to about the year 1400, but until comparatively recent times the amount of food allowed was very small. In the sixteenth century an ounce and a half of bread and a single glass of wine were the maximum allowance in many dioceses. The present relaxation (which allows a collation of eight ounces and the taking in the morning of a small piece of bread with tea or other warm drink) was introduced early in the last century.

The Law of Abstinence. As the Church uses the word, "abstinence" signifies depriving ourselves of meat, that thus the body may practise penance and the soul be thereby sanctified. Besides the days on which the obligation of fasting is imposed, the Church has always observed days of abstinence. In the rigorous monastic life of the early Middle Ages it was deemed a relaxation to keep Sunday as a day of mere abstinence, without fasting; all the other days of the year were fasting-days for those austere monks, except from Easter to Pentecost, when abstinence alone was observed and the strict rules of fasting were dispensed with.

From Apostolic times Friday has been a day of abstinence, and the reason is obvious to every Christian. Our Blessed Redeemer died on that day for our sins, and we should commemorate His sufferings and offer some expiation ourselves by voluntary mortification.

In some parts of the world, at a very early date, Friday was a day not only of abstinence but of fasting; and on Wednesdays and Saturdays the use of meat was forbidden. But the severity of these regulations led to their gradual modification; the observing of Wednesday as an abstinence day has almost entirely disappeared; and at the present time the Holy See has granted permission in many countries (including our own) too use meet freely on Saturdays.

Fasting and Abstinence Days. The following are days on which fasting and abstinence are prescribed, outside of Lent:

1). The Ember Days, sometimes called the Quarter Tenses (Latin, "Quatuor Tempora," the four times), come at intervals of about three months. They are the Wednesday, Friday and Saturday which follow December 13, the first Sunday in Lent, Pentecost and September 14

The observance of these days is an ancient practice. They are mentioned by Pope St. Leo as being so old in his time that he believed that they had an Apostolic origin; and he stated that the object of these days of fasting is to purify our souls by penance at the beginning of each quarter of the year. They were introduced into England by St. Augustine of Canterbury, the Apostle of that country. The ordinations of the clergy commonly occur on the Saturdays of the Ember Days, while the whole Church is devoted to prayer and penance, to secure as it were, the blessing of God on His new ministers.

Why are they called "Ember Days"? The word has nothing to do with embers or ashes. It may be from the Anglo-Saxon "ymbren," a circle or revolution; or it may be a corruption of "quatuor tempora"; for in Dutch the name is "Quatertemper," in German "Quatember," and in Danish "Kvatember" — whence the translation to Ember Days is easy.

2). In this country the following days are also observed as days of fasting and abstinence in most of our dioceses, although the rule is not the same in all: The Fridays in Advent, and the vigils of Pentecost, the Assumption, All Saints' and Christmas.

Our Church is a merciful mother. Her wisdom recognizes the needs of our weak human nature in these strenuous twentieth-century days. She knows that the rigorous practices of the ages of faith would not be easy for us, and so she accommodates her laws to our weakness, requiring of us only what is reasonable. But while the details of her penitential rules may vary from age to age, their spirit remains the same. Whatever may be the conditions of our lives, we must practise penance in some form. We must devote ourselves to earnest prayer and frequent good works if our circumstances forbid grave austerities. While we may avail ourselves of the dispensations granted by the Church, we must comply with her laws as far as they bind us. She teaches that for each of us there is a constant warfare against the lower elements in our nature; and some degree of mortification is necessary if we would be victors in that conflict.

CHAPTER LIV

INDULGENCES

THE Catholic doctrine and practice of Indulgences deserve and need a thorough explanation. Few points in our religion are so little understood. Many of the devotions performed by the faithful have been enriched by the Church with these spiritual favors; we find that certain prayers or pious works procure an indulgence of forty days, or seven years, or in some cases a plenary indulgence — and a large proportion of Catholics will fulfill the prescribed conditions and gain the indulgence without having a very clear idea of what they are gaining.

There is no Catholic teaching which has been so persistently misrepresented by non-Catholic writers. The average essayist who attempts to treat of the events which led up to the so-called Reformation generally assails this matter of indulgences with much vehemence. According to such authorities, the strenuous and whole-souled Luther rose in his might against papal decrees which gave a full forgiveness of sin to those who paid for it. The indulgences granted by Leo X were even, they say, "a license to commit sin." The Roman power in the sixteenth century is alleged to have been so degraded that it publicly proclaimed that the giving of money for the building of St. Peter's Church would ensure "the pardon of all past sins and the condoning of all future offences," no matter how grievous they might be. Such are the statements gravely set forth by "historians" — and every word of them is a falsehood.

The Meaning of an Indulgence. What is an indulgence? It is *not* a forgiving of sins already committed. It is *not* a license or permission to commit sin, nor a pardon for sins that may be committed in the future. It is *not* a pardon for sin at all.

It is a remission of the punishment which is still due to sin after its guilt has been taken away by the sacrament of Penance. This remission is made by applying to the repentant sinner's soul the "treasure of merit" which the Church possesses.

Now this definition requires some explanation, and

of an accurate kind; for the matter is somewhat abstruse, and misunderstanding is easy.

An indulgence never forgives sin. The guilt and the eternal punishment of sin must be taken away by other means, chiefly by the sacraments of Baptism and Penance; and, as we know, these cannot be of any avail to the soul in actual sin unless it is aroused to sincere and supernatural sorrow and a firm purpose of amendment. Before an indulgence can be gained, the soul must be free from mortal sin; that is, the guilt must be washed away and the eternal penalty which is deserved must be remitted — and until this is done there can be no question of an indulgence.

An indulgence cannot give a permission for future sins. The very thought of any such license is abominable and blasphemous. The Church strives to overcome evil, to inculcate virtue; and if she should countenance or connive at vice in any form she would be an agent of the devil, not the "mystical Body of Christ."

We see, then, that an indulgence cannot be "an encouragement to sin," or "a license or permission to sin," as some of our non-Catholic critics have asserted. It is rather a very salutary and powerful motive to repentance and to virtue.

Temporal Punishment. An indulgence takes away temporal punishment. The teaching of our faith is that after God through His Church's sacraments has forgiven our sins, after the eternal punishment has been remitted, a temporal punishment often remains. It does not remain after sins have been remitted through Baptism; this first of the sacraments annuls both guilt and penalty entirely. If a sinner received Baptism validly and worthily, and died before sinning again, there would be for him no Purgatory, no delay in entering Heaven.

But the forgiveness imparted in the sacrament of Penance is less efficacious. After the guilt of mortal sin has been washed away by it, although there is no longer any fear of eternal punishment for the sins forgiven, there may remain a temporal penalty which (unless it be remitted) must be expiated before Heaven can be attained. It may be "worked out" wholly or partially in this world — by penances, mortifications, devotions, almsdeeds and other good works. If it remains on the soul at death it necessitates a stay in Purgatory — how long, in any particular case, we do not know; or it may be remitted by the Church through indulgences — and this remission may be accomplished while we are living in this world, or (through the charity of others) after we have been sentenced by Divine Justice to purgatorial pains.

The Treasury of Merit. When the Catholic Church grants indulgences, she is able to do so because she has access to an infinite store of merit, gained by our Blessed Saviour and the saints. Our Redeemer's merits were sufficient, of course, to satisfy for all guilt and all penalty due to sin; His Church dispenses them to us. The Blessed Virgin Mary lived a life of perfect holiness; she did not need the abundant merits which she acquired, for she had no sins to atone for — and the Church can use her merits also for us. Many of the saints (not only the great and famous ones, but the multitudes concerning whose names or histories we know nothing) acquired far more merit before God than was needed for their own salvation. Now these merits have not ceased to exist. They are not lost. They are stored up, as it were, by Almighty God, and the Church makes use of them for those who need them, since those who gained them do not require them — just as if in some Utopian commonwealth all the surplus wealth of the successful citizens should be set apart for the poor and needy, and portioned out to them according to their necessities.

Two Kinds of Indulgences. Indulgences may be either plenary (Latin "plenus," full, entire), which remit all the temporal punishment; or partial, which take away only a part of it. For the gaining of a plenary indulgence especially, it is necessary that it should be proclaimed by the Church and that the required conditions be fulfilled — one of these being the detestation of all sin and the purpose of avoiding even the least venial sin. Thus we can seldom be certain that we have gained the whole of a plenary indulgence, as we cannot be usually sure that we have thoroughly compiled with these conditions.

Indulgences may be also considered as temporal and perpetual, personal, local, etc., but these divisions refer mainly to their duration and extent, and need not interest us now. Nor can we explain in detail the almost innumerable particular indulgences which the Church has granted in the course of centuries.

Who Can Grant Indulgences? The principal legislative power in the Church, the centre of her authority, is the Roman See; and to it primarily belongs the power of granting indulgences. This is shared, however, by other rulers in the Church to a limited extent. Plenary indulgences are usually granted by the Pope alone, though he may permit others to do so. Cardinals, certain Roman Congregations, papal delegates, primates, archbishops and bishops who are in charge of a diocese have a restricted power of granting partial indulgences.

How Indulgences are Gained. A person desiring to obtain any indulgence must, of course, be a member of the Church. He must perform the work enjoined exactly as it is prescribed. He must be in the state of grace at least before he finishes that work. For the gaining of plenary indulgences, as stated above, there must be also an earnest detestation of all sin and a firm purpose of avoiding it; and for these indulgences, in most cases, the Church insists on confession, Holy Communion and prayer for the Pope's intention. The nature and amount of this prayer is not specified, but usually five Our Fathers and five Hail Marys are deemed sufficient.

The History of Indulgences. The present practice of the Church regarding indulgences is the evolution of twenty centuries. Changes have been introduced, but they are changes of circumstances, not of principles.

In primitive times the discipline of the Church towards sinners was very severe. Heavy penalties, known as "canonical penances," were exacted for grave sins; but if the penitent manifested extraordinary signs of contrition, these penalties were shortened and lessened, and this was done especially when persecutions were going on. It frequently happened in those days that thousands of Christians were in prison, suffering much and awaiting death. Their martyrdom was sure to affect their eternal salvation. They often wrote to the Pope or bishops a "letter of peace," offering their merits and sufferings as a substitute for the canonical penances demanded of some other Christians who were being disciplined for sins. The penalties imposed upon these latter were then remitted, and they were not only restored to full membership in the Church, but they received remission of their temporal punishment in the sight of God. St. Cyprian, bishop of Carthage, tells us: "God can set down to the sinner's account whatever the martyrs have asked and the bishops have done for them."

Later on, as the law of canonical penances was made less rigorous, the Church often allowed a lesser work in place of a greater. Alms to the poor the endowing of churches and monasteries, pilgrimages to holy places, and even short prayers — all of these were considered equivalent to many days or even years of severe penance; and here we find the reason why indulgences are entitled "of forty days," "of one year," etc. These words do not imply, as some might think, that by a certain prayer or good work we take away forty days or a year of Purgatory for ourselves or another. They mean that we get as much benefit (for ourselves or for a soul in Purgatory) as we would if we performed the severe canonical penances of former times for forty days or one year.

Plenary indulgences may seem to have been granted only from about the eleventh century, and they were probably first given to the Crusaders. Pope Urban II decreed that "their journey would take the place of all penance," and later Pontiffs gave similar spiritual privileges to those who went to fight for the Holy Sepulchre or gave money for these expeditions.

From that epoch the history of indulgences became better known. They were given very freely by many Popes and for various reasons — for the dedication of churches, the canonization of saints, etc. Later on, certain great and popular devotions were enriched with indulgences, so that now they are attached to almost every pious practice. Even articles of devotion, such as crucifixes, medals, etc., may have these spiritual benefits annexed to them, for the advantage of the faithful who use them devoutly.

Indulgences for the Souls. The application of indulgences to departed souls which are in a state of penitential suffering is of rather ancient date. We find a mention of it in the ninth century, when Popes Pascal I and John VIII bestowed such indulgences on the souls of those who had died in defence of the Church or Christian civilization; and in succeeding ages it became customary to proclaim nearly all indulgences as applicable not only to the living person who performed the prescribed work, but also to such departed ones as he wished to aid.

How does the Church possess such power? These souls in Purgatory are no longer subjects of the Church on earth; how, then, can she legislate in their favor? The answer is not difficult. She has no actual power over these souls. She cannot help them directly nor by any law-making authority. She only entreats God to accept the superabundant merits of Christ and His saints, and to dispense these merits for the entire or partial relief of those who are in Purgatory. She leaves the giving of these merits to God, trusting to His infinite mercy for the relief of His friends who are suffering in penitential fires.

This beautiful doctrine and practice of our Church shows us the loving maternal spirit which animates her. Penance is necessary for us, her children; for even when God's mercy has extended forgiveness to us, we still have reparation to make and a penalty to pay. But the Church wishes to make our penalty small, and she can do so because we are members of a great spiritual society which not only has been heaping up a vast treasure of merit for nearly two thousand years, but has access also to the infinite merits of our Lord Jesus Christ. We are a part of the great corporation which controls that spiritual treasure; and as we are needy, as we ourselves deserve little from God's hands except punishment, the Church gives us a share in this accumulated merit. And even after our earthly life is over, if we need God's mercy, we receive it by the prayers of His Church, of which we shall still be members. He will lessen or totally remit our deserved punishment because of the indulgences gained for us by those who are still on earth and still able to merit.

Chapter LV

PILGRIMAGES

The old Tabard Inn and Chaucer's motley band of travelers — old-world shrines with glowing lamps and throngs of pious worshippers — plodding wayfarers on lonely roads, "with scrip and staff and sandal shoon" — princes and "knights of high degree" journeying in beggar guise to Eastern lands to kneel at the Saviour's sepulchre — such are the visions that rise before us when we speak of pilgrims and pilgrimages.

The pious practice of making journeys to distant shrines, of arousing or increasing devotion by visiting a holy place, is by no means exclusively Catholic. It has its origin in the fact that religious impressions naturally become stronger in the places that have been hallowed by religious events. We know that mere change of scene has a stimulating effect on the mind of man; and that when the place visited is one of historic interest, it brings before the mind, more vividly than would a printed page, the events that have made it famous. What is true of merely natural impressions is even more true of those that are religious and devotional. To behold with our own eyes the very places that were once sanctified by the living presence of our Blessed Saviour; to kneel at the shrines that were the scenes of apparitions of the Blessed Mother of God; to join in the prayers of assembled thousands, of every rank and condition, from the remotest parts of the earth — all this is full of inspiration for the pious mind; all this fills the soul with a religious fervor and exaltation that could hardly be attained elsewhere.

The Shrines of Other Creeds. In nearly every form of religion it has been found that journeys to supposedly holy places are a very potent help to devotion. The place where the god or the hero had lived or had wrought some mighty deed, or where wonders were supposed to be vouchsafed in answer to prayer, became the goal of pious worshippers.

The Jewish law imposed upon the heads of families as an obligation a pilgrimage to Jerusalem for the celebration of certain great festivals. The Romans had their shrines of Jupiter

Capitolinus at Rome, of Apollo at Delphi, of Diana at Ephesus. To visit Mecca at least once in his lifetime is the ambition of the pious Mussulman. The great temples of India have their countless throngs of worshippers who have come to offer their homage to the Hindoo gods and to pray at the shrines of Buddha.

In encouraging the making of pilgrimages, then, our Church has made use of a practice which has produced good results in other creeds. In all her history pious pilgrims have journeyed to distant shrines. The early Christians longed to see the cave of Bethlehem and the grotto of the Sepulchre; and almost from the time of our Lord's ascension they came in endless procession to Palestine, even from the outposts of Christendom. A pilgrimage to the Holy Places was often the fulfillment of a vow, and sometimes the performing of an imposed penance. And as the centuries rolled on, places of devotion were multiplied in every Christian country. Scenes of apparitions, hermitages of saints, churches which possessed the treasured relics of the apostles and martyrs — everywhere these became the centres of pilgrimages. And, in answer to the fervor and faith of those who prayed at these shrines, God's mercy and power were undoubtedly manifested in many miracles.

The Results of Pilgrimages. Important natural benefits have also resulted from the wanderings of the pious pilgrims of the Middle Ages. A knowledge of geography and languages, an increase of commerce, the spreading of religion and science, and the founding of certain religious orders were the results of this intercommunication of men from all parts of Europe; and the desire of being able to visit Palestine unmolested by Moslem hordes was one of the principal motives for the Crusades. The humble pilgrim who vowed a journey to the Holy Sepulchre was the forerunner of the lordly knight who set lance in rest that the sacred places of Christendom might be freed from Paynim rule.

In the Middle Ages the practice of going on pilgrimages became so common that it grew at times into an abuse. Thousands of pilgrims hastened from country to country, neglecting their duties to home and family — duties, which, if fulfilled, would be, doubtless, far more profitable to their souls than prayers offered at this shrine or that. The author of the "Imitation of

Christ" declares: "Who wanders much is little hallowed." Long before, the great St. John Chrysostom had not hesitated to say that "there is need for none to cross the sea or fare upon a long journey; let each of us at home invoke God earnestly, and He will hear our prayers"; and St. Jerome, speaking of the pilgrimages to the Holy Places, gave utterance to a phrase that has become a proverb: "From Jerusalem and from Britain heaven is equally open."

Recommended by the Church. But this does not mean that pilgrimages are in themselves useless. If abuses be guarded against, our holy Church favors and recommends them. She looks upon them as an excellent means of devotion and penance, and of consequent purification and spiritual benefit; and even in this material age the pilgrimage, as an expression of faith and religious zeal, has by no means fallen into disuse.

Does the Church ever require us to make pilgrimages? Not at the present day; for she looks upon them as being in no way necessary, though sometimes advisable. God is everywhere, and He is not to be sought exclusively in one place; His mercy and love, in answer to our prayers, may be manifested in our own homes and churches as benignly as at Lourdes or St. Anne de Beaupré. But nevertheless, our Church approves and recommends pilgrimages as a useful means of devotion, because she recognizes the fact that God has often granted and still grants favors in the form of graces, miracles and worldly blessings at particular places, as a reward for the perseverance and fervor of those who have journeyed thither, and as an aid in increasing the devotion of the faithful to our Blessed Lord, to His Virgin Mother, and to His servants who are specially honored at certain shrines.

Some Shrines of Pilgrimage. While it will not be possible here to make any extended reference to the various pilgrim-shrines of the world, we can at least mention a few of the most famous. The land hallowed by the life and death of our Blessed Lord has always been pre-eminently the "Holy Land" for all Christians. And, next to the sacred places of Palestine, the Vatican hill where "the vast and wondrous dome" marks the spot where rests the body of the Prince of the Apostles, has long been the goal of pilgrim devotion. In many parts of the earth, in the New World as well as the Old, are churches erected in honor of the Blessed Mother of God, which have become centres of devotion; for example, La Salette in France, Guadalupe in Spain, the Mexican shrine of the same name, and, greatest of all, Lourdes — where a million visitors journey every year to pay their homage to Mary Immaculate and to profit by her intercession. And other saints have been honored as well by the zeal of devout pilgrims. England cherishes the memory of the martyred Becket at Canterbury; Spain has its shrine of St. James the Apostle at Compostella; Ireland has its "St. Patrick's Purgatory" in bleak Donegal. In our own country a pilgrim-shrine has been established at Auriesville, New York, where three heroic Jesuits were tortured and slain by the savage Mohawks. Canada has its famous Beaupré, where the intercession of "la bonne Sainte Anne" is sought by thousands; and in several places that are nearer to us the votaries of the gracious mother of the Virgin seek alleviation of suffering by offering prayers before her altar.

We see, then, that the old simple Catholic faith is as strong now as it was in those dim days of long ago when in their thousands, along the roads of Europe or over the stormy seas to Palestine, the pious pilgrims journeyed, filled with an ardent desire to see the places hallowed by the Saviour, to kneel at sacred shrines, to offer their fatigue and sufferings as an expiation for their sins, and to secure the mercy of God and the intercession of the saints by fervent prayer.

Chapter LVI

AN UNMARRIED CLERGY

There is such a wide distinction between the mode of life of the Catholic priest and that of the clergy of other Christian denominations that we are apt to look upon his celibate state as something which is essential to his sacred character and profession. We are familiar with the idea that the priest is one who has voluntarily sacrificed all that man holds dear in worldly relationship in order thereby to be better able to devote himself to God's service; but it would be erroneous to imagine that the fact of his priesthood necessitates his living a single life. Our priests in the Latin Church have vowed themselves to celibacy; by receiving ordination they have rendered themselves forever incapable of valid marriage; but this is because the church has made laws to that effect, and not through any divine decree or institution.

The practice of clerical celibacy and the law which confirms it have been the slow growth of centuries — and, as we shall see, they are not by any means universal. There are many thousands of Catholic priests (not schismatics, but real Catholics) who are lawfully married and are living in the married state; but this is the case only in Eastern churches which have a ritual and a system of legislation different from the Roman. The uniform practice and rule of the "Latin Church" is that those who serve the altar and who are promoted to subdeaconship shall be unmarried and shall so remain.

Why Our Priests Do Not Marry. What are the reasons for clerical celibacy? Why is it that the Church insists on this rigorous and difficult rule? Rigorous and difficult it undoubtedly is, for it requires the constant repression of natural instincts and affections. The Church has imposed celibacy on her clergy that they may serve God with less restraint and with undivided heart. As St. Paul says, "He that is without a wife is solicitous for the things that belong to the Lord, how he may please God; but he that is with a wife is solicitous for the things of the world, how he may please his wife, and he is divided."

They are expected to practice chastity because the state of virginity is holier than that of marriage. This does not mean that the married state is not praiseworthy and honorable; but our Blessed Lord Himself tells us (and the Apostles reiterate His teaching) that the life of those who practise virginity is superior to that of those who are married. The Church has always taught the same doctrine. Council after Council has extolled the holy state of celibacy, and the great Council of Trent affirmed as a matter of faith that it is holier than marriage.

But this, while it shows that the unmarried state is preferable and even specially desirable for the priests of the Church, does not of itself compel them to observe it. This has been done by direct legislation, which required several centuries to reach its present development.

The Church's Law. The church imposes a law of celibacy upon her ministers, but she has not always done so. During at least one-half of her history the legislation was not in its present form; and even now it is not extended to all parts of the Church's domain and is not enforced in regard to all her clergy.

In the first days of the Church there was no law restricting the marriage of the clergy except that a bishop was required to be "a man of one wife"; that is, to have been married only once. It is quite likely that several of the Apostles were married. We read in the Gospel of the curing of Peter's mother-in-law by our Blessed Lord — and if the chief of the Apostles had a mother-in-law he undoubtedly had at some time a wife. It is supposed, however, that she was dead before he was called to be an Apostle, as there is no mention of her in the Scriptural account of Peter's life.

The first trace which we can find of positive legislation is in the fourth century. At the Council of Nice and other synods of about the same time a regulation was made prohibiting the marriage of the clergy after ordination; but the validity of the marriage was not denied or assailed by this rule. It merely provided that the priest who contracted it was to be degraded to the lay state. But gradually the sentiment of the whole Western Church became more rigorous. It was felt that a married clergy was in no way desirable; and under various Popes laws were made for the clergy of the Latin rite which rendered invalid any marriage attempted by a subdeacon or one in higher orders. The marriage of a cleric below the rank of subdeacon was and is valid, but it renders him incapable of receiving that or the succeeding orders while his wife lives — except in the case that, by mutual agreement, she enters a religious community of women and he a monastic house.

In the eyes of the Church a widower is a single man, and therefore is eligible to Holy Orders; if he is otherwise capable, his previous marriage is not an obstacle to his becoming a priest.

Catholic Priests Who are Married. Are there any married priests in the Catholic Church? Yes, several thousands. They are really married, and they are not living in opposition to God's or the Church's law. These are the clergy of several Oriental churches which are united to ours in faith and government, though differing from it in ritual and laws.

We shall not go into the details of the legislation of the separated Eastern churches — the schismatic sects which have a clergy and Mass and sacraments as we have, but which have cut themselves off from communion with Rome. In nearly all of these the pastors of parishes are married men — the members of the religious orders are not; while the bishops are also generally unmarried.

In nearly all the Oriental churches which are in communion with the Holy See, marriage before receiving deaconship is not an obstacle to that or the succeeding orders; but marriage is not allowed afterwards. If the candidate is not married he is ordained only on condition of making a promise of perpetual chastity. If the wife of a priest dies, he is not permitted to remarry in some Churches; while in others his second marriage is considered valid, but necessitates his retirement from priestly duties.

The result of these long-established customs in the Eastern Catholic Churches is that the candidate for Holy Orders, before receiving deaconship, usually withdraws from the seminary and is married — after which he returns, resumes his studies, and is finally ordained.

The Reasons for Celibacy. Why is it that the Church has

sought to make at least the priests of the Latin rite observe the rule of celibacy? Because the value of the priest's ministry is thereby enhanced. He is giving a practical lesson in disinterestedness and self-sacrifice. He has given up the things of the world which are most highly valued by men — the love of wife and children — that he may be the better able to devote himself to the salvation of souls. He has no earthly ties that might conflict with his duty to his spiritual flock. The burden which rests on the sinner's soul may be freely revealed to him without fear that the secret will be shared with the confessor's wife. Pestilence has no terrors for the unmarried priest — he has no family to whom the contagion might be transmitted; and so, when the call comes summoning him to the small-pox or typhus sufferer, or when his duty lies in the cholera-camp, he has no fear. He is risking nothing but his own life, and that he has already consecrated to God. And when the quest for souls leads him into distant pagan lands he has an advantage over the married missionary. He is a soldier in "light marching order." He takes no family with him, to be an encumbrance in his work, to require support and shelter in his field of labor; he leaves no wife and children behind him whose welfare would be a source of anxiety while he is far from them. If death comes in the course of his work, whether by accident or disease or martyrdom, the unmarried priest need not care; he has no worldly ties to lessen his peace of soul — no dependents whose future well-being would be affected by his living or dying.

Difficult Not Impossible. Is not this law difficult of observance, since it is opposed to a primary function and instinct of man's nature? Is it not impossible to bind the clergy by such a rule without leading to sins and irregularities immeasurably worse than honorable marriage would be?

These are questions which non-Catholics of an inquiring mind will frequently ask. We answer to the first question, that it is assuredly difficult. To observe the law of priestly celibacy requires a strong will, a divine vocation, a spirit of self-sacrifice, great watchfulness, frequent and fervent prayer, and God's grace. But only the difficult things obtain much merit or deserve much reward.

To the second question we answer decidedly, No. It is

not impossible nor even impracticable to bind the clergy to the unmarried state and to keep them pure and decent. We do not attempt to deny that abuses and scandals have arisen — that in some lands and in some epochs there have even been many lapses from virtue on the part of priests. Some countries have been worse than others — discipline has sometimes been relaxed, ecclesiastical training has sometimes been neglected, luxury and avarice have occasionally led to the preferment of the unworthy, and worse vices have naturally followed in their train. But we affirm most emphatically that the history of our Church shows that by far the greater part of her clergy have been faithful to their obligations, models of priestly virtue, ornaments of the mystical Body of Christ. The priests of Ireland, of Germany, of France and Belgium and the hard-working ones who have done God's work in our own land have been worthy of all praise, faithful to their holy vocation. There have been exceptions, we know; but they have been few and far between; and when scandals have arisen, the very sensation which they produced demonstrated their infrequency.

What a grand testimony is given by the apostate Renan to the virtue of the clergy who were his instructors in his boyhood and youth. "I spent thirteen years of my life under the care of priests, and I never saw the shadow of a scandal. I have known no priests but good priests."

Thank God, most of us can say the same.

CHAPTER LVII

CHRISTIAN SYMBOLS

When we enter a Catholic church and examine its architecture, we find that in many parts of it there are ornamental details of various kinds — representations of animals and plants, crosses, monograms, and many other things. All of these have a most instructive symbolism and an interesting history. They are emblematic of the great truths of Christianity, of our Saviour, of His Blessed Mother and the Saints, of our holy Church, and of the virtues which that Church teaches us.

The use of symbols in Christian art and architecture goes back to the very infancy of the Church. In the chapels of the Roman catacombs and in the subterranean churches of St. Clement, St. Praxedes, and other temples of early Christianity, crude mural paintings are still to be seen, containing ornaments and emblems typifying the faith of those who worshipped there. And in later centuries, when great cathedrals raised their domes and spires to heaven in every country of Europe, these mighty temples were enriched with a wealth of symbolic ornaments in sculpture, carving and painting. At the present day, in our own churches, many of these are still used in the details of architecture, in windows and interior decoration.

When you visit your own parish church, spare a few minutes from your prayer-book to look around at the symbolic ornaments which you will find there. This will not be a distraction; on the contrary, it will be a help to greater devotion.

They Teach Religion. This chapter will explain the meaning of some of these symbols, which St. Augustine has well called "libri idiotarum" — "the books of the unlearned," because they are admirably adapted to present the truths of religion to the faithful, many of whom in past centuries were unable to read a printed page.

First among them there is the most important of all Christian symbols — the Cross, the sign of salvation, the sacred emblem of our redemption; but this is treated at considerable length elsewhere in this book. We shall treat briefly of the others that are most common in our churches.

Animals as Symbols. The Lamb has been an emblem of our Saviour from the earliest period of Christian art. In the Jewish sacrifices it prefigured the coming Messias, and when St. John the Baptist pointed Him out to the multitude he cried out: "Behold the Lamb of God." The Lamb is sometimes represented standing, bearing a cross or banner inscribed with these words; or lying, as if slain, on a book closed with seven seals, as described in the Apocalypse. It is also a general symbol of modesty and innocence, and it is therefore used as an emblem of the martyr-virgin St. Agnes, whose name signifies a lamb.

Lamb

The Dove is the special symbol of the Holy Ghost. "And lo! The Holy Spirit descended from heaven upon Him in the form of a Dove," at the baptism of Christ; and we see it also in pictures of the Annunciation, to signify the Incarnation of our Blessed Saviour by the power of the Holy Ghost.

Dove

The Pelican, which, according to legend, feeds its young with its own blood, is an emblem of our redemption through the sufferings of our Lord, and particularly of the Blessed Eucharist, in which He nourishes our souls with His Body and Blood.

The Lion typifies our Saviour, the "Lion of the fold of Judah." As will be told further on, it is also a symbol of the Evangelist St. Mark. It is emblematic of solitude, and is therefore sometimes shown in pictures of hermit-saints.

Pelican

The Dragon always represents Satan and sin. It is shown as being conquered by the powers of good, as in the Scriptural account of St. Michael the Archangel and in the medieval legend of St. George. The Serpent, another emblem of sin, is sometimes placed beneath the feet of the Blessed Virgin, to symbolize that "the seed of the woman shall crush his head." The Serpent, however, when twined around a cross, is emblematic of the brazen serpent raised up by Moses in the desert — a prophetic figure of our crucified Saviour.

Symbolic Plants. There are various plants and flowers that have a symbolic meaning. The Olive Branch is an emblem of peace, and is often shown in the hand of the Archangel Gabriel. The Palm is the special badge of martyrs. "I saw a great multitude which no man could number, of all nations and tribes and tongues, clothed with white robes, and palms in their hands." Thus did St. John describe the vast army of martyrs before the throne of God.

The Lily, wherever seen, has but one meaning — chastity. We find it in pictures of the Annunciation, of St. Joseph (whose staff, according to an ancient legend, bloomed into lilies), and sometimes in representations of saints notable for their purity — for example, St. Anthony of Padua and St. Aloysius.

The Rose is an emblem of love and beauty, and is symbolical of the Blessed Virgin under her title of "Mystical Rose"; it is also used in pictures of St. Elizabeth of Hungary (because of the well-known legend), and of other saints.

Other Emblems. A Crown, of course, denotes kingly power. We see it in pictures of Mary as Queen of Heaven, of our Blessed Lord when His kingship is to be emphasized, and of saints of royal blood. The crown of the Blessed Virgin is often shown with twelve stars, after the description in the Apocalypse; and from the same vision of St. John we get the crescent moon shown beneath the feet of Mary: "A woman clothed with the sun, having the moon beneath her feet, and upon her head a crown of twelve stars."

A Ship symbolizes the Church, the bark of Peter, buffeted by tempests but guided by God Himself. The Anchor was an emblem of hope long before the beginning of Christianity, because it is the chief reliance of mariners in time of danger. Hence it has been adopted by the Church as a symbol, and is often combined with two others to denote the three great theological virtues — the Cross for faith, the

Symbols of Faith, Hope, Charity

Anchor for hope, the Heart for charity.

Ears of wheat and bunches of grapes are often used as ornaments around the altar and on the sacred vestments. These are symbols of the Holy Eucharist, the true Body and Blood of our Lord under the appearance of the bread which is made from wheat and the wine which we obtain from grapes. The Chalice, often surmounted by a Host, has the same signification.

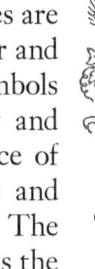

Grapes and Wheat

A Banner is an emblem of victory. It belongs to the military saints, and is also borne by our Lord in pictures of His Resurrection. A Candlestick typifies Christ and His Church, the "light of the world." It is sometimes represented with seven branches, symbolic of the seven gifts of the Holy Ghost or of the Sacraments. A Skull or a Scourge is emblematic of penance, and a Scallop-Shell, of pilgrimage.

Chalice and Host

The Sign of the Fish. A favorite emblem of early Christina times was a fish, generally resembling a dolphin. The Greek word for fish is Ichthus, spelt in Greek with five letters only: I-ch-th-u-s. These form what is called an acrostic, being the initial letters of the words: "Iesous Christos, Theou Uios, Soter" — or, in English, "Jesus Christ, Son of God, Saviour"; and thus the fish was taken as a symbol of our Blessed Lord, and is so found in many ancient inscriptions in the catacombs and elsewhere. The fish, because it lives in water, is also an emblem of the Sacrament of Baptism; of the vocation of the Apostles, the "fishers of men"; and of Christians in general, typified by the miraculous draught of fishes mentioned in the Gospel of St. John.

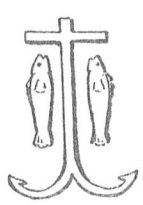

Sign of the Fish
From the Catacombs

The sign of the crossed keys, with or without the papal tiara, is symbolic of the power of the Pope "to bind and to loose." "I will give to thee the keys of the kingdom of heaven."

Emblematic Monograms. Various letters and monograms,

Monogram or Symbol Of the Blessed Virgin Mary

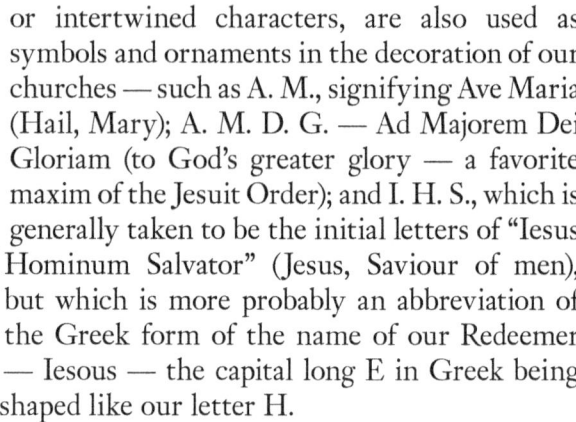

Alpha And Omega

Chrisma

or intertwined characters, are also used as symbols and ornaments in the decoration of our churches — such as A. M., signifying Ave Maria (Hail, Mary); A. M. D. G. — Ad Majorem Dei Gloriam (to God's greater glory — a favorite maxim of the Jesuit Order); and I. H. S., which is generally taken to be the initial letters of "Iesus Hominum Salvator" (Jesus, Saviour of men), but which is more probably an abbreviation of the Greek form of the name of our Redeemer — Iesous — the capital long E in Greek being shaped like our letter H.

We also see frequently the letters Alpha and Omega, the first and last of the Greek alphabet, signifying God, the Beginning and End of all things; and also the "chrisma," or monogram of the Greek letters Chi and Ro, shaped like our X and P, but equivalent to CH and R in Latin or English.

Symbols of the Saints. The pictures and images of saints in our churches are often ornamented with emblems illustrative of some virtue of the saint or some event in his career. Generally they are crowned with a halo or nimbus, symbolizing the light of grace and sanctity. In many representations of martyr-saints the instrument of their martyrdom is shown. Thus we have the sword or axe for many saints, the arrows of St. Sebastian, the gridiron of St. Lawrence, and the toothed wheel of St. Catherine.

For saints who were not martyrs, emblems are used which typify the virtues which they practised, the work which they did, or the rank which they held — a banner and cross for missionaries, a mitre and pastoral staff for bishops, a crucifix for preachers, a crown of thorns for those whose lives were full of mortification.

Symbols of the Evangelists. In some ecclesiastical decorations we may find four emblems, generally winged — the head of a man, a lion, an ox and an eagle. This is symbolism of a very ancient date, having its origin in St. John's Apocalypse. It represents the four writers of the holy Gospels. The human head indicates St. Matthew — for he begins his Gospel with the human ancestry of our Blessed Lord. The lion, the dweller in the desert, is emblematic of St. Mark, who opens his narrative with the mission of St. John the Baptist, "the voice of one crying in the wilderness." The sacrificial ox is the symbol of St. Luke — for his Gospel begins with the account of the priest Zachary. And the eagle, soaring far into the heavens, is the emblem of the inspiration of St. John, who carries us, in the opening words of his Gospel, to Heaven itself: "In the beginning was the Word, and the Word was with God, and the Word was God."

St. Matthew

St. Luke

St. Mark

St. John

Chapter LVIII

THE CATHOLIC BIBLE

We Catholics should be well informed as to our Church's teaching concerning the Holy Scriptures, which are one of the two great foundations of our faith. This is more necessary at the present time than ever before. In the early days of Protestantism the Church had to combat the error of the "reformers" that the word of God was contained in the Bible alone; but in these irreligious days, when so many so-called Protestants have come to treat the Bible as an ordinary book, when some of them even regard it as "a series of Oriental myths," we Catholics should know what our Church holds and teaches concerning it.

The Written Word of God. The Bible consists of a number of writings, or "books," written in different ages by men who were inspired by God. The books written before the coming of our Lord form the Old Testament; those written by His Apostles and Evangelists, the New. In the Catholic Bible there are forty-five books in the former and twenty-seven in the latter. The Protestant versions usually exclude seven books of the Old Testament and part of two others. The Latin Bible was translated from the Hebrew and Chaldean originals by St. Jerome. It came gradually into use throughout the Christian world, and hence is known as the Vulgate or "common" version. It was finally approved, and all other versions were excluded, by the great Council of Trent.

Our Church holds, and has always held, that the Sacred Scriptures are the written word of God. In the words of the Council, she believes and teaches concerning the books of the Old and New Testaments, that "God is the author if each" — and, believing this, she also believes that the Scriptures can contain nothing but perfect truth in faith and morals.

But if this be so, does it follow that God's word is contained only in them? By no means. Our Church affirms that there is an unwritten word of God also, which we call Apostolic Tradition; and she maintains that it is the duty of a Christian to receive the one and the other with equal veneration.

How do we know that this teaching of our Church is true? From the whole history and the whole structure of the Old and New Testaments. If our Lord had meant that His Church should be guided by a book alone, why did He not at once provide the Church with the book? He did not do so. He commanded the world to listen to the living voice of His Apostles. "He that heareth you, heareth Me." For about twenty years after the Ascension there was not a single book of the New Testament in existence; and the various Epistles were written by the Apostles at infrequent intervals thereafter, to give to widely scattered churches instruction on points of doctrine and morals, and to correct prevailing errors and abuses. There is no mention of even an incomplete collection of the New Testament books until the year 180. All that these early Christians had was the living voice of the Church, contained in the preaching and teaching of the Apostles and their successors. As there was no New Testament during all those years, and as a large part of Christian doctrine is in no way contained in the Old Testament, it is evident that the Scriptures could not have been in those days the sole deposit of Christian faith.

Interpreting the Scriptures. The Bible, in the words of St. Peter, contains "things hard to be understood." Who is to be its interpreter? Is it the individual, as Protestantism asserts, or is it the Church of God? A favorite and most impractical theory of the early "reformers" was that each Christian should interpret the Scriptures for himself. The Catholic teaching is that this is the work of the Church, the divinely appointed teacher of truth, against which "the gates of hell shall not prevail." What has been the outcome of the Protestant idea of "private judgment"? If God had intended that each man should be his own interpreter — if the Holy Spirit were to guide each — the result would be, undoubtedly, that all would agree; for the Spirit of God could not teach truth to one and error to another. But what has been the actual result? Division and confusion, the multiplication of sects and heresies — united in nothing save their antagonism to the Catholic Church — and finally, the total rejection, by many, of the inspiration and the authority of the Bible.

"But your Church has condemned the reading of the

Bible." This is true — in a certain sense. Her practice has varied with varying circumstances. She has forbidden at times the unguided use of the Scriptures. Parts of the Bible are evidently unsuited to the very young or the ignorant; and Pope Clement XI consequently condemned the proposition that "the reading of the Scriptures is for all." The watchful discipline of our Church has been exercised to keep her children from error or from moral evil. During the Middle Ages, when heresies were rife and corrupt translations of the Bible were numerous, the indiscriminate reading of the Scriptures was forbidden by various Councils. The Church, looking upon herself as the interpreter of God's word, strove to guard her children from the dangers which would arise from such reading. But when the Vulgate version was authorized she insisted upon its use by the faithful in general, with the recommendation that such explanatory notes should be appended as should preclude all danger of abuse.

Moreover, we Catholics hold that the reading of the Bible is not strictly necessary. The Apostles established the Church and converted a part of the pagan world without a Bible. Many nations have received the faith without being able to read. If the study of the Scriptures had been a requisite for conversion or salvation, a great part of the world would have been left without this means of grace, at least until the invention of printing. The Catholic Church, then, regards the Bible as one source of our holy faith, but holds that its use by all her children is by no means necessary, and not even advisable, except when its meaning is expounded and interpreted by her infallible authority.

The "Chained Bible." Rather amusing (and somewhat exasperating) is the old and oft-repeated assertion that "the Catholic Church chained the Bible." She did, undoubtedly. The statement is perfectly true. Each church, in the Middle Ages, possessed usually a single copy of the Scriptures, a ponderous folio volume; and this was often chained to a reading-desk — for the same reason that money is put into an iron safe; because it was worth stealing. A Bible copied by hand on parchment required three years' labor, and was valued at about $1500. Would it not have been unwise, to say the least, to leave it "lying around loose"?

MISCELLANEOUS

The Douay Bible. The translation of the Holy Scriptures used among English-speaking Catholics is commonly called the Douay version — though somewhat incorrectly, for the Bible was not translated into English at Douay, and only part of it was published there. Besides, the text in use at the present day has been considerably altered from that which originally bore the name of the Douay Bible.

The college at Douay, in France, was founded by exiled English priests in 1568. Within a few years political troubles caused the removal of its members to Rheims, and it was in the latter city that several of them undertook the work of preparing an English version of the Scriptures. The New Testament was published at Rheims in 1582, and the Old Testament at Douay in 1609.

The language of this first edition was fairly accurate, but was in some places uncouth and defective in style, following too closely the idioms of the language from which the translation was made. Consequently amended editions and even partially new translations were made, and of these the most widely used is that of Dr. Challoner, published in 1750, and plentifully provided with his notes, which have been added to since that time by various other editors.

The first Bible published in America for English-speaking Catholics, a reproduction of Challoner's second edition, was issued at Philadelphia in 1790; and between 1849 and 1547 Archbishop Kenrick published an excellent revision of the Douay version.

How does our Catholic Bible compare with the so-called "Authorized Version" (a revision, made in 1711, of the "King James" Bible), commonly used by the Protestant sects? The style of our Bible is often inferior; its matter is often superior in accuracy. The Doctors of Rheims and Douay made a closely literal and usually correct translation of the Latin text of the Vulgate, and their crudity of style and occasional slight errors have been largely eliminated by succeeding editors. The Protestant Bible is a masterpiece of English literature, generally beautiful in style and diction; but its text is distorted here and there to support Protestant doctrines — and it is, after all, only a part of the whole Bible, rejecting several books which our Church has declared to be a part of the written revelation of the Word of God. Being a masterpiece of literature does not make the "Authorized Version" a trustworthy guide to faith or to salvation.

Chapter LIX

CHURCH MUSIC

It is eminently proper that man, in his worship of God, should render to Him all that is most sublime and most beautiful. His homage can be expressed not only in words but in sweet sounds. In every form of worship since the world began, his natural devotional instinct urged him to honor Divinity by means of music as well as by the other arts, and to heighten his religious exaltation by the chanting of hymns and the sound of musical instruments.

All true religious music is an exalted prayer — an effective expression of religious feeling. In nearly all rites, whether Jewish, pagan or Christian, the elements of public worship have been sacrifice, prayer, ceremonies, chanting and instrumental music. In Catholic worship these elements constitute an organic whole, in which, however, music forms a part only on solemn occasions; and in order that it may be fittingly used it must be in accord with the regulations of proper authority.

An Auxiliary to Worship. Church music has, in common with secular music, the combination of tones in melody and harmony, the variation as to rhythm, measure and time, the distribution of power (known as dynamics), tone-color in voice and instrumentation, and the simpler and more complex styles of composition. All these, however, must be well adapted to the service at which they are used, to the words of the hymn or prayer, and to the devotion of the heart; otherwise they are unfit for use in the house of God. They must be calculated to edify the faithful, and must not be in any way opposed to the spirit of true worship. Music must be an auxiliary to the other means of giving honor to God; and if it be so it does not interfere with the Church's ceremonies or detract from their religious spirit, but, on the contrary, it imparts to them the greatest splendor and effectiveness. Appropriate music raises man above the sordid world, directs his mind and heart to the sacred words and ceremonies of his Church's worship, and fills him with a spirit of exalted devotion. Realizing this, our Church has indeed made her music appropriate to the spirit of her services, adapting it to the nature of the religious functions at which it is used, to the season of the ecclesiastical year and to the solemnity of the feast — making it grand and exultant on festivals of joy, and mournful in seasons of penance and in services for the dead.

In Jewish Worship. Under the Old Law music formed a prominent feature in the Jewish rites, and this was in compliance with the commands of God Himself. Religious songs of victory are mentioned in the books of Exodus and Judges; and later on the ceremonial was enriched by David with hymns and the use of instruments, and reached its highest development under his son Solomon in the sublime ritual practised in the great temple of Jerusalem.

In the Early Church. We know very little concerning the music of the primitive Christian Church. On account of many circumstances that Church was restricted in its religious manifestations, for the greater part of the first three centuries was a time of bitter persecution, when Christians worshipped God in secret and in peril of their lives. Tertullian tells us, however, that in his day psalms were sung in the divine service, and the pagan Pliny knew that Christians honored their God before dawn by the chanting of hymns. The extensive use of music in church ceremonies came later, and is to be largely attributed to St. Ambrose, the great Bishop of Milan, who introduced the singing of psalms "after the manner of the East." Under the fostering care of our Church sacred music developed most wonderfully during the succeeding centuries.

St. Jerome, who seldom failed to criticize when criticism was needed, speaks of singers of his day in words to which some of our modern choirs and church soloists may well hearken: "Let the servant of God sing in such manner that the words of the text rather than the voice of the singer may cause delight, and that the evil spirit of Saul may depart from those that are under its dominion, and may not enter into those who make a theatre of the house of the Lord." Can it be possible that the prophetic soul of the Saint foresaw the evils of some of the church music of to-day, wherein hymns to the Blessed Sacrament are chanted to the dulcet strains of "Juanita," and the sublime words of the Credo are sung to the liveliest melodies of Offenbach?

The Organ. The majestic tones of the organ have been considered from very early times to be particularly appropriate for religious services. The word "organ" is used occasionally in the Old Testament, but is somewhat of a mistranslation; in Jewish worship it signified any kind of wind instrument, as a pipe or trumpet, for organs resembling those of the present day did not then exist.

Nothing is known as to the exact date of the introduction of organ music into Catholic services. St. Augustine speaks of it as being in use in his time, and gives testimony to the delight he experienced in listening to it; he even seems to reproach himself because of the pleasure derived from it, asking himself whether it would not be perhaps more perfect to deny himself that gratification.

There is no authority whatever for the legend that the organ was invented by St. Cecilia, although modern art often depicts the Roman virgin-martyr seated at the keyboard of such an instrument. Probably in her day organs did not exist in any form, and the present form of keyboard was not devised until fully a thousand years later.

The organ was, in fact, the invention of many minds, and centuries were required for its development. It was evolved from the syrinx, or set of pipes bound together, such as we see represented in pictures of the pagan god Pan. A wind-box and bellows were attached, and the various pipes were caused to sound by means of a sliding perforated plate. This is said by some to have been invented by a certain Cresibius. A hydraulic organ, in which the bellows were actuated by water, is mentioned by Tertullian, who attributed the idea to the famous Archimedes.

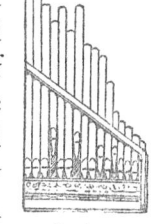

Syrinx

In the year 757 Constantine V, one of the Byzantine Emperors, sent an organ as a gift to Pepin, King of France, and another was sent later to his son Charlemagne.

The Development of the Organ. It was undoubtedly the

giving of these instruments to these great monarchs of the West that led to the general introduction of them into the service of the Church throughout Europe. A great organ with four hundred pipes and twenty-six bellows was built at Winchester, in England, in 951. From the eleventh century organs were used generally in cathedrals and monastic churches, although the idea was opposed by some great teachers of the Church, notably St. Thomas Aquinas. A vigorous effort was made to have legislation passed against them at the Council of Trent, but a majority of the bishops voted otherwise, and the Council simply enacted that the music should be grave and devotional. Similar injunctions were made by Benedict XIV in 1749, and strict regulations were put into effect a few years ago by the "Motu Proprio" of Pius X, which will be discussed further on.

Among the early Protestant denominations there was much discussion and dissension regarding the use of organs. The Lutherans and Anglicans retained them, but many other sects banished them from their churches. At the present day, however, many of even the stricter Methodist and Presbyterian branches have introduced them again, in an endeavor to add some attractiveness to their cold and barren ritual.

To proceed with the account of the organ's development: The blowing of the bellows, even for the largest instruments, was done by hand for many centuries. The Winchester organ mentioned above required seventy men, working in relays. The simple device of weighting the bellows was discovered only at the beginning of the sixteenth century. Portable organs were in use in the tenth century, and a little later the kind known as reed organs, using vibrating metal tongues instead of pipes, came into use. Organs with two or more manuals or keyboards were constructed about the year 1350, and soon afterwards the device known as the coupler was introduced, by which when a key is depressed a corresponding key is pulled down on another keyboard. The pedal keys, played with the feet, date back to the fourteenth century, but the invention which gives the organ its greatest effectiveness, namely the stops, was probably brought into use only about the year 1500. The enclosing of a part of the organ in a box with movable shutters, known as the swell, by moving which the volume of sound is diminished or increased, was the invention of a Londoner named Jordan, in 1712.

Orchestras in Churches. Are musical instruments, other than the organ, allowed in church services? Yes, under certain restrictions. After the introduction of the organ it alone was used for some centuries as an accompaniment to the solemn chanting of the choir. The nature of the organ is to a great extent a protection against its misuse. Its resonance and fullness lend themselves admirably to the majesty of the divine service. It can be sweeping and powerful, or delicate and sweet; but its tone is always more appropriate for sacred music than the combined tones of the brass and wind instruments of an orchestra. After the sixteenth century, and possibly earlier in some places, orchestral instruments found entrance into some churches, but laws were soon passed against them on account of the frivolous and sensuous character of the music produced by means of them. At the present day, as a result of the legislation contained in the "Motu Proprio" of Pius X, they may be used only by permission of the bishop and within due limits.

The Gregorian Chant. This is the distinctive song of the Church, the interpreter in melody of her prayerful devotion. It is so called from its great founder, St. Gregory the Great, and is also known by the name of Plain, Roman or Choral Chant. It is a grave melody, usually solemn in nature, sung in unison — that is, without harmonizing parts — set to the rhythm of the words, and without strictly measured time. As prayer is an utterance by the believing heart, expressing its faith, so the chant, which is the more solemn mode of liturgical prayer, owes to faith its power and its beauty.

The leading characteristics of the Gregorian Chant are its melody, its tone and its rhythm. Concerning the first of these, the Church, strictly speaking, authorizes in her liturgy no other music than pure melody; that is, the singers always chant in unison and at the same pitch. Voices of different pitch singing in harmonic chords may indeed be tolerated; but, however beautiful the effect, the Church does not consider such music appropriate to the sacred chant, with the exception of the so-called "Palestrina music," which will be alluded to further on.

The melody of the Gregorian Chant is at the same time recitative and meditative; it recites the words of the text and meditates upon them. Sometimes it proceeds with great dispatch, as in the singing of the psalms, usually assigning one note for each syllable; at other times it dwells upon the words, pouring out its meaning in rich and musical cadences, based rhythmically upon the syllables of the liturgical words. It is thereby accommodated to the spirit of the Church's services — now dwelling on the sacred word in sustained meditation, now sending forth a rapid current of melodious praise.

The Beauty of the Chant. As regards the tone used, the ecclesiastical chant is full of variety, for it was created for the purpose of beautifying the Church's services, which are of many kinds. Adoration, thanksgiving, supplication, sorrow, joy and triumph find in the Gregorian tones their fitting expression. The melody accommodates itself to the word and phrase, to the spirit of the Church, and to the nature of the prayer and praise which are being offered to God. Whether it be the Gloria, the jubilant song of the Angels — the Credo, which is the Church's public act of faith — the Sanctus, in which we here on earth join in adoration with the celestial spirits — the Agnus Dei, the appeal for mercy addressed to Him Who has taken away sin — the Libera, which is the intercessory prayer for the faithful departed — in each of these the spirit of the words and the devotion of the Church are brought out clearly by the grand and simple melodies of the Gregorian Chant. How beautiful in its solemn and reverential strains is the Preface of the Mass, in which the priest offers the Church's thanksgiving and homage before the throne of God! How replete with sadness and sorrow is the chant of the Lamentations in the office of Holy Week! How expressive of fear and desolation are the mournful notes of the "Dies Irae"! All these varying moods of the Church's praise and prayer are portrayed in the Gregorian Chant without any of the artifices of vocal or instrumental harmonizing that are employed in secular music. Its melodies have sprung from the minds of Saints, singing from the inspiration of the Spirit of God.

The simple Gregorian Chant was considered by the composer Halevy "the most beautiful religious melody that exists on earth." Mozart, who wrote many Masses of great merit and beauty, declared that he would gladly exchange all his musical reputation for the fame of having composed the Preface of the Mass.

As to rhythm, the Gregorian Chant differs from our modern music in that it follows the natural accenting of the words — that is, the longer notes are used for the accented syllables of the text, and there is no strict rule as to the time. Thus the melody of the Chant accentuates the meaning of the words of the liturgy, and does not becloud or conceal it, as is too often the case in secular music.

The Notation of the Chant. The admirable system now in use for the writing of all music originated in the chant of our Church. The ladder or scale of sound is represented to the eye by a pictorial ladder of rounds or steps, called a staff. In the Gregorian Chant four lines and three intervening spaces are used; in modern musical notation this has been increased to five lines and four spaces.

In the Gregorian staff the seven steps correspond to the seven different notes of the musical octave, and if any of these is defined by having assigned to it the pitch and name of one of the sounds of the octave, all the rest thereby receive their pitch and name. This defining is done by means of two signs called "clefs," that is, keys — representing the notes "do" and "fa," prefixed to any line of the staff.

The Gregorian Chant uses notes differing in form from those used in ordinary musical notation — a square note, called "brevis," or short; a square note with a tail, called "longs," or long; and a diamond-shaped note called "semi-brevis," having about half the value of the square note. Unlike the notes in modern music, these Gregorian notes have not strictly measured value; the sense of the words and the spirit of the season cause the text to be sung rapidly or slowly, and the music of the chant is merely intended to aid in expressing such sense and spirit.

The History of the Gregorian Chant. It is probable that

some of the psalm-tunes of our Church are derived from those used in the worship of the Old Law. The Apostles, who had been members of the Jewish Church, were the founders of the Christian Church; and it is reasonable to suppose that the chant, as well as the words, was preserved by them and handed on to their successors.

As soon as the Church was freed from persecution we find her occupied in establishing due uniformity in her liturgy. Pope Damasus, about the year 380, decreed that the psalms should be chanted by alternate choirs (as is done at the present day in monastic churches), and that the Gloria Patri should be added to each. St. Ambrose, Bishop of Milan, was one of the great founders of the system of church music. St. Augustine gives testimony to the beauty of the Ambrosian chant. "the sweet song of Thy Church stirred and penetrated my being; the voices streamed into my ears and caused truth to flow into my heart." But it is to St. Gregory the Great, Pope from 590 to 604, that we are principally indebted for the beautiful harmonies that have since borne the name of Gregorian. He is said to have discovered the octave as the naturally complete succession of sounds, to have to distinguished the various notes by means of letters, and to have added many new chants to those already in use.

The idea of the staff of four lines and of the movable clefs is due to a Benedictine monk, Guido d'Arezzo, in the eleventh century. He also is said to have given the names to the first six notes of the octave. The note "do" was originally called "ut," and the six names are taken from the Vesper hymn of the feast of St. John the Baptist:

> UT queant laxis REsonare fibris
> MIra gestorum FAmuli tuorum,
> SOLve polluti LAbii reatum,
>   Sancte Joannes.

As the centuries went on, the beauty and solemnity of the chant of the Church were impaired in many ways — by the growing use of measured rhythm, thereby making the words subordinate to the music — by the introduction of counterpoint or harmony, with its seductive beauty — and by the mingling in the liturgy of popular worldly music, both vocal and instrumental. Therefore at the Council of Trent, in the sixteenth century, the reform of church music was considered, and a little later, by authority of Paul V, the "Graduale Romanum" was printed, the great work of Giovanni Pierluigi da Palestrina.

The Music of Palestrina. This greatest of all composers of religious music was born in Italy about 1510. He was for some years a member of the papal choir, and afterwards of those of the churches of St. John Lateran and St. Mary Major. He was a friend of St. Philip Neri, and gained from him that insight into the spirit of the liturgy that enabled him to send it forth in music as it had never been done before. He made his compositions the medium for the expression of the state of his own soul, trained by his companionship with one of the greatest of modern saints.

After the Council of Trent, St. Pius V entrusted the reform of church music to a commission of Cardinals, among whom was St. Charles Borromeo. This holy and learned prelate became acquainted with Palestrina and with his music, and recognized that the latter was admirably adapted to the Church's liturgy. Masses, hymns and psalm-tunes were produced in great numbers by the gifted composer. His complete works comprise no less than thirty-three volumes. The distinguishing features of his music are the absence of all themes resembling secular melodies or reminiscent of them, and the rejection of musical forms that would obscure the liturgical text. His creations will stand forth for all time as the embodiment of the devotional spirit of the Church. To him belongs the double glory of having restored the sacred chant to its former grand and simple beauty, and of introducing harmonized music of such power and expressiveness that it became a proper accompaniment to Christian devotion.

Pius X on Church Music. This great Pope, who wrought so many changes in spiritual matters in the Church, and whose pontificate will go into history as an era of religious awakening, issued a decree in 1903, known as the "Motu Proprio" — which words signify "of his own accord," indicating that the Pontiff acted without consultation with Cardinals or others. This decree states clearly what Church music should be. "Sacred music should possess in the highest degree the qualities proper to the liturgy. It must be holy, and must therefore exclude all worldliness." The Holy Father declared that "the Church has always recognized and honored progress in the arts, admitting to the service of religion everything good and beautiful discovered by genius in the course of ages. Consequently modern music is also admitted in the Church, since it oftentimes affords compositions of such excellence, sobriety and gravity that they are in no way unworthy of liturgical functions. But care must be taken that musical compositions in this style contain nothing worldly, be free from reminiscences of theatrical *motifs*, and be not fashioned after the manner of secular pieces." Music in church must be in conformity with the spirit of divine worship. It must be Church music, not theatrical. Marches, operatic airs, ambitious solos and the crash of instruments are out of place in the worship of God, and the melodies that bring memories of the theatre and the concert-hall are nothing but a distraction to those who wish to pray.

According to the "Motu Proprio," the liturgical text must be sung as it is in the books of the Church, without alteration or transposing of the words, without undue repetition, and in an intelligible manner. The day of the two score Amens has gone by, and the endless and meaningless repeating of disconnected phrases of the Gloria or Credo is also, happily, a thing of the past.

Singing by the People. Pius X expressed himself as warmly in favor of congregational singing within proper limits; but it was his will that this should be largely the singing of the Gregorian Chant. Hymns in other languages than Latin may not be substituted at Mass, although they are permitted at some other services. In the "Motu Proprio" the Pontiff said: "Special efforts are to be made to restore the use of the Gregorian Chant by the people, so that the faithful may take a more active part in the ecclesiastical offices, as was the case in early times."

The History of Congregational Singing. We may consider this important matter with reference to its history, its revival at the present time, and the results of that revival.

The first testimony as to this ancient practice is found in the

Epistle of St. Paul to the Ephesians: "Speak to yourselves in psalms and hymns and spiritual canticles, singing and making melody in your hearts to the Lord." This is understood by the commentators as referring to congregational singing in the religious meetings of the faithful. In these services of the primitive Church both sexes took part in the singing. Although St. Paul had ordered that women should keep silence in church, his words applied only to instructing or exhorting. And in the times of persecution, as already stated, the Christians were accustomed to use psalms and hymns in the worship of God.

St. Ambrose introduced the practice of congregational singing from the East into his diocese of Milan, and it was soon spread throughout the Western Church. For many centuries Latin was used exclusively, but in later times rhyming hymns in the language of the country came into vogue in some parts of Europe. The frequent pilgrimages and the religious plays subsequently fostered such singing among the people.

After a time, in some parts of the Church, decrees were passed against such singing. At the Council of Laodicea, in the fourth century, it was declared that "besides the appointed singers who mount the ambo and sing from the book, others shall not sing in the church." The ambo was the raised platform from which the lectors read the Scriptures to the people, and on which the chanters sang. The reason for this decree was that the unskillful singing of the people interfered with the harmony of the chanters. However, it did not come into force everywhere. Centuries later, especially after the Reformation, the use of the language of the country became rather common, particularly in Germany.

The second Plenary Council of Baltimore, in 1866, urged pastors to have the elements of the Gregorian Chant taught in the schools, so that "the number of those who can sing the chant well may be increased, and that the greater part of the people shall thus learn to sing Vespers and the like with the ministers and the choir." The same wish was expressed by the third Plenary Council of Baltimore, in 1884.

These words show us that the people are to be instructed in the Gregorian Chant — that is, to take part in the liturgical offices of the Church, such as High Mass, Vespers and Benediction. Congregational singing at low Masses and at other services has always been practised more or less in some of our churches. It is to be hoped, therefore, that means will be found to teach the people to sing the "Ordinary of the Mass" in plain chant — namely, the Kyrie, Gloria, Credo, Sanctus and Agnus Dei, besides the various responses, leaving the changeable parts, such as the Introit, Offertory and Communion, to the trained choir; and also to sing the psalms and hymns at Vespers, the changing antiphons to be chanted by the choir.

Well-ordered singing by the people is assuredly edifying and devotional, although it is not the aim of the Church to teach them to sing rather than to pray. The problem, however, is full of difficulty, especially as regards to our American people, who, as a class, cannot be considered musical.

Women in Church Choirs. Are women to be allowed to sing in the choirs of our churches? If the choir were really the "official choir," stationed in the sanctuary, they would not be admissible; but our ordinary choirs may be considered as representing the congregation — and as women may certainly take part in congregational singing, their presence in our choirs would seem to be excusable under certain conditions. Of course, in theory, choirs composed of men and boys are preferable, and this is recommended by the "Motu Proprio"; but in many of our parishes, especially the smaller, it would be difficult to organize and maintain these. Therefore, for the present at least, the assistance of female singers is usually tolerated; and assuredly our churches are greatly indebted to the zeal and faithfulness of the gentler sex for the generally creditable manner in which the musical part of the liturgy is performed.

This, then, is a brief and necessarily imperfect account of the music of our Church, which adds so much beauty and grandeur to her solemn services. Daily in monasteries and convent chapels the Divine Office is sung by those who have given their lives to God. All over the world, Sunday after Sunday, the praise of God is sent up before His throne in sacred song. In grand cathedrals the diapason of great organs fills the house of God with mighty harmonies. In parish churches and in mission chapels the homage of the faithful is offered to their Lord in the sweet and simple melody of the sacred chant.

When we listen to such earthly harmonies, well may we hope that one day we may hear that perfect sacred music to which these are only a prelude — the chanting of the Seraphim who offer their homage of song and praise before the eternal throne of God.

CHAPTER LX

PSALMS AND HYMNS

A HYMN meant originally a song of praise in honor of gods or heroes. It had a religious character which distinguished it from a mere laudatory ode in honor of a living man. Among the Jews it is not certain that hymns, in the modern sense, were sung, for the word as used in the Old Testament includes psalms and canticles.

From very early times psalms and hymns were sung in Christian assemblies. We have alluded elsewhere to the testimony of Pliny, who, in a letter to the Emperor Trajan, in the year 104, mentions the Christian custom of singing a hymn to Christ as God in their "meetings before the dawn."

How Psalms are Used. The Psalms of David, during the centuries of persecution, were the most natural expression of the Church's sorrow and hope when trials weighed heavily upon her, of her joy in the midst of tribulation, and of her faith in the Redeemer Whose coming the Psalmist had prophesied.

These still form the greater part of the Church's liturgy. They are used in the Divine Office, and portions of them constantly occur in the words of the Mass. In the recitation of the Office they are chanted antiphonally; that is, alternate verses are said or sung by each half of the choir. This custom is attributed by some authors to St. Ignatius, a famous martyr of the early Church; by others it is said to have been introduced at Antioch during the reign of Constantine, by two monks named Flavian and Diodorus. In the Western Church this method of chanting was first practised at Milan, in the time of the great St. Ambrose. It is related that the Roman Empress Justina, an Arian heretic, sought to imprison Ambrose. His people gathered around him in his church to protect him, and spent several days in the alternate singing of the verses of psalms and hymns.

The Sacred Canticles. Besides the 150 psalms, the Breviary contains thirteen canticles taken from the Old Testament and three from the New. Some of these have been used in the Office since about the year 800, while others were added very recently in the revision of the Breviary under Pius X.

Our Church also uses other canticles which are not found in the Scriptures — the "Te Deum," the "Trisagion" and the "Gloria in Excelsis." The Te Deum, according to an old legend, was sung by Saints Ambrose and Augustine after the baptism of the latter — but there is no foundation whatever for the story. The canticle has been attributed to a certain Nicetius, bishop of Treves in France, and also to St. Hilary of Poictiers. It is recited at the end of Matins on most of the days of the year.

The Trisagion ("O Holy God, holy and strong, holy and immortal, have mercy on us") is said in Greek and Latin by the celebrant at the veneration of the cross on Good Friday, and is used in the prayers at Prime in the office on penitential days. It has been adopted into the Western Church from the Greek liturgy, and is traceable back to the fifth century.

The Gloria, or Greater Doxology, is used in the Mass, and is an amplification of the hymn of the angels at Bethlehem. It is a translation of an old Greek hymn, and was originally sung only at Christmas. Later it was extended to other joyful feasts, but up to the eleventh century it could be used by bishops only, except at Easter.

Hymns of the Breviary. About the sixth century the use of metrical hymns, often with rhyming stanzas, became common. Some of these go back even to an earlier date, being attributed to St. Ambrose.

The Breviary contains a great number of hymns — 173 in all; and many of them are of great beauty. Some occur frequently in the Office, while others are used only once in the year, on particular feasts. We shall confine our attention to those that are used in the public services of the Church, and that are thereby more or less familiar to our readers.

The beautiful hymns in honor of the Blessed Eucharist are mostly the work of the "Angelic Doctor," St. Thomas Aquinas, in the thirteenth century. Among them are the "Adore Te Devote," the "Pange, Lingua," which is sung in processions of the Blessed Sacrament, and of which the last stanzas form the "Tantum Ergo" at Benediction, and the "Verbum Supernum Prodiens," of which the last portion, the "O Salutaris," is usually sung at Benediction.

The anthems sung in honor of the Blessed Virgin at the end of Vespers are the "Salve, Regina," used during most of the year, and probably written by Hermannus Contractus, a German monk, about 1050; the "Alma Redemptoris Mater," by the same author, sung during and after Advent; the "Ave, Regina Coelorum," by an unknown author, sung from the Purification to Holy Week; and the "Regina Coeli," used during the Easter time, dating back probably to the tenth century.

Other well-known hymns to the Blessed Virgin are the "Ave, Maris Stella" ("Hail, Star of the Sea"); attributed to Fortunatus, bishop of Poictiers, in the sixth century — and the mournful "Stabat Mater," used frequently in our churches at the Stations of the Cross. This was composed by Giacopone da Todi, a disciple of St. Francis, in the thirteenth century, and has furnished the text for the immortal music of Rossini.

Hymns of the Missal. The "Dies Iræ" ("Day of Wrath") used at Masses for the dead, goes back to the thirteenth century, and was composed by a certain Thomas of Celano. It is written in rhyming three-line stanzas, giving a vivid description of the General Judgment, and the sounding of the Angel's trumpet, the resurrection of the dead, and the gathering of all mankind before the dread tribunal of the Judge; and it ends with a prayer for the eternal rest of the departed.

The "Veni, Creator Spiritus," the hymn to the Holy Ghost, is usually sung in our churches before the sermon, to invoke the aid and blessing of the Spirit of Wisdom, It is also used in the Mass and Office of Pentecost. By some it is attributed to Charlemagne, but it is more probably the work of St. Gregory the Great.

On Holy Saturday, at the blessing of the paschal candle, the "Exsultet" is sung — a long unrhymed hymn of praise and prayer. It is ascribed by some to St. Augustine, but it is probably of somewhat later date.

The "Lauda Sion Salvatorem," used in the Mass of Corpus Christi, is the work of the great St. Thomas Aquinas. He was a master of Latinity, as of nearly every other branch of knowledge. His hymns in honor of the Blessed Sacrament are unsurpassed in poetic beauty. In stanzas of faultless rhythm and rhyme they give a clear statement of the Church's teaching regarding the Real Presence, combined with a spirit of prayerful devotion worthy of their saintly author.

St. Thomas and St. Bonaventure. There is a story connected with the composing of these hymns in honor of the Blessed Sacrament. When Urban IV established the office and festival of Corpus Christi in 1264, he directed St. Thomas, a Dominican, and St. Bonaventure, a Franciscan, to prepare appropriate words for the Church's ritual. When the task had been completed the two Doctors of the Church appeared before the Pontiff to submit the result of their labors. St. Thomas was requested to read his composition; and as the holy Bonaventure listened to the exquisite cadences of the "Pange, Lingua" and the "Lauda, Sion," he quietly tore his own manuscript into small pieces; and when the Dominican had finished and the Franciscan was called upon, he replied with saintly humility that his hymns were unworthy to be compared with those which had just been read.

The beautiful "Adeste, Fideles," so familiar to us at Christmas season, is not of ancient origin. It is probably of French or German authorship, and was first used in London in the chapel of the Portuguese Legation in 1797.

Our English Hymns. Of many of the hymns in our own tongue, the less said the better. Few of them possess any artistic merit, and many of them are decidedly bad in wording and music. Those recited as a part of the "Little Office of the Blessed Virgin" are excellent examples, both in rhyme and rhythm, of "how not to do it." In an effort to imitate the short metre of the Latin originals, the translator (who is deservedly unknown) has produced a series of jerky stanzas distinguished by really atrocious attempts at rhyming. For the benefit of our sodalities, a rewriting of this Office is much to be desired.

However, there are some excellent English hymns. "Lead, Kindly Light" was written by John Henry Newman, afterwards

Cardinal, before his conversion to Catholicism. In beautiful and mystical language it expresses his seeking for the light of truth which shone so radiantly into his soul a few years later.

The hymn "Holy God, We Praise Thy Name" is a free translation of the "Te Deum." It was composed by the Rev. Clarence Walworth before his conversion, and first appeared in a Protestant hymnal in 1853. Its sonorous chords are well suited to male voices, and it is commonly sung at the meetings and services of Holy Name societies and other men's sodalities.

Chapter LXI

THE MARRIAGE LAWS

Our holy Church does not look upon marriage merely as a Sacrament. She considers it also as a contract, and the most important of all contracts. There is nothing in her code of laws that has received so much attention from her teachers and law-givers. The nature and beauty of marriage as a Sacrament are explained and extolled in the homilies of the Fathers; and the zeal of the Church for the validity and inviolability of the marriage contract is manifest in the decrees of Councils and Popes.

The Marriage Contract and the Law. The contract of marriage between certain persons is null and void by the law of God, both natural and revealed. This is the belief of all races and creeds. For example, the attempted marriage of a father and his daughter, or of a brother and his sister, would be of itself invalid. But the Catholic Church goes further. She teaches that the contract of marriage may be rendered null by impediments which are instituted by her laws. According to her doctrine, marriage between baptized persons is a Sacrament, and therefore it falls under her authority. Just as the civil government may pronounce certain contracts void, for the general good, so the Church may interfere with the freedom of the marriage contract for the same purpose.

The Power of the State. Has the State any right to nullify marriages? None whatever. It has the right to regulate them — for instance, to require the obtaining of a license and the subsequent registration of the marriage — and it can lawfully inflict penalties for the non-observance of these rules; but it has no right and no power to annul a valid marriage. And so the divorce-mill that grinds so merrily at Reno and that works almost as freely elsewhere in our land is a feature of our laws that has no justification whatever.

The Kinds of Impediments. We shall now consider the impediments to this sacramental contract. As said above, some of them exist because of the natural law or the revealed law of God, some because the Church has so ruled. Impediments are of two kinds. Some render a marriage merely unlawful, but do not affect its validity; these are called hindering impediments. Others render it absolutely null, and are known as "diriment"' or destroying impediments.

The Hindering Impediments. The principal impediments of the first-mentioned class, merely impeding the marriage but not affecting its validity, are as follows:

1. Time. So far as concerns the solemn celebration of a marriage, it is not permitted during the so-called "closed time" — Advent and the following days until after Epiphany, Lent, and the octave of Easter. This is an ancient practice of the Church, especially as regards Lent; the rule concerning Advent was not everywhere in force in the early centuries. Our law as it stands at present dates back to the Council of Trent.

2. The Church's prohibition. This includes the marriage of a Catholic with a baptized non-Catholic — which is valid if performed by proper authority, but which requires a dispensation to be lawful — and also marriage without banns, which is likewise valid but illegal unless permission is secured to celebrate it without such publication. According to the present law, three publications of the banns, on different days and at the public services of the Church, are ordinarily required, and a dispensation is necessary if any of these be omitted.

3. A simple vow of chastity, such as may be made privately or in religious societies that are not Orders in the strict sense — such as the Sisters of Mercy.

4. A previous engagement to another person — provided that it has been entered into in writing before ecclesiastical authority, as will be explained further on, when we consider the new marriage laws.

The Diriment Impediments. The impediments that render a marriage altogether invalid are the following:

1. Error. Suppose that a man went through the form of marriage with a woman, mistaking her for another; he would not be married to either.

2. Condition. This refers to the case where a person unknowingly goes through a form of marriage with a slave, in

regions where slavery is legal. This marriage would be invalid.

3. A solemn vow of chastity, or Sacred Orders; for the obligation resulting from a solemn vow made to God is an obstacle to marriage unless a dispensation is given. Such a vow is one that is made publicly and for life in a regularly constituted religious order, or at the reception of Holy Orders. The rule of the Church requiring celibacy for her clergy in Sacred Orders is explained elsewhere in this book, in the chapter on "An Unmarried Clergy."

4. Consanguinity. This includes both blood relationship and certain legal and spiritual relationships as well. The rule is that, by natural law, marriages are forbidden in the direct line of descent; that is, a man cannot marry any one from whom he is descended or who is descended from him; and for such relationships no dispensation can be given. And a man cannot marry what are called near collateral relatives — his sister, cousin, niece, aunt, etc., as far as the fourth degree inclusively, which means third cousins. As regards dispensations for such marriages, none can be given for the first degree of collateral relationship — brother and sister; for this is forbidden by the natural law. Cousins are of the second degree; second cousins are of the third degree, etc.; and for these relationships dispensations may be granted by the Church. For very near relationships, such as first cousins, this is rarely done.

Legal relationship, that is, resulting from adoption, impedes marriage between the adopter and the adopted; and either party cannot marry the wife of the other, nor the child of the other while he or she is under parental care. Dispensations may be given, when necessary from this form of impediment.

Spiritual relationship is caused by sponsorship at the administration of Baptism or Confirmation. This impediment goes back to the sixth century, though its rules have been changed since that time. Without dispensation, a person cannot marry his or her god-parent; the latter cannot marry the father or mother of the person for whom he or she has been sponsor; and the one who administers private Baptism cannot marry the person baptized.

5. Affinity. This is an impediment that prevents a valid

marriage (unless by dispensation) with certain blood-relatives of a previous wife or husband — or with those of a party with whom illicit intercourse had previously taken place. The first, or lawful affinity, renders marriage invalid to the fourth degree of kindred — that is, a man cannot marry without dispensation even the third cousin of his deceased wife. Unlawful affinity makes the marriage null to the second degree only, or as far as first cousin or aunt.

6. Public decorum — an impediment arising from an engagement. It prevents the marriage of a person to the parents, brother, sister or child of the party to whom he or she had been previously engaged. This impediment loses much of its force under the new marriage laws, which consider only solemn and formal engagements, as will be explained further on.

7. Crime. This means, for example, a conspiracy between a wife and a man, resulting in the murder of the woman's husband, with the intention that the guilty parties may subsequently marry; or adultery with the same expressed intention of marriage after her husband's death; or a combination of both crimes for the same end. These are gruesome details of human wickedness — but such things have happened. Any of these crimes, committed with the intention of subsequent marriage, is an impediment to matrimony.

8. Difference of worship (in Latin "disparitas cultus") — which signifies that one party is a Catholic and the other is unbaptized. Unless by dispensation, such a marriage is null.

9. Grave fear renders a marriage invalid. A contract forced by fear of death or of grave injury is not a contract at all.

10. A previous marriage prevents another marriage until the death of the former wife or husband has become morally certain.

11. Extreme youth is an impediment to matrimony. The general rule of the Church is, for boys, that they cannot validly marry until they have completed their fourteenth year, and for girls, their twelfth year — which rule seems extremely mild to us who dwell in the Temperate Zone.

12. Physical impotency, incurable and existing before the

attempted marriage, renders it null.

13. Violence, the forcible carrying off or detention of a woman, renders a marriage invalid so long as she remains in the power of the aggressor, because she is considered as being unable to act of her own free will.

14. Clandestinity. This means that a marriage ceremony is void unless it is performed by the parish priest of the parties, or by their bishop, or by the delegate of either. This rule goes back to the Council of Trent, and was made even more strict by the matrimonial legislation of Pius X.

The New Marriage Laws. This new code of rules was put into force to bring about uniformity. The laws of the Council of Trent were effective only where they had been promulgated; and as in a large part of the world this had not been done, there was a great difference in the marriage regulations and requirements between countries which were under these laws and those which were not.

This was especially true in the case of a secret marriage — that is, one not performed by the parish priest or bishop of the parties, and therefore coming under the last-mentioned impediment, clandestinity. Where the legislation of Trent was in force, such a marriage was absolutely void. Where this legislation had not been put into effect, such a marriage was illegal, sometimes sinful, but nevertheless valid, provided that there was no other impediment. Thus what might be a real marriage in one country might be no marriage at all in another. There was also much confusion concerning the effect of a betrothal or promise of marriage, which became an impediment to the marriage of either party to a third person.

To simplify matters and to promote uniformity in marriage laws throughout the Catholic world, the decree of Pius X, known as the "Tametsi," from its opening word, was drawn up with the greatest care, requiring the continual labor of an expert commission for more than two years.

The Law About Betrothals. A valid betrothal has these effects in Church law. It makes the marriage of either party with a third person unlawful, but not invalid; but if the third person be a near blood-relative of the party with whom the betrothal was contracted (a mother, sister, daughter, father, brother or son), the marriage is invalid.

But what is a valid betrothal? Before the issuing of the new decree, it meant simply a mutual promise of marriage, whether before ecclesiastical authority or not, whether before witnesses or not, whether written or verbal; and hence ensued many difficulties. It was not easy to determine what was a real promise and what was rather a conditional expression of future intention.

All this haziness has been cleared away by the new law. It declares that no previous betrothal or promise of any kind whatever shall have any effect on a marriage unless such betrothal be contracted in writing, signed by both parties and by the parish priest or bishop, or at least two witnesses. And as, in our country at least, few couples will go to their pastor or appear before witnesses to advertise the fact that they are "engaged," we may consider that the impediment arising from a previous betrothal is practically done away with altogether.

The result is that a private engagement of the two parties has now no effect whatever upon the marriage of one of them to a third person.

Difficulties Under the Old Law. In the greater part of the United States, previous to the decree of Pius X, there had been no promulgation of the laws of the Council of Trent, and hence marriages, even though sinful and unlawful, were valid when they were performed before Protestant ministers, justices or other officials, provided that both of the parties were baptized — that is, both Catholics, or one a Catholic and the other a baptized Protestant.

You can imagine the difficulties that pastors and confessors met with in investigating such cases — in trying to determine whether a certain party was married or not. Take a case like this: A Catholic woman went to a Protestant minister to be married to a Protestant man. Later the man disappeared. The Catholic woman cannot ascertain definitely whether the said Protestant had ever been baptized or not. Having made her peace with God and the Church (for she had incurred excommunication) she wishes to marry a Catholic.

Under the law as it was before 1908, she could marry thus if the Protestant party was unbaptized, for there had been no real marriage with him; she could not if he was a baptized Protestant, for her marriage with him was valid, even though contracted before a minister. And as she cannot find out whether he was baptized or not, she can do nothing.

The Substance of the New Law. All the difficulties, inquiries, delays and disappointments resulting from the old system of law have been removed (for marriages since Easter, 1908) by the new decree, which declares that no marriage is a marriage at all unless it be performed by a parish priest in his own parish, or by a bishop in his own diocese, or by a delegate of either, in the presence of at least two witnesses. If those subject to the Church's law go elsewhere to be married, there is no marriage at all.

This rule, concerning those who can assist at marriages, is a striking feature of the new law. One would think, for instance, that a Catholic priest would be able to marry a couple validly anywhere in his own diocese. He cannot. He may perform the ceremony only in his own parish; and if he should attempt to do so outside of its limits without the permission of the parish priest or bishop of that place, there would be no marriage.

Suppose that a priest in his own parish or a bishop in his own diocese should join in marriage a couple who do not reside therein. It will be a valid marriage, but it is illicit if it infringes on the rights of the pastor of the parties.

What is to be said of the right and power of an assistant priest, a curate, to officiate at marriages? He acts only as the pastor's delegate. This delegation, however, is taken for granted from the fact that he is appointed an assistant in the care of souls.

One's Own Parish. What is required that a person shall belong to a certain parish? If he or she has a real "domicile," a residence therein with the intention of remaining, or has dwelt within its limits for at least a month, the party is considered as belonging to that parish.

When the parties reside in different parishes, the marriage is celebrated in the parish of the bride, unless some sufficient reason excuses from the rule.

If the persons have no fixed abode, the parish priest must refer the matter to the bishop, except in case of necessity, and receive permission to officiate at the ceremony. Any pastor in his parish or any bishop in his diocese may give permission to another to perform a marriage.

Marriage Without a Priest. The Sacrament of Matrimony differs from all other Sacraments in one important feature. In all the others, the Sacrament is administered by a person (bishop, priest or layman, as the case may be) to another, and the person who performs the sacramental rite is called the "minister" of the Sacrament. In Matrimony, the parties who marry are themselves the ministers of the Sacrament. By their expressed mutual consent they marry themselves. The officiating priest sanctions their union in the name of the Church and bestows her benediction upon it, but does not marry the parties.

As this sanction and benediction are not essential to the Sacrament, they may be omitted altogether under certain conditions without affecting the validity or lawfulness of the marriage. This is indicated in a striking provision of the new law. If a couple wish to marry in a locality where for a month there has been no priest qualified to join them in matrimony, they may simply express their mutual consent to be man and wife in the presence of two witnesses, and they are thereby validly and lawfully united in Catholic marriage.

It is required that afterwards, if an opportunity presents itself, they shall see that the marriage is properly recorded, and shall have the ritual prayers read over them — without, however, any necessity of renewing their consent. They are also advised to receive the nuptial blessing at a marriage Mass; but their lawful marriage dates from the moment when they stood in the presence of witnesses and took each other as man and wife.

The Registering of Marriages. It is the strict duty of the parish priest to inscribe the record of the marriage immediately in the parish register, giving all essential details. If the parties were baptized in the parish where the marriage takes place, an entry must be made also in the Register of Baptisms, testifying to the marriage; or if either or both were baptized elsewhere, a notification of their marriage must be sent to the parish or parishes where the baptisms occurred, that it may be registered beside the record of each baptism.

In a country like ours, where persons move about frequently from parish to parish and from State to State, and where many are emigrants from other lands, this rule is not easy of fulfillment; but the difficulty does not exempt pastors from the obligation of complying with the law. Hence it is necessary in all cases that persons who intend to be married shall know positively where they were baptized, so that the priest who joins them in marriage may be able to forward the records to the proper places.

The Subjects of the Law. The decree of Pius X binds all persons who have been baptized in the Catholic Church, and all converts from heresy or schism. This includes even those who have fallen away from the Church and no longer call themselves Catholics. It binds also all Catholics who wish to marry non-Catholics, whether these are baptized or unbaptized.

The Church does not exact compliance with these laws from those who are not and have never been Catholics, in regard to marriages which they contract among themselves.

Therefore, the points to be remembered are these:

1. No marriage is valid unless celebrated in the presence of the parish priest or bishop of the place, or the delegate of either — except in the case mentioned above, where no priest is available.

2. No previous engagement, unless made legally before Church authority or solemnly before witnesses, is any barrier to a lawful marriage to another party.

3. Non-Catholics who have never been Catholics are not affected by the law.

These are the essential features, and they reveal in a most eminent degree the wisdom of the Church's legislators and the zeal and vigilance of the Holy See for the safeguarding of the contract which joins a Catholic man and woman in sacramental union "for better, for worse, for richer, for poorer, in sickness and in health, till death do them part."

Chapter LXII

RELIGIOUS SOCIETIES

Our Church, like every society that has work to be done, knows full well that "in union there is strength." Results that would be impossible of accomplishment by individuals become possible and even easy when united effort is made. Individual energy, even in spiritual things, is apt to be misdirected; or, at least, it is likely to be of benefit only to him who makes it, and to produce little or no good result in others. But when the religious efforts of individuals are combined with similar zeal on the part of others by the forming of religious societies, and when the work of the whole body is carefully guided and regulated, great good is accomplished, both in the individual member and in the whole society. God's glory is promoted, and the members are sanctified to a degree that would not be possible except as a result of such united effort.

For All Classes. The religious societies established by our Church are almost beyond counting. She has organized them for every class — for men and women, for the married and single, for children, for those living in the world and those consecrated to God in religion. She sets before these societies a great variety of objects — works of charity for some, devotional exercises for others; zeal for the spiritual improvement of mankind and for the spread of Christian virtues; aid to missionary enterprises; prayers and good works for the souls in Purgatory — such are some of the secondary objects of Catholic societies, all tending towards their great primary object — the sanctification of their members and the glory of God.

The Kinds of Societies. The Catholic societies for the laity are divided into three classes: First, Confraternities, which are religious associations of the faithful canonically established by Church authority to accomplish certain works of piety or charity; and when a confraternity has received the right to unite to itself sodalities existing in other localities and to communicate to them the spiritual advantages it enjoys, it is called an Archconfraternity. Second, Pious Associations, which have in general the same objects, but which are not "canonically erected"; these are variously known as pious unions, leagues, sodalities, etc. Third, societies which are not distinctively religious, even though all their members are Catholics.

In the second class, the "Pious Associations," are the Society of St. Vincent de Paul, the Society for the Propagation of the Faith, and the Apostleship of Prayer, otherwise known as the League of the Sacred Heart. In the third class are included the various beneficial organizations that have been established within recent years — notable among which are the Knights of Columbus, the Catholic Knights of America, the Catholic Foresters and the Catholic Benevolent Legion. We shall be obliged to confine our attention to the best-known societies of the first two classes.

The Federation of Catholic Societies. The Catholic societies of the United States have formed themselves into a union known as the American Federation of Catholic Societies, for the promotion of their religious, civil and social interests. The Federation has no political motive, but merely seeks to foster Christian education and Catholic interests, to overcome bigotry, to spread a knowledge of Catholic doctrine and principles, and to combat the social evils of the day. It was first advocated in 1899, and was established at a convention in Cincinnati in 1901. It is said to represent nearly two millions of Catholics, and has exercised a widespread and salutary influence since its inception.

The Holy Name Society. "At the Name of Jesus every knee shall bend." The greatest organization intended especially for Catholic laymen is the Society of the Holy Name of Jesus. It has been a wonderful power for good ever since its establishment centuries ago. At no time have its beneficial results been more in evidence than at the present day; in no place has it effected more good than in our own country.

The Holy Name Society (or, to give it its full title, the Confraternity of the Most Holy Name of God and Jesus) was established by the Dominicans, and has always been under their especial charge. It owes its origin, indirectly at least, to a decree of the Council of Lyons, in 1274, which provided for the instruction of the faithful regarding devotion and reverence towards the

Name of Jesus. Shortly after the issuing of the Council's decree, Pope Gregory X directed Blessed John Vercelli, Master-General of the Dominicans, to apply the energies of his order to this work. The society had a gradual growth in the fourteenth and fifteenth centuries. The first public procession in honor of the Holy Name took place at Lisbon in 1433. In 1564 Pius IV approved the confraternity and granted indulgences to it; and since that time it has been further enriched with spiritual favors by many Pontiffs.

The members bind themselves to labor for the glory of the Holy Name; to pronounce it always with reverence; to abstain from all sinful speech, and to strive that others shall also refrain from evil speaking. The spiritual advantages are many. Masses are offered for living and dead members; plenary indulgences are granted on the day of admission into the society and on certain festivals during the year; and partial indulgences may be gained for almost every act of worship or charity performed by the members.

It is a society for Catholic men living in the world, and its aim is to help them so to live that their every-day duties to God and their neighbor will be well performed — that their lives will be lives of many Christian virtue and of good example, resounding to the greater glory of God.

The League of the Sacred Heart. This is also known as the Apostleship of Prayer, and is one of the most widely spread of Catholic societies. It is purely spiritual in its aims, being intended to promote the practice of prayer for the mutual intentions of its members, and the increasing of love for our Blessed Saviour in return for the love which His Sacred Heart has lavished upon mankind.

It was founded at Vals, in France, in 1844, and was put substantially into its present form by Father Henri Ramiére, a Jesuit, in 1861. It was approved by Pius IX in 1879, and its statutes were revised and again approved by Leo XIII in 1896. It is under the special care of the Society of Jesus, and to the zeal and wise direction of that great Order it undoubtedly owes much of its marvelous success.

The supreme officer, known as the Moderator General, is the Superior General of the Jesuits, who usually deputes his authority to an assistant. The management of the society is largely carried on through the "Messenger of the Sacred Heart," a periodical which is published in different parts of the world and in various languages. Diocesan directors promote the work in their own territories, and the separate societies are known as "centres," each in charge of a local director. Under him are promoters, each caring for a band of members and distributing the "mystery leaflets" which instruct the members concerning the monthly practices of piety expected of them.

The religious duties of the association are a daily offering of prayers and good works, the daily recitation of a decade of the beads for the special intention of the Holy Father, as recommended in the monthly bulletin of the society, and the making of a "Communion of Reparation" on an assigned day of the month or week. The first Friday of each month is observed as a day of special devotion, the Mass of the Sacred Heart being usually celebrated; and evening services are held at which the members assist.

The growth of this society has been phenomenal. Over 62,500 local centres exist in various parts of the world, of which about 6,700 are in the United States. There are no less than twenty-five million members in this world-wide organization, and four millions of these are Americans.

Our Blessed Lord has assured us that "where two or three are gathered together in His Name, there is He in the midst of them." How pleasing, then, must be the united service of these millions of His children! Each month the intentions and good works of the society are printed in a bulletin, and the number and variety of these are astounding. Millions of separate petitions, millions of prayers of thanksgiving ascend day by day to the throne of our Saviour from the League of His Sacred Heart.

This society has had a large share in bringing about that great spiritual renovation which is the most consoling feature of our Church's life during the last few years. Frequent Communion is its watchword. Some of our readers can remember when the person who approached the altar-rail as often as once a month was looked upon as somewhat of a devotee. All this changed — and largely through the League of the Sacred Heart. Frequent Communion has become the rule, rather than the exception, for practical Catholics. When, in future ages, the history of our Church in the nineteenth and twentieth centuries shall be reviewed, the wonderful spread of the devotion to the Sacred Heart of Jesus and the resulting increase of devotion to the Blessed Sacrament will be the salient points of that history.

The Children of Mary. It is rather a curious fact that the Children of Mary, now distinctively a girls' society, had its origin in a sodality for young men. In Rome, about the year 1500, a number of students at the Roman College were formed by their Jesuit teachers into a religious organization for practices of devotion and works of charity. This society was approved by Gregory XIII in 1584, and was enriched with indulgences, especially by Benedict XIV. In 1830, at Paris, a pious nun named Catherine Labouré was favored with a vision in which the Miraculous Medal of the Blessed Virgin was given to her as the badge of an association for young girls. The indulgences which had been previously given to the men's sodality, known as the "Prima Primaria," were extended to the girls' sodality, and further evidences of approval were given by Pope Leo XIII. The society exists in nearly every country, and its branches flourish in almost every parish here in the United States. It has been productive of untold good among our young girls, and membership in it has become recognized as the badge of devout Catholic maidenhood.

The Rosary and Scapular Societies. These are commonly united in our parishes into a single organization, but they are in reality distinct bodies, established at different times and for somewhat different objects.

The Confraternity of the Holy Rosary was instituted in the fifteenth century, and the first branch of which there is a definite record was founded in the city of Cologne, in Germany, in 1474, by a zealous priest named Sprenger. A Dominican, Alan de Rupe, was largely instrumental in establishing the devotion of the Rosary as we now have it; and it was through him and other members of his order that societies of the Rosary were formed throughout Europe.

The members of this society partake of the merit of all the good works performed throughout the world by the members (both male and female) of the Dominican Order. Branches exist in many of our parishes, and with us it is largely a woman's society. It has received many indulgences from various Pontiffs; and Pope Leo XIII, in 1898, renewed and confirmed these in an important decree.

The only obligation for the members is the reciting of the beads — the fifteen mysteries within a week; and even this does not bind in any way under penalty of sin. In return for this simple service they share in a vast treasure of merit gained by the great Order of Preachers, which has ever been unsurpassed in untiring effort for the spread of the faith of Christ and in zeal for souls.

Other Rosary Societies. There are other societies which have the same object and practise of the same devotion. The "Perpetual Rosary" has existed since the seventeenth century. It assigns to each member a certain time of the day or night for the recitation of the beads, so that a continual Rosary will be offered to our Blessed Mother. Another society, the "Living Rosary," dates from 1826, and divides its members into "circles" of fifteen, each of whom is to recite a single decade each day, thus ensuring the recitation of the whole Rosary by each circle — a maximum of prayer, as it were, with a minimum of effort.

The Scapular Society. The "Confraternity of Our Lady of Mount Carmel," — for such is the real title of the Scapular Society — is much older than the Rosary Confraternity. It is known to have existed in the thirteenth century, and may be even older. The origin and rules of the scapular and scapular medal are fully treated elsewhere in this book, in the chapter on "Scapulars."

The Purgatorian Societies. Devotion to the suffering members of the Church in Purgatory is almost as old as the Church herself, for the doctrine of the Communion of Saints has always been asserted as a part of Catholic teaching. The Church of the catacombs had its prayers for the dead. The religious societies of the Middle Ages practised special works of charity for deceased members; and it was customary for churches and monastic houses, even of different orders, to enter into an agreement to pray and offer Masses mutually for the souls of all who were enrolled in a "register of brotherhood." This led to the institution of "Purgatorian societies" exclusively for the laity, and the first of these of which there is a clear record was established in Germany in 1355.

There have been, and still are, many distinct associations of this nature. Prominent among them are the Confraternity of "the Passion of Christ and of the Sorrowful Mother," instituted at Rome in 1448; "Our Lady of Suffrage," 1592; the "Archconfraternity of Death and Prayer," 1538; the Franciscan "Mass Association of Ingoldstadt," founded in 1726, which has many thousands of members and provides for the saying of more than two thousand Masses daily; the "Archconfraternity for the Relief of the Poor Souls in Purgatory," under the direction of the Redemptorist Fathers, established in 1841; and a society intended especially for the relief of the most needy and abandoned souls in Purgatory, founded at Montligeon, France, in 1884. All of these associations have been enriched with numerous indulgences by the Holy See, and priests who belong to them are in some cases entitled to the "privileged altar," which means that a plenary indulgence is granted to the soul for which the Mass is offered.

Thus does our holy Church provide for her children, even when they have passed from this world. It is a consoling thought, when we approach the end of our earthly career and dread the purgation which may be our due, that prayers and Masses are offered daily all over the Christian world, in the fruits of which we shall have a share.

The Society of the Holy Family. The "Archconfraternity of the Holy Family" is more widely established in Europe than it is in America. Its object is the sanctification of Christian families, and its membership includes men, women and children. It was founded at Liège, Belgium, in 1844, by Henri-Hubert Belletable, an army officer. He was a married man, living in the midst of the world, obliged to mingle with companions of all kinds — "even as you and I"; and he realized that the only hope for society was the bringing of religion into the daily and family life of men.

The association grew rapidly, and was placed under the direction of the Redemptorist Fathers. Pius IX, in the year 1847, approved it and granted indulgences to its members. It has about 1400 branches throughout the world, and nearly five million members.

Another society which has the same object was established in 1861 at Lyons, and was enlarged and approved by Leo XIII in 1892. It is known as "The Pious Association of Christian Families."

The Society of St. Vincent De Paul. This is an organization of Catholic laymen which is almost world-wide in extent, and is engaged in ministering to the needs of the poor. It was founded at Paris in 1833 by Antoine-Frederic Ozanam, a brilliant young professor, who brought together several of the students of the Sorbonne for charitable work, under the title of "The Conference of Charity" — later adopting the name of "The Society of St. Vincent de Paul" and choosing that grand exemplar of Christian charity as the patron and model of the society.

Its special field, from the beginning, has been "the service of God in the persons of the poor," who are visited in their homes and assisted according to their needs. The membership is of three classes: Active, subscribing and honorary — the last two being those who cannot devote themselves personally to the work, but who assist the active members by their influence, their contributions and their prayers.

The branches of the society in parishes are known as "Conferences"; and when there are several of these in a city they are usually controlled by a "particular Council." A further plan of administration has been undertaken in this country, which calls for a "Superior Council of the United States" for the whole country, a "Metropolitan Central Council" in each ecclesiastical province, and a "Diocesan Council" in each diocese.

The society has now more than two hundred thousand members. It exists in every European country and in almost every other part of the world. The American branch was organized in St. Louis in 1846; and throughout this country at the present time about $400,000 is annually gathered and spent — and, remember, it is all spent for the poor, and not for salaries and "expenses."

Chapter LXIII

THE CANONIZATON OF A SAINT

In another chapter of this book we discussed the doctrine of the veneration of saints, and explained what Catholics do and do not believe concerning these "chosen friends of God." From the earliest ages of Christianity the saints have been honored publicly and privately by the Church. In the first three centuries public veneration was usually given only to martyrs; but when the days of persecution were over, the Church's practice regarding the saints took a wider scope. She began to give public homage to holy men and women who, in the religious state, had given up all things to follow their Master — to zealous missionaries who had carried the Gospel into pagan lands — to learned Fathers and Doctors who had explained the same Gospel in words of heavenly wisdom — and even to men and women of the laity who had lived lives of eminent sanctity.

We must remember that the saints whose names are on the authoritative list of the Church are not the only saints. They are only the famous ones. Their virtues were so great that the fame of them became widespread, and a spirit of devotion sprang up in the hearts of the faithful which in time led the Holy See to examine into the lives and works of these servants of God, and to command public veneration of them. But in heaven there are countless millions of souls — and every one of these souls is a saint. While we do not honor each of them separately, we honor them collectively. The special homage that is manifested in public veneration is only for those upon whose sanctity the Church has set the seal of her approval, and whose eternal blessedness is vouched for by her infallible voice.

Beatification and Canonization. In order that the prayers of the faithful may not be, as it were, misdirected — that is, offered to one who is not really a saint — the Church has commanded that no public homage shall be given to any individual who has not been "beatified" or "canonized." Beatification consists in the issuing of a decree permitting public religious honor to a certain person in a certain place, gives him the title of "Blessed," and generally allows Masses to be celebrated and offices to be recited in his honor, but only in that place. Canonization is a precept of the Sovereign Pontiff commanding that public veneration be paid to a certain person by the whole Church, and gives him the title of "Saint." In brief, beatification is a permission to honor a person locally; canonization is the declaration that person is a saint, to be venerated by the universal Church.

By Decree of the Pope. It is the Pope, and only he, who issues a decree of beatification or canonization. In early centuries bishops had the right or exercised the privilege of declaring, in their own dioceses, that certain persons were deserving of religious honor or "beatification"; but the need of uniformity in this important part of Catholic worship gradually caused the abolition of this practice, and Pope Urban VIII, in 1634, reserved to the Holy See all legislation concerning the veneration of saints.

Is the Pope infallible in issuing a decree of canonization? Or, in other words, can he make a mistake in declaring a certain person a saint? It is the general opinion of theologians that when the Sovereign Pontiff declares that a certain person is in heaven he is preserved by the Holy Ghost from the possibility of error. The veneration paid to the saints is a part of the Church's worship of God, for when we honor them we honor God Himself; and it is eminently proper that this worship should have in it nothing erroneous. This infallibility in canonizing, however, has not thus far been defined by the Church as an article of faith; and it is certain that the Pope is not necessarily infallible when he issues a decree of mere beatification.

The Process of Canonization. How is a saint canonized? It is a long and laborious process, calling for ample deliberation and most absolute proofs of sanctity. It may last for years, and even for centuries. There are two parts to the procedure. The first is the beatification, during which the servant of God receives first the title of Venerable, and later that of Blessed. The second is the canonization proper, when he is finally enrolled in the list of those honored by the universal Church, and he is thereafter called a Saint.

The canonization of a martyr differs considerably from that of a person who was not a martyr. It is usually more quickly completed. There is less question of miracles as proofs of sanctity; his martyrdom for the faith is the essential point, and must be clearly proven.

A servant of God who is a non-martyr is called a "confessor" — that is, one who has confessed and manifested his faith by the eminent holiness of his life; or, in the case of a woman, a virgin or non-virgin, according as her life has been spent in a state of celibacy or not. The beatifying and canonizing of these classes is a very complicated process, and a brief outline of it will be given, to show the scrupulous care which our Church exercises, to the end that her public homage shall be offered only to those who are really saints of God.

The Investigations. Inquiries are first made by authority of the bishop of the place wherein the person lived. These are of three kinds — as to his reputation for sanctity and miracles — to prove that he has not, thus far, been publicly venerated (this being prohibited before beatification) — and regarding his writings, if there are any. The result of these inquires is sent to Rome, to the Congregation of Rites, and are there translated into Italian and copied; and a Cardinal is deputed by the Pope as "relator" or manager of the cause. The writings of the person (if any) are carefully examined by theologians, and an advocate and a "procurator of the cause" are appointed, who prepare all the documents that concern the case. These are printed and distributed to the Cardinals who form the Congregation of Rites, forty days before the date assigned for their discussion. And all this is merely to ascertain whether the cause is to be introduced or not.

If the Congregation is of the opinion that the matter should be carried further, a commission is appointed to introduce it, and the Holy Father signs the approval of the said commission, using (according to custom) his baptismal name, not his papal title. The servant of God is thereafter known by the title of "Venerable."

Letters are sent to the Church authorities of the place or places wherein the person spent his life, directing them to make further inquiries concerning his sanctity and miracles, in general and in particular. The Congregation also examines the proofs that no public veneration has been paid him. The results of all these inquiries, which must be completed within eighteen months, are examined, and lengthy documents are prepared by the "advocate of the cause," demonstrating the validity of all that has been thus far done. These are discussed at a special meeting of the Congregation, and it is the duty of the "promoter of the faith" (sometimes called jacosely "The advocate of the devil") to present difficulties and objections against the further consideration of the case.

The Signature of the Pope. Then comes the important part of the process, to which all that has preceded has been only a preparation. Three meetings of the Congregation of Rites are held, at the last of which the Pope himself presides. At these the question is debated: "Is there evidence that the Venerable Servant of God practised virtues both theological and cardinal, and in a heroic degree?" At each meeting a majority of those who take part must vote in the affirmative in order that the matter may be carried further. Complete reports of each meeting must be prepared and printed. And at the last meeting the Pope is asked to sign the solemn decree that there exists evidence of heroic virtue. The Holy Father, after fervent prayer, confirms by his signature the decision of the Congregation.

Two Miracles are Needed. Even then, the case is far from complete. At least two important miracles wrought through the intercession of the servant of God must be proved. The evidence regarding these must be very clear, and is carefully and thoroughly discussed in three separate meetings. Again three reports are made, and a decree is issued, confirmed by the Pope, that there is proof of miracles.

At a final meeting of the Congregation a last debate is held and a vote is taken; and on an appointed day the solemn ceremony of beatification takes place in the Vatican Basilica, on which occasion the Sovereign Pontiff issues a decree permitting public veneration (usually in certain places only) of the servant of God, who is thenceforth known as Blessed.

The Canonization. After the solemn beatification it is necessary that two more well-authenticated miracles shall be proved to have taken place through the intercession of the one who has been declared Blessed. When these have been discussed and confirmed at three meetings of the Congregation, another special meeting is held, at which the members consider the advisability of giving public universal veneration to the servant of God. And finally the Pope issues a "Bill of Canonization," by which he no longer permits but commands the public veneration of the Saint; and a great ceremony usually takes place in St. Peter's Church, at which the first Mass in honor of the new Saint is celebrated and his image is solemnly venerated.

We see, then, what laborious and lengthy deliberation our Church uses when it is a question of adding a new name to the long list of her saints. She does not hurry, for she does not need to do so; she will endure "all days, even to the consummation of the world." In some cases centuries have elapsed, and the cause is not yet completed. Sir Thomas More, the brave Englishman of nearly four hundred years ago, who "served his country well and his God better," and who went smiling to his death because he died for the faith of the Catholic Church, was declared Blessed as late as 1886, and has not yet been proclaimed a Saint. The causes of many other undoubted martyrs have not yet been presented to the Holy See. Many saintly confessors and virgins, who would seem to deserve richly all the honors that the Church could give them, have not been canonized. The vast number of cases presented to the Roman Congregation and the extreme care which must be exercised in considering them causes the list to grow but slowly.

It is comforting thought that we are members of the same great Church as are the saints who are with God in heaven. We are still here in the conflict, in the midst of sorrow and sin; they have won and obtained their eternal reward — and they are our friends and our intercessors before the throne of God.

"I saw a great multitude, which no man could number, of all nations and tribes and peoples ant tongues, standing before the Throne and in the sight of the Lamb."

Chapter LXIV

CHURCH BUILDINGS AND THEIR PARTS

A CHURCH is a building set apart for worship, and the name is used only for such structures as are for the general use of the faithful, as distinguished from chapels, which are for some community or family, or oratories, which are for private devotion.

The use of churches may be said to be as old as Christianity, for places of Christian meeting are frequently mentioned in the New Testament. At first, private houses were used for this purpose; and this state of things continued probably for three centuries. In the days of persecution the Christians usually worshipped underground, in the recesses of the excavations known as the Catacombs, which were also used as burial-places, and they registered their assemblies as "collegia," or burial-societies, so that they might hold property as legal corporations. About the beginning of the third century we find mention of churches properly so called; for when the final and greatest persecution broke out under the Emperor Diocletian, an edict of that tyrant ordered the destruction of Christian churches throughout the Empire.

Early Churches. As soon as peace had come to the Church under Constantine, the erection of magnificent temples of the true faith began everywhere. These early churches always had the sanctuary at the east end, so that the worshippers might pray in the ancient fashion, facing the east, whence the light of faith had come to them. At this end was the apse (Greek "apsis," a wheel), within which the altar was placed. Behind this was the bishop's throne, and the priests occupied seats in a semicircle. This part was celled the "presbyterium" — the priests' place, the name of the sanctuary being of much later date. Just forward of this was the choir, wherein the singers were placed. In those early days the Blessed Sacrament was not kept on the altar, but in a cell or chapel near the apse. The baptistery was usually a separate building, often octagonal or round, with a pool in which the Sacrament was administered by immersion. Fine examples of such detached baptisteries, though of much later date, are to be seen at Florence, Pisa and elsewhere

The laity were placed in the nave, the body of the church, which derived its name from the Latin "navis," a ship, from its shape and from the symbolism of a ship as emblematic of the Church. This part of the building was divided into sections by low partitions — the nearest to the presbyterium being for virgins and consecrated widows. Next came the parts for men and for women — carefully separated from each other in those days; and in the rear were the catechumens (those preparing to embrace the faith) and the penitents, who were also arranged in a certain order according to their guilt.

The Kinds of Churches. The principal churches are called, in Church law, basilicas (Greek "basilike," a palace or handsome building), which may be greater or patriarchal, or minor basilicas. The chief church of a diocese, wherein the bishop customarily officiates, is known as a cathedral (Latin "cathedra," a chair). An abbatial church is the seat of an abbot; and if a church had a chapter of canons for the daily solemn chanting of the Divine Office, as is usual in many dioceses of Europe and elsewhere, it is called a collegiate church. A parish church, of course, is the chief place of worship in a parish; other churches within its limits, attended from the parish church, are often known as mission churches; and other places in which Mass is said are, in our country, called stations.

Some Styles of Architecture. Let us devote the remainder of this chapter to an explanation of the principal features of our present-day churches, so that the various parts of these edifices may be familiar to us. There are several distinct styles of architecture in common use in our country — and, unfortunately, some of our churches are a mixture of details of many styles and of no style at all.

Grecian Architecture. This ancient form of construction is not often used in its purest form for Catholic churches at the present day, though Roman modifications of it are common enough. Its essential features are the columned portico, the low-pitched roof overhanging it, and the plain or pilastered side walls of massive construction, to carry the weight of the broad roof. The front columns support a triangular "pediment," of which the sunken panel, called a "tympanum," is often highly ornamented with sculptures.

There are three distinct types of Grecian architecture, differing mostly according to the columns used. The Doric has columns of simple design, fluted, with a capital consisting of a projecting curved moulding surmounted by a flat square block called an abacus. The Ionic has also fluted columns with moulded base and a capital with curled ornaments known as volutes. The Corinthian is the richest form of Grecian architecture. The capitals of the columns are carved exquisitely into leaves, surmounted by a gracefully moulded abacus. There is a legend that this beautiful form of capital took its origin from a basket filled with acanthus leaves.

Roman Architecture. In imperial Roman times all these styles of columns came into use and are to be found in ancient buildings; but the distinctive feature of Roman architecture was the round arches supported on rows of columns. The Roman style later developed into the Italian Renaissance, marked also by round arches and by the attachment of columns and fluted pilasters to the fronts of buildings. In the early Middle Ages the contact of Rome with the East resulted in the introduction of the Byzantine style, of which a fine specimen is the cathedral of St. Mark, in Venice.

Gothic Architecture. This has as its distinguishing feature the pointed arch. The nations of Europe, after their conversion to Christianity, devoted their energies to the construction of great churches; and when the light of learning had begun to shine upon them they developed this new and beautiful style of architecture, full of grace and captivating harmony. It is distinguished by comparative lightness of material, as well as by art and boldness and engineering skill in execution. The heavy piers and massive walls of earlier days were replaced by graceful clustered columns carrying on exquisite capitals lofty and beautiful pointed arches; by buttresses, both solid and "flying"; by grouped windows with slender mullions between, and complicated tracery; by great "rose windows" of circular shape; and by mighty towers, buttressed and pinnacled and often surmounted by graceful spires, "like angels' fingers, pointing ever heavenward" — sometimes at the front of the church, sometimes at the intersection of the nave and transept. Wonderful examples of this beautiful style of architecture are to be found throughout Europe, and nowhere are they more numerous than in once-Catholic England, where the services of a mutilated Christianity have replaced the Holy Sacrifice and the Divine Office in majestic cathedrals that were built by Catholic hands for Catholic worship.

The Gothic style has varied in detail in different countries, and has passed through many modifications in the course of centuries. Space will not permit even a brief description of each of these. In England we may distinguish the Norman, the Early Pointed (also called Lancet or Early English), the Middle Pointed style, the Flowing or Curvilinear, and the Third Pointed or Perpendicular. Similar changes took place in French architecture, resulting in the majestic cathedrals of Paris, Amiens, Rheims and Chartres, varying much in design an detail, but each an exquisite specimen of the handiwork of the men who built well because they built for God.

Details of Our Own Churches. Now let us, in imagination, approach a church — our own parish church. Above us, it may be, rises the tower. If this has a belfry and spire, the whole is called a steeple. It may be battlemented — in which case the openings in the battlement are embrasures, the intervening blocks are merlons. The pointed caps at the corners of a tower or parapet are called pinnacles (Latin, little feathers), and the topmost ornaments of these are finials. Carven ends of water-spouts are gargoyles — often grotesque figures of animals or diabolic faces. An outside shelter at the door is a porch or portico. Projecting stone braces against the walls are called buttresses, and if these stand apart from the wall which they support and are connected with it by cross-braces or arches, they are flying buttresses.

Let us go into the church, and find the proper names of its interior parts, not already mentioned. The nave stretches before us, bounded on each side by a row of columns and arches. A column is to be distinguished from a pillar — the latter being usually a square or several-sided pier (although a very heavy round pier may also be called a pillar), while a column is always a round shaft of more slender form, with a base and capital. A portion of a pillar or column affixed to a wall is a pilaster. Arches may vary in shape, according to the style of architecture, the Roman arch being a semicircle, the Gothic of pointed form. The central stone of an arch is the keystone; the lowest stones are the springers; the flat under-surface of an arch is the soffit; and the wall-space above the sides of the arches is a spandrel. The columns and arches divide the whole nave into bays. If there are columns but no arches, the wall-space above is the entablature, composed ordinarily of an architrave, a frieze and a cornice. If the church has a ceiling, ornaments hanging therefrom are pendents, and deep panels therein are coffers. If the roof is formed of interlacing arches, the construction is called groining.

The parts of the church beyond the rows of pillars are the aisles; and as the roofs over these are usually lower than the nave roof, the upper part of the nave, if provided with windows, is the clerestory. The part which crosses the nave and thus makes the church cross-shaped is the transept. Brackets projecting from the walls to carry pilasters, etc., are known as corbels. If the church has a dome, a turret surmounting this to admit light is called a lantern.

The part of the church containing the main altar is the sanctuary or chancel (Latin "cancellus," a lattice, because in past ages it could be screened off from the body of the church by the "rood-screen," so called because it supported a large "rood" or crucifix). As already mentioned, the further end of the sanctuary, if of semicircular or polygonal form, is the apse. Over the altar there may be a "baldacchino" or "ciborium," a canopy supported on columns. A reredos is the carved screen or ornamental work behind an altar. Around the sanctuary there may be "stalls" or seats for the clergy; and near by is the sacristy or vestry — the room for keeping the vestments and sacred vessels. This is usually provided with a basin for receiving ablutions — the water in which the sacred linens, etc., are washed; this is a "sacrarium" or "piscina" (Latin, fish-pool). An underground vaulted room such as is sometimes used for burial, is a crypt. An enclosed square outside the church, with a colonnaded shelter-roof around it, is a cloister.

Chapter LXV

THE CONSECRATION OF A CHURCH

The consecration of a Catholic church is a solemn and impressive ceremony, with rites which are symbolical of the sacred uses to which the edifice will be devoted. The various parts of this service are of very ancient date, and are substantially the same to-day as they were centuries ago.

A building which is to be used for the worship of God should be sanctified by prayer. When Moses constructed the movable Tabernacle for the people of Israel in the desert, he dedicated it to the service of the Almighty with much ceremony; and when the temple of Sion was built by Solomon it was consecrated to God with pomp and grandeur that lasted for many days, "and the majesty of the Lord filled the temple."

As these sanctuaries of the Old Law were a type of the Christian Church, so the rites of their dedication were a foreshadowing of the solemn service by which our churches are set apart for the worship of God.

On the day of the consecration of a church, some of the assisting clergy are deputed as chanters or choir, to intone the many psalms, responses and antiphons which form a part of the service.

Outside the Church. The Bishop and priests leave the church in procession, except one priest attired in deacon's vestments, who remains within. The doors are then closed. The Bishop, assisted by the clergy, chants an invocation to the Trinity: "Be with us, one Almighty God, Father, Son and Holy Ghost," after which he offers a prayer asking God's blessing on the work which he is beginning.

The intercession of the Saints is invoked by the recital of their Litany, after which the Bishop blesses some holy water; and with the words: "Thou shalt sprinkle me with hyssop, O Lord, and I shall be cleansed; Thou shalt wash me, and I shall be made whiter than snow," the Bishop and clergy form a procession and go entirely around the church, the outer walls of which are sprinkled with the holy water. The choir chants a beautiful "responsory," as follows: "The house of the Lord is founded on the summit of mountains, and is exalted above all hills, and all nations shall come to it, and they shall all say, Glory to Thee, O Lord. And coming, they shall come with joy, bearing their sheaves."

The Bishop offers before the church-door a prayer asking God's protection on the new house which He has founded — that here true service may always be rendered to Him. He then strikes the door with his pastoral staff, saying in the words of the psalm, "Lift up your gates, and the King of Glory shall enter." The deacon inside the church answers through the closed door, "Who is this King of Glory?" To which the Bishop responds, "The strong and powerful Lord, the Lord strong in battle." Another circuit of the church is made, with sprinkling as before, and the choir chants, "Bless, O Lord, this house which I have built to Thy name; hear in the high throne of Thy glory the prayers of those coming into this place; O Lord, if Thy people shall be converted and shall do penance and shall come and pray in this place, hear them."

After another prayer the Bishop again knocks at the church-door with his staff, speaking as above, and the deacon answers in the same manner. The procession goes again around the church in a direction opposite to that previously taken, and during its progress the choir sings, "Thou, the Lord of all, Who needest nothing, hast wished Thy temple to be made among us; preserve this house spotless forever, O Lord. Thou hast chosen this house for the invoking of Thy name therein, that it may be a house of prayer and petition for Thy people." A third time the Bishop strikes the door, and the dialogue with the deacon within the church takes place; but this time the door is opened. As the Bishop passes the threshold he makes the sign of the cross with his staff, saying, "Behold the sign of the cross; may all phantoms flee away."

The Entrance. During the entrance into the church the choir intones two beautiful anthems, the first being a solemn invocation of the Holy Trinity: "Peace eternal from the Eternal upon this house. May peace perpetual, O Word of the Father, be on this house. May the loving Consoler bestow peace on this house." The second is taken, very appropriately, from the

Gospel narrative of the humble publican who received our Lord: "Zaccheus, make haste and descend, because I shall remain to-day in thy house. And he descended in haste and received Him joyfully into his house. To-day on this house salvation has been bestowed by God."

Then the grand hymn to the Holy Ghost, the "Veni Creator," is chanted, followed by litanies, prayers and an antiphon: "O how this place is to be dreaded: Truly, this is none other than the house of God and the gate of heaven." The beautiful Canticle of Zachary is then recited: "Blessed be the Lord God of Israel, because He hath visited and hath made the redemption of His people."

The Ashes on the Floor. A very striking ceremony then takes place. Ashes have been previously strewn on the floor of the church in the form of a "St. Andrew's cross," or X, and the Bishop, with his pastoral staff, marks in them the letters of the Greek and Roman alphabets, beginning at the corners nearest to the door — from A to Z of the Roman alphabet and from Alpha to Omega of the Greek. This is symbolic of the two great branches of the Catholic Church, the Eastern and the Western, which differ in language and details of ritual, but are one in doctrine and government; and it also typifies the universality of the Church of God, teaching in all languages the Gospel of the Cross of Christ.

The Consecration of the Altar. A most important feature of the ceremonies is the consecration of the altar, the most essential part of a Catholic church — the place where the Holy Sacrifice of the Mass, the central point of Catholic worship, is offered up. This is a lengthy ceremony, full of beautiful symbolism, and containing many rites of great antiquity. In this blessing a special kind of holy water is used, called Gregorian, or Water of Consecration, which is not employed in any other service. It contains not only salt, as does ordinary holy water, but also ashes and wine; and the salt, ashes and wine are solemnly blessed with appropriate prayers before being mingled with the water.

After the reciting of a beautiful prayer asking for the outpouring of God's grace upon this house, the Bishop goes in procession with the clergy to the church-door, and marks on the inside with the sign of the cross, to indicate that this temple of God is protected by His cross against all dangers and the attacks of the Evil One.

The actual blessing of the altar then begins with the recital of the psalm which is said ordinarily at the beginning of the Mass: "I shall go unto the altar of God, to God Who rejoiceth my youth." The Bishop makes the sign of the cross five times upon different parts of the table of the altar, which is bare, dedicating it to God Almighty, to the glorious Virgin Mary, to all the Saints, and particularly to the name and memory of the Saint in whose honor it is erected. A prayer is said in which is mentioned "the stone on which the patriarch Jacob offered sacrifice," and the Bishop then goes around the altar seven times (symbolic of the seven gifts of the Holy Ghost), sprinkling it with holy water, while the psalm "Miserere" is recited. He then makes a circuit of the interior of the church three times, sprinkling the walls all around, during which ceremony several psalms are recited and appropriate antiphons are chanted by the choir, such as "My house shall be called a house of prayer. I will narrate Thy name to my brethren, in the midst of Thy church will I praise Thee." Then comes a long and beautiful Preface, invoking the descent of the Holy Ghost upon this church, and enumerating the spiritual blessings which will come from its dedication to the worship of God.

The Relics in the Altar. When the altar is consecrated, a small sealed metal box containing relics of at least two saints, is enclosed within it. These relics are guaranteed to be genuine by the Roman authorities who send them to the various dioceses of the world. A square cavity is made in the front part of the altar table, and a stone lid is fitted to this, to be cemented into place.

What is the reason of this placing of relics in the altar? It is said to go back to the days of persecution. In the catacombs, the underground chambers where the Christians were forced to hide from their enemies, were many tombs containing the bodies of martyrs and other saints; and when the priests celebrated the Divine Mysteries, the flat-topped stone tombs made very convenient altars. When the persecutions were over, and the

Church was able to build her altars in the light of day, the same form was retained; the altar was a tomb, containing the body of some holy servant of God, but, as churches multiplied, it was impossible to provide a whole body for each altar; and so the custom began of placing in each a small portion of the earthly remains of some canonized saint, whose intercession is thereby sought by those who will hereafter worship at that altar.

The Bishop uses some of the holy water described above, to make cement with which the relics are to be sealed within the altar-stone — in which work he is assisted by a stone-mason who is present for that purpose. The relics have been previously deposited in a chapel or other place, and a procession is formed to transport them to the sanctuary. The choir chants these appropriate words: "O how glorious is the Kingdom in which all the Saints rejoice with Christ; clothed in white robes, they follow the Lamb whithersoever He goeth. Arise, ye Saints of God, from your abodes; sanctify these places, bless the people, and guard us sinners in peace. Enter into the City of God, for a new church is built for you, where the people ought to adore the majesty of God."

A discourse or proclamation is then read by the Bishop, explaining the holiness of a place consecrated to God. It recounts the fact that the tabernacle of Moses was dedicated for the offering of sacrifices — not to be used for worldly things; and the faithful are urged to look upon this new temple as worthy of even greater honor.

Two decrees of the Council of Trent are read aloud by one of the clergy, declaring that the Church's anathemas shall fall upon any one converting to his own use any of her property, and that the faithful are under obligation to provide for the proper support of the new house of God.

At the entrance of the church the Bishop makes the sign of the cross with Chrism on the outside of the door, with a solemn blessing: "Mayest thou be a gate blessed, sanctified, consecrated, sealed, dedicated to the Lord God; a gate of entrance to salvation and peace."

When the relics have reached the sanctuary, two psalms

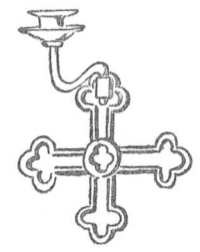

Cross on Wall of Consecrated Church

are recited, and the Bishop signs with holy Chrism the cavity or "sepulchre" of the altar-stone, and places the sacred relics within it. The cover or stone tablet which closes the cavity is anointed in like manner, and is then cemented into place; during which ceremony the choir chants appropriate verses, such as "The bodies of the Saints are buried in peace, and their names shall live forever."

The solemn incensing of the altar then takes place; it is begun by the Bishop, and is performed all through the remainder of the service by one of the priests, who makes the circuit of the altar continuously, except when the Bishop resumes the incensing at intervals.

The altar-stone is then anointed with holy Chrism in the form of a cross in five places on its upper side.

The Crosses on the Walls. When a church is to be consecrated, twelve crosses, generally cut into slabs of marble, are placed on the interior walls, about six or eight feet from the floor, and at the top of each is a candlestick holding a candle. The Bishop anoints each of these with Chrism, and also incenses them, going in procession from one to another, and saying at each unction: "May this temple be sanctified and consecrated, in the name of the Father, and of the Son, and of the Holy Ghost."

The blessing of the altar is then resumed. Five crosses are formed of grains of incense on the altar-stone, and on each of these a cross is made of small wax tapers, which are then lighted, so that, when these burn down, the crosses of incense will be ignited and consumed. The ashes are then scraped off the stone. A beautiful Preface is intoned by the Bishop, asking for God's blessing on His new temple and for the presence therein of His Angels and the Holy Spirit; and after two more unctions and two prayers the Bishop usually celebrates the first Mass on the newly-consecrated altar. This Mass is a special one, "for the Dedication of a Church." An announcement is then made of the indulgences which may be gained — a year for each visit on the day of the consecration, and forty days on each anniversary of it.

Such are the impressive ceremonies which our Church uses for the sanctifying of a temple of God. It is sprinkled, within and without, with holy water; the door and walls are signed with blessed Chrism; the altar is anointed with the same holy oil, and is made a tomb of one of God's illustrious servants. The odor of incense fills the house of God; and the solemn prayers of the Church are used to consecrate both temple and altar to His service forever. "This is none other than the House of God and the Gate of Heaven."

Chapter LXVI

OTHER RITES THAN OURS

We have hitherto confined our attention to the practices which are in vogue in our part of the world — the externals of Catholicity as we see and use them in our churches. We have explained the meaning and reviewed the history of Catholic customs and observances which are familiar to us. But there are millions of Catholics whose rites and ceremonies differ greatly from ours. Among them the outward form of the Church's worship varies considerably from that which we use. Their services are conducted in strange tongues; their Mass is celebrated with a ceremonial which would be unrecognizable by us if we were present at it; their sacraments are administered in a different manner from that in which we receive these same sacraments according to the Latin rite.

And yet these people are Catholics — fervent and faithful members of the flock of Christ. Their services are not heretical nor schismatic. Their Mass is the real unbloody Sacrifice of the Body and Blood of our Saviour; their sacraments are the same as ours, instituted by the same Divine Founder and producing the same spiritual effects — and the Mass and the sacraments are lawful, for those who use these various rites are in full communion with Christ's Vicar on earth.

There are also in many parts of the world, particularly in the East, schismatic sects which fell away centuries ago from the Church's unity and denied her authority over them, but which have preserved much of her doctrine and have clung steadfastly to the ancient rituals which they possessed before their separation from Catholicity. In nearly all of these schismatic Churches of the Orient there is undoubtedly a real priesthood, a true Sacrifice of the Mass and valid sacraments. But we shall pay special attention only to the religious bodies that are Catholic — that are in union with the Roman See, and nevertheless use in their liturgy languages which are strange to us and ceremonies different from ours.

The Languages Used by Catholics. There are, in all, nine languages used at the present day in Catholic worship. Latin is used in our Roman rite, and in those known as the Milanese and the Mozarabic. Greek is largely, though not exclusively, the language of the Byzantine rite. Syriac is the liturgical tongue of those who follow the Syrian, Maronite, Chaldean and Malabar rites. Armenian is used in all churches of the Armenian rite. Coptic is the Church's language in parts of northeastern Africa. Arabic is used by the Melchites who follow the Byzantine rite. Slavonic is in use in the Byzantine worship of the Slav races, and in the Roman rite as practised in Dalmatia. The inhabitants of the Asiatic province of Georgia, following the Byzantine liturgy, worship in their ancient Georgian tongue, and the people of Wallachia, in Roumania, with a similar ritual, use an old form of Roumanian.

Other Rites in Latin. During the Middle Ages and later, there was a great diversity of rites in Catholic worship. The Gallican rite was used at one time over nearly all of northwestern Europe, and our present Roman rite is largely a modification of it. The Milanese rite (also known as the Ambrosian, from the great Bishop of Milan) flourished in northern Italy, and the Mozarabic rite prevailed in parts of Spain. All of these used the Latin language. Many provinces, dioceses and religious orders also had ceremonials of their own.

St. Pius V, in 1570, ordered the publication of the Roman Missal, and decreed that all these varying Latin rites should be abolished, excepting those that could show an existence of at least two centuries. Some dioceses, therefore, have kept a distinct ritual; the Ambrosian and Mozarabic rites are still in daily use; and certain religious orders have rites of their own, as follows:

The Benedictine rite, which is very ancient, but which concerns only the Breviary. St. Benedict regulated the canonical hours for his monks, and his rules are still obligatory on all religious houses of the various Benedictine branches.

The Carmelite rite, also called the Rule of the Holy Sepulchre, began in the twelfth century. It varies somewhat from the Roman rite in the giving of Extreme Unction, and considerably in the Mass, the Office and the calendar of saints.

The Cistercian rite originated at Citeaux, France, in 1134. In the Breviary it follows the rule of St. Benedict, and in the Mass and the administration of Penance and Extreme Unction it varies somewhat from the Roman rite.

The Dominican rite goes back to the thirteenth century. When the order was founded, each house at first followed the rites of its own locality, and these were then very diverse in the different countries of Europe. The superiors of the order, therefore, sought to bring about uniformity, and formulated the ritual which the Dominicans still use. Many of our readers may have assisted at a low Mass in this rite. The celebrant goes to the altar wearing the amice on his head, like a hood or cowl; the introductory psalm "Judica me" is omitted, the Confiteor is shorter than ours, and some of the prayers and ceremonies are different from those of the Roman rite. The High Mass and the Office also differ considerably from ours.

The Franciscans, Capuchin Friars Minor, Premonstratensians and Servites also have rites in their Masses and Offices varying more or less from the Roman usage.

The Mass in Greek. The ancient tongue of Homer is the liturgical language of a large portion of the Catholic world. The Uniat Greeks, or those united to the See of Rome, are to be found in parts of Syria, at Jerusalem, in Russia, Bulgaria and Greece. There are small colonies of them in various places in southern Italy — the descendants of Greek fugitives who were driven thither by the Mohammedans nearly four hundred years ago.

The Greek used in their ceremonial is not the form in common use in Greece at the present day. It is the ancient classical Greek, which is not easily understood except by the learned. The ritual of their Mass differs greatly from ours, and is fully as old and as venerable as that with which we are familiar. It has many beautiful and symbolic ceremonies which would demand much space if we were to attempt to describe them.

At their Mass the bread is leavened or "raised" with yeast, in which it differs from that used in the Roman rite, which is simply wheaten flour mixed with water and baked in the form of a thin wafer. The Greeks consecrate a large oblong loaf which is divided, near the end of the Mass, into many small parts, so that the faithful may receive Holy Communion. All this seems very strange to us, simply because it is unfamiliar; but what they receive under this form is precisely what we receive — the Body and Blood of our Lord Jesus Christ.

The Greeks use three different liturgies, according to the feast or the season of the year — that known as the Rite of St. John Chrysostom, throughout most of the year; that of St. Basil on some days of Lent; and the "Liturgy of the Pre-Sanctified" on certain Lenten days when Mass is not said.

The Mass in Syriac. There are several branches of the Catholic Church which use the ancient Syriac tongue, though their ceremonials differ considerably from each other. The Syrian Uniats worship in the ancient "Liturgy of St. James." In far-away India there are Christians, of the Malabar rite, who use Syriac. The Maronites, a people who live on the slopes of Mount Lebanon and who have been remarkable for their unswerving devotion to the Holy See, have a ritual of their own. The language of these tribes to-day is Arabic; but in their liturgies they preserve the language which our Blessed Saviour spoke — for Syriac was the vernacular tongue of Palestine in the time of Christ, Hebrew having ceased to be in common use.

The Maronites use incense at low Masses as well as at the more solemn functions, and the celebrant and the server chant certain parts and responses of the Mass in a weird harmony which is thoroughly Oriental in its spirit.

Other Asiatic Liturgies. Mass is said in ancient Syro-Chaldaic by certain Catholic communities in the eastern and northern parts of Asiatic Turkey, as well as by Nestorian heretics in the same localities, and in ancient Georgian, in the Byzantine rite, by the inhabitants of Georgia, in Asia. Armenian is the liturgical language of the Christians of that long-persecuted tribe, both Catholics and heretics, of whom the latter far outnumber the former. They inhabit the parts of Asia Minor near the Black Sea, and various parts of Palestine; and they are also found in the provinces of European Turkey, Austria and Russia. Their ritual is beautiful in many respects, and some of its details can be traced back at least to the fourth century.

Slavonic and Roumanian. The old Slavonic language is the medium of worship for a small body of Catholics in Russia, and is also used in the ritual of the Dalmatians, dwelling near the Adriatic, who, after their conversion in the ninth century, received the privilege of holding the services of the Church in their own tongue. It is also the ecclesiastical language of parts of schismatic Russia and of some separated sects in European Turkey.

The privilege of using their own ancient tongue was also extended to the inhabitants of Wallachia, in the kingdom of Roumania in eastern Europe. With the tacit consent of Rome they have been saying Mass for many centuries in an old form of their language.

The African Christians. In "darkest Africa," not only in the Nile region but in more remote parts, are some Christian communities which have held to the faith of Christ more or less perfectly, despite long isolation from the Catholic world and centuries of warfare with Mohammedanism. Some of them are Catholic; others have drifted into schism and heresy, and the Christianity which they have preserved is mingled with superstition and error.

The Christians who dwell along the Nile, whether Catholics or schismatics, follow the Coptic rite and use the language which bears the same name. It is said by some to be the ancient tongue of the Pharaohs, and is now a dead language — the vernacular of those regions being everywhere Arabic. A small proportion of the Copts are Catholics, but the great majority are out of communion with the Church. They have a beautiful and complex liturgy, which goes back to very early times.

Further south we find the Christians of semi-barbarous Abyssinia. This strange and little-known people has held fast to at least a part of Christian truth for many centuries. Some of them are Catholics, but the greater part of the nation is schismatic, and among these are found various superstitions and semi-pagan practices. Their liturgy differs in nearly every detail from all those previously mentioned.

The Wisdom of Our Church. These are the principal forms of liturgy used in the Catholic world, apart from the Roman rite, which prevails throughout the greater part of Catholic Christendom. How well we see in this not only the unity but the wisdom of our holy Church! She has not interfered with the ancient rituals which are cherished by these Oriental Catholics, for she knows that the small details of rite and ceremony are not essential to faith, and that they may develop differently in different surroundings. She realizes that the faith of the Catholic Greek or Syrian or Copt is precisely the same as ours, though the outward expression of it may seem strange and unfamiliar to our eyes and ears. The language or the ceremonies used in religious service are not of paramount importance. They are only accidentals.

And so, all over the world, the grand ritual of our Faith goes on — expressed, indeed, in various ancient tongues, performed in various ways. The bishops and the priests are vested differently in each of these Oriental Churches; the Mass is celebrated and the Sacraments are administered with a symbolism unknown to us. But the bishops are real bishops, the priests are real priests, the Mass is the same Mass as ours, and the Sacraments are the same channels of grace as are those which we receive who are of the Latin rite.

INDEX

Ablegates, 13
Absolution, at Funerals, 282
Absolution, Form of, 65
Abstinence, 304
Abyssinian Rite, 392
Acolyte, 76
Acts, the, 282
"Adeste, Fideles," 349
"Ad Limina" Visits, 15
Adoration of the Cross, 151
"Adoro Te Devote," 347
Advent, 137
Affairs of Religious, Cong. of, 11
African Rites, 392
Agnus Dei, 212
"Agnus Dei," at Mass, 109
Aisle, 379
Alb, 172
Alleluia, at Mass, 99
All Saints' Day, 133
All Souls' Day, 133
"Alma Redemptoris Mater," 348
Alpha and Omega, Symbols, 326
Altar, 113
Altar-Bread, 102
Altar Cards, 116
Altar, Consecration of, 383
Altar Linens, 114
Altar, Privileged, 204
Altar Stone, 113 , 270
Ambo, 100
Ambrosian Rite, 389
Ambry, 188
A. M. D. G., 326
Amice, 172
A. M. (Monogram), 326

Anchorites, 22
Anchor, Symbol of Hope, 324
Angelus, 294
Anniversary Mass of Requiem, 294
Annunciation, Feast of the, 127, 132
Antependium, 114
Apostles' Creed, 279
Apostleship of Prayer, 363
Apostolic Blessing, 73
Apostolic Chancery, 12
Apostolic Delegates, 12
Apostolic Legates, 12
Apostolic Vicars, 13
Apse, 375
Arch, 379
Archbishops, 14
Archconfraternities, 361
Architecture, 376
Armenian Liturgy, 389
Ascension Day, 133
Ashes, 2335
Ashes, at Consecration of Church, 383
Asiatic Liturgies, 389
Asperges, 164, 167
Assumption, Feast of the, 133
Augustinians, 27
Auxiliary Bishops, 15
"Ave, Maris Stella," 348
"Ave, Regina Coelorum," 348

Baldacchino, 379
Balm, or Balsam, 56
Banner, Symbol, 325
Baptismal Font, 45

Baptismal Water, 165
Baptismal Water, Blessing of, 152
Baptism, Ceremonies of, 44
Baptistery, 375
Basilica, 376
Beads, 194
Beatification, 370
Bell, at Mass, 106
Bells, Blessing of, 229
Bells, Church, 223
"Benedicamus Domino" at Mass, 111
Benedictines, 27
Betrothals, 355
Bible, 328
Biretta, 171
Bishops, 14
Bishops and Regulars, Congreg. of, 11
Blessed Virgin, Litany of the, 287
Blessed Virgin, Medals of the, 234
Blessing, at Mass, 111
Blessing, Nuptial, 90
Blessing of New Fire, 152
Blessings, Ritual, 248
Books, Liturgical, 238
Bread for Mass, 102
Breviary, 243
Bugia, 191
Burse, 118
Buttress, 378
Byzantine Rite, 389

CALENDAR, Gregorian, 128
Calendar, the Church's, 126
Camera, Apostolic, 12
Candlemas Day, 190
Candle, at Baptism, 47
Candles, 189
Candles, at Mass, etc., 115, 190
Candles, St. Blaise, 249
Candlestick, Symbolism of, 325

Candles, Votive, 191
Canon of the Mass, 241
Canonization, 370
Canticles, 346
Cappa Magna, 177
Cardinals, 10
Cassock, 171
Cassock, Bishop's, 178
Catafalque, 294
Cathedral, 376
Celibacy, 317
Censer, 219
Censor of Books, 18
Ceremonies, Congregation of, 11
Chalice, 117
Chalice, Symbolism of, 325
Chancel, 379
Chancellor, Diocesan, 18
Chancery, Apostolic, 12
Chant, Gregorian, 337
Chaplain, 19
Chasuble, 173
Children of Mary, 365
Chimes, 224
Choir (Part of Church), 375
Choir (Singers), 344
Chrism, Holy, 56, 184
Chrisma, Monogram, 326
Christian Brothers, 37
Christmas Day, 141
Church Bells, 223
Church Buildings, 375
Church, Consecration of a, 381
Churches, Kinds of, 376
Churching of Women, 298
Church Music, 333
Ciborium (Canopy), 379
Ciborium (Vessel), 118
Cincture, 172
Circumcision, Feast of the, 127
Cistercians, 30
Clementine Instruction, 273

INDEX

Clerestory, 379
Clergy, 3
Cloister, 380
Closed Times, 89, 352
Coadjutor Bishops, 15
Collation, 303
Collects, 99
Colors, Liturgical, 170
Column, 378
Commemoration of the Dead, at Mass, 108
Commemoration of the Living, at Mass, 105
Committee of Vigilance, 19
Communion, in the Mass, 110
Communion of Saints, 259
Communion Paten, 119
Conclave, 7
Concursus, 19
Confession, 61
Confessional, 66
Confirmation, Ceremonies of, 54
Confiteor, 281
Confraternities, 361
Congregational Singing, 342
Congregations, Roman, 11
Consecration, in the Mass, 105
Consecration of a church, 381
Consistory, Sacred, 11
Consultors, Diocesan, 18
Cope, 174
Coptic Rite, 389
Corporal, 118
Corporation, Parish, 19
Corpus Christi, Feast of, 133
Council, Congregation of the, 11
Credence Table, 115
Creed, in the Mass, 100
Creed, the Apostles', 279
Crib, Christmas, 145
Crosier, 176
Cross, 157

Cross, Adoration of the, 151
Cross, Archiepiscopal, 14
Crosses, Varieties of, 159
Cross, Pectoral, 17, 177
Cross, Sign of the, 45
Cross, Symbol of Faith, 322
Cross, the True, 158
Crown, Symbolism of, 324
Crucifix, 157
Crucifix, Altar, 115
Cruets, 116
Crypt, 379
Curates, 19

DAILY Prayers, 276
Dalmatic, 82, 175
Datary, 12
Deacon, 81
Dead, Services for the, 291
Deans, Board of, 19
Defender of the Marriage Tie, 18
Delegates, Apostolic, 12
"Dies Iræ," 100, 294, 348
Diocesan Attorney, 18
Diocesan Bishops, 14
Domestic Prelates, 17
Domicile, 357
Dominicans, 29
Douay Bible, 331
Dove, Symbolism of, 323
Dragon, Symbolism of, 323

EASTER, Date of, 126
Election of a Pope, 6
Election of Bishops, 16
Elevation, at Mass, 106
Ember Days, 305
Embolism, 109, 278
Embrasure, 378
"Ephpheta," 45
Epiphany, Feast of the, 127
Episcopacy, 4

Epistle, in the Mass, 99
Espousal of the Bl. Virgin, Feast of, 134
Eucharist, Symbols of the, 323
Evangelists, Symbols of the, 327
Examiners, Board of, 18
Exorcism at Baptism, 46
Exorcist, 78
Expectation of the Bl. Virgin, Feast, 135
Expedition, Tribunals of, 12
Exposition, Mass of, 274
"Exsultet," 152, 348
Extraordinary Eccl. Affairs, Cong. of, 11
Extreme Unction, Ceremonies of, 69

FASTING, 302
Favor, Signature of, 12
Federation of Catholic Societies, 362
Festivals, Kinds of, 131
First Fridays, Devotion of the, 256
Fish, Signs of the, 325
Five Scapulars, the, 203
Forty Hours' Adoration, 272
Franciscans, 28

GARGOYLES, 378
Gaudete Sunday, 139
Gloria, 98, 347
Gloves, Bishop's, 177
Good Friday, 151
Gospel at Mass, 100
Gospel, Last, 111
Gothic Architecture, 377
Grace, Tribunals of, 12
Gradual, in the Mass, 99
Grapes, Symbolism of, 325
Greater Doxology, 98, 347
Greater Patriarchs, 14

Grecian Architecture, 376
Greek Rite, 389
Gregorian Calendar, 128
Gregorian Chant, 337
Gregorian Water, 165, 383
Gremiale, 178

HAIL Mary, 278
Halo, 326
Hearts of Jesus and Mary, Scapular of, 210
Heart, Symbol of Charity, 325
Help of Christians, Our Lady, Feast of, 134
Help of the Sick, Scapular of, 207
Hermits, 21
Hierarchy, 3
Holydays of Obligation, 132
Holy Face, Scapular of the, 210
Holy Family, Society of the, 367
"Holy God, We Praise Thy Name," 350
Holy Name of Jesus, Feast of the, 132
Holy Name of Jesus, Litany of the, 286
Holy Name of Jesus, Society of the, 362
Holy Name of Mary, Feast of the, 135
Holy Office, Congregation of the, 11
Holy Oils, 183
Holy Orders, Ceremonies of, 74
Holy Rosary, Feast of the, 135
Holy Thursday, 150
Holy Saturday, 151
Holy Water, 163
Holy Week, 149
Humeral Veil, 174
Hymns, 333

INDEX

I. H. S., 326
Images, Veneration of, 262
Immaculate Conception, Feast of the, 134
Immaculate Conception, Medal of the, 234
Immaculate Conception, Scapular of, 207
Immaculate Heart of Mary, Scapular of, 208
Impediments, Matrimonial, 351
Incense, 219
Incensing at Mass, 98, 219
Indulgence "in Articulo Mortis," 73
Indulgences, 307
Indulgences for Souls in Purgatory, 311
Infallibility of the Pope, 5
"In Partibus Infidelium," Bishops, 15
Inquisition, Congregation of the, 11
I. N. R. I., 162
Insignia of an Archbishop, 14
Insignia of the Pope, 9
Intentions for Masses, 94
Introit of the Mass, 97
Invocation of Saints, 258
Irremovable Rectors, 19
"Ite, Missa Est," 111

Jesuits, 33
Jurisdiction, for Confession, 64
Justice, Signature of, 12
Justice, Tribunals of, 12

Keys, Symbolism of, 325
Kiss of Peace, 110
Kyrie Eleison, 98

Laetare Sunday, 148
Lamb, Symbolism of, 323

Lamentations, 149
Lamps, 191
Languages, Liturgical, 388
Last Gospel, 111
Latin, at Mass, 121
"Lauda, Sion, Salvatorem," 100, 348
Lavabo, in the Mass, 116
"Lead, Kindly Light," 349
League of the Sacred Heart, 362
Lector, 77
Legates, Apostolic, 12
Lent, 147
Libera, 295
Lily, Symbolism of, 324
Lion, Symbolism of, 323
Litanies, 284
Liturgical Books, 238
Liturgies, 388
Living Rosary, the, 366
Lord's Prayer, the, 276
Loreto, Litany of, 287
"Lumen Christi," 152
Luna, 119

Major Orders, 79
Malabar Rite, 389
Maniple, 173
Maronite Liturgy, 389
Marriage Laws, 351
Mass, 92
Mass for Peace, 274
Masses, Intentions for, 94
Masses, Kinds of, 95
Mass, Fruits of the, 94
"Mass of the Pre-Sanctified," 151
Mass, Nuptial, 87
Mass, Requiem, 96
Matrimonial Court, 18
Matrimonial Impediments, 351
Matrimony, Ceremonies of, 87
Maundy Thursday, 150
Medals, 231

Melchites, 389
Merlons, 378
Metropolitans, 14
Milanese Rite, 389
Minor Orders, 74
Miraculous Medal, the, 234
Missal, 116, 238
"Missa pro Pace," 274
Mitre, 16, 176
Monasteries, 22
Monastic Rules, 23
Monks, 24
Monograms, 325
Monsignors, 17
Monstrance, 119
"Month's Mind" Mass, 294
Most Blessed Trinity, Scapular of the, 206
Mother of Good Counsel, Scapular of, 209
"Motu Proprio" on Church Music, 341
Mount Carmel, Our Lady of, Feast of, 135
Mount Carmel, Scapular of, 200
Mozarabic Rite, 389
Mozzetta, 178
Music, Church, 333
Mysteries of the Rosary, 195

NAILS of the True Cross, 159
Names, Baptismal, 52
Nativity of the Blessed Virgin, Feast, 135
Nave, 376
New Fire, Blessing of the, 152
Nicene Creed, 101
Nimbus, 326
Notes, Musical, 339
Nuncio, 12
Nuptial Mass and Blessing, 89

OATH at Ordination, 85
Offertory, 102
Office, Divine, 243
Office, Holy, Congregation of the, 11
Oil in Lamps, 191
Oil of Catechumens, 184
Oil of the Sick, 69, 185
Oils, Holy, 183
Oil-Stock, 72
Olive-Branch, Symbolism of, 324
"Orate, Fratres" in Mass, 103
Orchestras in Churches, 337
Orders, Holy, Ceremonies of, 74
Orders, Minor, 76
Orders, Religious, 27
Orders, Sacred, 79
Organ, 335
"O Salutaris," 348
Ostensorium, 119
Our Father, the, 276
Our Lady of Mount Carmel, Confraternity, 366
Our Lady of Mount Carmel, Feast of, 135
Our Lady of Mount Carmel, Scapular of, 200
Our Lady of Ransom, Feast of, 135
Our Lady of Ransom, Scapular of, 206
Our Lady of the Snows, Feast of, 135

Palestrina, Music of, 341
Pall, 118
Pallium, 14
Palm-Branch, Symbolism of, 216, 324
Palms, 216
Palm Sunday, 217
"Pange, Lingua," 347

INDEX

"Papa," 8
Papacy, 4
Papal Consistory, 11
Parish, 19
Paschal Candle, 152
Passing Bell, 225
Passion, Black Scapular of the, 207
Passion, Red Scapular of the, 208
Passionists, 31
Passion Sunday, 149
Pastor, 19
Paten, 117
Paten, Communion, 119
Pater Noster, in the Mass, 109
Patriarchs, 14
Pectoral Cross, 17, 177
Pelican, Symbolism of, 323
Penitentiary, Sacred, 12
Permanent Rectors, 19
Perpetual Rosary, 366
Peterspence, 9
Pilaster, 379
Pilgrimages, 313
Pillar, 378
Pinnacle, 378
Pious Associations, 361
Piscina, 379
Placeat, in Mass, 111
Plain Chant, 337
Pontiff, Sovereign, 8
Pope, 4
Porter, Order of, 76
Portico, 378
Postcommunion, 111
Prayers at Meals, 283
Prayers, Daily, 276
Precious Blood, Scapular of the, 208
Preface, in the Mass, 104
Prelates, Domestic, 17
Presbyterium, 375
Presentation of Bl. Virgin, Feast, 128
Priesthood, Ordination to, 83
Primates, 14
Privileged Altar, 204
Privileges, Scapular, 201
Processional Cross, 161
Procurator Fiscalis, 18
Propagation of the Faith, Cong. of, 11
Protonotary Apostolic, 17
Psalms, 346
Purgatorian Societies, 366
Purification of Bl. Virgin, Feast 127
Pyx, 119

QUARTER Tenses, 305

READER, Order of, 77
Rector, 19
Redemptorists, 32
"Regina Coeli," 227, 348
Relics in Altars, 384
Relics, Veneration of, 267
Religious Life for Women, 40
Religious Orders, 27
Religious Medals, 231
Religious Societies, 361
Reliquary, 270
Repose, Altar of, 150
Reposition, Mass of, 274
Requiem Mass, 293
Requisites for Mass, 113
Reredos, 379
Ring, Bishop's, 17
Ring, Wedding, 88
Rites, 388
Rites, Congregation of, 11
Ritual, 247
Rochet, 177
Rogation Days, 285

INDEX

Roman Architecture, 377
Roman Congregations, 11
Rood-Screen, 379
Rosary, 193
Rosary, Confraternity of the, 365
Rosary, Holy, Feast of the, 135
Rosary, Living, 366
Rosary, Perpetual, 366
Rose, Symbolism of, 324
Rota, 12
Roumanian Liturgy, 392
Rubrics, 238
Rules, Monastic, 23

SABBATINE Indulgence, 201
Sacerdotale, 247
Sacramentals, 154
Sacraments, Congregation of the, 11
Sacrarium, 379
Sacred College, 10
Sacred Heart, Devotion to the, 252
Sacred Heart, Feast of the, 253
Sacred Heart, League of the, 363
Sacred Heart, Litany of the, 289
Sacred Heart, Scapular of the, 209
Sacred Orders, 74
Sacred Penitentiary, 12
Sacristy, 379
Saints, Canonization of, 370
Saints, Communion of, 259
Saints, Invocation of, 257
Saints, Litany of the, 286
Salt, 45, 166
Salve Regina, 348
Sance Bell, 107
Sanctuary, 375
Sanctuary Lamp, 188
Sanctus, in the Mass, 104
Sandals, Bishop's, 177
Scapular Confraternity, 366
Scapular Medal, 204

Scapular Privileges, 201
Scapulars, 198
Seal of Confession, 65
Secretariate of State, Papal, 12
Secret Prayers, at Mass, 103
Segnatura, 12
Seminaries and Universities, Cong. of, 11
Sequences, at Mass, 99
Sermon, 100
Serpent, Symbolism of, 323
Services for the Dead, 291
"Servus Servorum Dei," 9
Seven Dolors, 134
Seven Dolors, Feasts of the, 134
Seven Dolors, Scapular of the, 206
Ship, Symbolism of, 324
Shrines of Pilgrimage, 313
Signature of Favor, 12
Signature of Justice, 12
Sign of the Cross, 154
Sign of the Cross, at Baptism, 45
Sign of the Fish, Symbolism of, 325
Skull, Symbolism of, 325
Slavonic Rite, 392
Societies, Religious, 361
Society of Jesus, 33
Soutane, 171
Sovereign Pontiff, 8
Spire, 378
Sponsors at Baptism, 49
Sponsors at Confirmation, 57
"Stabat Mater," 100, 348
Stations of the Cross, 179
St. Benedict, Medal of, 233
St. Benedict, Scapular of, 207
St. Blaise, Blessing of, 248
St. Dominic, Scapular of, 210
Steeple, 378
St. John the Baptist, Feast of, 133
St. Joseph, Feast of, 132

INDEX 403

St. Joseph, Litany of, 289
St. Joseph, Scapular of, 209
St. Michael Archangel, Scapular of, 209
Stole, 173
Stole, Broad, 175
Stole, Deacon's, 82
Sts. Peter and Paul, Feast of, 133
St. Vincent de Paul, Society of, 368
Studies, Congregation of, 11
Subdeacon, 79
Surplice, 174
Swastika, 157
Symbols, 322
Syriac Rite, 389
Syrinx, 335

TABERNACLE, 114
"Tametsi" Decree, 355
"Tantum Ergo," 347
"Te Deum," 347
Tenebrae, 149
Theological Virtues, Symbols of the, 324
Third Orders, 198
Tiara, 8
Titular Archbishops, 14
Titular Bishops, 15
Tonsure, 74
Tower, Church, 378
Tract, in the Mass, 99
Transept, 379
Trappists, 30
Treasury of Merit, 309
Tribunals, Roman, 12
Trinity Sunday, 133
Triple Candle, 152

Trisagion, 347
True Cross, History of the, 158
Tunic, 81, 175

VEIL, Chalice 118
Veil, Humeral, 174
Veil, Tabernacle, 114
Veneration of Images, 262
Veneration of Relics, 267
"Veni, Creator Spiritus," 348
"Veni Sancte Spiritus," 100
"Verbum Supernum Prodiens," 347
Vestments, 169
Vestry, 379
Veto, Power of, 7
"Vexilla Regis," 151
Vicar General, 18
Vicars, Apostolic, 13
"Victimae Paschali," 99
Vigilance, Committee of, 19
Vigil of Christmas, 142
Visitation of Bl. Virgin, Feast of the, 134
Visits "ad Limina," 15
Votive Candles, 191
Vows, Baptismal, 46
Vows of Sisterhoods, 42
Vulgate, 328

WASHING of Fingers at Mass, 103
Water, Gregorian, 165, 383
Water, Holy, 163
Way of the Cross, 179
Wheat, Symbolism of, 325
Wine, 102
Women in Church Choirs, 344

www.ingramcontent.com/pod-product-compliance
Lightning Source LLC
Chambersburg PA
CBHW020729160426
43192CB00006B/160